Lecture Notes in Computer Science 11947

More information about this series at http://www.springer.com/series/7407

Shivam Bhasin · Avi Mendelson ·
Mridul Nandi (Eds.)

Security, Privacy, and Applied Cryptography Engineering

9th International Conference, SPACE 2019
Gandhinagar, India, December 3–7, 2019
Proceedings

 Springer

Editors
Shivam Bhasin ⓘ
Temasek Laboratories
Nanyang Technological University
Singapore, Singapore

Avi Mendelson
Computer Science Department
Technion
Haifa, Israel

Mridul Nandi ⓘ
Indian Statistical Institute
Kolkata, India

ISSN 0302-9743 ISSN 1611-3349 (electronic)
Lecture Notes in Computer Science
ISBN 978-3-030-35868-6 ISBN 978-3-030-35869-3 (eBook)
https://doi.org/10.1007/978-3-030-35869-3

LNCS Sublibrary: SL1 – Theoretical Computer Science and General Issues

This Springer imprint is published by the registered company Springer Nature Switzerland AG
The registered company address is: Gewerbestrasse 11, 6330 Cham, Switzerland

Preface

The Conference on Security, Privacy, and Applied Cryptography Engineering 2019 (SPACE 2019), was held during December 3–7, 2019, at the Dhirubhai Ambani Institute of Information and Communication Technology, Gandhinagar, India. This annual event is devoted to various aspects of security, privacy, applied cryptography, and cryptographic engineering. This is a challenging field, requiring expertise from diverse domains, ranging from mathematics to solid-state circuit design.

This year we received 26 submissions from 10 different countries. The submissions were evaluated based on their significance, novelty, technical quality, and relevance to the SPACE conference. The submissions were reviewed in a double-blind mode by at least 3 members of the 36-member Program Committee. The Program Committee was aided by 9 additional reviewers. The Program Committee meetings were held electronically, with intensive discussions. After an extensive review process, 12 papers were accepted for presentation at the conference, with an acceptance rate of 46.15%.

The program also included five invited talks and four tutorials on several aspects of applied cryptology, delivered by world-renowned researchers: Yu Sasaki, Francesco Regazzoni, Makoto Nagata, Sahar Kvatinsky, Avinash L. Varna, Debrup Chakraborty, Shashwat Raizada, and Stjepan Picek. We sincerely thank the invited speakers for accepting our invitations in spite of their busy schedules. As in previous editions, SPACE 2019 was organized in cooperation with the International Association for Cryptologic Research (IACR). We are thankful to the Dhirubhai Ambani Institute of Information and Communication Technology, Gandhinagar, for being the gracious host of SPACE 2019.

There is a long list of volunteers who invested their time and energy to put together the conference, and who deserve accolades for their efforts. We are grateful to all the members of the Program Committee and the additional reviewers for all their hard work in the evaluation of the submitted papers. We thank Cool Press Ltd, owner of the EasyChair conference management system, for allowing us to use it for SPACE 2019, which was a great help. We thank our publisher Springer for agreeing to continue to publish the SPACE proceedings as a volume in the *Lecture Notes in Computer Science* (LNCS) series. We are grateful to the local Organizing Committee, especially to the general chair, Anish Mathuria, who invested a lot of time and effort in order for the conference to run smoothly. Our sincere gratitude to Debdeep Mukhopadhyay, Veezhinathan Kamakoti, and Sanjay Burman for being constantly involved in SPACE since its very inception and responsible for SPACE reaching its current status.

Last, but certainly not least, our sincere thanks go to all the authors who submitted papers to SPACE 2019, and to all the attendees. The conference was made possible by you, and it is dedicated to you. We sincerely hope you find the proceedings stimulating and inspiring.

October 2019   Shivam Bhasin
                                                                 Avi Mendelson
                                                                 Mridul Nandi

Organization

Program Committee

Reza Azarderakhsh	Florida Atlantic University, USA
Lejla Batina	Radboud University, The Netherlands
Shivam Bhasin	Temasek Labs @ NTU, Singapore
Billy Brumley	Tampere University, Finland
Arun Balaji Buduru	Indraprastha Institute of Information Technology Delhi (IIIT-D), India
Claude Carlet	University of Paris 8, France
Avik Chakraborti	Indian Statistical Institute, India
Rajat Subhra Chakraborty	IIT Kharagpur, India
Donghoon Chang	NIST, USA
Anupam Chattopadhyay	Nanyang Technological University, Singapore
Jean-Luc Danger	Institut Télécom/Télécom ParisTech, CNRS/LTCI, France
Thomas De Cnudde	COSIC - ESAT, K.U. Leuven, Belgium
Sylvain Guilley	GET/ENST, CNRS/LTCI, Télécom Paris, France
Matthias Hiller	Fraunhofer AISEC, Germany
Naofumi Homma	Tohoku University, Japan
Dirmanto Jap	Nanyang Technological University, Singapore
Shahar Kvatinsky	Technion - Israel Institute of Technology, Israel
Eik List	Bauhaus-University Weimar, Germany
Subhamoy Maitra	Indian Statistical Institute, India
Mitsuru Matsui	Mitsubishi Electric, Japan
Anisur Rahaman Molla	Indian Statistical Institute, India
Pratyay Mukherjee	University of California, Berkeley, USA
Debdeep Mukhopadhyay	IIT Kharagpur, India
Mridul Nandi	Indian Statistical Institute, India
Leo Perrin	Inria, France
Stjepan Picek	Delft University of Technology, The Netherlands
Chester Rebeiro	IIT Madras, India
Somitra Sanadhya	IIT Ropar, India
Vishal Saraswat	Robert Bosch Engineering and Business Solutions Pvt. Ltd (RBEI/ESY), India
Santanu Sarkar	IIT Madras, India
Sourav Sen Gupta	Nanyang Technological University, Singapore
Sujoy Sinharoy	University of Birmingham, USA
Yuval Yarom	The University of Adelaide, Data61/CSIRO, Australia
Amr Youssef	Concordia University, Canada
Fan Zhang	Zhejiang University, China

Additional Reviewers

Barua, Rana
Datta, Nilanjan
Delgado-Lozano, Ignacio M.
Galal, Hisham
Garb, Kathrin
Ghosh, Satrajit
Guilley, Sylvain
Hamburg, Michael
Jati, Arpan
Mendelson, Avi

Muhammad, Elsheikh
Pandit, Tapas
Ravi, Prasanna
Saha, Sayandeep
Sengupta, Abhrajit
Stebila, Douglas
Tolba, Mohamed
Tuveri, Nicola
Ueno, Rei
Yli-äyry, Ville

Contents

Deployment of EMC-Compliant IC Chip Techniques in Design
for Hardware Security: Invited Paper.............................. 1
  Makoto Nagata

Real Processing-In-Memory with Memristive Memory Processing Unit 5
  Shahar Kvatinsky

Challenges in Deep Learning-Based Profiled Side-Channel Analysis 9
  Stjepan Picek

A Study of Persistent Fault Analysis 13
  Andrea Caforio and Subhadeep Banik

Internal State Recovery Attack on Stream Ciphers: Breaking BIVIUM...... 34
  Shravani Shahapure, Virendra Sule, and R. D. Daruwala

Related-Key Differential Cryptanalysis of Full Round CRAFT 50
  Muhammad ElSheikh and Amr M. Youssef

SpookChain: Chaining a Sponge-Based AEAD
with Beyond-Birthday Security 67
  *Gaëtan Cassiers, Chun Guo, Olivier Pereira, Thomas Peters,
  and François-Xavier Standaert*

One Trace Is All It Takes: Machine Learning-Based Side-Channel
Attack on EdDSA.. 86
  Léo Weissbart, Stjepan Picek, and Lejla Batina

An Efficient Parallel Implementation of Impossible-Differential
Cryptanalysis for Five-Round AES-128 106
  *Debranjan Pal, Dishank Agrawal, Abhijit Das,
  and Dipanwita Roy Chowdhury*

Automated Classification of Web-Application Attacks
for Intrusion Detection....................................... 123
  *Harsh Bhagwani, Rohit Negi, Aneet Kumar Dutta, Anand Handa,
  Nitesh Kumar, and Sandeep Kumar Shukla*

Formal Analysis of PUF Instances Leveraging Correlation-Spectra
in Boolean Functions.. 142
  Durba Chatterjee, Aritra Hazra, and Debdeep Mukhopadhyay

ProTro: A Probabilistic Counter Based Hardware Trojan Attack
on FPGA Based MACSec Enabled Ethernet Switch 159
    *Vidya Govindan, Sandhya Koteshwara, Amitabh Das, Keshab K. Parhi,
    and Rajat Subhra Chakraborty*

Encrypted Classification Using Secure K-Nearest Neighbour Computation . . . 176
    B. Praeep Kumar Reddy and Ayantika Chatterjee

A Few Negative Results on Constructions of MDS Matrices Using Low
XOR Matrices 195
    Kishan Chand Gupta, Sumit Kumar Pandey, and Susanta Samanta

Revisiting the Security of LPN Based RFID Authentication Protocol
and Potential Exploits in Hardware Implementations 214
    *Krishna Bagadia, Urbi Chatterjee, Debapriya Basu Roy,
    Debdeep Mukhopadhyay, and Rajat Subhra Chakraborty*

Invited Abstracts

Length Preserving Symmetric Encryption: Is It Important? 233
    Debrup Chakraborty

Towards Automatic Application of Side Channel Countermeasures 234
    Francesco Regazzoni

Author Index 237

Deployment of EMC-Compliant IC Chip Techniques in Design for Hardware Security
Invited Paper

Makoto Nagata[✉]

Kobe University, 1-1 Rokkodai, Nada, Kobe 657-8501, Japan
nagata@cs.kobe-u.ac.jp

Abstract. IC chips are key enablers of densely networked smart society and need to be more compliant to security and safety. The talk will start from Electromagnetic Compatibility (EMC) techniques of IC chips on the safety side, toward EMC aware design, analysis and implementation. Then, the challenges will be discussed about the deployment of such EMC techniques in the design of IC chips for the higher level of hardware security. In detail, the talk will start with Silicon experiments on electromagnetic susceptibility (noise immunity) and electromagnetic interference (noise emission) of IC chips in automotive applications, covering on-chip/in-place noise measurement (OCM) and chip-package-system board (C-P-S) simulation techniques. Then, the talk will evolve for side channel leakage analysis and resiliency by design in cryptographic IC chips.

Keywords: Hardware security · Electromagnetic compatibility · Side channel leakage · Cryptography · Semiconductor integrated circuit

1 Outline

Semiconductor integrated circuit (IC) chips are strongly requested to hold safety and security features with of critical importance in the fields such as automotive, aerospace/aviation, healthcare and medical applications (Fig. 1).

Fig. 1. Semiconductor IC chips in mission critical application [1]. (Copyright 2019, IEEE.)

© Springer Nature Switzerland AG 2019
S. Bhasin et al. (Eds.): SPACE 2019, LNCS 11947, pp. 1–4, 2019.
https://doi.org/10.1007/978-3-030-35869-3_1

Electromagnetic compatibility (EMC) of an IC chip covers radio wave noise interference (EMI) and susceptibility (EMS). When circuits operate, power supply (PS) current is dynamically consumed, and leads to the emanation of electromagnetic (EM) waves through the interaction with parasitic antennas on metallic wiring associated with a power delivery network (PDN). On the other hand, external EM waves can be captured by the same parasitic antennas that may introduce disturbances on the operation of ICs through modulated PS currents. These bidirectional influence of EM waves on IC chips needs to be predicted and protected by design for the safety as well as for the security.

The knowledge and techniques of EMC on IC chips are very much relevant to hardware security, in the context of physical side channel information leakage and attack preventions [2]. PS current flows from an external power source to ICs on a die through PDNs. The current can be observed through the power lines on a printed circuit board (PCB), power pins of an IC chip package, power pads and power wirings in an IC chip. Electromagnetic (EM) waves are also radiated from an IC chip in operation. Those paths and nodes unintentionally provide the vulnerability of security functions like cryptographic engines in hardware, through a variety form of side channel attacks by an adversary, as sketched in Fig. 2.

There are a variety of technical and scientific achievements to solve EMC problems in semiconductor IC chip developments, which can be applied for the mitigation of side channel attacks in secure IC chips. This presentation will focus on following two major aspects of EMC techniques.

(1) Chip-package-system board (C-P-S) simulation technique.
(2) On-chip waveform measurement (OCM) technique.

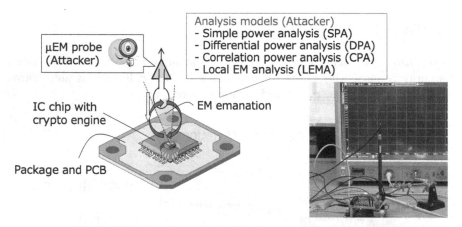

Fig. 2. Side-channel passive attacks [1]. (Copyright 2019, IEEE.)

The C-P-S simulation involves active PS current and passive PDN impedance models and evaluates dynamic PS noise of an IC chip. The model is capable for a full chip level PDNs where security and other circuits may belong to individual power domains (Fig. 3). The EM simulation is extensively extended for the side channel leakage analysis (SCA) of cryptographic engines.

The OCM evaluates PS noise waveforms of cryptographic engines in-place on an IC chip. The measured waveforms provide in-depth understanding of PS side channel leakage mechanisms, and also guarantee the efficacy and accuracy of the C-P-S simulation technique. The voltage and time resolution of 100 μV and 100 ps has been achieved.

An IC chip as the test vehicle of these techniques embeds advance encryption standard (AES) cores and OCM circuitry and actualizes Si demonstration. The whole flow and evaluation examples will be detailed in the presentation. The techniques outlined here can be the basis for the design of protection circuitry against side channel attacks and also for the resiliency by design against active attacks such as fault injection [3].

The challenges have been pursued to establish the pre-silicon evaluation of cryptographic engines about the level of leakage in the development of very large scale integration (VLSI) chips [4], where the large number of logic gates (e.g. 1 million or more) and the large number of payloads (e.g. 10k or more) need to be handled in the simulation flow.

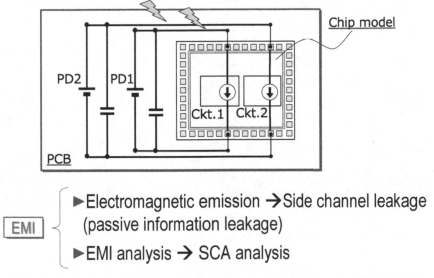

Fig. 3. Electromagnetic interference simulation model [1]. (Copyright 2019, IEEE.)

Acknowledgements. This work was in part based on results obtained from a project commissioned by the New Energy and Industrial Technology Development Organization (NEDO). The authors would like to deeply thank K. Matsuda, A. Tsukioka, Dr. D. Fujimoto and Prof. N. Miura for their valuable help and valuable scientific discussions.

References

1. Nagata, M.: Power noise simulation of IC chips for hardware security. In: 2019 IEEE International Symposium on Electromagnetic Compatibility, Signal and Power Integrity (EMC+SIPI 2019), Tutorial, FR-AM-3-2, 26 July 2019
2. Nagata, M., Fujimoto, D., Miura, N., Homma, N., Hayashi, Y., Sakiyama, K.: Protecting cryptographic integrated circuits with side-channel information. IEICE Electron. Express **14**(2), 1–13 (2017)
3. Nagata, M., Miki, T., Miura, N.: On-chip physical attack protection circuits for hardware security (Invited). In: Proceedings of IEEE Custom Integrated Circuits Conference (CICC 2019), #15-5, pp. 1-6, April 2019
4. Tsukioka, A., et al.: A fast side-channel leakage simulation technique based on IC chip power noise modeling. In: Proceedings of the 2019 IEEE International Symposium on Electromagnetic Compatibility, Signal and Power Integrity (EMC+SIPI 2019), Abstract Reviewed Paper, TH-PM-3-4, July 2019

Real Processing-In-Memory with Memristive Memory Processing Unit

Shahar Kvatinsky[✉]

Technion – Israel Institute of Technology, 3200003 Haifa, Israel
shahar@ee.technion.ac.il

Abstract. Memristive technologies are attractive candidates to replace conventional memory technologies and can also be used to perform logic and arithmetic operations. In this extended abstract, we discuss how memristors are used to combine data storage and computation in the memory, thus enabling a novel non-von Neumann architecture called the 'memristive memory processing unit' (mMPU). The mMPU relies on a memristive logic technique called 'memristor aided logic' (MAGIC) that requires no modification to the memory array structure. By greatly reducing the data transfer between the CPU and the memory, the mMPU alleviates the primary restriction on performance and energy efficiency in modern computing systems.

Keywords: Memristors · RRAM · mMPU · MAGIC

1   The Memory Wall and Processing-In-Memory

General purpose computing systems are typically designed in von Neumann architecture, or an ameliorated version of it, which separates the memory and processing space. In these systems, programs are executed by moving data between the processing unit and memory using specific operations (load/store). While this programming model is simple, the performance of the system is limited by the memory access time, which is substantially higher than the computing time itself. This performance bottleneck has become even more severe over the years because CPU speed has improved much more than memory speed and bandwidth. Moreover, many modern workloads have high and unstructured data volumes with limited locality, reducing the effectiveness of data caching.

This separation of the processing and memory space – and thus the required transfer of data between them – constitute two main bottlenecks in current computing systems: speed (*'memory wall'*) and energy efficiency (*'power wall'*). A promising approach to overcome these challenges is to push the computation closer to the memory. Both DRAM and emerging non-volatile memory have ample intrinsic parallelism, which goes unutilized today because of the pin-limited integrated circuit interface. *Processing-In-Memory* (PIM) can tap this intrinsic parallelism, avoiding the need for high-latency and high-energy chip-to-chip transfers, thus yielding massively parallel, high-performance, energy-efficient processing [1].

© Springer Nature Switzerland AG 2019
S. Bhasin et al. (Eds.): SPACE 2019, LNCS 11947, pp. 5–8, 2019.
https://doi.org/10.1007/978-3-030-35869-3_2

Early research into PIM dates back to the '90s, but only recently with the advancements in technologies it seems that PIM may become an efficient solution to the aforementioned walls. This extended abstract deals with the use of emerging memory technologies, namely, memristive memory technologies, to perform PIM. Figure 1 shows the evolution from von Neumann architecture to near-memory processing techniques and to the proposed PIM technique in this extended abstract, where the computation is done inside the memory arrays.

2   Memristors and Memristor Aided Logic

2.1   Memristors

Memristive emerging memory technologies are different types of technologies that store data in the form of resistance [2]. For example, high resistance can be considered as logical 0, while low resistance as logical 1. Note that multilevel cells with multiple resistive values can also be used. These technologies differ in their physical mechanism and can be based on mechanisms such as oxygen vacancy ion drift (RRAM), thermal effects (PCM), and magnetic tunnel junctions (STT MRAM). All of these technologies can be fabricated in CMOS back-end-of-line and are nonvolatile and relatively fast.

In addition to their obvious potential for memory applications, they have also potential to be used in other applications, such as neuromorphic computing [3, 4], cytomorphic electronics [5, 6], and logic gates [7, 8].

2.2   Memristor Aided Logic (MAGIC)

Recently, we have proposed *Memristor-Aided loGIC* (MAGIC) [9], a stateful, in-memory, flexible logic family. In MAGIC, only a single voltage V_G is used to perform a NOR logic operation and there are separate input and output memristors, as shown in Fig. 2. Additionally, MAGIC gates do not require additional devices to perform the operation (unlike some memristive logic families that require an additional resistor for each wordline). Since NOR is a complete logic function, a MAGIC NOR operation is sufficient to execute any Boolean operation. Hence, MAGIC NOR can be the basis for performing all desired processing within memory by dividing the desired function into a sequence of MAGIC NOR operations. These basic NOR operations are executed one after the other using the memory cells as computation elements. MAGIC can also be used to perform logic operations in parallel on sets of data. The crossbar array is structured such that applying the operating voltage V_G on any two selected rows and grounding a third row will result in NOR operations being performed on all columns that were not isolated by applying an isolation voltage V_{ISO}. Note that due to the symmetry of memristive crossbar arrays (*i.e.*, transpose memory), performing NOR operations on column vectors is similarly feasible.

3   Memristive Memory Processing Unit (mMPU)

The mMPU [10, 11] is a standard RRAM memory with a few modifications that enable the support of MAGIC-based PIM instructions. In other words, the mMPU functions as a standard memory that supports memory operations (*i.e.*, read and write) with additional PIM capabilities, and thus it is backward compatible with the von Neumann computing scheme.

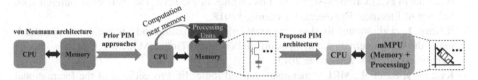

Fig. 1. Architectural evolution of eliminating the von Neumann bottleneck by moving processing into the memory. Moving from von Neumann machines with separate computation and storage to near data processing, and finally to the proposed architecture that eliminates a significant amount of data transfer using the same cells that store the data to perform logical operations within the mMPU.

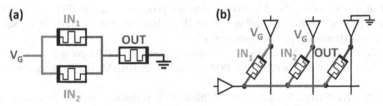

Fig. 2. Schematic of (a) MAGIC NOR gate and (b) MAGIC NOR gate within a memristive memory array. IN_1 and IN_2 are the input memristors and OUT is the output memristor. A single voltage V_G is applied to perform the NOR operation [9].

To support PIM instructions, the memory controller [12, 18, 19], the memory protocol [13], and the peripheral circuits (*i.e.*, voltage drivers and row/column decoders) must be modified to support MAGIC instructions [14, 15]. The mapping of data is also modified to maintain persistency and coherence. Note, however, that the memory crossbar array structure itself is not modified. The mMPU is useful to accelerate different applications such as image processing [16, 17].

References

1. Balasubramonian, R., Grot, B.: Near-data processing. IEEE Micro **36**(1), 4–5 (2016)
2. Kvatinsky, S., et al.: The desired memristor for circuit designers. IEEE Circ. Syst. Mag. **13**(2), 17–22 (2013)
3. Greenberg-Toledo, T., Mazor, R., Haj Ali, A., Kvatinsky, S.: Supporting the momentum algorithm using a memristor-based synapse. IEEE Trans. Circ. Syst. I Regul. Pap. **66**(4), 1571–1583 (2019)
4. Rosenthal, E., Greshnikov, S., Soudry, D., Kvatinsky, S.: A fully analog memristor-based multilayer neural network with online backpropagation training. In: Proceeding of the IEEE International Symposium on Circuits and Systems, pp. 1394–1397, May 2016

5. Abo Hanna, H., Danial, L., Kvatinsky, S., Daniel, R.: Modeling biochemical reactions and gene networks with memristors. In: Proceeding of the IEEE Symposium on Biological Circuits and Systems, pp. 1–4, October 2017
6. Abo Hanna, H., Danial, L., Kvatinsky, S., Daniel, R.: Memristors as artificial biochemical reactions in cytomorphic systems. In: Proceedings of the IEEE International Conference on Science of Electrical Engineering, December 2018
7. Reuben, J., et al.: Memristive logic: a framework for evaluation and comparison. In: Proceeding of the IEEE International Symposium on Power and Timing Modeling, Optimization and Simulation, pp. 1–8, September 2017
8. Kvatinsky, S., et al.: MRL – memristor ratioed logic. In: Proceedings of the International Cellular Nanoscale Networks and their Applications, pp. 1–6, August 2012
9. Kvatinsky, S., et al.: MAGIC - memristor-aided logic. IEEE Trans. Circ. Syst. II Exp. Briefs **61**(11), 895–899 (2014)
10. Ben Hur, R., Kvatinsky, S.: Memory processing unit for in-memory processing. In: Proceedings of the IEEE International Symposium on Nanoscale Architectures, pp. 171–172, July 2016
11. Haj Ali, A., et al.: Not in name alone: a memristive memory processing unit for real in-memory processing. IEEE Micro **38**(5), 13–21 (2018)
12. Ben-Hur, R., Kvatinsky, S.: Memristive memory processing unit (MPU) controller for in-memory processing. In: Proceedings of the IEEE International Conference on Science of Electrical Engineering, pp. 1–5, November 2016
13. Talati, N., Ha, H., Perach, B., Ronen, R., Kvatinsky, S.: CONCEPT: a column oriented memory controller for efficient memory and PIM operations in RRAM. IEEE Micro **39**(1), 33–43 (2019)
14. Wald, N., Kvatinsky, S.: Influence of parameter variations and environment for real processing-in-memory using memristor aided logic (MAGIC). Microelectron. J. **86**, 22–33 (2019)
15. Talati, N., et al.: Practical challenges in delivering the promises of real processing-in-memory machines. In: Proceedings of the Design Automation and Test in Europe, pp. 1628–1633, March 2018
16. Haj Ali, A., et al.: Efficient algorithms for in-memory fixed point multiplication using MAGIC. In: Proceeding of the IEEE International Symposium on Circuits and Systems, pp. 1–5, May 2018
17. Haj Ali, A., et al.: IMAGING - in-memory algorithms for image processing. IEEE Trans. Circ. Syst. I Regul. Pap. **65**(12), 4258–4271 (2018)
18. Ben Hur, R., et al.: SIMPLE MAGIC: synthesis and mapping of boolean functions for memristor aided logic (MAGIC). In: Proceeding of the IEEE International Conference on Computer Aided Design, pp. 225–232, November 2017
19. Ben-Hur, R., et al.: SIMPLER MAGIC: synthesis and mapping of in-memory logic executed in a single row to improve throughput. IEEE Trans. Comput. Aided Des. Integr. Circ. Syst. (in press)

Challenges in Deep Learning-Based Profiled Side-Channel Analysis

Stjepan Picek[✉]

Delft University of Technology, Delft, The Netherlands
stjepan@computer.org

Abstract. In recent years, profiled side-channel attacks based on machine learning proved to be very successful in breaking cryptographic implementations in various settings. Still, despite successful attacks even in the presence of countermeasures, there are many open questions. A large part of the research concentrates on improving the performance of attacks while little is done to understand them and even more importantly, use that knowledge in the design of more secure implementations. In this paper, we start by briefly recollecting on the state-of-the-art in machine learning-based side-channel analysis. Afterward, we discuss several challenges we believe will play an important role in future research.

1 Introduction

In side-channel analysis (SCA), the attacker exploits weaknesses in physical implementations of cryptographic algorithms [12]. This is possible by exploiting unintentional leakages in physical channels like power consumption [9] or electromagnetic radiation [19].

In profiled side-channel attacks, a powerful attacker has a device (the clone device) with knowledge about the secret key implemented and can obtain a set of profiling traces. From there, he builds a profiled model, which is then used to conduct an attack on another device (the device under attack). Consequently, profiled attacks have two phases (1) profiling phase where a model is constructed and (2) attack phase where the constructed model is used to attack the actual target device. Profiled SCA performs the worst-case security analysis as it considers the most powerful side-channel attacker with access to an open (since the keys are chosen/known by the attacker) clone device. The best-known profiled attack is the template attack, which is based on the Bayesian rule. Template attack is considered to be the most powerful attack from the information-theoretic point of view when the attacker has an unbounded number of measurements in the profiling phase [3]. To cope with certain statistical difficulties that can arise in template attack, there is a variant of it commonly known as the pooled template attack [4]. Finally, the third example of profiled attacks is the stochastic attack, which uses linear regression in the profiling phase [20].

These three techniques represent a standard set of techniques in profiled SCA. Besides these techniques, the SCA community also started using different

© Springer Nature Switzerland AG 2019
S. Bhasin et al. (Eds.): SPACE 2019, LNCS 11947, pp. 9–12, 2019.
https://doi.org/10.1007/978-3-030-35869-3_3

machine learning techniques. Common examples are the Naive Bayes [15], Support Vector Machines [7], Random Forest [10], and multilayer perceptron [6,13]. The multilayer perceptron algorithm (when having multiple hidden layers) also represents the first setting for deep learning-based attacks in profiled SCA. In 2016, Maghrebi et al. conducted a more detailed study of deep learning techniques in profiled SCA where they also used techniques like convolutional neural networks (CNN) or recurrent neural networks [11]. The reported results were in favor of CNNs, and from that time, a large part of the SCA community started to use CNNs, see, e.g., [2,17]. Such a direction seems to pay off as current state-of-the-art results suggest CNNs indeed perform very well and can break implementations protected with countermeasures [2,8,22].

2   State-of-the-Art and Future Challenges

We emphasize that we do not provide a complete overview of the state-of-the-art nor all related works tackling certain aspects of the future research directions we discuss. Rather, we concentrate on challenges we consider to be important and then offer more precise research questions within those.

Currently, the most explored research direction in machine learning-based SCA uses deep learning techniques like multilayer perceptron and convolutional neural networks to mount as powerful as possible attacks. A common setting is to use publicly available datasets (the more difficult dataset the more attractive target) and report the guessing entropy results (i.e., how many traces we require to break the target). There, we mention research by Kim et al. that showed how to add noise to the input to improve the performance of CNNs [8]. More recently, Zaid et al. proposed a methodology for CNN-based attacks where they achieved state-of-the-art results [22]. Some of their results are so good that it remains questionable whether truly better attacks on those datasets and in such scenarios are even possible (as minimal improvements in guessing entropy are not so relevant in practice). Still, there is room for improvements if we consider not only the number of measurements necessary to mount the attack but also to:

- Reduce the complexity of deep learning models. For example, Zaid et al. reported CNN models with much smaller number of parameters than commonly needed [22].
- Limit the number of measurements available to the attacker not only in the attack phase (which is usually done) but also in the training phase. By doing so, we force the attacker to use as powerful as possible deep learning models and at the same time, we reduce the computational complexity as the training phase would last shorter [16].
- Consider more difficult targets and more realistic settings. Indeed, a quite common procedure in profiled SCA research is to use only a single device for both profiling and attacking as well as to have the same key on both "devices". While this makes the setting easier for research, it also makes the results less reliable. Recent results indicate that settings using different devices and keys,

commonly known as portability settings, are significantly more difficult for machine learning attacks [1,5].

Next, despite strong results in deep learning-based SCA, we still do not understand much that is happening inside the deep learning process and as such, we do not know how to make the attacks even stronger. Common examples of questions one could ask are:

- How to know when to stop the training phase (as simply observing loss and accuracy is not necessarily revealing the SCA performance)?
- How to understand what did deep learning model learn and how different results one can expect from some other target?
- How to better connect the performance as measured by side-channel metrics and machine learning metrics?
- How to select the best deep learning architectures (from both performance and complexity perspectives) for certain scenarios and how to conduct good hyperparameter tuning?

We note there are several works partially considering such questions but the answers are far from complete [14,18,21].

Finally, while improving the performance of attacks is important, we must not forget that the end goal is to provide more security. As such, we should consider how to use the knowledge from the most powerful machine learning-based attacks to construct stronger countermeasures and how to use machine learning constructively in SCA (i.e., not only to attack).

References

1. Bhasin, S., Chattopadhyay, A., Heuser, A., Jap, D., Picek, S., Shrivastwa, R.R.: Mind the portability: a warriors guide through realistic profiled side-channel analysis. Cryptology ePrint Archive, Report 2019/661 (2019). https://eprint.iacr.org/2019/661
2. Cagli, E., Dumas, C., Prouff, E.: Convolutional neural networks with data augmentation against jitter-based countermeasures. In: Fischer, W., Homma, N. (eds.) CHES 2017. LNCS, vol. 10529, pp. 45–68. Springer, Cham (2017). https://doi.org/10.1007/978-3-319-66787-4_3
3. Chari, S., Rao, J.R., Rohatgi, P.: Template attacks. In: Kaliski, B.S., Koç, K., Paar, C. (eds.) CHES 2002. LNCS, vol. 2523, pp. 13–28. Springer, Heidelberg (2003). https://doi.org/10.1007/3-540-36400-5_3
4. Choudary, O., Kuhn, M.G.: Efficient template attacks. In: Francillon, A., Rohatgi, P. (eds.) CARDIS 2013. LNCS, vol. 8419, pp. 253–270. Springer, Cham (2014). https://doi.org/10.1007/978-3-319-08302-5_17
5. Das, D., Golder, A., Danial, J., Ghosh, S., Raychowdhury, A., Sen, S.: X-DeepSCA: cross-device deep learning side channel attack. In: Proceedings of the 56th Annual Design Automation Conference 2019, DAC 2019, pp. 134:1–134:6. ACM, New York (2019)
6. Gilmore, R., Hanley, N., O'Neill, M.: Neural network based attack on a masked implementation of AES. In: 2015 IEEE International Symposium on Hardware Oriented Security and Trust (HOST), pp. 106–111, May 2015

7. Hospodar, G., De Mulder, E., Gierlichs, B.: Least squares support vector machines for side-channel analysis. Center for Advanced Security Research Darmstadt, pp. 99–104, January 2011

8. Kim, J., Picek, S., Heuser, A., Bhasin, S., Hanjalic, A.: Make some noise. Unleashing the power of convolutional neural networks for profiled side-channel analysis. IACR Trans. Cryptogr. Hardw. Embed. Syst. **2019**(3), 148–179 (2019)

9. Kocher, P., Jaffe, J., Jun, B.: Differential power analysis. In: Wiener, M. (ed.) CRYPTO 1999. LNCS, vol. 1666, pp. 388–397. Springer, Heidelberg (1999). https://doi.org/10.1007/3-540-48405-1_25

10. Lerman, L., Medeiros, S.F., Bontempi, G., Markowitch, O.: A machine learning approach against a masked AES. In: Francillon, A., Rohatgi, P. (eds.) CARDIS 2013. LNCS, vol. 8419, pp. 61–75. Springer, Cham (2014). https://doi.org/10.1007/978-3-319-08302-5_5

11. Maghrebi, H., Portigliatti, T., Prouff, E.: Breaking cryptographic implementations using deep learning techniques. In: Carlet, C., Hasan, M.A., Saraswat, V. (eds.) SPACE 2016. LNCS, vol. 10076, pp. 3–26. Springer, Cham (2016). https://doi.org/10.1007/978-3-319-49445-6_1

12. Mangard, S., Oswald, E., Popp, T.: Power Analysis Attacks: Revealing the Secrets of Smart Cards. Springer, New York (2006). ISBN 0-387-30857-1. http://www.dpabook.org/

13. Martinasek, Z., Zeman, V.: Innovative method of the power analysis. Radioengineering **22**(2), 586–594 (2013)

14. Masure, L., Dumas, C., Prouff, E.: A comprehensive study of deep learning for side-channel analysis. Cryptology ePrint Archive, Report 2019/439 (2019). https://eprint.iacr.org/2019/439

15. Picek, S., Heuser, A., Guilley, S.: Template attack versus Bayes classifier. J. Cryptogr. Eng. **7**(4), 343–351 (2017)

16. Picek, S., Heuser, A., Guilley, S.: Profiling side-channel analysis in the restricted attacker framework. Cryptology ePrint Archive, Report 2019/168 (2019). https://eprint.iacr.org/2019/168

17. Picek, S., Heuser, A., Jovic, A., Bhasin, S., Regazzoni, F.: The curse of class imbalance and conflicting metrics with machine learning for side-channel evaluations. IACR Trans. Cryptogr. Hardw. Embed. Syst. **2019**(1), 209–237 (2019)

18. Picek, S., Samiotis, I.P., Kim, J., Heuser, A., Bhasin, S., Legay, A.: On the performance of convolutional neural networks for side-channel analysis. In: Chattopadhyay, A., Rebeiro, C., Yarom, Y. (eds.) SPACE 2018. LNCS, vol. 11348, pp. 157–176. Springer, Cham (2018). https://doi.org/10.1007/978-3-030-05072-6_10

19. Quisquater, J.-J., Samyde, D.: ElectroMagnetic analysis (EMA): measures and counter-measures for smart cards. In: Attali, I., Jensen, T. (eds.) E-smart 2001. LNCS, vol. 2140, pp. 200–210. Springer, Heidelberg (2001). https://doi.org/10.1007/3-540-45418-7_17

20. Schindler, W., Lemke, K., Paar, C.: A stochastic model for differential side channel cryptanalysis. In: Rao, J.R., Sunar, B. (eds.) CHES 2005. LNCS, vol. 3659, pp. 30–46. Springer, Heidelberg (2005). https://doi.org/10.1007/11545262_3

21. van der Valk, D., Picek, S.: Bias-variance decomposition in machine learning-based side-channel analysis. Cryptology ePrint Archive, Report 2019/570 (2019). https://eprint.iacr.org/2019/570

22. Zaid, G., Bossuet, L., Habrard, A., Venelli, A.: Methodology for efficient CNN architectures in profiling attacks. Cryptology ePrint Archive, Report 2019/803 (2019). https://eprint.iacr.org/2019/803

A Study of Persistent Fault Analysis

Andrea Caforio and Subhadeep Banik[✉]

LASEC, École Polytechnique Fédérale de Lausanne, Lausanne, Switzerland
{andrea.caforio,subhadeep.banik}@epfl.ch

Abstract. Persistent faults mark a new class of injections that perturb lookup tables within block ciphers with the overall goal of recovering the encryption key. Unlike earlier fault types persistent faults remain intact over many encryptions until the affected device is rebooted, thus allowing an adversary to collect a multitude of correct and faulty ciphertexts. It was shown to be an efficient and effective attack against substitution-permutation networks. In this paper, the scope of persistent faults is further broadened and explored. More specifically, we show how to construct a key-recovery attack on generic Feistel schemes in the presence of persistent faults. In a second step, we leverage these faults to reverse-engineer AES- and PRESENT-like ciphers in a chosen-key setting, in which some of the computational layers, like substitution tables, are kept secret. Finally, we propose a novel, dedicated, and low-overhead countermeasure that provides adequate protection for hardware implementations against persistent fault injections.

Keywords: Fault analysis · PFA · Feistel networks · Reverse engineering · AES · PRESENT · Countermeasures

1 Introduction

Fault injections and their accompanying analysis techniques rank amongst the most devastating attacks against cryptographic implementations. They saw their inception in 1996 when Boneh et al. demonstrated how to use computation errors during the CRT step of RSA to recover a prime factor of the public modulus [5]. In the following year, Biham and Shamir gave a method to exploit the difference between a faulty and correct DES ciphertext to gain information about the encryption key, this type of analysis became known as differential fault analysis [3]. Usually very few ciphertext pairs are needed to mount a DFA attack successfully; however, the faults have to be precisely targeted, often at rather small memory regions or specific registers, and during particular rounds of a block cipher computation. Other attacks assume a permanent fault model that is most commonly induced by defective hardware [9].

Persistent faults attempt to bridge the gap between short-lived and permanent faults as they remain intact over multiple encryptions but vanish once the device is rebooted. Persistent fault analysis gained traction at CHES 2018, in a

© Springer Nature Switzerland AG 2019
S. Bhasin et al. (Eds.): SPACE 2019, LNCS 11947, pp. 13–33, 2019.
https://doi.org/10.1007/978-3-030-35869-3_4

work by Zhang et al. [16]. Their attack exploits the statistical imbalance in a collected set of ciphertexts, caused by one or more overwritten s-box elements, to recover the last round-key of substitution-permutation networks. The idea is based on the fact that in most SPN ciphers, like AES, a skewed substitution layer distribution translates directly into the ciphertexts. To see this, suppose the element u does not appear anymore in the s-box output due to the persistent fault injection, as a consequence, $u \oplus k$ is an impossible ciphertext word, where k is a last round-key word. Hence, after enough collected ciphertexts from the faulty device, k can be uniquely identified. The authors subsequently show that around 1500 ciphertexts are sufficient to recover the last round-key of AES in the presence of a single overwritten s-box element. They further demonstrate how to use the rowhammer attack [10] in order to provoke persistent fault injections in the s-box of vulnerable AES implementations.

In this paper, we show how persistent faults can be used to attack generic Feistel schemes where an altered s-box distribution is not directly visible in the collected ciphertext set. In a next step, we tackle the task of reverse engineering concealed parts of block ciphers. In particular, we demonstrate how to leverage persistent fault injections to recover a hidden PRESENT s-box and its permutation layer, as well as the substitution box of AES in a reduced-round setting. These reverse engineering attacks take place in the chosen-key setting and exploit particular behaviours within the key-schedule routines of both PRESENT and AES. Lastly, we propose a novel, low-overhead hardware countermeasure that adequately protects bijective substitution boxes against persistent fault injections.

2   Persistent Fault Analysis on Feistel Schemes

The standard techniques of persistent fault analysis do not apply to Feistel networks due to the fact that the both the left and right side of the output are masked by previous round function outputs. Indeed any Feistel round is a permutation over bit strings of length equal to the block size of the cipher, irrespective of whether the component s-box used in it is bijective or not. As a consequence, the skewed distribution of a faulty substitution box does not appear in the collected ciphertexts. However, if we loosen the ciphertext-only requirement, persistent fault can become a feasible danger. More specifically, we allow the attacker a single device reset and the possibility to re-encrypt plaintexts.

Consider a generic r-round Feistel scheme whose substitution layer consists of b identical or different $n \times m$ s-boxes $S_1, S_2, \ldots, S_b$. The last round of such a construction is depicted in Fig. 1, with $x_l \| x_r$ being the input to the last round and $y_l \| y_r$ the corresponding ciphertext. Both $x_l \| x_r$ and $y_l \| y_r$ can be further decomposed into b blocks of m bits such that

$$x_l = |x_l^1, \ldots, x_l^b|, \ x_r = |x_r^1, \ldots, x_r^b|,$$
$$y_l = |y_l^1, \ldots, y_l^b|, \ y_r = |y_r^1, \ldots, y_r^b|.$$

For most ciphers $n = m$. However, for block ciphers like DES, $n = 6$ and $m = 4$. So we first expand x_r using an expansion function to a string d_r of length nb bits. Thereafter, we can write $d_r = |d_r^1, d_r^2, \ldots, d_r^b|$, where each d_r^i is of length n bits.

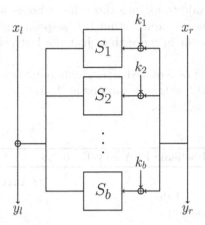

Fig. 1. Last round of a generic Feistel scheme

2.1   Different S-Boxes

We first treat the case where $S_1, S_2, \ldots, S_b$ are pairwise different substitution boxes. The key observation is that in the presence of persistent faults some ciphertexts remain uncorrupted.

Suppose a single fault has been injected into one box. The probability that this element is not accessed in each round lies at $(1 - \frac{1}{2^n})^r$. Furthermore, the probability that the faulty element is only accessed in the very last round is given by $\frac{1}{2^n}(1 - \frac{1}{2^n})^{r-1}$.

Example 1 (DES). The data encryption standard [8] is a 16-round Feistel network whose substitution layer consists eight pairwise different 6×4 s-boxes. The probability that a faulty element in one box is not accessed in all rounds stands at $(1 - \frac{1}{2^6})^{16} \approx 0.777$. Additionally, the probability that the faulty element is only accessed in the last round is given by $\frac{1}{2^6}(1 - \frac{1}{2^6})^{15} \approx 0.0123$.

For illustration purposes assume that entry e of S_b has been altered. The faulty s-box is denoted by S_b'. The injected element does not need to be known to the attacker. Let $y_l||y_r$ be a ciphertext from a faultless device, i.e. one with S_b, and $y_l'||y_r'$ the encryption of the same plaintext on a faulty device, i.e. one with S_b' that only accessed faulty element of S_b' in the last round. As a consequence we have that $y_l \oplus y_l'$ is of the form

$$y_l \oplus y_l' = |a_1, a_2, \ldots, a_b|,$$

where a_i is a block of m bits with the property that $a_i = 0$ for $0 \leq i < b$ and $a_b = S_b(y_r^b \oplus k_b) \oplus S_b'(y_r^b \oplus k_b)$. In other words, incorrect ciphertexts that accessed the faulty entry e of S_b' only in the last round can be identified when given the corresponding correct ciphertext. In such a case k_b can be recovered via $k_b = y_r^b \oplus e$. In the case where we have l faulty elements $e_1, \ldots, e_l$, k_b can be recovered up-to l candidates. Note that to recover the remaining parts of the last round-key further injections into the other s-boxes are needed. Also note that there is a negligible probability that a false-positive, i.e. a ciphertext that accessed the faulty element in more than just the last round, is of the desired form.

The expected number of required ciphertexts pairs is given by the reciprocal $2^n(1 - \frac{1}{2^n})^{-(r-1)}$. For DES this value stands at $2^6(1 - \frac{1}{2^6})^{-15} \approx 82$. Algorithm 1 summarizes the developed ideas.

Algorithm 1. Feistel Scheme PFA Key-Recovery

---

1 $p, cl, cr \leftarrow (\cdot)$ // Initialize empty lists
2 **for** $i \leftarrow 0$; $i < n$; $i \leftarrow i + 1$ **do**
3 $\quad$ $p(i) \leftarrow$ random plaintext
4 $\quad$ $y_l \| y_r \leftarrow E(p(i))$
5 $\quad$ $cl(i), cr(i) \leftarrow y_l, y_r$

6 Overwrite element e of S_t in E

7 **for** $i \leftarrow 0$; $i < n$; $i \leftarrow i + 1$ **do**
8 $\quad$ $y_l' \| y_r' \leftarrow E(p(i))$
9 $\quad$ $|a_1, \ldots, a_b| \leftarrow y_l \oplus y_l'$
10 $\quad$ **if** $(a_j = 0, j \in \{1, \ldots, b\} \setminus \{t\}) \wedge (a_t \neq 0)$ **then**
11 $\quad\quad$ **return** $y_r^t \oplus e$

2.2 A Single S-Box

In the case where $S_1 = \cdots = S_b$ the probability that the faulty element is only accessed by y_r^b in the last round is now given by $\frac{1}{2^n}(1 - \frac{1}{2^n})^{br-1}$, which can significantly increase the number of required ciphertext pairs. However, unlike in the previous case, one fault injection is enough to recover the entire last round-key. Furthermore, the overwritten element does not need to be known by the attacker either and can be brute-forced. In summary, if the attacker is allowed slightly more powers persistent faults can be exploited to recover the last round-key of Feistel schemes as well.

3 Reverse Engineering

The idea of leveraging fault injections for reverse-engineering, (in short FIRE), was introduced by San Pedro et al. [14] in an attempt to use a corrupted last round computation of either AES or DES to recover their hidden s-boxes. The attack itself is differential in its nature and requires many thousands of faults in order to be successful. The attack was later improved by Le Boulder et al. [12], their attack requires fewer faults in the penultimate instead of the last round of DES to recover all eight hidden substitution boxes. The concept of ineffective fault analysis where a particular byte of the intermediate state is stuck at zero is used by Clavier et al. to recover a hidden s-box of AES [6]. Finally, Tiessen et al. [15] used integral cryptanalysis to retrieve a secret AES substitution box when the cipher is reduced to four rounds.

In this section, we present a chosen-key attack that, in combination with persistent faults, aims to recover hidden substitution boxes and permutations of block ciphers more efficiently than an ordinary exhaustive search. Consider a PRESENT-like [4] construction in which the s-box or the permutation layer are fixed but secret bijective functions over $\{0,1\}^4$ and $\{0,1\}^{64}$ respectively. We demonstrate how persistent faults can be used to reverse-engineer such a construction.

3.1 Brute-Force

We first consider the method of a simple exhaustive search in order to recover the substitution box. There are $2^n!$ bijective s-boxes over $\{0,1\}^n$, and hence the computational complexity of exhaustive search grows out of bound very quickly. For instance, there are $16! \approx 2^{44.25}$ possible arrangements for a small 4×4 s-box. However, already for a 8×8 s-box, as deployed in AES, there exist $256! \approx 2^{1684}$ possibilities. For non-bijective $n \times m$ substitution tables we have $\frac{2^n!}{(2^{n-m}!)^{2^m}}$ potential arrangements. For one of the 6×4 DES s-boxes this values stands at $\frac{64!}{(4!)^{16}} \approx 2^{222.64}$.

3.2 S-Box Recovery of 16-Round PRESENT

PRESENT is an ultra-lightweight block cipher designed by Bogdanov et al. [4] that operates on 64-bit blocks with a key size of either 80 or 128 bits meant for usage in low-energy and space-restricted devices. It operates over 31 rounds with a substitution layer consisting of a single 4×4 s-box that is applied on all 16 nibbles of the intermediate state. For the remainder, we will focus on the 80-bit version and in particular on its key schedule routine. Algorithm 2 depicts its key schedule procedure. Let $|k_{79}k_{78}\ldots k_1k_0|$ be the individual bits of the master key in big endian notation. In each round the 64 most significant bits yield the current round-key. The key is then rotated 61 positions to the left, followed by the substitution of the four most significant bits $|k_{79}k_{78}k_{77}k_{76}|$ by $S(|k_{79}k_{78}k_{77}k_{76}|)$. Finally, the bits $|k_{19}k_{18}k_{17}k_{16}k_{75}|$ are xored with the binary representation of the round counter i.

As a warm-up we consider the s-box recovery in a reduced 16-round setting of PRESENT in the presence of persistent faults in the known-key setting such that the last round-key can be *exactly* determined. Assume the faults are injected into the target device before the key schedule takes place and that the encryption key can be switched out without necessitating a reboot of the device, i.e. the injected faults do not disappear.

Algorithm 2. 80-Bit PRESENT Key-Schedule

---

1 **for** $i = 1$; $i \leq 32$; $i \leftarrow i + 1$ **do**
2      $K_i \leftarrow |k_{79}k_{78} \ldots k_{16}|$
3      $|k_{79}k_{78} \ldots k_1 k_0| \leftarrow |k_{18}k_{17} \ldots k_{20}k_{19}|$
4      $|k_{79}k_{78}k_{77}k_{76}| \leftarrow S(|k_{79}k_{78}k_{77}k_{76}|)$
5      $|k_{19}k_{18}k_{17}k_{16}k_{15}| \leftarrow |k_{19}k_{18}k_{17}k_{16}k_{15}| \oplus i$

Due to its simplicity, the PRESENT key schedule exhibits some peculiarities. For instance, Hernandez et al. [11] showed that there exist keys that expand into very similar round-keys. This is partly due to the fact that some key bits only enter the substitution box during relatively late rounds and only appear in a few round-keys.

We want to stress another property of the key schedule routine. It is not hard to see that during the first 16 rounds no key bit enters the substitution box more than once, hence all s-box accesses during the second 16 rounds only depend on the values of the first 16 accesses. As a consequence, it is possible to compute keys that only access a single s-box element during the first half which in turn leads to the fact that the pattern of the latter half of s-box accesses is entirely determined by this single s-box value that was accessed during the first half.

Definition 1 (Low-Diffusion Key). *A low-diffusion key $\widetilde{K}$ is a PRESENT master key that, if fed into the key schedule routine, causes only one element of the s-box table to be accessed during the first 16 key schedule rounds.*

Naturally, there can only be 16 low-diffusion keys in total $\widetilde{K}_0, \ldots, \widetilde{K}_{15}$ one for each substitution box element, i.e. key $\widetilde{K}_i$ only accesses s-box entry i during the first 16 rounds of the key schedule. See Algorithm 7 in the appendix on how to calculate all the 16 low-diffusion keys.

The existence of low-diffusion keys immediately suggests a s-box recovery procedure in a reduced 16-round setting. Given a faulty device E, for each low-diffusion key $\widetilde{K}_i$, $0 \leq i < 16$ we recover the last round-key k through PFA then iterate over all possible values of $S(i) = j$ and compare whether an offline key schedule calculation is equal to k. Algorithm 3 depicts the described method. Note that we assume that the faults remain intact after re-keying, if this is not the case the persistent faults have to be injected again for each iteration. Further note that only a few dozens of ciphertexts are required to recover the last round-key through PFA in PRESENT with high probability.

3.3   S-Box Recovery of Full-Round PRESENT

The attack from the previous section does not directly apply to a full 31-round setting, however we can use persistent faults to engineer a new s-box recovery algorithms applicable to different fault models. The intuition is still based on the particular behaviour of low-diffusion keys, especially their behaviour throughout the key schedule computation.

Algorithm 3. 16-Round PRESENT S-Box Recovery

---

1 $S(i) \leftarrow 0$, for $0 \leq i < 16$
2 **for** $i = 0$; $i < 16$; $i \leftarrow i + 1$ **do**
3     $k \leftarrow \text{PFA}(E_{\widetilde{K}_i})$ // Recover last round-key through PFA
4   **for** $j = 0$; $j < 16$; $j \leftarrow j + 1$ **do**
5        $S(i) = j$ // Assign j to i-th s-box entry
         // Offline key schedule using s-box S
         // and low-diffusion key $\widetilde{K}_i$
6   **if** $\text{KeySchedule}_S(\widetilde{K}_i) = k$ **then**
7 | **break**

Definition 2 (Access Rate). *The access rate of a low-diffusion key, denoted by* $r_{\widetilde{K}_i}(j)$, *is the number of accessed s-box elements by the key* $\widetilde{K}_i$ *during the key schedule routine when* $S(i) = j$.

Table 1 depicts each low-diffusion key alongside their respective access rates.

Table 1. Low-diffusion keys and their access rates

i	$\widetilde{K}_i$	$r_{\widetilde{K}_i}(j)$															
		0	1	2	3	4	5	6	7	8	9	10	11	12	13	14	15
0	0x037bf04d5c0567402460	16	15	13	13	11	11	11	11	15	14	12	13	11	11	11	11
1	0x026ae06f7e012300ace8	16	15	13	13	11	11	11	11	16	15	13	13	11	11	11	11
2	0x0159d009180defc13570	16	15	13	13	11	11	11	11	15	14	12	13	11	11	11	11
3	0x0048c02b3a09ab81bdf8	16	15	13	13	11	11	11	11	15	14	12	13	11	11	11	11
4	0x073fb0c5d41476420640	16	15	13	13	11	11	11	11	15	14	13	14	11	11	11	11
5	0x062ea0e7f61032028ec8	16	15	14	14	11	11	11	11	15	14	12	13	11	11	11	11
6	0x051d9081901cfec31750	16	16	14	14	11	11	11	11	15	14	13	14	11	11	11	11
7	0x040c80a3b218ba839fd8	16	15	14	14	11	11	11	11	15	15	13	14	11	11	11	11
8	0x0bf3715c4c2745446020	16	15	13	13	12	12	12	11	15	14	12	13	12	12	11	11
9	0x0ae2617e6e230104e8a8	16	15	13	13	12	12	11	11	15	14	12	13	12	12	12	11
10	0x09d15118082fcdc57130	16	15	13	13	12	12	11	12	15	14	12	13	12	12	11	11
11	0x08c0413a2a2b8985f9b8	16	15	13	13	12	12	11	11	15	14	12	13	12	12	11	12
12	0x0fb731d4c43654464200	16	15	13	13	12	11	12	12	15	14	12	13	11	11	12	12
13	0x0ea621f6e6321006ca88	16	15	13	13	11	11	12	12	15	14	12	13	12	11	12	12
14	0x0d951190803edcc75310	16	15	13	13	11	12	12	12	15	14	12	13	11	11	12	12
15	0x0c8401b2a23a9887db98	16	15	13	13	11	11	12	12	15	14	12	13	11	12	12	12

Definition 3 (Access Pattern). *Denote by* $p_{\widetilde{K}_i}(j)$ *the set of accessed s-box entries during the key schedule for low-diffusion key* $\widetilde{K}_i$ *with* $S(i) = j$.

Example 2. The access pattern for $\widetilde{K}_0$ and $S(0) = 12$ is given by

$$p_{\widetilde{K}_0}(12) = \{0, 1, 2, 3, 4, 5, 6, 7, 12, 14, 15\}.$$

We look at the case where the adversary manages to inject a single chosen fault at a precise position in the substitution table, i.e. one element is overwritten. The online stage for this attack is the same as the previous one; we use the persistent attack module with the set of known keys $\widetilde{K}_i$ to extract the last round-key.

Note that a brute-force search in this setting, to recover the secret s-box, requires in the worst case $15! \approx 2^{40.25}$ trials in order to recover the remaining s-box entries. This value can be significantly improved if the encryption key can be chosen. Let the injected fault be of the form $S(i) = j$ such that $r_{\widetilde{K}_i}(j) = 11$. In this case there are only 10 remaining s-box entries in the entire key schedule routine that are accessed for the low-diffusion key $\widetilde{K}_i$. The strategy is to randomly assign values to these 10 entries, after which it is possible to compute the last round-key from $\widetilde{K}_i$ using an offline key schedule computation: the assigned values are correct if this computed key matches the last round-key obtained through PFA. Now, there are $\frac{15!}{5!} \approx 2^{33.34}$ potential arrangements that have to be checked in the worst case since due to the low-diffusion key and the fault injection only 10 s-box entries need to be assigned from a set of 15 potential values. This results in a reduction by a factor of 120 compared to the brute-force approach. The remaining 5 elements can then be safely brute-forced. Thus the computational complexity of this method is around $2^{33.34} + 5! \approx 2^{33.34}$ offline key schedule computations. Algorithm 4 formally depicts the described strategy: it makes use of the following definition.

Definition 4 (m-Permutation). *Let L be a collection of n elements. A m-permutation of L, denoted by $\Pi_{n,m}(L)$, is the set of all possible ways to choose m elements from L without repetition.*

Algorithm 4. Single-Fault S-Box Recovery

---

1   Choose $i \in \{0, 1, 2, 3, 4, 5, 6, 7\}$
2   Overwrite $S(i) = j$ such that $r_{\widetilde{K}_i}(j) = 11$

    // Recover last round-key k
    // and overwritten element v through PFA
3   $k, v \leftarrow \text{PFA}(E_{\widetilde{K}_i})$
4   $L \leftarrow \{0, \ldots, 15\} \setminus \{v\}$
5   $S'(l) = 0,\ 0 \leq l \leq 15;\ S'(i) = j$
6   **for each** $\pi \in \Pi_{15,10}(L)$ **do**
7      $z \leftarrow 0$
8   **for each** $p \in p_{\widetilde{K}_i}(j)$ **do**
9        $S'(p) \leftarrow \pi(z),\ z \leftarrow z + 1$
10   **if** $\text{KeySchedule}_{S'}(\widetilde{K}_i) = k$ **then**
11   **return** S'

3.4   Permutation Layer Recovery of PRESENT

On paper, recovering the permutation layer appears to be a harder task due to the sheer amount $64! \approx 2^{296}$ of possibilities. Let $C = \{c_1, \ldots, c_n\}$ be a set of n ciphertexts from the faulty device. Denote by $|c(i), c(j), c(k), c(l)|$ the nibble that is created by extracting the bits i, j, k, l from a ciphertext c. Further, denote by $C(i, j, k, l)$ the set of nibbles that is generated by extracting bits i, j, k, l from each ciphertext, i.e.

$$C(i, j, k, l) = \{|c_1(i), c_1(j), c_1(k), c_1(l)|, \ldots, |c_n(i), c_n(j), c_n(k), c_n(l)|\}.$$

Suppose an random entry in the S-box is overwritten due to a fault. If each bit in a nibble i, j, k, l stems from the same s-box then we have necessarily $|C(i, j, k, l)| < 16$ due to the persistent fault injection. This is obviously due to the fact that overwriting the entry of a bijective 4×4 s-box decreases the number of unique outputs to less than 16. For all other nibbles the set is of size 16 for a large enough n. In this fashion we recover the hidden permutation up to a reordering of the bits i, j, k, l of each nibble, which naturally gives rise to 4! possibilities for each nibble and hence $4!^{16}$ possibilities for the entire 16 nibbles. Furthermore a reordering of the 16 s-boxes is also required that gives rise to 16! possibilities, which leaves us with a remaining complexity of $24^{16} \times 16! \approx 2^{118}$ to recover the entire permutation. Algorithm 5 depicts this strategy.

Algorithm 5. PRESENT Permutation Recovery

---

1 $L \leftarrow \{0, 1, 2, \ldots, 63\}$
2 $C \leftarrow \{c_1, \ldots, c_n\}$ // Set of n ciphertexts from faulty device
   // Iterate over all permutations of size 4
3 for each $\pi_0, \pi_1, \pi_2, \pi_3 \in \Pi_4(L)$ do
4   if $|C(\pi_0, \pi_1, \pi_2, \pi_3)| < 16$ then
5   output $|\pi_0, \pi_1, \pi_2, \pi_3|$
6          $L \leftarrow L \setminus |\pi_0, \pi_1, \pi_2, \pi_3|$

The question is now, how large do we have to choose n in order to guarantee with high probability that only the correct nibbles are chosen? This is a classical instance of the coupon collector's problem where we want to quantify the number of uniform trials until some number of elements have been picked. In the case of Algorithm 5, how many ciphertexts are required until $|C(i, j, k, l)| = 16$ with high probability for an incorrect nibble? Let T the number of trials until 16 substitution box entries have occurred for a specific ciphertext nibble. The expected number of picks $E[T]$ is given by

$$E[T] = 16H_{16} \approx 54.1,$$

where H_{16} is the 16-th Harmonic number. Similarly, we can quantify the variance $\mathrm{Var}[T]$, which is upper-bounded by

$$\mathrm{Var}[T] < \frac{\pi^2}{6}16^2 \approx 421.1.$$

Finally, we can use the Chebyshev's inequality to specify the bound on the error probability.

$$\Pr[T \geq kE[T]] \leq \Pr\left[|T - E[T]| \geq (k-1)E[T]\right]$$
$$\leq \frac{\mathrm{Var}[T]}{((k-1)E[T])^2}$$
$$< \frac{16\pi^2}{6(k-1)^2 H_{16}^2},$$

where $k \geq 2$. Table 2 depicts $\Pr[T \geq kE[T]]$ for multiple choices of k. Evidently, a few hundred ciphertexts should suffice for a successful run of Algorithm 5.

Table 2. $\Pr[T \geq kE[T]]$ for several n

k	2	3	4	5	10	20
$\Pr[T \geq kE[T]]$	0.1439	0.0359	0.0159	0.0089	0.0017	0.0003

Knowing the nibbles that directly originated from one s-box, it is possible to further reduce the permutation space with multiple injections. Firstly, note that if 0 is overwritten then the last round-key bits $\kappa = |\kappa(i), \kappa(j), \kappa(k), \kappa(l)|$ is determined exactly (where we have already determined that bits i, j, k, l emanate from the same s-box). This is a direct consequence of the fact that all 4-bit permutations of 0 remain 0, hence $0 \oplus \kappa$ does not appear in the ciphertext nibble. The same also holds if 15 is overwritten (in that case $15 \oplus \kappa$ does not appear in the ciphertext nibble). Once the last round-key has been established, the last round substitution layer output bits $s = |\kappa(i) \oplus c(i), \kappa(j) \oplus c(j), \kappa(k) \oplus c(k), \kappa(l) \oplus c(l)|$ is also available. Figure 2 illustrates the situation.

Let L_a be the list of collected s-box outputs s for one nibble when entry a of the s-box has been overwritten. There exists a small set of potential 4-bit permutations that produce the values in L_a assuming element a never appears in the s-box output. For example let the entry 1 in the s-box table be overwritten. Then we know that the s-box never outputs 1. We are interested in the determining the order in which the output bits of some s-box is shuffled to map to bits i, j, k, l of the ciphertext (denote this permutation by π_s). Now if some $s = s_0$ is not present in L_1, then we can reduce the search space for π_s to only those permutations that map 1 to s_0. For example if $s_0 = 8$ (the nibble which has 1 in the msb), then π_s is essentially the set of all 4 bit permutations that map the lsb to the msb.

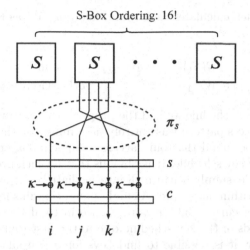

Fig. 2. Permutation layer recovery in PRESENT

It is not too difficult to see that repeating the above experiments for $a = 2, 4, 8$ gives us the unique 4-bit permutation π_s. This means with four injections we can retrieve the 4-bit permutation after each s-box, which reduces the overall search space down to a reordering of the s-boxes, i.e. $16! \approx 2^{44}$ possibilities. This set is small enough to be brute forced using appropriate computational resources.

3.5   Reduced-Round AES S-Box Recovery

The ideas developed so far can be adapted in order to recover a hidden AES s-box in a reduced-round setting. We consider the 128-bit Rijndael key schedule procedure as it is deployed in the final AES specification [7]. The routine acts in eleven rounds, one for each round-key, and works on 32-bit words. Let K_0, K_1, K_2 and K_3 denote the four 32-bit words of the master key with $W_0, \ldots, W_{43}$ being the 32-bit round-key output words. Further, let rc be a list of ten round constants.

The key schedule also makes use of two external transformations R and S. R designates the rotation of a 32-bit word, consisting of four bytes $|b_0, b_1, b_2, b_3|$, by one position to the left, such that

$$R(|b_0, b_1, b_2, b_3|) = |b_1, b_2, b_3, b_0|$$

while S is the substitution of each byte in a 32-bit word by its corresponding s-box value such that

$$S(|b_0, b_1, b_2, b_3|) = |S(b_0), S(b_1), S(b_2), S(b_3)|.$$

The key schedule then calculates each round-key word W_i as follows

$$W_i = \begin{cases} K_i, & i < 4 \\ W_{i-4} \oplus R(S(W_{i-1})) \oplus rc_{i/4}, & i \geq 4 \text{ and } i \equiv 0 \bmod 4 \\ W_{i-4} \oplus W_{i-1}, & \text{otherwise.} \end{cases}$$

In the PRESENT key schedule we had the property that during the first sixteen rounds the s-box access pattern was entirely determined by the master key thus special keys could be found that only access a single s-box entry during those initial rounds of the key schedule. It is obvious that no such property is given in the AES key schedule, simply because all intermediate key states are affected by the s-box accesses within one round. A single round contains four s-box accesses one for each byte of current 32-bit word, hence in total there are 40 accesses over all eleven rounds of the key schedule due to the first round not performing no lookup. However, it is possible to find keys for which all four lookups of a single round go to the same element for the first few rounds of the key schedule routine.

We consider the following adapted fault model, where the 0 is injected at a *known* position i in the substitution table such that $S(i) = 0$, which has the following lemma as a consequence.

Lemma 1. *Given a AES master key of the form*

$$K_0 = \text{0x01000000}, \ K_1 = \text{0x02000000},$$
$$K_2 = \text{0x02000000}, \ K_3 = |a, a, a, a|,$$

where $a \in \{0, 1\}^8$ *are the individual bytes of the word, and a faulty substitution box* S *with* $S(a) = 0$. *The s-box access pattern during first six rounds of the key schedule is given by*

$$W_3 = |a, a, a, a|, \ W_7 = |a, a, a, a|,$$
$$W_{11} = |a, a, a, a|, \ W_{15} = |a, a, a, b|,$$
$$W_{19} = |a, a, c, d|, \ W_{23} = |a, e, f, g|,$$

where $b, c, d, e, f, g \in \{0, 1\}^8$ *are bytes and given by*

$$b = a \oplus \text{0x06}, \qquad c = a \oplus S(b),$$
$$d = a \oplus \text{0x08}, \qquad e = a \oplus S(a \oplus S(b)),$$
$$f = a \oplus S(b) \oplus S(\text{0x08}), \quad g = \text{0x1a}.$$

This means that the set of input entries of the s-box accessed during the first 6 rounds is given by the byte-values a, b, c, d, e, f, g.

Proof. Due to space constraints, we present a proof in Appendix B.

By leveraging those keys we can device a s-box recovery attack on a reduced-round version of AES that is similar to the algorithms in Sects. 3.2 and 3.3. We use PFA to recover last round-key, then guess partial locations of the s-box table to do an offline key schedule to calculate the last round-key and see if both the above keys match. Algorithm 6 shows a five-round s-box recovery, which recovers three elements of the substitution box.

Algorithm 6. 5-Round AES S-Box Recovery

---

1 Inject 0 at position a in substitution box of E_K
2 $S(i) \leftarrow 0$, for $0 \leq i < 256$
3 $a \in \{0, \ldots, 255\}$
4 $K_0 \leftarrow$ 0x01000000, $K_1 \leftarrow$ 0x02000000, $K_2 \leftarrow$ 0x02000000, $K_3 \leftarrow |a, a, a, a|$
5 $K \leftarrow K_0 || K_1 || K_2 || K_3$

    // Retrieve round-key k and active s-box elements L through PFA
6 $k, L \leftarrow \text{PFA}(E_K)$

7 **for each** $x \in L$ **do**
8   **for each** $y \in L \setminus \{x\}$ **do**
9   **for each** $z \in L \setminus \{x, y\}$ **do**
10             $S(a \oplus \text{0x06}) = x$, $S(a \oplus \text{0x08}) = y$, $S(a \oplus S(a \oplus \text{0x06})) = z$
11   **if** $\text{KeySchedule}_S(K) = k$ **then**
12   **return** S

The number of key schedule operations in Algorithm 6 depends the numbers of cipher rounds, i.e. since only one assignment is made to the s-box table for the 4 round attack, we require 255 key schedule operations. For the 5 round attack, 3 entries are assigned and so $\frac{255!}{252!} \approx 2^{24}$ offline key schedule computations. Similarly 6 assignments are required for the 6 round attack and so and $\frac{255!}{249!} \approx 2^{48}$ operations are required.

The above routine needs to be repeated for multiple values of a to recover the full S-box table. For example in both the 5/6 round attacks, we successfully assign 2 entries $(a \oplus \text{0x06})$ and $(a \oplus \text{0x08})$ in each execution of the above routine. Thus at most 128 executions of the above routine with judiciously chosen values of a are sufficient to extract the entire table.

4 Countermeasures

We propose a novel, low-overhead and dedicated countermeasure against persistent fault injections in bijective substitution boxes that is not susceptible to further injections through redundant lookup tables. The need for this arises through the fact that common fault injection countermeasures, like area redundancy and masking of intermediate values, have been shown to be ineffective [13,16].

We assume the fault model where one or more entries of the s-box have been altered. In such a scenario there are necessarily at least two entries in the s-box that bear the same value such that $S(x) = S(y)$ with $x \neq y$, i.e. if two different values enter the substitution layer and are equal after the transformation an error is detected. This necessitates that all input and output are compared to each other. Figure 3 depicts such a construction. Once a fault has been detected the device can engage in remedy procedures such as outputting random ciphertexts until the next reboot. We will see that the number of encryptions is so low that no information about the last round-key can be inferred through persistent fault analysis techniques.

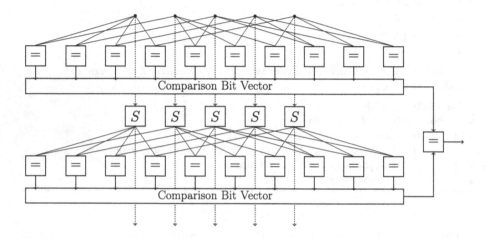

Fig. 3. Pairwise comparison network

If there is one or more overwritten elements in the substitution layer it is possible to quantify the probability that the fault is detected in a particular round by the following lemma.

Lemma 2. *Denote by S a faulty $n \times n$ s-box with t altered entries $v_1, \ldots, v_t$ such that $S(v_i) = S(u_i)$ for some $u_i \notin \{v_1, v_2, \ldots, v_t\}$. Let $p_{n,m,t}$ be the probability that at least one pair of equal entries is accessed in one round. The value is given by*

$$
p_{n,m,t} = 1 - \left(\frac{2^n - 2t}{2^n} \right)^m
$$

$$
- \sum_{i=1}^{t} \left(2^i \binom{t}{i} \right)
$$

$$
\times \sum_{k_1}^{m} \sum_{k_2}^{m-k_1} \cdots \sum_{k_i}^{m-\sum_{j=1}^{i-1}} \binom{m}{k_1} \cdots \binom{m - \sum_{j=1}^{i-1} k_j}{k_i}
$$

$$\times \left(\frac{1}{2^n}\right)^{\sum_{j=1}^{i} k_j} \left(\frac{2^n - 2t}{2^n}\right)^{m - \sum_{j=1}^{i} k_j}\Bigg)$$

Proof. Suppose there are t pairs of equal entries. An error is not detected if none of the $2t$ elements of these pairs are accessed in round, which happens with probability $\left(\frac{2^n - 2t}{2^n}\right)^m$, or exactly one element is accessed from i pairs, which happens with probability

$$\sum_{k_1}^{m} \sum_{k_2}^{m-k_1} \cdots \sum_{k_i}^{m - \sum_{j=1}^{i-1} k_j} \binom{m}{k_1} \cdots \binom{m - \sum_{j=1}^{i-1} k_j}{k_i}.$$

Summing over all $1 \leq i \leq t$ then yields $p_{n,m,t}$.

We can further calculate the probability that one or more faults are detected over r round function invocations in a block cipher.

Corollary 1. *Given a r-round block cipher whose substitution box bears t equalized entries. Denote by $p_{n,m,t}^r$ the probability that an error is detected. It is given by*

$$p_{n,m,t}^r = 1 - (1 - p_{n,m,t})^r.$$

The expected value of required encryption until an injected fault is detected lies at $\frac{1}{p_{n,m,t}^r}$. Table 3 shows the detection probabilities for a varying number of overwritten elements t for both AES $p_{8,16,t}^{10}$ and PRESENT $p_{4,16,t}^{31}$.

Table 3. $p_{n,m,t}^r$ for AES and PRESENT

	$p_{n,m,t}^r$					
	$t = 1$	$t = 2$	$t = 3$	$t = 4$	$t = 5$	$t = 6$
$p_{8,16,t}^{10}$ (AES)	0.0341	0.0671	0.0990	0.1288	0.1597	0.1884
$p_{4,16,t}^{31}$ (PRESENT)	≈ 1	≈ 1	≈ 1	≈ 1	≈ 1	≈ 1

The sixteen substitution box accesses per AES round already yield a relatively good fault detection probability whose expected value is well below the number of ciphertexts that are required for a successful persistent fault analysis attack. However, it is possible to perform additional redundant accesses, i.e. increasing m, to further increase the detection probability.

4.1   Reducing the Hardware Cost

For both AES and PRESENT it is necessary to perform $\binom{16}{2} = 120$ pairwise byte or nibble comparisons. This necessitates a rather large overhead in hardware implementations. A naive circuit that compares bytes can be built out of 8 XNOR gates and 7 AND gates, thus doing 120 comparisons would result in a

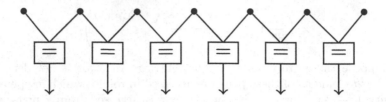

Fig. 4. Adjacent comparison network

total of 1800 logic gates, which requires a significant amount of chip area. As an alternative construction, we propose a modification in which that only adjacent bytes are compared, as seen in Fig. 4.

In such a pattern there are only fifteen comparisons, which in turn changes the detection probability, which is now lower-bounded by $\frac{p_{n,m,t}}{8}$. For AES this bound is tight, the overall detection probability over 10 rounds then stands at $1 - (1 - \frac{p_{8,16,t}}{8})^{10} \approx 0.004335$. Hence in expectation we need $\frac{1}{0.004335} \approx 230$ encryptions until a faulty substitution box is detected. For PRESENT, this bound is not tight, it can be shown that in a single-fault setting the detection probability for one encryption is roughly 0.97, which means that in expectation 1 encryption suffices to detect the fault.

We measured the effectiveness of our countermeasure in the following experiment. We collected ciphertexts from a faulty device protected by our countermeasure until the fault is detected. Persistent fault analysis is then performed on those ciphertexts and the residual key-entropy of the last round key is evaluated. The experiment is further repeated for around 2^{20} random keys in order to obtain a probability for each entropy value. The results are tabulated as a function of the number of persistent faults t in Table 4 for AES and Table 5 for PRESENT. Our countermeasure offers a very strong protection of PRESENT already in the single-fault setting. For AES, it performs well on average but it is especially effective in the presence of more than one persistent fault injection.

Table 4. Probability of residual key entropy (AES)

	$[0, 15)$	$[15, 30)$	$[30, 45)$	$[45, 60)$	$[60, 75)$	$[75, 90)$	$[90, 105)$	$[105, 120)$	$[120, 128]$
$t = 1$	0.00195	0.00361	0.00856	0.01699	0.03708	0.07811	0.16763	0.35617	0.32989
$t = 2$	0.00000	0.00000	0.00008	0.00071	0.00343	0.01654	0.07612	0.35053	0.55261
$t = 3$	0.00000	0.00000	0.00000	0.00002	0.00020	0.00261	0.02669	0.26949	0.70104
$t = 4$	0.00000	0.00000	0.00000	0.00000	0.00001	0.00032	0.00860	0.18980	0.80127

Table 5. Probability of residual key entropy (PRESENT)

	$[56, 57)$	$[57, 58)$	$[58, 59)$	$[60, 61)$	$[61, 62)$	$[62, 63)$	$[63, 64)$	64
$t = 1$	0.00000	0.00000	0.00002	0.00032	0.00067	0.03099	0.00000	0.96798
$t = 2$	0.00000	0.00000	0.00000	0.00001	0.00001	0.00085	0.00000	0.99914

5   Implementation

The countermeasure we suggest is efficiently implementable in ASIC platforms with minimal overhead in hardware. For a round based implementation of AES, the architecture is straightforward and is exactly as depicted in Fig. 4. Comparing each of the adjacent bytes before and after the s-box operation to produce 15-bit vectors before and after the s-box, requires a total of $2 \cdot 15 = 30$ comparator blocks. Each such block can be constructed as the bitwise AND of the XNOR of the two input bytes, i.e.

$$c = \prod_{i=0}^{7}(a_i \oplus b_i \oplus 1),$$

where $\mathbf{a} = (a_0, a_1, \ldots, a_7)$ and $\mathbf{b} = (b_0, b_1, \ldots, b_7)$ are the input bytes and $c = 1$ if and only if $\mathbf{a} = \mathbf{b}$. The circuit to compare the two 15-bit vectors is similar, we perform a bitwise XNOR and compute the logical AND of the resultant bits to get the final fault integrity bit F. If $F = 1$ and all previous fault integrity checks have passed, the round function is allowed to output required result else it is replaced with the all 0 signal. We thus must have some way of ascertaining if all previous integrity checks have passed. To do that we introduce a fault integrity flip-flop, that is initialized to 1 at system reset, which is updated by ANDing the value of the current flip-flop state f_t with the current value of F, i.e $f_{t+1} = F \cdot f_t$. The advantage of this method is that once a fault integrity check fails, the integrity flip-flop is permanently set to 0, after which it becomes easy to replace s-box outputs with random bytes by xoring the term $(1 + f_t) \cdot \theta$, where θ is the output of a random byte generator. Since a bitwise AND of a t-bit signal requires $t - 1$ 2-input AND gates, the above comparison network requires $2 * 15 * 8 + 15 = 255$ two-input XNOR gates and $2 * 15 * 7 + 14 = 224$ two-input AND gates. The final randomizing of the round function output in case $f_t = 0$, requires a simple XOR of the function output with $(1 + f_t) \cdot \theta$ and hence requires a further 128 two-input AND and XOR gates. For the round based implementation of PRESENT, the cost is similar, except that the comparison network is built over nibbles rather than bytes.

For a serial architecture, the implementation is even more efficient and requires minimal hardware overhead. Take, for example the Atomic AES v 2.0 architecture proposed in [2], which performs one s-box operation in one clock cycle. The architecture has an internal round counter constructed with 5-bit full period LFSR that counts up from 0 to 30 for each round. Of these the 16 s-box operations are done in cycles 15 to 30, as the state bytes are shifted out serially through the first byte register implemented in the circuit. In each cycle labeled $t = 15 + j$ for $j \in [0, 14]$ the s-box input and output are each driven into byte registers C_{IN} and C_{OUT} respectively as shown in Fig. 5. As a result at round $t + 1$ one can make a comparison between adjacent byte inputs by simply comparing the values stored in C_{IN} and the current s-box input. A similar comparison can be made between the C_{OUT} and the current s-box output. For fault integrity, the result of the input and output byte comparisons should be equal to each other which is again implemented by an XNOR gate: which naturally outputs 1

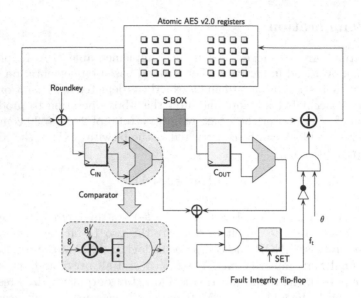

Fig. 5. Fault Integrity check for the Atomic AES v2.0 architecture

if the input-output pairs are both equal or both unequal. Moreover this equality must hold for the $15 \cdot 11 = 165$ comparisons made during an AES encryption operation. Thus we also have a fault integrity flip-flop which works exactly in the same manner as described in the round based circuit.

Table 6 tabulates the results of all implementations. The following design flow was used: first the design was implemented in VHDL. Then, a functional verification was first done using Mentor Graphics Modelsim software. The designs were synthesized using the standard cell library of the 90 nm logic process of STM (CORE90GPHVT v 2.1.a) with the Synopsys Design Compiler, with the compiler being specifically instructed to optimize the circuit for area. A timing simulation was done on the synthesized netlist. The frequency of operation was fixed at 10 MHz as established in [1], because at this frequency, for the STM 90 nm logic process, the energy consumption of block ciphers was found to be frequency-independent. The switching activity of each gate of the circuit was collected while running post-synthesis simulation. The average power was obtained using *Synopsys Power Compiler*, using the back annotated switching activity. Energy is calculated as the product of average power and time taken for one encryption. The table clearly shows that the overhead in terms of area, except for the round based implementation of PRESENT is well under 8%. In terms of other performance metrics, we see reasonably competitive figures.

Table 6. Performance Comparison of circuits before and after implementing fault integrity countermeasures. B refers to the basic circuit without countermeasures, C refers to the circuit after implementing countermeasures, TP_{max} refers to maximum throughput achievable on hardware. Note that the figures do not include an RNG used for randomization

#	Architecture	Type	Area (GE)	Overhead (in %)	Latency (cycles)	Energy (nJ)	TP_{max} (Gbps)
	AES						
1	Round based	B	12876	5.7	11	0.72	2.371
		C	13615		11	0.78	1.555
2	8-bit Serial	B	2060	4.0	246	3.20	0.086
		C	2143		246	3.23	0.075
	PRESENT						
1	Round based	B	1316	30.2	33	0.19	1.598
		C	1713		33	0.29	1.050
2	4-bit Serial	B	892	7.9	564	2.50	0.052
		C	963		564	2.71	0.046

6   Conclusion

Persistent fault analysis has been shown to be an efficient and devastating attack against substitution-permutation networks. In this paper, we further broadened and investigated the range of these kinds of injections. In other words, we showed how Feistel schemes can also fall prey to persistent faults and demonstrate how they can be used to accelerated reverse engineering endeavors. Finally, we presented a low-overhead countermeasure that efficiently protects bijective substitution boxes against persistent fault injections.

In conclusion, persistent faults offer an exciting new perspective on fault attacks in various fields from key-recovery attacks to reverse engineering tasks and the development of efficient and adequate countermeasures. It is thus an interesting exercise in future works to see to what extent persistent faults can be further leveraged.

Appendix

A   Calculation of Low-Diffusion Keys

Algorithm 7 depicts the routine that calculates all 16 low-diffusion keys for PRESENT.

Algorithm 7. Calculation of Low-Diffusion Keys

---

1 **for** $i = 0;\ i < 16;\ i \leftarrow i + 1$ **do**
2 $\quad \widetilde{K}_i \leftarrow 0$
3 $\quad$ **for** $j = 0;\ j < 16;\ j \leftarrow j + 1$ **do**
4 $\quad\quad r \leftarrow (15 + 19j) \bmod 80$
5 $\quad\quad \widetilde{K}_i = \widetilde{K}_i \oplus ((i \oplus j) \lll r)$
6 **return** $\widetilde{K}_i,\ 0 \leq i < 16$

B Proof of Lemma 1

Proof. The access pattern follows from a simple calculation of the intermediate round key words. Set $K_0 = \text{0x01000000}$, $K_1 = \text{0x02000000}$, $K_2 = \text{0x02000000}$, $K_3 = |a, a, a, a|$ and $S(a) = 0$.

$$W_0 = K_0 = \text{0x01000000}$$
$$W_1 = K_1 = \text{0x02000000}$$
$$W_2 = K_2 = \text{0x02000000}$$
$$W_3 = K_3 = |a, a, a, a|$$
$$W_4 = W_0 \oplus S(R(W_3)) \oplus rc_1 = \text{0x00000000}$$
$$W_5 = W_1 \oplus W_4 = \text{0x02000000}$$
$$W_6 = W_2 \oplus W_5 = \text{0x00000000}$$
$$W_7 = W_3 \oplus W_6 = |a, a, a, a|$$
$$W_8 = W_4 \oplus S(R(W_7)) \oplus rc_2 = \text{0x02000000}$$
$$W_9 = W_5 \oplus W_8 = \text{0x00000000}$$
$$W_{10} = W_6 \oplus W_9 = \text{0x00000000}$$
$$W_{11} = W_7 \oplus W_{10} = |a, a, a, a|$$
$$W_{12} = W_8 \oplus S(R(W_{11})) \oplus rc_3 = \text{0x06000000}$$
$$W_{13} = W_9 \oplus W_{12} = \text{0x06000000}$$
$$W_{14} = W_{10} \oplus W_{13} = \text{0x06000000}$$
$$W_{15} = W_{11} \oplus W_{14} = |a \oplus \text{0x06}, a, a, a|$$
$$W_{16} = W_{12} \oplus S(R(W_{15})) \oplus rc_4 = |\text{0x0e}, 0, 0, S(a \oplus \text{0x06})|$$
$$W_{17} = W_{13} \oplus W_{16} = |a \oplus \text{0x08}, 0, 0, S(a \oplus \text{0x06})|$$
$$W_{18} = W_{14} \oplus W_{17} = |a \oplus \text{0x0e}, 0, 0, S(a \oplus \text{0x06})|$$
$$W_{19} = W_{15} \oplus W_{18} = |a \oplus \text{0x08}, a, a, a \oplus S(a \oplus \text{0x06})|$$
$$W_{20} = W_{16} \oplus S(R(W_{19})) \oplus rc_5 = |\text{0x1e}, 0, S(a \oplus S(a \oplus \text{0x06})), S(\text{0x0b})|$$
$$W_{21} = W_{17} \oplus W_{20} = |\text{0x16}, 0, S(a \oplus S(a \oplus \text{0x06})), S(\text{0x0b}) \oplus S(a \oplus \text{0x06})|$$
$$W_{22} = W_{18} \oplus W_{21} = |\text{0x18}, 0, S(a \oplus S(a \oplus \text{0x06})), S(\text{0x0b})|$$
$$W_{23} = W_{19} \oplus W_{22} = |\text{0x1a}, a, a \oplus S(a \oplus S(a \oplus \text{0x06})), a \oplus S(a \oplus \text{0x06}) \oplus S(\text{0x0b})|$$

References

1. Banik, S., Bogdanov, A., Regazzoni, F.: Exploring energy efficiency of lightweight block ciphers. In: Dunkelman, O., Keliher, L. (eds.) SAC 2015. LNCS, vol. 9566, pp. 178–194. Springer, Cham (2016). https://doi.org/10.1007/978-3-319-31301-6_10
2. Banik, S., Bogdanov, A., Regazzoni, F.: Compact circuits for combined AES encryption/decryption. J. Cryptogr. Eng. **9**(1), 69–83 (2019). https://doi.org/10.1007/s13389-017-0176-3

3. Biham, E., Shamir, A.: Differential fault analysis of secret key cryptosystems. In: Kaliski, B.S. (ed.) CRYPTO 1997. LNCS, vol. 1294, pp. 513–525. Springer, Heidelberg (1997). https://doi.org/10.1007/BFb0052259

4. Bogdanov, A., et al.: PRESENT: an ultra-lightweight block cipher. In: Paillier, P., Verbauwhede, I. (eds.) CHES 2007. LNCS, vol. 4727, pp. 450–466. Springer, Heidelberg (2007). https://doi.org/10.1007/978-3-540-74735-2_31

5. Boneh, D., DeMillo, R.A., Lipton, R.J.: On the importance of checking cryptographic protocols for faults. In: Fumy, W. (ed.) EUROCRYPT 1997. LNCS, vol. 1233, pp. 37–51. Springer, Heidelberg (1997). https://doi.org/10.1007/3-540-69053-0_4

6. Clavier, C., Isorez, Q., Marion, D., Wurcker, A.: Complete reverse-engineering of AES-like block ciphers by SCARE and FIRE attacks. Cryptogr. Commun. Discrete Struct. Boolean Funct. Seq. 7(1), 121 (2015)

7. Daemen, J., Rijmen, V.: The block cipher Rijndael. In: Quisquater, J.-J., Schneier, B. (eds.) CARDIS 1998. LNCS, vol. 1820, pp. 277–284. Springer, Heidelberg (2000). https://doi.org/10.1007/10721064_26

8. Des: Data Encryption Standard. In: FIPS PUB 46, Federal Information Processing Standards Publication 46–2 (1977)

9. Dutta, A., Paul, G.: Deterministic hard fault attack on trivium. In: Yoshida, M., Mouri, K. (eds.) IWSEC 2014. LNCS, vol. 8639, pp. 134–145. Springer, Cham (2014). https://doi.org/10.1007/978-3-319-09843-2_11

10. Gruss, D., Maurice, C., Mangard, S.: Rowhammer.js: a remote software-induced fault attack in JavaScript. In: Caballero, J., Zurutuza, U., Rodríguez, R.J. (eds.) DIMVA 2016. LNCS, vol. 9721, pp. 300–321. Springer, Cham (2016). https://doi.org/10.1007/978-3-319-40667-1_15

11. Hernandez-Castro, J.C., Peris-Lopez, P., Aumasson, J.-P.: On the key schedule strength of PRESENT. In: Garcia-Alfaro, J., Navarro-Arribas, G., Cuppens-Boulahia, N., de Capitani di Vimercati, S. (eds.) DPM/SETOP 2011. LNCS, vol. 7122, pp. 253–263. Springer, Heidelberg (2012). https://doi.org/10.1007/978-3-642-28879-1_17

12. Le Bouder, H., Guilley, S., Robisson, B., Tria, A.: Fault injection to reverse engineer DES-like cryptosystems. In: Danger, J.-L., Debbabi, M., Marion, J.-Y., Garcia-Alfaro, J., Zincir Heywood, N. (eds.) FPS -2013. LNCS, vol. 8352, pp. 105–121. Springer, Cham (2014). https://doi.org/10.1007/978-3-319-05302-8_7

13. Pan, J., Bhasin, S., Zhang, F., Ren, K.: One Fault is All it Needs: Breaking Higher-Order Masking with Persistent Fault Analysis. Cryptology ePrint Archive, Report 2019/008 (2019). https://eprint.iacr.org/2019/008

14. San Pedro, M., Soos, M., Guilley, S.: FIRE: fault injection for reverse engineering. In: Ardagna, C.A., Zhou, J. (eds.) WISTP 2011. LNCS, vol. 6633, pp. 280–293. Springer, Heidelberg (2011). https://doi.org/10.1007/978-3-642-21040-2_20

15. Tiessen, T., Knudsen, L.R., Kölbl, S., Lauridsen, M.M.: Security of the AES with a secret S-Box. In: Leander, G. (ed.) FSE 2015. LNCS, vol. 9054, pp. 175–189. Springer, Heidelberg (2015). https://doi.org/10.1007/978-3-662-48116-5_9

16. Zhang, F., et al.: Persistent fault analysis on block ciphers. IACR Transactions on Cryptographic Hardware and Embedded Systems, pp. 150–172 (2018)

Internal State Recovery Attack on Stream Ciphers: Breaking BIVIUM

Shravani Shahapure[1]([✉]), Virendra Sule[2], and R. D. Daruwala[1]

[1] Department of Electronics, Veer Jijamata Technological Institute,
Matunga, Mumbai 400031, India
shravani@iitb.ac.in
[2] Department of Electrical Engineering, Indian Institute of Technology Bombay,
Powai, Mumbai 400076, India

Abstract. This paper proposes an attack on shift register based stream ciphers. The attack consists of recovering the internal state of the registers at a starting clock instant from which the output stream is available. For a given output stream the evolution of the output function at the clocking times is first computed in symbolic form as a sequence of Boolean functions from the symbolic state update map of the internal state dynamics. Then the Boolean equations are solved using a Boolean solver which returns all possible internal states which match the output stream. Once the internal state (or most of its assignments) are obtained this way the internal state is reversed sequentially to the initial condition. The resulting equations give solutions to key bits solved by comparing the IV bits with unknown variable equations. This discovers most of the key bits and reduces the unknown key bits to a very small number. Then by brute force search on the remaining key bits the output stream is regenerated to recognize the remaining key bits when the output stream exactly matches. In case when all the bits of the internal state are solved from the Boolean equations of the output stream, but there are more than one solutions to the internal state, the correct initial state is recognized when the IV bits match exactly with the initial condition obtained by reversing the internal state. The attack is practically useful when the all computations involved in steps such as solutions of the Boolean equations from the output stream, the symbolic equation generation from the output function for the length of output stream, symbolic reversing of the internal state with small number of unknown variables are feasible. This paper shows feasibility of this approach for the stream cipher BIVIUM with 80 bits of key and shows that a complete recovery of the key is feasible in practical time by parallel search requiring memory space which is feasible in modern day clusters.

Keywords: Stream ciphers · Shift registers · Boolean polynomial systems · Implicants

© Springer Nature Switzerland AG 2019
S. Bhasin et al. (Eds.): SPACE 2019, LNCS 11947, pp. 34–49, 2019.
https://doi.org/10.1007/978-3-030-35869-3_5

1   Introduction

The aim of this paper is to demonstrate a complete key recovery attack on the stream cipher Bivium by solving the internal state of the cipher using a Boolean model of the cipher and solving all Boolean assignments of a system of equations compatible with the output stream. This attack is in principle a universal methodology for cryptanalysis of nonlinear combiners or NLFSR based stream ciphers. But in practice it may work only when computation of a Boolean model of the output functions for the length of output stream is feasible, as well as computing all solution of the Boolean system for the output stream with partially solved bits is also feasible. This paper shows that the structure of the Boolean system of Bivium with 177 variables in the internal state fails to withstand this attack. We show how 80 bit Bivium key can be estimated to be recovered from 177 variable internal state within a time of 49 h by a parallel brute force search of special 40 bits equivalent to parallel 2^{40} searches requiring 5.4 TB of memory space. Similarly a parallel search over 2^{42} threads generated from implicants obtained from the first 14 of the same equations can recover the key in 17 h but requires 30 TB of memory. The first of these attacks can be accomplished in a practically feasible memory space available with state of the art clusters. Since the memory space required does not increase drastically for implicant based search a combination of the two searches may be utilized to bring the computation to a feasible space and time requirement. No previous record of an algebraic system solver to the best of author's knowledge has achieved these performances.

Creating a record of breaking Bivium is a case study for establishing the effectiveness of the algorithmic methods used in this paper. Aim of this paper is much beyond just breaking Bivium and is to find heuristics for solving all solutions of the non linear system of 177 Boolean variables arising from Bivium key stream. To get a perspective we list the main contributions of this paper as

1. Showing that the implicant based solver announced in [14] is effective in solving the system of Boolean equations and get all solutions in realistically feasible time and memory space. No other algebraic approach has reported equivalent success in finding all solutions of such large nonlinear equations. (The timings shown in Tables 1 and 2 of performances are of actual computations on a 2.5 GHz desktop computer with standard Intel processor and RAM).
2. Discovering two different heuristics for decomposing the Boolean equations due to their structure. These heuristics are otherwise quite general and can be useful for solving Boolean systems in cryptanalysis of other stream ciphers as well as in other applications.
3. Estimating a practically feasible record of breaking Bivium by parallel computation by actually carrying out sample computations of threads for estimating average times and memory space requirements. No such practically feasible records of breaking Bivium are believed to be known.

Key recovery problem of cryptanalysis of stream ciphers requires solving the hard computational problem of finding all solutions of Boolean equations arising from the knowledge of the output stream. Most well known algebraic cryptanalysis approaches are either not scalable for realistic number of variables of actual cipher models and hence can only show results of scaled down ciphers. Often their limitation is also due to not being able to represent all solutions of the system of equations which are essential for key recovery. Our aim in this paper is to demonstrate that the implicant based approach to solving Boolean systems is scalable, parallel and can represent all solutions and succeeds in solving the realistic size equations arising in Bivium. Hence this algorithm should also be useful in solving similar complex Boolean systems depending on the structure which permitted certain heuristics in decomposition of the equations.

1.1   The Key Recovery Problem

A stream cipher which uses shift registers for its state evolution is a finite state dynamical system with an output. In most cases such a system can be described by a finite state map $F : \mathbb{F}_2^n \to \mathbb{F}_2^n$ and a function $f : \mathbb{F}_2^n \to \mathbb{F}_2$ giving a state output system

$$
\begin{aligned}
x(k+1) &= F(x(k)) \\
w(k) &= f(x(k))
\end{aligned}
\tag{1}
$$

where $x(k)$ is the internal state (of all the shift registers) and $w(k)$ is the output (key stream bit) of the cipher at an instant k. The symmetric key K of the cipher is a fixed subset of known bits of the initial state $x(0)$. The remaining state is filled with bits known as IV (initializing vector) and possibly fixed bits. Hence apart from K all the bits of the initial state $x(0)$ are known. Assuming that the algorithm (or model) of the cipher is known, the key recovery problem is stated as follows:

Problem 1 (Key Recovery Problem). Given an instant $k_0 > 0$, the IV of the stream cipher and the output stream $w(k_0), w(k_0 + 1), \ldots, w(k_0 + m)$ for some $m > 0$ find the key K.

Key recovery problem arises from the known plaintext attack on the cipher when the encryption of the plaintext stream $p(k)$ is carried out as $c(k) = p(k) \oplus w(k)$ by modulo 2 addition of bits. For the attack described in this paper it is not necessary that the output stream $w(k)$ be known for consecutive instants $k_0, k_0 + 1, \ldots$. Any sample of outputs $w(k)$ with known instances $k \geq k_0$ is sufficient to formulate this attack. The state $x(k_0)$ is called the *internal state* at k_0. This paper describes solution of the key recovery problem by computing all solutions of the internal state $x(k_0)$.

1.2   Internal State Recovery Problem

The most logical strategy to solve the key recovery problem is to solve the internal state recovery problem for a known model of the stream cipher.

Since the secret key is a part of the initial condition, computation of internal states of the cipher at other times either by mathematical analysis or by side channel attack is the only way available to the cryptanalyst to attack the cipher. In a practical cipher implementation, the secret key is well guarded from the side channel measurements but the internal state can be vulnerable to attack hence even knowledge of the internal state by side channel attack can be utilized to attack the cipher. On the other hand computation of the internal state from a known output stream is the most practical attack since it does not assume extra information or measurement than is naturally possible.

This makes the internal state recovery problem a realistic problem of cryptanalysis of stream ciphers. The Mathematical statement of this problem is as follows.

Problem 2 (Internal State Recovery Problem). Given an instant $k_0 > 0$ and an output stream $w(k)$ for $k = k_0, k_0 + 1, k_0 + 2, \ldots, k_0 + m$ corresponding to an unknown key K and known IV, find the internal state $x(k_0)$.

Internal State Recovery Attack. This attack in principle works as follows. (This attack is most convenient for stream cipher models in which the state transition map F is invertible. In that case the internal states which satisfy output equations can be inverted symbolically to recover key bits. When the state map F is not invertible the modification required is discussed in the next subsection). Let G denote the inverse map. Then it follows that $G(x(k + 1)) = x(k)$ when $x(k + 1) = F(x(k))$.

1. Compute all solutions $\tilde{x}(k_0)$ of the internal state from a Boolean system of equations which model the output stream $w(k)$ for $k \geq k_0$.
2. For those solutions $\tilde{x}(k_0)$ in which all bits of the state are determined, compute the initial state $\tilde{x}(0) = G^{k_0}(\tilde{x}(k_0))$ using the inverse map. Compare the bits of $\tilde{x}(0)$ at the indices of IV and fixed bits. If these match then the key bits of the $\tilde{x}(0)$ give correct key recovery.
3. In solutions $x(k_0)$ where only partial bits are recovered, the remaining bits of $x(k_0)$ are free for the same output stream. Then reverse the internal state $x(k_0)$ symbolically using the map G to $x(0)$ and solve the remaining bits using known IV bits of $x(0)$ to recover the remaining key bits.

The solutions $x(k_0)$ of the Boolean equations corresponding to the output stream are usually very small in number and when computation of such solutions is practically feasible, they contain almost all assignments of the internal state leaving a very small number of unknown (free) variables of the internal state. Hence the computation of the initial states symbolically in terms of such small number of variables is also practically feasible.

Role of Symbolic Computation. Symbolic computation is required in the above procedure at two different stages. First the construction of the Boolean equations for a given output stream $w(k_0 + j)$ for $j = 1, 2, \ldots$ has to be computed by compositions described by

$$w(k_0 + j) = f_j(x(k_0)) = f(F^{j-1}(x(k_0))$$

where $f_0(x(k_0))$ is defined as $f(x(k_0))$. These compositions are symbolic Boolean computations. Next the reversing of the internal state $x(k_0)$ to the initial condition $x(0)$ as $G^{k_0}(x(k_0))$ may also involve symbolic free variables in $x(k_0)$ if not all variables of $x(k_0)$ are assigned by the Boolean equations defined by the output stream. Our central observation in this paper which leads to a successful attack on Bivium is that these symbolic computations and the solutions of Boolean equations are practically feasible for Bivium.

There is another way to solve the key recovery problem by using a different symbolic computation. In this method the initial condition $x(0)$ with known IV bits and unknown key bits is symbolically updated using the map $F(.)$ to get $x(k_0 + j)$ symbolically in terms of unknown key bits. Then the solution of the Boolean equations directly solves the key bits. However in Bivium $k_0 = 4 \times 177 + 1 = 709$ where 177 is the number of internal state variables. In a previous article an author attempted to update the initial state with 80 unknown key bits but the symbolic computation could not be scaled up to $k_0 = 709$. Hence such a simplistic attack is not practically feasible. It is for this reason that the internal state recovery attack is the most feasible attack.

Cryptanalysis approaches which utilize algebraic equations usually require symbolic computation as discussed above. However symbolic computation and its scalability for realistic size models has not yet been fully understood and appreciated as the problem of solving large algebraic systems. Efficient and scalable symbolic computation is likely to have a deep impact in cryptanalysis and can reduce algebraic problems to smallest possible sizes.

Case of Non Invertible State Map. When the state map is not invertible previous states before k_0 cannot be represented by a map G as above. However for an internal state $x(k_0)$ there exist attractor states $x(k_0 - 1)$ such that $F(x(k_0 - 1)) = x(k_0)$. This gives equations for solving the previous states. Since the components of map F are much simple and sparse compared to the output equations, these equations can be solved for assignments in $x(k0 - 1)$ (by implicants) much easily compared to output equations. Many internal states $x(k_0)$ which are not feasible for the key and IV specified may not have solution to previous states. Repeating such inverse computations will result into multiple initial states from which the correct initial state can be recognised by the associated IV values and give correct key bits from the rest of the variables. Many back computations of the internal state in the case of such maps may not correspond to possible state for the key and IV hence the threads may terminate even before reaching the initial state. In the present case study of Bivium the internal state map is invertible. Hence this procedure is not necessary.

1.3   Previous Work and Challenges of Algebraic Cryptanalysis.

Since recent times algebraic model based cryptanalysis of stream ciphers has come on the scene in a big way [1–3]. These are primarily based on Gorbener basis computation of algebraic equations or XL (extended linearization) and the advances to the method of fast algebraic attacks. Other approaches for algebraic attacks involve decomposition of Boolean equations [1,8]. A major hurdle for algebraic attacks is the scalability of the methods for realistic sizes of the number of states of practical ciphers. Algebraic operations involved in computations are also not easy for parallelization of solving large systems. Another modern alternative to the algebraic attack which is being vigorously researched is the satisfiability (SAT) based solution of the algebraic system. This method has been tested for cryptanalysis of many ciphers including the Bivium case study [6,7,9]. The nonlinear equations resulting from the output stream data can be expressed as a multivariable quadratic (degree at most two) system of polynomial equations over the binary field. However finding all satisfying assignments of such a system is known to be an NP hard problem in general and hence is expected to be infeasible as number of variable are as large as in realistic ciphers. SAT approach is also being developed for overcoming challenges of parallelization [12]. SAT approach (based on available algorithms) has the difficulty that these are meant for solving the decision problem while cryptanalysis requires computing all solutions. The SAT methods need re-initialization for computing every new solution. Another difficulty is that the SAT algorithms work on CNF model of the algebraic equation hence cannot handle the ANF forms of functions more commonly available in algebraic models. Conversion of ANF to CNF distroys the natural structure of equations which may be useful for scaling up the procedure. It is important to note that apart from the difficulty in solving these equations in a given practical time limit such as 48 h (say), the true hurdle is the scalability of the method to successfully solve these equations with the number of variables in a realistic cipher without crashing the program. A logical approach to make any method (algorithm) scalable is to execute the algorithm in parallel using a large cluster which offers sufficient memory. However unless the algorithm has inherent parallel computational features it is not likely to be scalable when the number of variables are large enough. In this sense the currently available algebraic methods have not been successful at scalability.

1.4   Approach of the Present Paper

This paper utilizes a Boolean approach (called Implicant based approach) [14] for solving the algebraic equations resulting from the output stream to solve the internal state. This approach is inherently parallel and results in all solutions of equations. The approach becomes scalable for solving the large system with the help of heuristics suggested. Previously this approach succeeded in completely solving the 80 bit Bivium key from a keystream starting with $k = 0$ [15]. However this was not the most realistic case of cryptanalysis. This paper shows that for $k_0 = 709$ using an in house implementation of the Implicant algorithm, the internal state recovery is feasible for Bivium and gives estimates of successful breaks of Bivium if carried out on a parallel cluster with realistic memory requirement for search. The main reason for this success is the exploitation of the structure of

Boolean equations resulting from the keystream from $k_0 = 709$. No other alge-braic solver is believed to have solved these equations with realistic feasibility constraints of time and memory as reported in this paper to the knowledge of authors. The implicant based approach for solving Boolean systems has resulted from several fundamental results on Boolean equations whose theory has been well known in books and references therein such as [10,11,13].

The heuristics discovered in solving the Boolean equations in this paper and for internal state recovery are quite general and are applicable to solve output equations of other stream ciphers as well as in many other applications by par-allel computation. Whenever a stream cipher algorithm is amenable to offline computation of Boolean equations for the output stream then the number of parallel searches (the memory required for parallel computation) for solving the Boolean equations can be reduced using the heuristics presented in this paper.

2   Internal State Recovery

We now explain the attack of this paper to solve key recovery problem by internal state recovery. This method is suitable for stream ciphers whose internal state update map F in Eq. (1) is invertible. Note that when the map F is invertible then even if k_0 is a large enough time instant, an internal state $x(k_0)$ can be inverted fast to the initial state by repeated inversions to compute the previous state $x(k_0 - 1) = F^{-1}(x(k_0))$. The overall methodology of internal state recovery attack requires another computation which is difficult for scalability in the prac-tical cases. This computation is that of computing a symbolic model for output equations in terms of the internal state.

2.1   Computation of Symbolic Model or Equations for Internal State

For any instant k in time, the output of the stream cipher is given by the output equation

$$w(k) = f(x(k))$$

with internal state $x(k)$. Then the output at the next instant $k + 1$ is given by

$$w(k + 1) = f(x(k + 1)) = f(F(x(k)))$$

the last composition $f \circ F(.)$ of the function f with the map F is also denoted as $F^* f(.)$ (called action of map F on f) and is a new function of the internal state.

This step of computing the new function $F^* f(.)$ from a given function involves symbolic computation in which the arguments of f are not specified any value but have to obey formal rules of arithmetic in the field $\mathbb{F}_2$. By repeated composition we can define a sequence of new functions starting from f as follows.

$$f_0(x) = f(x)$$
$$f_{k+1}(x) = F^* f_k(x)$$

for $k = 1, 2, 3, \ldots$. This sequence of functions in principle can be computed from the model of the stream cipher offline since it can be performed starting at any instant k. However the map action $F^* f$ is an expensive computation practically. The symbolic terms of the iterated functions f_k grow fast in number hence require increasing memory.

Although performing a number of such iterations or actions $F^* f_k$ is one of the expensive computations required in this attack it is worth noting that this computation can be carried out offline. Hence given the cipher model (1) the sequence of functions $f_k, k = 0, 1, 2, \ldots$ can be assumed to be pre-computed before the internal state recovery attack. The symbolic model (or equations) for computation of the internal state is then given by the following system

$$w(k_0 + j + 1) = F^* f(x(k_0 + j)) \tag{2}$$

for $j = 0, 1, 2, \ldots, m$ while $w(k_0) = f(x(k_0))$. In this model the right hand side (RHS) consists of the iterates of the output function f of the model (1) and is a precomputed. The left hand side (LHS) however consists of the output values $w(k)$ which are available only as the online data stream generated with help of a key and an IV of the session of operation. Hence the LHS is only available online. Due to this dichotomy between online and pre-computation of the model, the symbolic model computation (2) of the output is a practically feasible problem for any stream cipher modeled by state update maps $F(.)$ to get enough number of Boolean equations in (2) to solve the internal state $x(k_0)$. Note that it is not necessary to have a consecutive stream of outputs $w(j)$ and the Boolean functions corresponding to them. Any collection of sufficient number of outputs $w(j)$ for known indices of $j \geq k_0$ are sufficient to solve for all internal states $x(k_0)$ provided all the internal state variables are reflected in these equations.

2.2   Computing all Internal States by Implicant Based Algorithm

Next the Eq. (2) need to be solved and all the solutions need to be represented in symbolic form for assignments of solved variables and identifying free variables. This task is achieved by using the Implicant based solver algorithm on the system of Boolean equations above resulting from the output stream. This algorithm has been announced in previous articles. It is briefly described here for convenience. The RHS of these equations are Boolean functions f_k with unknown internal state x. For an equation $w(k) = f_k(x)$ denoted as E_k an implicant of E_k is a term $t(x)$ of unknown variables in x such that the assignment of variables for $t(x) = 1$ satisfies E_k. For example, consider an equation E given by

$$1 = w + x + y$$

in variables w, x, y. Then $t = w'x'y$ is an implicant of E. For an equation E given by $f(x) = c$ where c is a constant $0, 1$, a set $I(E)$ of implicants of E is called a complete set of implicants of E if whenever E is satisfied for any assignments of x there exists an implicant t in $I(E)$ such that the assignments $t = 1$ satisfy E. Moreover such a set is called orthogonal if the implicants are orthogonal i.e.

$t_i t_j = 0$ for $i \neq j$. When $I(E)$ is a complete set of orthogonal implicants of E then there is exactly one implicant t which gives a satisfying assignment for every satisfaction of E. For instance for the above equation the set of terms

$$\{wx'y', w'xy, w'x'y, wxy\}$$

is a complete orthogonal set of implicants of E and when E is satisfied exactly one of the implicants $t = 1$ since the set is orthogonal. Hence the set of all assignments for satisfying the equation E is given by set

$$S(E) = \sqcup_{t \in I(E)} \{X | t(X) = 1\}$$

where $\sqcup$ denotes disjoint union. To represent all solutions of multiple equations we need the concept of implicant of simulteneous equations such that all the equations are satisfied by the assignments when the implicant becomes 1. For example if E_1 and E_2 are two equations with non overlapping variables and $I(E_1)$ and $I(E_2)$ are their complete sets of implicants then a complete set of implicants of simultaneous equations is

$$I(E_1, E_2) = \{ts, t \in I(E_1), s \in I(E_2)\}$$

Implicant Algorithm for all Solutions of a Boolean System. For one equation E we described above a complete set of orthogonal implicants $I(E)$. Next a set of all solutions of the simultaneous equations E_1, E_2 is described by a complete set of implicants denoted as $I(E_1, E_2)$. For equations with non-overlapping variables this set was just the product set of $I(E_1)$ and $I(E_2)$ as shown above. However when E_1 and E_2 have overlapping variables then

$$I(E_1, E_2) = \{ts | t \in I(E_1), s \in I(E_2/t_1)\} = \{ts | t \in I(E_1/s), s \in I(E_2)\}$$

where E_2/t denotes the equation obtained by substituting assignments $t(X) = 1$ in E_2. Here if E_2 is not satisfied by assignments of $t = 1$ then $I(E_2/t) = \emptyset$ while if E_2 is satisfied by assignments $t = 1$ then t is also an implicant of E_2. In general for a system of equations S the Implicant solver can be briefly described by the following recursive algorithm (1).

It is beyond the scope of this paper to describe this algorithm fully beyond these basic concepts. The algorithm has been announced and applied for solving complex Boolean systems in several papers. One of these [15], showed the solution of 80 bit system in unknown key variables for a hypothetical keystream starting at $k = 0$ however the system was complex enough with nonlinear terms as the registers build the feedback. Another demonstration of the effectiveness of the implicant algorithm is in paper [16] for solving XOR linear systems with $O(n^2)$ computation time.

Computation of Internal State $x(k_0)$ and $x(0)$. Consider the Boolean Eq. (2) called the Boolean system corresponding to an output stream $w(k_0 + j)$. The implicant algorithm shall return the set I of all orthogonal implicants such

---

Algorithm 1. Implicant algorithm ImplicantSolve(S)

Input: Boolean system of equations S
Output: A complete set of orthogonal implicants $I(S)$
1 $I(S) = \emptyset$
2 Select one equation E in S and find an orthogonal implicant set $I(E)$
3 Repeat
4 **for** *Implicant t in $I(E)$* **do**
5   Compute S/t. % Reduce the system by assignments defined by $t = 1$
6   **if** *S/t has a contradiction in an equation* **then**
7   Go to End
8   % choose next t in $I(E)$
9   **else**
10   delete all equations that are satisfied to get a reduced system $S(t)$
11   % this reduces the system by variables assigned by $t = 1$ and also by deleted equations
12   **while** *$S(t)$ has equations left to be solved* **do**
13         $S := S(t)$
14         $I(t) = $ ImplicantSolve(S)
15   Return $I(S) = I(S) \cup \{t \times I(S)\}$
16   % $t \times I(S)$ is the set of product implicants $\{ts | s \in I(S)\}$
17   End
18   Until all t in $I(E)$ are processed

---

that for each t in I the assignments $t(X) = 1$ satisfy all equations of the Boolean system and such that if there is any assignment of variables $X = a$ for which all equations are satisfied then there is an implicant t in I such $t(a) = 1$. In this way I represents all solutions of the Boolean system. Hence once this set I is computed all internal states $x(k_0)$ which give rise to the same given output stream are available. The key recovery problem is then solved by reversing each of the internal states $x(k_0)$ by the inverse map G to compute $x(0)$ and recognizing the correct initial state by matching the IV, as explained in introduction. This attack succeeds in practice when the number of implicants i.e. the size of the set is I is small and the the assignments determined by $t = 1$ do not leave too many free state variables. In short it is expected that the inverse computation of $x(0)$ by the map G is feasible. In the next section we show that this attack succeeds in the case of Bivium. We conclude by describing this algorithm (2) for solving the key recovery problem. Note that the

3 Bivium Cryptanalysis

In this section we discuss the Divium case study in detail. The model of the cipher in terms of state update map (1), output function of the cipher and the inverse map are first described. Then the Boolean system corresponding to the output stream is described followed by heuristics for solving these equations.

Algorithm 2. Key recover algorithm

Input: Functions of the Boolean system (2), inverse map G, k_0 output stream
   $w(k_0 + j), j = 1, \ldots, m$

Output: Key bits from the initial state

1 Prepare the Boolean system (2) denoted S for the output stream for input to
   the Implicant algorithm
2 Compute the set of all orthogonal implicants $I(S)$ (output of Implicant
   algorithm $I(S) = \text{ImplicantSolve}(S)$)
3 Choose t in $I(S)$ to fix $x(k_0)$ for assignments defined by $t = 1$. (some
   components of $x(k_0)$ may be free and treated as unknowns)
4 Compute symbolically $x(0) = G^{k_0}(x(k_0))$
5 Solve the Boolean equations for unknown variables in $x(k_0)$ by matching the
   known IV bits of $x(0)$. Discover the unknown key bits of from known bits of
   $x(k_0)$ and solved bits after matching IV bits in $x(0)$.
6 % most of the key bits may be discovered in this steps
7 If the equations of unknown bits in $x(k_0)$ after matching IV bits in $x(0)$ have no
   solution, reject the implicant t and choose the next implicant in $I(S)$. select
   $x(k_0)$ corresponding to the implicant and repeat above steps.
8 If after solving the equations a small number of key bits are not discovered.
   Then these are free bits of key and signify multiple solutions of key for
   generating same output stream with same IV.
9 End the process when $x(k_0)$ is found for which the equations matching IV bits
   in $x(0)$ are consistent. Solve all possible unknown bits of key.

3.1   Bivium State Model and the Inverse

Bivium cipher has been described in detail in [7]. We shall describe the model
equations of Bivium in the form (1). The state consists of 177 variables
$x_1, \ldots, x_{177}$. The key forms first 80 bits $x_1, \ldots, x_{80}$ of $x(0)$, IV forms 80 bits
$x_{94}, \ldots, x_{173}$ of $x(0)$ while variables $x_{81}, \ldots, x_{93}$ and $x_{174}, \ldots, x_{177}$ are set to
zero in $x(0)$. State update map F is

$$
\begin{aligned}
x_1(k+1) &= x_{162}(k) \oplus x_{177}(k) \oplus x_{175}(k)x_{176}(k) \oplus x_{69}(k) \\
x_2(k+1) &= x_1(k) \\
&\vdots \\
&= \vdots \\
x_{93}(k+1) &= x_{92}(k) \\
x_{94}(k+1) &= x_{66}(k) \oplus x_{93}(k) \oplus x_{91}(k)x_{92}(k) \oplus x_{171}(k) \\
x_{95}(k+1) &= x_{94}(k) \\
&\vdots \\
&= \vdots \\
x_{177}(k+1) &= x_{176}(k)
\end{aligned}
\tag{3}
$$

The ouput map is

$$
w(k) = x_{66}(k) \oplus x_{93}(k) \oplus x_{162}(k) \oplus x_{177}
$$

The inverse of the update map G is

$$
\begin{aligned}
x_1(k) &= x_2(k+1) \\
\vdots\ &= \vdots \\
x_{92}(k) &= x_{93}(k+1) \\
x_{93}(k) &= x_{94}(k+1) \oplus x_{66}(k+1) \oplus x_{91}(k+1)x_{92}(k+1) \oplus x_{177}(k+1) \\
x_{94}(k) &= x_{95}(k+1) \\
\vdots\ &= \vdots \\
x_{176}(k) &= x_{177}(k+1) \\
x_{177}(k) &= x_1(k+1) \oplus x_{162}(k+1) \oplus x_{175}(k+1)x_{176}(k+1) \oplus x_{69}(k+1)
\end{aligned}
\tag{4}
$$

Thus the inverse map G of Bivium is no more complex in degree than forward update map F.

3.2 Boolean System

The functions involved in the Boolean system (2) can be computed offline. The system of equations is determined by the output stream $w(k)$ for $k \geq k_0 = 709$. A sample set of equations is given in the appendix where the list of equations $f_j(x(k)) = w(k)$ are written in terms of the list of functions $f_j(k) \oplus w(k)$. We shall call this the Boolean system of equations in terms of the internal state $x(k)$ referring to the same system of Eq. (2).

The procedure described in algorithm (2) for the key recovery problem is used to discover the key bits once all internal states $x(k_0)$ are solved from the Boolean system. Following features were discovered in the Bivium case study which were advantageous to complete the computation and hence can be considered as yardsticks of complexity (or weakness) of Bivium.

1. Solution of the Boolean system (2) formed the major computational load. The equations had a structure which facilitated heuristics for solving the equations by parallel computation. (These heuristics are discussed below).
2. Assignments of all the bits of the internal state $x(k_0)$ were fixed by the implicants of the Boolean system. Free variables in $x(k_0)$ were absent. Hence the inverse computation of $x(0)$ was as fast as forward computation of $x(k_0)$ for a given key and IV since no symbolic computation was needed in inversion. Moreover complete key bit recovery was possible by matching the IV bits.
3. Number of implicants of the Boolean system in sample trials were very few (at most two). This is expected as sufficient number of bits of the output stream are available. Hence the major computation involved is in searching over the rare set of implicants which provide satisfying assignments of the Boolean system or solve $x(k_0)$. This computation was simplified by certain heuristics possible with the structure of equations.

These observations are elaborated further with results of computation. The structure of equations identified above in the Boolean system was not affected by change in key and IV as both are random looking.

Structure of Boolean System and Heuristics for Parallel Solution. The Boolean system (2) corresponding to an output stream has 177 unknown variables corresponding to bits of the internal state $x(k_0)$ and as many equations assuming a sufficiently long output stream. Some observations which shaped the heuristics of solving this systems were as follows.

1. First set of 66 equations in (2) are linear with 4 variables each.
2. These linear equations have 8 implicants each in these 4 variables irrespective of the value of output w.
3. First 15 of these equations have non-overlapping variables. Hence the largest set of all implicants to search from is $8^{15} = 2^{45}$. Each such search will thus fix $4 \times 15 = 60$ variables while rest of 117 variables will have to be solved using the Boolean solver. Using less number of equations will reduce the number of searches but will increase number of variables in the Boolean system.
4. A gross ranking of variables can be made by the number of equations in which that variable appears. If a variable appears in more equations its assignment is likely to simplify more equations. The Boolean system showed drastic improvements in time taken to solve once the top ranked variables were substituted.

Based on above observation following heuristics were developed for solving the Boolean system. The performance of solving the system are presented for each heuristic. A sample Boolean system and an output stream are shown in the appendix.

Searching over Possible Implicants Obtained with Constraints on Number of Searches. Presence of a set of linear equation in the Boolean system which have no overlapping variables suggests that by choosing a number of equations a set of implicants can be easily obtained in which an implicant satisfying the system must exist. For instance if all 15 linear equations each with 4 variables with non-overlapping variables are considered, then the total number of implicant (8 per equation) is $8^{15} = 2^{45}$. Hence a search over these implicants by reducing the system with assignments of these implicants becoming 1 will find at least one solution of the system. All these searches are parallel hence given a memory resource for executing 2^{45} threads one for each implicant the search for the internal state can be accomplished in time approximately equal to average time to decide whether the Boolean system has a solution and compute the solution when the assignments for variables arising in the implicant are substituted. The Table 1 shows such average time for different selection of equations.

For instance the table shows that a parallel search over 2^{42} implicants of 56 variable each (requiring 56×2^{42} bits (=30 TB) of memory) can recover the key of Bivium in 6150317 s. (or 17 h).

A general heuristic that follows from this observation for solving Boolean equations is thus to identify a subset of equations which have non-overlapping variables and search over the assignments defined by their implicants. The set of implicants is just a direct product of implicants of each of the equations. The

Table 1. Implicant based computation timings

No. of equations	No. of variable assignments	No. of implicant threads	Average Time for computation Sec	Memory required in terabytes
13	52	2^{39}	>2 days	3.95
14	56	2^{42}	61503	30.68
15	60	2^{45}	4926	261.16

set of implicants and the time required to compute the solution after substitution gives a time versus memory tradeoff.

Brute Force Search over Assignments of Top Ranked Variables. The variables of the Boolean system are spread in different equations unevenly. A variable is said to have rank r if it appears in r equations. For the Boolean system of Bivium a table of number of incidences of variables with equations was computed offline. Of these a certain number of top ranked variables (e.g. 44 variables of highest rank) were chosen. When the true internal state assignments for a known key and IV were substituted in the Boolean system it was observed that the Boolean system was rapidly solved by the solver.The Table 2 shows the time for solving the remaining variables of the system when certain number of top ranked variable assignments are substituted. The 40 bit brute force search

Table 2. Timing with assignment of top ranked variables

No. of top ranked variables in search	Time taken (Sec) to solve the system	Memory required in terabytes
40	177746	5.4
44	100642	96.7
45	50521	197.9
48	6642	>1000
52	663	>1000
56	26	>1000
60	13	>1000

approximately requires 5.4 TB of memory space and the Boolean solver can solve the complete set of equation in 49 h. This may be considered as a practically feasible attack. The implicant based search requires much less memory as compared to the brute force search. However if the memory is kept in practical limit such 3.95 TB as for search over implicants obtained from first 13 equations the computation time required for each thread is larger than 2 days. These two types of heuristics can be combined for parallely solving the equations keeping both memory and time in feasible limits. This heuristic for solving Boolean systems, to select a set of top ranked variables of the system small enough to carry out parallel brute force search over the assignments may be potentially effective in solving Boolean systems arising in several other Cryptanalysis problems.

4   Conclusion

An algorithm called Implicant based solver for Boolean systems was utilized to solve the Boolean system arising from the output stream of Bivium with 80 bits key. Two heuristics for searching the solutions are proposed based on the structure of equations of the system. It is shown that Bivium key can be recovered in practical time of about 49 h by a brute force search over top ranked 40 variables with 3.95 terabytes of memory, which is feasible for modern clusters. The important conclusions of this study are that the Implicant based solver has good scalability, the heuristic of searching implicants from equations without non-overlapping variables and the heuristic of searching over top ranked variables are powerful methodologies for Cryptanalysis. These two can be combined to get a better control over memory requirement and time of computation for parallel solution of Boolean systems. The case study shows that Bivium is weak against these algebraic attacks.

Acknowledgements. Author Virendra Sule gratefully acknowledges support of the project 15DITIR002 at the NCETIS at IIT Bombay, for the research reported in this paper.

References

1. Roy, D., Datta, P., Mukhopadhyay, S.: Algebraic cryptanalysis of stream ciphers using decomposition of Boolean function. J. Appl. Math. Comput. **49**(1–2), 397–417 (2015)
2. Bard, G.: Security and cryptology. Algebraic Cryptanalysis, 1st edn. Springer, Berlin (2009). https://doi.org/10.1007/978-0-387-88757-9
3. Courtois, N.T., O'Neil, S., Quisquater, J.-J.: Practical algebraic attacks on the hitag2 stream cipher. In: Samarati, P., Yung, M., Martinelli, F., Ardagna, C.A. (eds.) ISC 2009. LNCS, vol. 5735, pp. 167–176. Springer, Heidelberg (2009). https://doi.org/10.1007/978-3-642-04474-8_14
4. Mihaljević, M.J., Gangopadhyay, S., Paul, G., Imai, H.: Internal state recovery of grain-v1 employing normality order of the filter function. Inf. Secur. IET **6**(2), 55–64 (2012b)
5. Dudek, P., Kurkowski, M., Srebrny, M.: Towards parallel direct SAT-based cryptanalysis. In: Wyrzykowski, R., Dongarra, J., Karczewski, K., Waśniewski, J. (eds) Parallel Processing and Applied Mathematics. PPAM 2011. Lecture Notes in Computer Science, vol 7203. Springer, Berlin (2012)
6. Eibach, T., Pilz, E., Völkel, G.: Attacking bivium using SAT solvers. In: Kleine Büning, H., Zhao, X. (eds.) SAT 2008. LNCS, vol. 4996, pp. 63–76. Springer, Heidelberg (2008). https://doi.org/10.1007/978-3-540-79719-7_7

7. McDonald, C., Charnes, C., Pieprzyk, J.: Attacking Bivium with Minisat. Technical Report 2007/040, ECRYPT Stream Cipher Project (2007)
8. Koon-Ho Wong, K., Bard, G.V.: Improved algebraic cryptanalysis of QUAD, bivium and trivium via graph partitioning on equation systems. In: Steinfeld, R., Hawkes, P. (eds.) ACISP 2010. LNCS, vol. 6168, pp. 19–36. Springer, Heidelberg (2010). https://doi.org/10.1007/978-3-642-14081-5_2
9. McDonald, C., Charnes, C., Pieprzyk, J.: An Algebraic Analysis of Trivium Ciphers based on the Boolean Satisfiability Problem. https://eprint.iacr.org/2007/129.pdf
10. Brown, F.M.: Boolean Reasoning. The logic of Boolean equations. Dover, Illinois (2006)
11. Rudeanu, S.: Boolean Functions and Equations. North Holland, Amsterdam (1974)
12. Hammadi, Y., Wintersteiger, C.M.: Seven challenges in parallel SAT solving. Challenge paper AAAI 2012 Sub-Area spotlights track. Association of Advancement of Artificial Intelligence
13. Crama, Y., Hammer, P.L.: Boolean Models and Methods in Mathematics, Computer Science, and Engineering. Cambridge University Press, Cambridge (2010)
14. Sule, V.: An implicant based parallel all solution solver for Boolean satisfiability (2017). arxiv.org/1611.09590v3
15. Sule, V., Yadav, A.: Cryptanalysis of Bivium using a Boolean all solution solver. http://eprint.iacr.org/2017/1141
16. Jayashree, K., Virendra, S., Lande B.K.: Implicant based solver for XOR boolean linear systems, SpringSim-HPC 2017, April 23–26, Virginia Beach, VA, USA, pp. 556–567; Society for Modeling and Simulation, ISBN: 1-56555-361-6. (Refereed conference)

Related-Key Differential Cryptanalysis of Full Round CRAFT

Muhammad ElSheikh and Amr M. Youssef[(✉)]

Concordia Institute for Information Systems Engineering,
Concordia University, Montréal, QC, Canada
{m_elshei,youssef}@ciise.concordia.ca

Abstract. CRAFT is a lightweight tweakable block cipher introduced in
FSE 2019. One of the main design criteria of CRAFT is the efficient protection of its implementations against differential fault analysis. While the
authors of CRAFT provide several cryptanalysis results in several attack
models, they do not claim any security of CRAFT against related-key
differential attacks. In this paper, we utilize the simple key schedule of
CRAFT to propose a systematic method for constructing several repeatable
2-round related-key differential characteristics with probability 2^{-2}. We
then employ one of these characteristics to mount a key recovery attack
on full-round CRAFT using 2^{31} queries to the encryption oracle and 2^{85}
encryptions, and 2^{41} 64-bit blocks of memory.. Additionally, we manage
to use 8 related-key differential distinguishers, with 8 related-key differences, in order to mount a key recovery attack on the full-round cipher
with $2^{35.17}$ queries to the encryption oracle, 2^{32} encryptions and about
2^6 64-bit blocks of memory. Furthermore, we present another attack that
recovers the whole master key with $2^{36.09}$ queries to the encryption oracle
and only 11 encryptions with 2^7 blocks of memory using 16 related-key
differential distinguishers.

1 Introduction

Modern symmetric-key cryptographic primitives, such as the Advanced Encryption Standard (AES), which are likely designed for desktops and servers, cannot
be easily implemented on resource-constrained devices such as sensor networks,
healthcare equipment, Internet of Things (IoT) devices, and RFIDs. With the
rapidly increasing demand for such devices, the National Institute for Standards and Technology (NIST) has initiated a standardization process for new
lightweight cryptographic algorithms for use in resource-constrained devices.
SKINNY [3], PRESENT [7], SIMON [2], and GIFT [1] are examples of such
lightweight block ciphers that have been recently proposed.

The resistance against the differential cryptanalysis [6] is essential for any
proposed cryptographic block ciphers. In differential cryptanalysis, for an n-
bit primitive, an attacker is looking for a distinguisher ($\Delta P \rightarrow \Delta C$) where
an XOR difference of two plaintexts (ΔP) gives, after some rounds, another

© Springer Nature Switzerland AG 2019
S. Bhasin et al. (Eds.): SPACE 2019, LNCS 11947, pp. 50–66, 2019.
https://doi.org/10.1007/978-3-030-35869-3_6

XOR difference (ΔC) with probability higher than 2^{-n}. Using this distinguisher, a key recovery attack can be performed by guessing the round keys. One of the variations of this attack is the related-key differential cryptanalysis [5] in which the attacker has the ability to query the encryption oracle asking for the encryption of two plaintexts, the first plaintext is encrypted using the secret key, and the other one is encrypted using another key related to the secret key, where such relation is known or even chosen by the attacker.

At FSE 2019, Beierle *et al.* presented CRAFT [4], a new lightweight tweakable block cipher with a block size of 64 bits and a key length of 128 bits associated with 64 bits as a tweak. One of the main design criteria of CRAFT is the efficient protection of its implementations against differential fault analysis. In the design paper, the authors provide the security analysis of CRAFT against several cryptanalysis techniques such as differential, linear, impossible differential, zero correlation, and integral cryptanalysis in the single-key and related-tweak settings. While they do not claim any security of CRAFT against the related-key differential attacks, they presented a deterministic related-key/related-tweak differential characteristic. However, this characteristic cannot be used to mount a key recovery attack. In this paper, we study in details the security of CRAFT against the related-key differential attack. More precisely,

1. We utilize the simple key schedule of CRAFT to present a systematic method of how to select the key difference in addition to the input and the output differences of the 2-round structure of CRAFT such that the input difference is the same as the output difference. Thus, the resulting 2-round characteristic is repeatable. In the same time, we also try to maximize the probability of that characteristic. Thereby, we use it as a building block for constructing a longer characteristic. To illustrate the effectiveness of this method, we present 17 repeatable 2-round characteristics, each one of them has only one active Sbox and holds with probability equals to the maximum differential probability of an active Sbox of CRAFT (2^{-2}).
2. We extend one of these characteristics to a 28-round related-key differential characteristic with probability 2^{-28}. After that, we employ it to mount a key recovery attack on full-round CRAFT using 2^{31} queries to the encryption oracle and 2^{85} encryptions, and 2^{41} 64-bit blocks of memory.
3. We can speed up the key recovery attack against the full-round CRAFT using $2^{35.17}$ queries to the encryption oracle and 2^{32} full-round encryptions. To this end, we manage to use 8 different related-key differential characteristics (with 8 related-key differences) in order to recover 96 bits from the secret master key and then we get the full master key by testing the right 96-bit key along with the remaining 32 bits of the key using 2 plaintext/ciphertext pairs.
4. Furthermore, we can perform the previous attack without the exhaustive search step and recover the whole master key with $2^{36.09}$ queries to the encryption oracle and only 11 full-round encryptions (instead of 2^{32} in the above attack) using 16 different related-key differential characteristics (with 16 related-key differences). This attack has been verified experimentally.

It should also be noted that, independent of our work, a related-key attack on CRAFT has been recently presented in [8] but with data and time complexities higher than the complexities of our attack.

The rest of this paper is organized as follows. In Sect. 2, we briefly revisit the specifications of CRAFT. A systematic method to build a repeatable 2-round related-key characteristic is explained in Sect. 3. In Sect. 4, we describe the key recovery attack against the full rounds of CRAFT using a single related-key differential characteristic. Then, the details of our attack using multiple related-key differential characteristics are presented in Sect. 5. Finally, the paper is concluded in Sect. 6.

2   Specifications of CRAFT

CRAFT [4] is a lightweight tweakable block cipher with a block size of 64 bits, a key length (K) of 128 bits, and a tweak (T) of 64 bits. The internal state of the cipher can be represented as a 4×4 square array of nibbles or as a 16-nibble vector by concatenating the rows of the square array. The notation $I_{i,j}$ is used to denote the nibble located at row i and column j of the 4×4 array. Also, a single subscript I_i denotes the nibble in the i-th position of 16-nibble vector, i.e., $I_{i,j} = I_{4i+j}$.

Tweakey Schedule. The 128-bit key K is split into two 64-bit subkeys K^0 and K^1. Similar to the internal state, the subkeys K^0 and K^1 in addition to the 64-bit input tweak T are represented as as 4×4 square array of nibbles or as a 16-nibble vector using a similar indexing technique as for the internal state. Then, four 64-bit tweakeys TK^0, TK^1, TK^2 and TK^3 are derived from K^0 and K^1 with the associated T as follows:

$$TK^0 = K^0 \oplus T, \quad TK^1 = K^1 \oplus T, \quad TK^2 = K^0 \oplus Q(T), \quad TK^3 = K^1 \oplus Q(T).$$

where $Q(T)$ is a permutation on the nibbles of the input tweak T using a permutation $Q = [12, 10, 15, 5, 14, 8, 9, 2, 11, 3, 7, 4, 6, 0, 1, 13]$. In other words, the i-th nibble of $Q(T)$ $(T(Q)_i, 0 \le i \le 15)$ is equal to the $Q(i)$-th nibble of T $(Q(T)_i = T_{Q(i)})$. The tweakey $TK^{i \bmod 4}$ $(0 \le i \le 31)$ is used during the i-th round of the encryption operation in order to update the internal state.

Encryption Operation. The encryption operation proceeds as follows. First, the plaintext $m = m_0||m_1|| \cdots ||m_{14}||m_{15}$ (where m_i is a 4-bit nibble) is loaded into the internal state. Then, the internal state is updated by applying the full round function of CRAFT 31 times $(\mathcal{R}_i, 0 \le i \le 30)$. Finally, one more linear round $(\mathcal{R}'_{31})$ is applied on the internal state to compute the ciphertext as shown in Fig. 1, where RC_i is the round constant. The full round of CRAFT $(\mathcal{R}_i)$ consists of the following five operations: MixColumn, AddConstant$_i$, AddTweakey$_i$ PermuteNibbles and SubBox as described in Fig. 2. The last round $(\mathcal{R}'_{31})$ omits PermuteNibbles and SubBox operations from the full round. These operations are defined as follows,

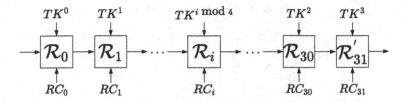

Fig. 1. Structure of CRAFT

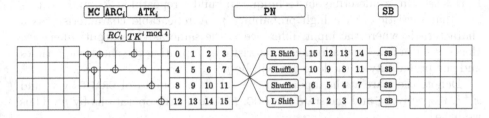

Fig. 2. One full round function of CRAFT

- MixColumn (MC): Each column of the internal state is multiplied by a binary matrix M,

$$M = \begin{bmatrix} 1 & 0 & 1 & 1 \\ 0 & 1 & 0 & 1 \\ 0 & 0 & 1 & 0 \\ 0 & 0 & 0 & 1 \end{bmatrix}$$

This operation can be described using the XOR operation as follows. For each column j $(0 \leq j \leq 3)$,

$$\begin{bmatrix} I_{0,j} \\ I_{1,j} \\ I_{2,j} \\ I_{3,j} \end{bmatrix} \mapsto \begin{bmatrix} I_{0,j} \oplus I_{2,j} \oplus I_{3,j} \\ I_{1,j} \oplus I_{3,j} \\ I_{2,j} \\ I_{3,j} \end{bmatrix}$$

- AddConstants$_i$ (ARC$_i$): In the i-th round $(0 \leq i \leq 31)$, the internal state nibbles I_4 and I_5 are XOR-ed with the two nibbles (a and b), respectively, where a and b represented the 2-nibble round constant $RC_i = (a, b)$. These round constants are generated using 4-bit and 3-bit LFSRs. The details of generating the round constants can be found in [4].
- AddTweakey$_i$ (ATK$_i$): Each nibble of the internal state is XOR-ed with the corresponding nibble of the tweakey $TK^{i \bmod 4}$.
- PermuteNibbles (PN): An permutation $\mathcal{P}$ is applied on the nibble positions of the internal state. In particular, for all $0 \leq i \leq 15$, I_i is replaced by $I_{\mathcal{P}(i)}$, where

$$\mathcal{P} = [15, 12, 13, 14, 10, 9, 8, 11, 6, 5, 4, 7, 1, 2, 3, 0].$$

- SubBox (SB): A nonlinear bijective mapping applied on every nibble of the internal state in parallel using the Sbox given in Table 1.

Table 1. 4-bit Sbox of CRAFT

x	0	1	2	3	4	5	6	7	8	9	a	b	c	d	e	f
$S(x)$	c	a	d	3	e	b	f	7	8	9	1	5	0	2	4	6

3   Related-Key Differential Characteristic of CRAFT

In this section, we describe our technique to build a repeatable 2-round related-key characteristic with a high probability p. A repeatable characteristic is a characteristic where the input difference is the same as the output difference. Hence, we can construct a long characteristic by repeating the short one n times and the probability of the long one will be p^n.

Denote the state at the input and the output of round i of CRAFT by x^i and x^{i+1}, respectively, and the state after MC, ARC$_i$ and ATK$_i$ operations by y^i. Thus we have

$$y^i = \text{ATK}_i \circ \text{ARC}_i \circ \text{MC}(x^i)$$
$$x^{i+1} = \text{SB} \circ \text{PN}(y^i)$$

In the related-key with a single tweak model of CRAFT, the tweak (T) has zero difference, and the subkeys (K^0, K^1) have the nonzero differences ΔK^0 and ΔK^1, respectively. Thereby, the four tweaks have nonzero differences as follows

$$\Delta TK^0 = \Delta TK^2 = \Delta K^0, \qquad \Delta TK^1 = \Delta TK^3 = \Delta K^1$$

A 2-Round Characteristic. Consider two consecutive rounds, i and $i+1$, where i is even. Thus $\Delta TK^{i \bmod 4} = \Delta K^0$ and $\Delta TK^{(i+1) \bmod 4} = \Delta K^1$. We start building a repeatable 2-round characteristic by setting the input and the output differences (Δx^i and Δx^{i+2}) of the 2-round with arbitrary nonzero values such that $\Delta x^i = \Delta x^{i+2}$. Then, we deterministically propagate the input difference Δx^i forward through the MC and ARC$_i$ operations and choose ΔK^0 such that $\Delta K^0 = \text{ARC}_i \circ \text{MC}(\Delta x^i)$. Thereby, we ensure that $\Delta y^i = 0$, $\Delta x^{i+1} = 0$ and $\Delta y^{i+1} = \Delta K^1$. From the other direction, we propagate the output difference Δx^{i+2} backward through SB and PN operations to obtain Δy^{i+1} and select ΔK^1 such that $\Delta K^1 = \Delta y^{i+1} = \text{PN}_i^{-1} \circ \text{SB}^{-1}(\Delta x^{i+2})$. It should be noted that the probability of propagating Δx^{i+2} backward to ΔK^1 is the same as the probability of propagating ΔK^1 forward to Δx^{i+2} due to the properties of the Sbox of CRAFT. Therefore, the overall probability of this characteristic depends on the probability of propagating Δx^{i+2} through SB^{-1} operation. In order to maximize the overall probability, we have to minimize the number of active nibbles in the input/output differences to only one active nibble with, e.g., difference value (α). Therefore, ΔK^1 also has a single active nibble with, e.g., difference value (β) such that $\Pr[\text{SB}^{-1}(\alpha) \rightarrow \beta] = p$. Finally, we select the value of the tuple (α, β) so that p is equal to the maximum differential probability for an active Sbox which is 2^{-2}.

Figure 3 depicts an example of such characteristics in which we set the input/output differences to zero except for the two nibbles Δx_{12}^i and Δx_{12}^{i+2}, which we set to α. Therefore, we select the difference of the subkey K^0 such that it has zero difference except the nibbles ΔK_0^0, ΔK_4^0 and ΔK_{12}^0 have a nonzero difference (α). For the subkey K^1, it will have zero difference in 15 nibbles and nonzero difference β in the nibble ΔK_1^1 such that $\Pr[\text{SB}^{-1}(\alpha) \rightarrow \beta] = 2^{-2}$.

Based on the differential distribution table (DDT) of the CRAFT's Sbox, the unordered tuples (α, β) can take one of the values from the following set:

$$(\alpha, \beta) \text{ or } (\beta, \alpha) \in \{(1,2), (2,4), (2,9), (2,c), (3,6), (5,7), (5,a),$$
$$(7,d), (a,a), (a,d), (a,f), (b,b), (e,e), (f,f)\}. \qquad (1)$$

We can also build a repeatable 2-round characteristic by setting the input and the output differences to zero differences $(\Delta x^i = \Delta x^{i+2} = 0)$, then selecting ΔK^0 such that it has only one active nibble with nonzero difference (α). After that, we obtain the value of the difference ΔK^1 which will have only one active nibble with nonzero difference (β) such that $\Delta K^1 = \text{ARC}_{i+1} \circ \text{MC} \circ \text{SB} \circ \text{PN}(\Delta K^0)$. Finally, we select the value of the tuple (α, β) from the previously mentioned set. Table 2 summarizes some examples for the obtained 2-round related-key differential characteristics.

In the following sections, we utilize the repeatable 2-round related-key differential characteristics derived here to mount two key recovery attacks against the full round of CRAFT.

4   Related-Key Differential Attack Using Single Difference

In this section, we employ the repeatable 2-round characteristic ($\mathbf{RK_0}$) with, e.g., the tuple $(\alpha, \beta) = (4, 2)$ to present a related-key differential attack against the full round of CRAFT. By repeating $\mathbf{RK_0}$ (14) times as depicted in Fig. 4, we are able to construct a 28-round related-key differential characteristic (covered from round 0 to round 27) with probability $(2^{-2})^{14} = 2^{-28}$. We have verified this characteristic experimentally.

Since the characteristic ends at x^{28} with all nibbles have zero differences. After that, we propagate this difference through the last 4 rounds, and we obtain the difference at the ciphertext (ΔC) in form of

$$(\delta_4, \delta_3, \delta_9, \delta_6, \delta_4, 0, \delta_8, \delta_6, 0, \delta_3, 0, 0, \delta_4, 0, \delta_7, \delta_6).$$

Thus, we can derive the following conditions:

$$\Delta C_5 = \Delta C_8 = \Delta C_{10} = \Delta C_{11} = \Delta C_{13} = 0,$$
$$\Delta C_1 = \Delta C_9,$$
$$\Delta C_0 = \Delta C_4 = \Delta C_{12},$$
$$\Delta C_3 = \Delta C_7 = \Delta C_{15}.$$

Our attack has two phases: Data Collection phase and Key Recovery phase.

Table 2. Examples of repeatable 2-round related-key differential characteristics of **CRAFT**, all of them hold with probability 2^{-2} starting from an even round i and (α, β) can take one of the values given by Eq. (1).

	$\Delta K^0 = \Delta TK^0 = \Delta TK^2$	$\Delta K^1 = \Delta TK^1 = \Delta TK^3$	$\Delta x^i = \Delta x^{i+2}$
RK$_0$	$(0,0,0,\alpha,0,0,0,0,0,0,0,0,0,0,0,0)$	$(0,0,\beta,0,0,0,\beta,0,0,0,0,0,0,0,0,\beta)$	$(0,0,0,0,0,0,0,0,0,0,0,0,0,0,0,0)$
RK$_1$	$(\alpha,0,0,0,\alpha,0,0,0,0,0,0,\alpha,0,0,0)$	$(0,\beta,0,0,0,0,0,0,0,0,0,0,0,0,0,0)$	$(0,0,0,0,0,0,0,0,0,0,0,\alpha,0,0,0)$
RK$_2$	$(0,\alpha,0,0,0,\alpha,0,0,0,0,0,0,\alpha,0,0)$	$(0,0,\beta,0,0,0,0,0,0,0,0,0,0,0,0,0)$	$(0,0,0,0,0,0,0,0,0,0,0,0,\alpha,0,0)$
RK$_3$	$(0,0,\alpha,0,0,0,\alpha,0,0,0,0,0,0,\alpha,0)$	$(0,0,0,\beta,0,0,0,0,0,0,0,0,0,0,0,0)$	$(0,0,0,0,0,0,0,0,0,0,0,0,0,\alpha,0)$
RK$_4$	$(0,0,0,\alpha,0,0,0,\alpha,0,0,0,0,0,0,0,\alpha)$	$(\beta,0,0,0,0,0,0,0,0,0,0,0,0,0,0,0)$	$(0,0,0,0,0,0,0,0,0,0,0,0,0,0,\alpha)$
RK$_5$	$(\alpha,0,0,0,0,0,\alpha,0,0,0,0,0,0,0,0)$	$(0,0,0,0,0,\beta,0,0,0,0,0,0,0,0,0,0)$	$(0,0,0,0,0,0,0,\alpha,0,0,0,0,0,0,0)$
RK$_6$	$(0,\alpha,0,0,0,0,0,\alpha,0,0,0,0,0,0,0)$	$(0,0,0,0,0,0,\beta,0,0,0,0,0,0,0,0,0)$	$(0,0,0,0,0,0,0,0,\alpha,0,0,0,0,0,0)$
RK$_7$	$(0,0,\alpha,0,0,0,0,0,\alpha,0,0,0,0,0,0)$	$(0,0,0,0,0,0,0,\beta,0,0,0,0,0,0,0,0)$	$(0,0,0,0,0,0,0,0,0,\alpha,0,0,0,0,0)$
RK$_8$	$(0,0,0,\alpha,0,0,0,0,0,\alpha,0,0,0,0,0)$	$(0,0,0,0,0,0,0,0,\beta,0,0,0,0,0,0,0)$	$(0,0,0,0,0,0,0,0,0,0,\alpha,0,0,0,0)$
RK$_9$	$(0,0,0,0,\alpha,0,0,0,0,0,\alpha,0,0,0,0)$	$(0,0,0,0,0,0,0,0,0,\beta,0,0,0,0,0,0)$	$(0,0,0,0,\alpha,0,0,0,\alpha,0,0,0,0,0,0)$
RK$_{10}$	$(0,0,0,0,0,\alpha,0,0,0,0,0,\alpha,0,0,0)$	$(0,0,0,0,0,0,0,0,0,0,\beta,0,0,0,0,0)$	$(0,0,0,0,0,\alpha,0,0,0,\alpha,0,0,0,0,0,0)$
RK$_{11}$	$(0,0,0,0,0,0,\alpha,0,0,0,0,0,\alpha,0,0)$	$(0,0,0,0,0,0,0,0,0,0,0,\beta,0,0,0,0)$	$(0,0,0,0,0,0,\alpha,0,0,0,\alpha,0,0,0,0,0)$
RK$_{12}$	$(0,0,0,0,0,0,0,\alpha,0,0,0,0,0,\alpha,0)$	$(0,0,0,0,0,0,0,0,0,0,0,0,\beta,0,0,0)$	$(0,0,0,0,0,0,0,\alpha,0,0,0,\alpha,0,0,0,0)$
RK$_{13}$	$(\alpha,0,0,0,0,0,0,0,0,0,0,0,0,0,0)$	$(0,0,0,0,0,0,0,0,0,0,0,0,0,0,0,\beta)$	$(\alpha,0,0,0,0,0,0,0,0,0,0,0,0,0,0,0)$
RK$_{14}$	$(0,\alpha,0,0,0,0,0,0,0,0,0,0,0,0,0)$	$(0,0,0,0,0,0,0,0,0,0,0,0,0,\beta,0,0)$	$(0,\alpha,0,0,0,0,0,0,0,0,0,0,0,0,0,0)$
RK$_{15}$	$(0,0,\alpha,0,0,0,0,0,0,0,0,0,0,0,0)$	$(0,0,0,0,0,0,0,0,0,0,0,0,0,\beta,0,0)$	$(0,0,\alpha,0,0,0,0,0,0,0,0,0,0,0,0,0)$
RK$_{16}$	$(0,0,0,\alpha,0,0,0,0,0,0,0,0,0,0,0)$	$(0,0,0,0,0,0,0,0,0,0,0,0,0,0,\beta,0)$	$(0,0,0,\alpha,0,0,0,0,0,0,0,0,0,0,0,0)$

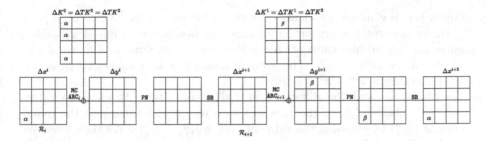

Fig. 3. A repeatable 2-round related-key characteristic of CRAFT with probability 2^{-2}.

4.1 Data Collection

We select a set of 2^m 64-bit plaintexts associated with a 64-bit tweak in which the plaintexts and the tweak can take any arbitrary values. Each plaintext is encrypted twice, using the secret master key $(K^0 || K^1)$ and using the secret master key XORed with the key differences $((K^0 \oplus \Delta K^0)||(K^1 \oplus \Delta K^1))$. Then, we compute the difference at the ciphertext (ΔC) and filter out the plaintext/ciphertext pairs that do not satisfy the conditions, obtained above, on ΔC. This step provides a $5 \times 4 + 4 + 2 \times 4 + 2 \times 4 = 40$ bits filtration. Suppose the number of the remaining plaintext/ciphertext pairs after this filtration is $2^{m'}$, then on average, $2^{m'} = 2^m \times 2^{-40} = 2^{m-40}$.

4.2 Key Recovery

We first prepare $2^{11 \times 4} = 2^{44}$ counters corresponding to the 44 bits of the key involved in the analysis. After that, for each ciphertext pair in the filtered $2^{m'}$ pairs obtained in the data collection phase, we apply the following procedure:

1. Guess the key nibbles (K_9^1, K_{12}^1) and partially decrypt the ciphertext to obtain the differences $(\Delta y_1^{30}, \Delta y_5^{30})$. The average number of the guessed keys that satisfy the condition $(\Delta y_1^{30} = \Delta y_5^{30})$ is $2^{2 \times 4} \times 2^{-4} = 2^4$.
2. Guess the key nibbles $(K_6^1, K_{14}^1, K_{15}^1)$ and partially decrypt the ciphertext to obtain the values and differences at the nibbles $(y_0^{30}, y_3^{30}, y_8^{30})$ and discard any key that does not lead to satisfy the condition of $(\Delta y_0^{30} = \Delta y_8^{30})$. The average number of the keys passing this filtration is $2^4 \times 2^{3 \times 4} \times 2^{-4} = 2^{12}$.
3. Guess the value of $(K_2^1 \oplus K_{10}^1)$ with associated value of K_{14}^1 passed the filtration on the previous step (step 2) and partially decrypt the ciphertext to obtain the values and the differences at the nibbles (y_4^{30}, y_{13}^{30}). Then filter out the keys if the difference(Δy_{13}^{30}) is not the same as the differences $(\Delta y_1^{30}, \Delta y_5^{30})$ that are obtained in the step (1). Thus, the average number of keys suggested by a pair after this step is $2^{12} \times 2^4 \times 2^{-4} = 2^{12}$.
4. Guess the key nibbles (K_8^0, K_{13}^0) and partially decrypt the nibbles (y_2^{30}, y_{13}^{30}) obtained on steps (2,3), respectively, and get the differences $(\Delta y_2^{29}, \Delta y_6^{29})$. The average number of the guessed keys that satisfy the condition of $(\Delta y_2^{29} = \Delta y_6^{29})$ is $2^{12} \times 2^{2 \times 4} \times 2^{-4} = 2^{16}$.

5. Guess the key nibble (K_7^1) and use the previous guessed value of K_{15}^1 to partially decrypt the ciphertext in order to obtain the value of y_{11}^{30}. Also, guess the key nibbles value of $(K_0^1 \oplus K_8^1)$ and use the previous guess of K_{12}^1 to obtain the value of y_{15}^{30}. The average number of keys suggested by a pair after this step is $2^{16} \times 2^{2 \times 4} = 2^{24}$.

6. Use the value and the difference at (y_3^{30}) from step (2) with the values $(y_{11}^{30}, y_{15}^{30})$ obtained from the previous step to get the value and the difference at (y_{14}^{29}) by guessing the value of $(K_3^0 \oplus K_{11}^0 \oplus K_{15}^0)$. We then filter out the keys if the difference(Δy_{14}^{29}) is not the same as the differences $(\Delta y_2^{29}, \Delta y_6^{29})$ that are obtained in the step (4). Thus, the average number of keys suggested by a pair after this step is $2^{24} \times 2^4 \times 2^{-4} = 2^{24}$.

7. Use the previously guessed value of the key nibble (K_{14}^1) to partially decrypt the nibble y_{14}^{29} to obtain the difference Δy_3^{28} and discard the keys if the condition of $(\Delta y_3^{28} = 4)$ is not satisfied. Consequently, the average number of keys suggested by a pair after this procedure will be decreased to $2^{24} \times 2^{-4} = 2^{20}$. Thus, we increment the corresponding 2^{20} counters.

After repeating the above procedure for $2^{m'}$ pairs, we select the key corresponding to the highest counter as a 44-bit right key. Then, we recover the 128-bit master key by testing the 44-bit right key along with the remaining 84 bits of the master key that are not involved in the analysis using 2 plaintext/ciphertext pairs.

4.3   Attack Complexity and Success Probability

In what follows, we present the complexity analysis of the attack in order to determine the required number of chosen plaintexts and the memory required to launch this attack.

Data Complexity. We utilize the concept of signal-to-noise ratio (S/N) [6] in order to determine the required number of chosen plaintext/ciphertext pairs (2^m). $S/N = \frac{2^k \times p}{\alpha \times \beta}$, where k is the number of key bits involved in the analysis, p is the probability of the differential characteristic, α is the number of guessed keys by a pair, and β is the ratio of the pairs that are not discarded. In our analysis, $k = 44$, $p = 2^{-28}$, $\alpha = 2^{20}$, and $\beta = 2^{-40}$. Therefore, we have $S/N = \frac{2^{44} \times 2^{-28}}{2^{20} \times 2^{-40}} = 2^{36}$. Due to this high S/N, we can use the recommendation of Biham and Shamir [6] that 3–4 right pairs are sufficient enough to mount a successful differential attack. Therefore, we select the number of plaintext/ciphertext pairs (2^m) equal to $4 \times p^{-1} = 2^{30}$. Consequently, the data complexity will be 2^{31} chosen plaintexts.

During the data collection phase, we discard the pairs that do not satisfy the conditions on the differences of the ciphertext. The probability of satisfying these conditions is 2^{-40}, i.e., there are, on average, $2^{m-40} = 2^{30-40} = 2^{-10}$ remaining pairs. This means that the right pairs only pass this filtration and $2^{m'} = 4$.

According to [9] and due to the high S/N, the success probability of the attack (P_s) can be calculated as $P_s \approx \Phi(\sqrt{p \times 2^m})$ where Φ is the cumulative distribution function of the standard normal distribution. Therefore, our differential attack will succeed with probability $P_s \approx 0.9772$.

Time Complexity. During the key recovery phase, we perform several partial decryption of some nibbles which we can consider as $\frac{1}{16}$ of 1-round decryption. The dominant time complexity of the key recovery procedure comes from step 6 in which we perform $2^{m'} \times 2^4 \times 2^{24} \times 2 = 2^{31}$ partial decryption of 3 nibbles. This time equals to $\frac{1}{16} \times \frac{1}{32} \times 2^{31} = 2^{22}$ 32-round encryptions. Then, we perform the exhaustive search over the remaining 2^{84} keys using 2 plaintext/ciphertext pairs. The time complexity of this step is $2 \times 2^{84} = 2^{85}$ 32-round encryptions. Therefore, the total time complexity of the attack is $2^{22} + 2^{85} \approx 2^{85}$ encryptions.

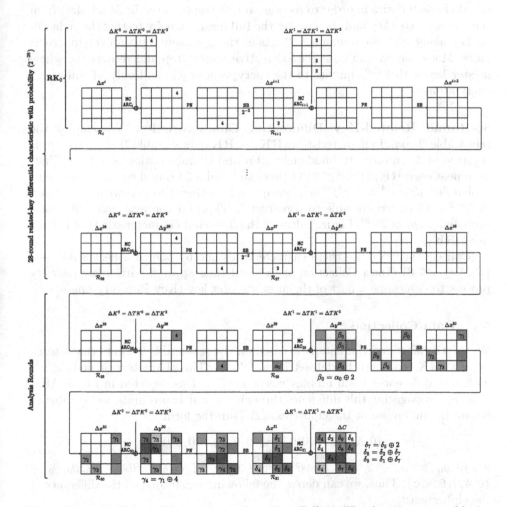

Fig. 4. The related-key differential attack against Full CRAFT using the repeatable 2-round related-key differential characteristic ($\mathbf{RK}_0$) where the colored cells are known values and differences.

Memory Complexity. The dominant part of the memory complexity comes from storing 2^{44} counters. Since the upper limit of each counter is $2^{m'} = 4$, we can store each counter in one byte. Therefore, we need $2^{44} \times \frac{8}{64} = 2^{41}$ 64-bit blocks of memory.

5 Related-Key Differential Attack Using Multiple Differences

In this section, we present a key recovery attack in the related-key model against the full-round CRAFT with $2^{35.17}$ queries to the encryption oracle and 2^{32} full-round encryptions. To this end, we manage to use 8 different related-key differential characteristics in order to recover 96 bits (represented in 24 nibbles) from the secret master key and then we get the full master key by testing the right 96-bit key along with the remaining 32 bits of the key using 2 plaintext/ciphertext pairs. Moreover, we can omit the exhaustive search step and recover the whole master key with $2^{36.09}$ queries to the encryption oracle and only 11 full-round encryptions.

30-Round Related-Key Differential Characteristics. We employ the repeatable 2-round characteristics ($\mathbf{RK_1}$ – $\mathbf{RK_8}$) (see Table 2) with the tuple $(\alpha, \beta) = (4, 2)$ in order to build eight 30-round characteristics as follows. First, we repeat each $\mathbf{RK}_i$ ($1 \leq i \leq 8$) 14 times to build a 28-round characteristic with probability $(2^{-2})^{14} = 2^{-28}$. Then, we append another 2 rounds with probability of (2^{-2}). Thus, we are able to construct a 30-round characteristic with total probability (p) of 2^{-30}. Figure 5 depicts the 30-round characteristic that is built using $\mathbf{RK_1}$.

Consequently, we use these characteristics one by one to collect 8 datasets $(\mathcal{D}_i, 1 \leq i \leq 8)$ (Data Collection phase) and then apply a partial-key recovery process to determine a part of the master secret key (Key Recovery phase).

5.1 Data Collection

We use the 30-round characteristic based on the repeatable 2-round characteristic, e.g., $\mathbf{RK_1}$ to build the dataset $\mathcal{D}_1$ as follows. This characteristic ends at x^{30} with zero differences in all nibbles except $\Delta x_{12}^{30} = 1$ as depicted in Fig. 5. After that, by propagating this difference through the last two rounds, we are able to obtain the difference at the ciphertext (ΔC) in the form

$$(0, \delta_0, \beta_0, \gamma_0, 0, 0, 0, \gamma_0, 0, 0, \beta_0, 0, 0, 0, 0, \gamma_0)$$

where $\delta_0 = \alpha_0 \oplus 2$ and based on the DDT of CRAFT Sbox, $\alpha_0, \beta_0, \gamma_0 \in \{0, 4, 7, 9, \mathsf{a}, \mathsf{c}\}$. Thus, we can derive the following conditions on the difference of the ciphertext:

$$\Delta C_i = 0, \ i \in \{0, 4, 5, 6, 8, 9, 11, 12, 13, 14\}, \quad \Delta C_1 = \delta_0,$$
$$\Delta C_2 = \Delta C_{10} = \beta_0, \quad\quad\quad\quad\quad\quad\quad\quad \Delta C_3 = \Delta C_7 = \Delta C_{15} = \gamma_0.$$

Consequently, we first select a set of $4 \times p^{-1} = 4 \times 2^{30} = 2^{32}$ arbitrary plaintexts $(\mathcal{L}_0)$ and then we create another set of 2^{32} plaintexts $(\mathcal{L}_1)$ by XORing each plaintext in the first set $\mathcal{L}_0$ with the input difference. After encrypting the two sets $(\mathcal{L}_0, \mathcal{L}_1)$ using $(K^0 \| K^1)$ and $((K^0 \oplus \Delta K^0) \| (K^1 \oplus \Delta K^1))$, respectively, we discard the pairs where the output difference does not match the required output difference (ΔC). The probability of getting (ΔC) is $2^{-(10 \times 4 + 4 + 2 \times 4)} \times (\frac{6}{16})^3 \approx 2^{-56.25}$. In other words, only the right pairs can pass this filtration. Thus, we collect, on average, 4 right pairs that follow the characteristic.

We repeat the same approach using the same set of plaintexts $(\mathcal{L}_0)$ with other sets of plaintexts $\mathcal{L}_i, (2 \leq i \leq 8)$, selected like $\mathcal{L}_1$, in order to construct the datasets $\mathcal{D}_i, (1 \leq i \leq 8)$ using the 30-round characteristic that has been built using $\mathbf{RK}_i, (1 \leq i \leq 8)$ in order to get 4 right pairs per each dataset.

5.2   Key Recovery

We first prepare 24 groups of counters in which each group consists of 16 counters. Each group corresponds to a nibble of the key involved in the analysis. After that, we perform the attack in three sequential stages as follows.

First Stage. In this stage, we manage to determine the nibbles $K_i^1, (8 \leq i \leq 15)$. For example, we determine the right value of K_{15}^1 as follows. We consider the group of counters corresponding to K_{15}^1, then for each right pair in the datasets $\mathcal{D}_1$ and $\mathcal{D}_5$, we guess K_{15}^1 and decrypt the ciphertext nibble (C_{15}) (see Figs. 5 and 6), then increment the counter corresponding to the guessed value if the difference $\Delta y_0^{30} = 5$. After repeating these steps for all the pairs, we select the value corresponding to the highest counters as the right value for K_{15}^1.

By repeating these steps, we are able to obtain the right values of the nibbles $K_i^1, (8 \leq i \leq 15)$. Table 3 summarizes which datasets are used to recover these nibbles.

Second Stage. After finishing the first stage, we have the right value of the key nibbles $K_8^1, K_9^1, K_{10}^1, K_{11}^1, K_{12}^1, K_{13}^1, K_{14}^1, K_{15}^1$. During this stage, we obtain the right value of another 8 nibbles $K_0^1, K_1^1, K_2^1, K_3^1, K_{12}^0, K_{13}^0, K_{14}^0, K_{15}^0$. To this end, we consider, for example, the groups of counters corresponding to the key nibbles K_1^1 and K_{12}^0, respectively. After that, we reuse the dataset $\mathcal{D}_1$ (see Fig. 5) in order to carry out the following steps:

1. Use the key nibbles K_9^1 and K_{13}^1 determined in the first stage to partially decrypt the ciphertext nibbles (C_9, C_{13}) and obtain the values of the nibbles x_9^{31} and x_{13}^{31}, respectively.
2. Guess K_1^1 and partially decrypt the ciphertext nibble C_1 to get the value and the difference at y_{12}^{30}, after that, increment the counter corresponding to the value of K_1^1 in case of $\Delta y_{12}^{30} = 5$.
3. Determine the right value of the key nibble K_1^1 by observing the highest counter.

Table 3. Key recovery

Key nibble	Dataset used	Key nibble	Dataset used
K_0^0	$\mathcal{D}_{13}$	K_0^1	$\mathcal{D}_4$
K_1^0	$\mathcal{D}_{14}$	K_1^1	$\mathcal{D}_1$
K_2^0	$\mathcal{D}_{15}$	K_2^1	$\mathcal{D}_2$
K_3^0	$\mathcal{D}_{16}$	K_3^1	$\mathcal{D}_3$
K_4^0	$\mathcal{D}_9$	K_4^1	$\mathcal{D}_7$
K_5^0	$\mathcal{D}_{10}$	K_5^1	$\mathcal{D}_6$
K_6^0	$\mathcal{D}_{11}$	K_6^1	$\mathcal{D}_5$
K_7^0	$\mathcal{D}_{12}$	K_7^1	$\mathcal{D}_8$
K_8^0	$\mathcal{D}_5$	K_8^1	$\mathcal{D}_3$
K_9^0	$\mathcal{D}_6$	K_9^1	$\mathcal{D}_2$
K_{10}^0	$\mathcal{D}_7$	K_{10}^1	$\mathcal{D}_1$
K_{11}^0	$\mathcal{D}_8$	K_{11}^1	$\mathcal{D}_4$
K_{12}^0	$\mathcal{D}_1$	K_{12}^1	$\mathcal{D}_2, \mathcal{D}_6$
K_{13}^0	$\mathcal{D}_2$	K_{13}^1	$\mathcal{D}_3, \mathcal{D}_7$
K_{14}^0	$\mathcal{D}_3$	K_{14}^1	$\mathcal{D}_4, \mathcal{D}_8$
K_{15}^0	$\mathcal{D}_4$	K_{15}^1	$\mathcal{D}_1, \mathcal{D}_5$

4. Guess K_{12}^0 and decrypt y_{12}^{30} to get the difference Δy_1^{29}, then increment the counter corresponding to the value of K_{12}^0 if $\Delta y_1^{29} = 2$.
5. Determine the right value of the key nibble K_{12}^0 by observing the highest counter.

In the same manner, we reuse the datasets $\mathcal{D}_2, \mathcal{D}_3$ and $\mathcal{D}_4$ to determine the right values of the key nibbles (K_2^1, K_{13}^0), (K_3^1, K_{14}^0), (K_0^1, K_{15}^0), respectively.

Third Stage. Similar to the second stage, we reuse the datasets $\mathcal{D}_5, \mathcal{D}_6, \mathcal{D}_7$ and $\mathcal{D}_8$ to recover the key nibbles $K_i^1, (4 \leq i \leq 7)$ and $K_j^0, (8 \leq j \leq 11)$ as follows. To recover the nibbles K_6^1 and K_8^0, we consider the groups of counters corresponding them, and we reuse the dataset $\mathcal{D}_5$ (see Fig. 6) in order to carry out the following steps:

1. Use the key nibble K_{14}^1 determined in the first stage to partially decrypt the ciphertext nibbles (C_{14}) to obtain the value of the nibble x_{14}^{31}.
2. Guess K_6^1 and get the value and difference at y_8^{30}, then increment the counter corresponding to the value of K_6^1 in case of $\Delta y_8^{30} = 5$.
3. Determine the right value of the key nibble K_6^1 by observing the highest counter.
4. Guess K_8^0 and decrypt y_8^{30} to get the difference Δy_6^{29}, then increment the counter corresponding to the value of K_8^0 if $\Delta y_6^{29} = 2$.

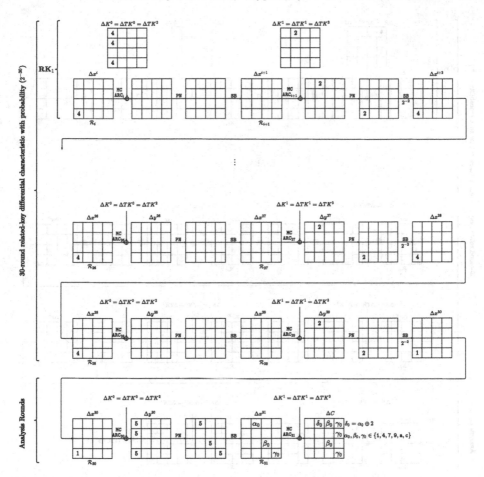

Fig. 5. Related-key differential attack against Full CRAFT using the dataset $(\mathcal{D}_1)$ to recover $K_1^1, K_{10}^1, K_{15}^1$, and K_{12}^0.

5. Determine the right value of the key nibble K_6^0 by observing the highest counter.

Using the same approach, we are able to determine the right values of the key nibbles (K_5^1, K_9^0), (K_4^1, K_{10}^0) and (K_7^1, K_{11}^0) using the datasets $\mathcal{D}_6, \mathcal{D}_7$ and $\mathcal{D}_8$, respectively.

5.3 Attack Complexity

Each set of plaintexts $\mathcal{L}_0, \cdots, \mathcal{L}_8$ contains 2^{32} plaintexts. Thus, we need $9 \times 2^{32} \approx 2^{35.17}$ queries to the encryption oracle.

During the first stage of the key recovery phase, we determine 4 nibbles using 32 right pairs and another 4 nibbles using 16 right pairs, therefore, we execute $2 \times (32 + 16) \times 2^4 = 2^{10.58}$ single nibble encryptions. For the second stage, we

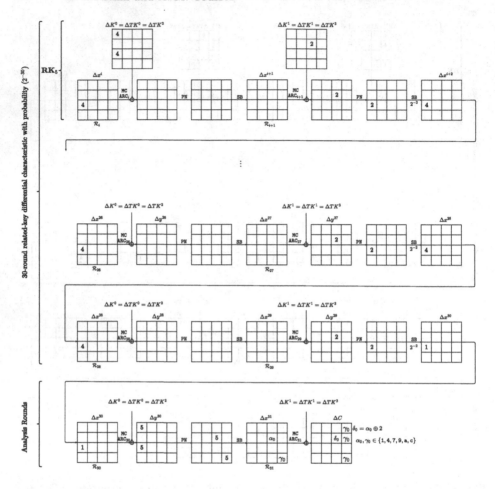

Fig. 6. Related-key differential attack against Full CRAFT using the dataset ($\mathcal{D}_5$) to recover K_6^1, K_{15}^1, and K_8^0.

recover another 8 nibbles using 4 right pairs per each nibble. This process needs $2 \times 4 \times 4 \times (2 + 2^4 + 2^4) = 2^{10.08}$ single nibble encryptions. The third stage needs $2 \times 4 \times 4 \times (1 + 2^4 + 2^4) = 2^{10.04}$ single nibble encryptions. Therefore, these three stages need $2^{12.32}$ single nibble encryptions which is equivalent to $2^{11.83} \times \frac{1}{16} \times \frac{1}{32} \approx 8$ full-round encryptions. After these stages, we run exhaustive search over the remaining 2^{32} keys using 2 plaintext/ciphertext pairs and this step needs $2^{32} = 2^{33}$ full-round encryptions.

The dominant part of the memory complexity of this stage is for storing $4 \times 8 = 32$ right pairs in addition to the 128-bit right key. Therefore, the memory complexity is $2 \times 32 + 2 = 66$ 64-bit blocks.

5.4   Omitting the Exhaustive Search Step

In this section, we describe how we can omit the exhaustive search over 2^{32} keys. To this end, we utilize the repeatable 2-round characteristics $\mathbf{RK}_9 - \mathbf{RK}_{16}$ to build another 8 30-round characteristics. Then, we employ these characteristics to construct the datasets $\mathcal{D}_1 - \mathcal{D}_{16}$ to get, on average, 4 right pairs per each dataset as we do before.

To determine the right value of the key nibbles $K_i^0, (0 \le i \le 7)$, we first prepare 16 counters per each nibble. Then, we partially decrypt some nibbles of the ciphertexts. After that, we guess the key nibble and increment the counters if a specific nibble at the state y^{29} has a difference equal to 2, as we do in the second and the third stages before. The ciphertext nibbles to be decrypted in addition to the position of the checked nibble at the state y^{29} and the used dataset depend on which key nibble we recover (see Table 3).

In this case, we need $17 \times 2^{32} \approx 2^{36.09}$ queries to the encryption oracle. In addition to the 8 full-round encryptions required during the previous three stages, we need $2 \times 4 \times 4 \times (6 + 2^4) = 2^{9.46}$ single nibble encryptions to recover the nibbles $K_0^0 - K_3^0$ and $2 \times 4 \times 4 \times (4 + 2^4) = 2^{9.32}$ single nibble encryptions to recover the nibbles $K_4^0 - K_7^0$. Thus, we need $8 + ((2^{9.46} + 2^{9.32}) \times \frac{1}{16} \times \frac{1}{32}) \approx 11$ full-round encryptions. Also, we need more $2 \times 4 \times 8 = 64$ block of memory to store the right pairs. Thus, the total memory complexity will be $66 + 64 = 130$ blocks of memory.

6   Conclusion

In this paper, we studied the security of the lightweight tweakable block cipher CRAFT against the related-key differential cryptanalysis. More precisely, we described a systematic method to build a repeatable 2-round related-key differential characteristic that holds with the probability of 2^{-2}. We utilized this method to build several 30-round related-key differential characteristics with probability 2^{-30}. Then, we employed these characteristics to mount a key recovery attack against the full round of CRAFT in practical time. Moreover, we have verified this attack experimentally.

References

1. Banik, S., Pandey, S.K., Peyrin, T., Sasaki, Y., Sim, S.M., Todo, Y.: GIFT: a small present. In: Fischer, W., Homma, N. (eds.) CHES 2017. LNCS, vol. 10529, pp. 321–345. Springer, Cham (2017). https://doi.org/10.1007/978-3-319-66787-4_16
2. Beaulieu, R., Treatman-Clark, S., Shors, D., Weeks, B., Smith, J., Wingers, L.: The SIMON and SPECK lightweight block ciphers. In: 2015 52nd ACM/EDAC/IEEE Design Automation Conference (DAC), pp. 1–6 (2015)
3. Beierle, C., et al.: The SKINNY family of block ciphers and its low-latency variant MANTIS. In: Robshaw, M., Katz, J. (eds.) CRYPTO 2016, Part II. LNCS, vol. 9815, pp. 123–153. Springer, Heidelberg (2016). https://doi.org/10.1007/978-3-662-53008-5_5

4. Beierle, C., Leander, G., Moradi, A., Rasoolzadeh, S.: CRAFT: lightweight tweakable block cipher with efficient protection against DFA attacks. IACR Trans. Symmetric Cryptol. **2019**(1), 5–45 (2019). https://tosc.iacr.org/index.php/ToSC/article/view/7396
5. Biham, E.: New types of cryptanalytic attacks using related keys. J. Cryptol. **7**(4), 229–246 (1994)
6. Biham, E., Shamir, A.: Differential Cryptanalysis of the Data Encryption Standard. Springer, New York (1993)
7. Bogdanov, A., et al.: PRESENT: an ultra-lightweight block cipher. In: Paillier, P., Verbauwhede, I. (eds.) CHES 2007. LNCS, vol. 4727, pp. 450–466. Springer, Heidelberg (2007). https://doi.org/10.1007/978-3-540-74735-2_31
8. Hadipour, H., Sadeghi, S., Niknam, M.M., Bagheri, N.: Comprehensive security analysis of CRAFT. Cryptology ePrint Archive, Report 2019/741 (2019). https://eprint.iacr.org/2019/741
9. Selçuk, A.A.: On probability of success in linear and differential cryptanalysis. J. Cryptol. **21**(1), 131–147 (2008)

SpookChain: Chaining a Sponge-Based AEAD with Beyond-Birthday Security

Gaëtan Cassiers, Chun Guo, Olivier Pereira[⊠], Thomas Peters,
and François-Xavier Standaert

UCLouvain – ICTEAM – Crypto Group, 1348 Louvain-la-Neuve, Belgium
{olivier.pereira,thomas.peters}@uclouvain.be

Abstract. We present SpookChain, a new *online authenticated encryption* (OAE) mode that offers several appealing features:
- SpookChain is fully online: it supports the processing of long messages by segments of arbitrary size, and the processing of each segment is online itself, with memory requirements in encryption and decryption being independent of the segment size.
- SpookChain is, to the best of our knowledge, the first concrete mode that is proven to offer dOAE security, a requirement for OAE that, at least guarantees security for new segments as soon as one of the previously processed segments contains a fresh element (nonce, plaintext or associated data).
- SpookChain offers beyond birthday multi-user security (w.r.t. the secret key length), a requirement that we define for the first time in the context of OAE, and which is increasingly appealing in a world where communications are encrypted by default.
- SpookChain is also expected to be remarkably lightweight to implement when protection against side-channel attacks is required.

1 Introduction

Online Authenticated Encryption. Online authenticated encryption (OAE), first formally studied by Bellare et al. [1], aims at offering confidentiality and authenticity under the constraint that the amount of memory that is needed to encrypt and decrypt messages is limited to a constant that can be much smaller than the size of the messages and ciphertexts that may be processed. Encryption and decryption then need to be possible while only storing small segments of the plaintext or ciphertext.

The design of OAE is motivated by numerous applications. For instance, a user willing to watch a movie stored on a remote server will not wait until the full movie, which may be a few gigabytes big, is downloaded, but rather buffer segments of a few megabytes, which will be decrypted and authenticated before being watched, even if the rest of the movie keeps being downloaded in background.

In switched packet networks, it is also common to use a transport layer that provides an in-order stream communication where data is sent and received by

© Springer Nature Switzerland AG 2019
S. Bhasin et al. (Eds.): SPACE 2019, LNCS 11947, pp. 67–85, 2019.
https://doi.org/10.1007/978-3-030-35869-3_7

chunks (which correspond to a packet in the underlying network), and it is then a common approach to secure this stream by enforcing confidentiality and authenticity at the chunk level. An OAE offers here the convenience of securely linking the chunks together as part of a unique stream. For instance, in its latest version, the widely used TLS protocol [10] performs a nonce-based AEAD for each segment (named record) where the nonce contains the record number. Another example is the SSH protocol which uses a similar technique (although it predates the AEAD definition). Online authenticated encryption appears thus as a natural abstraction of the goal of those protocols where, while data is conceptually a stream, it is split into segments (that are sent and received in-order) that match the characteristics of the underlying network for performance reasons.

Eventually, OAE may be required in environments in which the available memory is much smaller than the size of the messages that need to be processed: this may be the case in FPGA or ASIC implementations for instance.

dOAE *security*. Following the tradition of modern authenticated encryption, we are interested in designing a nonce based OAE (that is, deterministic encryption and decryption processes that are initialized with the help of a nonce that is expected to be unique), which still offers some form of security when nonces are repeated (contrary to the normal use of the OAE). Indeed, even if the requirement of a nonce is much less stringent than the requirement of a uniformly random IV, it appears that this uniqueness requirement remains notoriously hard to guarantee in practice [4,11].

First security definitions for OAE that incorporate some protection against repeated nonces have been proposed by Fleischmann et al. [6], and have been recently revised and extended by Hoang et al. [8] who propose two new definitions: dOAE, and OAE2 (a third one, nOAE, focuses on nonce-respecting adversaries). OAE2 is the strongest of these notions, and requires two passes on each message segment that cannot be processed online, meaning that the memory available in the encryption and decryption devices must be at least as big as the size of a segment. We are interested in minimizing the memory requirements in order to obtain a scheme that is suitable for the most memory constrained environments. Of course, minimal memory requirements can be obtained by defining very small segments, but this comes at the cost of an increased ciphertext expansion since authentication tags need to be provided per segment. So, our goal is to obtain minimum memory requirements while keeping the flexibility to define the segment size as a function of the latency and/or ciphertext expansion that one is willing to tolerate in a given application. We refer to OAE schemes that offer constant memory requirements, independent of the segment size, as *fully online*.

Fully online encryption is compatible with the second notion proposed by Hoang et al., namely dOAE security, a notion that was inspired by the general duplex design approach [3]. In a nutshell (a more detailed presentation will be offered in the next section), dOAE guarantees security for a segment as long as there is at least one fresh element (nonce, plaintext or associated data) in a prior segment. So, for instance, even if a nonce is repeated, security remains guaranteed if there is a unique element in the associated data.

Multi-user Security. As encryption has become a default choice for communication in an always increasingly connected world, the importance of multi-user security has become paramount: it is not exceptional to have an encryption scheme used with billions of keys.

SpookChain offers beyond birthday multi-user security, that is, it keeps offering security even when using a number of keys that is (much) larger than the square-root of the size of the key space. As dOAE was only defined in the single user setting, we extend the notion to the multi-user setting, a contribution that offers an interest independent of SpookChain itself.

Previous sponge or duplex-based AEs, see e.g., Keyak [2], attempted chaining for online functionality. But SpookChain provides the first rigorous security analysis for such chains in the multi-user setting (even for nOAE). Prior Duplex [5] analysis did not explicitly consider this setting. We leave similar treatments on the other permutation-based AEs as open questions.

Side-Channel Attack Resistant Implementations. Side-channel attacks have also become a major concern, as it is more and more common to have devices spread in the nature within adversarial reach, and as it has become standard to have sensitive information belonging to independent organizations being processed on a single hardware platform. As a result, the built-in side-channel attack resistance of authenticated encryption schemes has been pointed out as a core criterion in the ongoing NIST lightweight cryptography competition [9].

SpookChain builds on the TETSponge mode [7], which is a used in the Spook proposal to this NIST competition. SpookChain incorporates many of the features offered by TETSponge, while actually offering some extra efficiency benefits. TETSponge mixes two components: one is a tweakable block cipher (TBC) that is required to be strongly protected against side channel attacks, and is used only twice per encrypted message (independently of the size of the message). The plaintext and associated data are themselves processed using a variant of the sponge-based duplex mode, with minimal protections against side-channel attacks. As the heavily protected TBC is expected to be more expensive than the sponge by 2–3 orders of magnitude, the efficiency benefits of TETSponge are most important when longer messages are processed or, considering an OAE setting, when segments are relatively long. SpookChain mitigates this effect by only requiring a single use of the heavily protected TBC per additional segment (2 TBC calls are still needed for the initial segment).

As a result, in settings where multiple ordered messages need to be sent (e.g., in an SSH or TLS communication), SpookChain offers not only an effective way of splitting the conversation in multiple segments that are linked together, but also comes with efficiency benefits (which are most visible when side-channel attacks are a concern) compared to a solution in which messages would be encrypted independently of each other.

Paper Organization. Section 2 introduces our notations and defines the components and security notions that are needed for the presentation of SpookChain. The SpookChain mode itself is presented in Sect. 3, together with security analysis in Sect. 4.

2 Preliminaries

We use the following notations. Let $A \in \{0,1\}^*$ be a bitstring and $r > 0$ be an integer. $|A|$ denotes the bit-length of the bit-string A, i.e. the value a such that $A \in \{0,1\}^a$. The concatenation of the bit-strings A and B is $A\|B$. The empty string is ϵ. If $A \neq \epsilon$ (i.e. $|A| > 0$), $A[1]\| \dots \|A[\alpha] \overset{r}{\leftarrow} A$ denotes that A is parsed into r-bit blocks such that $A = A[1]\| \dots \|A[\alpha]$ and $|A[i]| = r$, for $i = 1, \dots, \alpha-1$, and $0 < |A[\alpha]| \leq r$, hence $\alpha = \lceil a/r \rceil$. Moreover, if $r \leq a$, $\mathsf{msb}_r(A)$ (resp. $\mathsf{lsb}_r(A)$) is an r-bit string composed of the r most (resp. least) significant bits of A.

Let $\boldsymbol{A} \in \mathcal{A}^*$. Λ denotes the empty vector, $\Lambda = ()$. $|\boldsymbol{A}|$ denotes the number of components of $\boldsymbol{A}$ in $\mathcal{A}$, i.e. the value L such that $\boldsymbol{A} \in \mathcal{A}^L$. Therefore, $\boldsymbol{A} = (A_1, \dots, A_{|\boldsymbol{A}|})$ and $\boldsymbol{A}[i] := A_i$ is its i-th component, for $i = 1$ to $|\boldsymbol{A}|$. Moreover, given $A \in \mathcal{A}$, $\boldsymbol{A}\|A = (A_1, \dots, A_{|\boldsymbol{A}|}, A)$ in $\mathcal{A}^{L+1}$. For instance, if $\mathcal{A} = \{0,1\}^*$, we simply have $\mathcal{A}^* = \{0,1\}^{**}$ such that if $A_i \in \{0,1\}^{a_i}$, then $|\boldsymbol{A}[i]| = a_i$. For $\boldsymbol{A} = (\epsilon, \epsilon)$, we have $|\boldsymbol{A}| = 2$ and then $\boldsymbol{A} \neq \Lambda$, but $|\boldsymbol{A}[1]| = |\boldsymbol{A}[2]| = 0$.

2.1 Primitives

A Tweakable Block Cipher (TBC) with key space $\{0,1\}^\kappa$, tweak space $\{0,1\}^t$, and domain $\{0,1\}^n$, also denoted (κ, t, n)-TBC, is a mapping $\widetilde{\mathsf{E}} : \{0,1\}^\kappa \times \{0,1\}^t \times \{0,1\}^n \to \{0,1\}^n$ such that for any key $K \in \{0,1\}^\kappa$ and any tweak $T \in \{0,1\}^t$, $X \mapsto \widetilde{\mathsf{E}}(K,T,X)$ is a permutation of $\{0,1\}^n$. We only focus on (n,n,n)-TBC in this paper. An ideal TBC $\widetilde{\mathsf{IC}} : \{0,1\}^n \times \{0,1\}^n \times \{0,1\}^n \to \{0,1\}^n$ is a TBC sampled uniformly at random from all (n,n,n)-TBCs: the spirit is the same as ideal (block) ciphers. In this case, $\widetilde{\mathsf{IC}}_K^T$ is a random independent permutation of $\{0,1\}^n$ for each $(K,T) \in \{0,1\}^n \times \{0,1\}^n$ even if the key K is *public*.

A random key-less permutation π, as used in sponge designs, refers to a permutation of $\{0,1\}^\ell$ drawn uniformly at random among the set of all permutations of $\{0,1\}^\ell$. The permutation π is then seen as an ideal object.

Chaining authenticated encryption is made segment by segment as formally defined next.

Definition 1 (Segmented-AE [8]). *A segmented-AE scheme is a triple $\Pi = (\mathcal{K}, \mathcal{E}, \mathcal{D})$ where the key space $\mathcal{K}$ is a non-empty set with an associated distribution and both encryption $\mathcal{E} = (\mathcal{E}.\mathsf{init}, \mathcal{E}.\mathsf{next}, \mathcal{E}.\mathsf{last})$ and decryption $\mathcal{D} = (\mathcal{D}.\mathsf{init}, \mathcal{D}.\mathsf{next}, \mathcal{D}.\mathsf{last})$ are specified by triple of deterministic algorithms such that*

$$\mathcal{E}_K.\mathsf{init} : \mathcal{N} \to \mathcal{S} \qquad\qquad \mathcal{D}_K.\mathsf{init} : \mathcal{N} \to \mathcal{S}$$
$$\mathcal{E}_K.\mathsf{next} : \mathcal{S} \times \mathcal{A} \times \mathcal{M} \to \mathcal{C} \times \mathcal{S} \qquad \mathcal{D}_K.\mathsf{next} : \mathcal{S} \times \mathcal{A} \times \mathcal{C} \to \mathcal{M} \cup \{\bot\} \times \mathcal{S}$$
$$\mathcal{E}_K.\mathsf{last} : \mathcal{S} \times \mathcal{A} \times \mathcal{M} \to \mathcal{C} \qquad\quad \mathcal{D}_K.\mathsf{last} : \mathcal{S} \times \mathcal{A} \times \mathcal{C} \to \mathcal{M} \cup \{\bot\}$$

where $K \leftarrow \mathcal{K}$, $\mathcal{N}$ is the nonce space, $\mathcal{S}$ is the state space, $\mathcal{A}$ is associated data space, $\mathcal{M}$ is the message space and $\mathcal{C}$ is the ciphertext space.

In order to encrypt a chain $(A_1, M_1), \ldots, (A_L, M_L) \in \mathcal{A} \times \mathcal{M}$, for some L, given a nonce $N \in \mathcal{N}$, we start by generating an initial state $S_0 \leftarrow \mathcal{E}_K.\mathsf{init}(N)$, then we iterate $(S_i, C_i) \leftarrow \mathcal{E}_K.\mathsf{next}(S_{i-1}, A_i, M_i)$, for $i = 1, \ldots, L-1$, and eventually we finalize by $C_L \leftarrow \mathcal{E}_K.\mathsf{last}(S_{L-1}, A_L, M_L)$ resulting in $C_1, \ldots, C_L \in \mathcal{C}$. This process denoted by $\boldsymbol{C} \leftarrow \mathcal{E}_K(N, \boldsymbol{A}, \boldsymbol{M})$, where $\boldsymbol{A} = (A_1, \ldots, A_L) \in \mathcal{A}^L$, $\boldsymbol{M} = (M_1, \ldots, M_L) \in \mathcal{M}^L$ and $\boldsymbol{C} = (C_1, \ldots, C_L) \in \mathcal{C}^L$ is the induced encryption chain. Similarly, we have the induced decryption chain $\boldsymbol{M} \leftarrow \mathcal{D}_K(N, \boldsymbol{A}, \boldsymbol{C})$, where all $\boldsymbol{M}[i] \in \mathcal{M} \cup \{\bot\}$. Since L is not fixed, the induced chain algorithm $\mathcal{E}_K$ (resp. $\mathcal{D}_K$) runs on the domains $\mathcal{N}$, $\mathcal{A}^*$ and $\mathcal{M}^*$ (resp. $\mathcal{C}^*$).

Throughout the paper any segmented-AE is assumed to be correct meaning that, for all $K \leftarrow \mathcal{K}$, the induced chaining is correct: for any $N \in \mathcal{N}$, any $\boldsymbol{A} \in \mathcal{A}^*$ and any $\boldsymbol{M} \in \mathcal{M}^*$, $|\boldsymbol{A}| = |\boldsymbol{M}|$ implies $\boldsymbol{M} = \mathcal{D}_K(N, \boldsymbol{A}, \mathcal{E}_K(N, \boldsymbol{A}, \boldsymbol{M}))$.

Ciphertext Expansion. The ciphertext expansion τ is the constant value such that, for any ciphertext C computed by a segmented-AE on input (S, A, M), we have $|M| + \tau = |C|$. In our case, we have $\tau = n$ since our ciphertext $C = (c, Z)$, where $c \in \{0, 1\}^{|M|}$ and Z is an integrity tag output by an (n, n, n)-TBC.

2.2   dOAE Security

We extend the dOAE security given by Hoang et al. [8] to the multi-user (i.e. multi-key) setting. Since we get the original definition in the single-user setting, i.e. when there is only one key in our model, we only proceed with our natural extension. However, we recall the original definition [8] for completeness in Appendix A, Fig. 6.

dOAE Privacy. We recall the intuition behind the dOAE privacy of [8]. A dOAE-secure scheme should produce pseudorandom segments into a chain of segment ciphertexts under partial misuse of prefix chains. More precisely, an adversary can make adaptive encryption queries segment-by-segment. To start a new chain, the adversary makes an *initial* query on a nonce N which may be repeated. The adversary can also make some segment encryption queries to continue an encrypted prefix chain $(N, (A_1, A_2), (C_1, C_2))$ of $(N, (A_1, A_2), (M_1, M_2))$ with a *next* segment (A, M). As long as the prefix $(N, (A_1, A_2, A), (M_1, M_2, \star))$ is fresh, which means that it never appears before, the adversary gets $C \leftarrow \{0, 1\}^{|M|+\tau}$, where τ is the ciphertext expansion of the scheme. However, if some prefix $(N, (A_1, A_2, A), (M_1, M_2, M'))$ already exists, the adversary gets $\bot$, if $M \neq M'$, or the already defined segment ciphertext C, otherwise. This latter case allows the adversary to adaptively build two chains with a common prefix that could be forked later from different associated data, like for instance from $(N, (A_1, A_2, A'), (M_1, M_2, \star))$ with A' different than the A above. Eventually, the adversary may also make a *last* segment encryption queries on any chain to add a final segment. If a chain ends with a *last* segment it cannot be further augmented. The restriction between last segment queries is the same as between next segment queries. Nevertheless, assuming the existence of a prefix chain for $(N, (A_1, A_2), (M_1, M_2))$, it is accepted to make both a next segment encryption query on (A, M) and a last segment encryption query on (A, M'), even if the associated data are common but $M \neq M'$. So there is a full prefix-misuse resistance between next and last segments.

To enhance the dOAE privacy to the multi-user setting, we only have to properly deal with the chaining generated from different keys. Moreover, we merge both types of queries into a single *encryption segment* procedure as the specifications of both queries are very similar. More precisely, the procedure Enc.seg$(i, j, A, M, 0)$ (resp. Enc.seg$(i, j, A, M, 1)$) corresponds to an encryption query for a next (resp. last) segment (A, M) using the key K_i, and where j allows keeping track of the current state in the continuing chain. For convenience, even though a last segment has signature $C \leftarrow \mathcal{E}_K.\text{last}(S, A, M)$ we abuse the notation and use $(C, \perp) \leftarrow \mathcal{E}_K.\text{last}(S, A, M)$, where the update state $\perp$ indicates that no further segment is allowed in that chain.

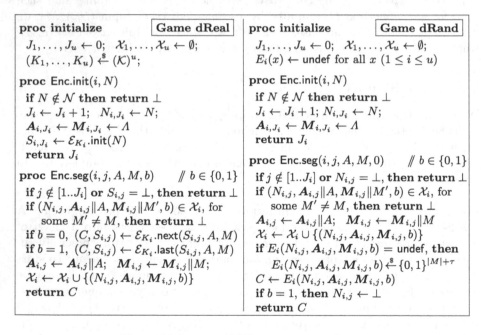

Fig. 1. Multi-user dOAE privacy experiments.

dOAE Integrity. Under the same restriction on the encryption queries it should be unfeasible to output a valid chain $(N, \boldsymbol{A}, \boldsymbol{C})$ for some key K_i, meaning that all the internal segments are valid for K_i, as long as the chain is fresh for i. The multi-user **dForge** experiment given in Fig. 2 follows the multi-user **dReal** experiment where we have to keep track of all the ciphertext chains returned to the adversary, and augmented with a final procedure as in [8]. Formally, we define the authenticity advantage $\mathbf{Adv}_{\mathsf{AEAD}}^{\mathsf{doae\text{-}auth}}(\mathscr{D}) = \Pr[\mathbf{dForge}_{\mathsf{AEAD}}(\mathscr{D}) \Rightarrow \mathsf{true}]$.

---

proc initialize   **Game dForge**

$J_1, \ldots, J_u \leftarrow 0; \quad \mathcal{X}_1, \ldots, \mathcal{X}_u \leftarrow \emptyset; \quad (K_1, \ldots, K_u) \stackrel{\$}{\leftarrow} (\mathcal{K})^u;$

proc Enc.init(i, N)

  if $N \notin \mathcal{N}$ then return $\perp$
  $J_i \leftarrow J_i + 1; \quad N_{i,J_i} \leftarrow N; \quad \boldsymbol{A}_{i,J_i} \leftarrow \boldsymbol{M}_{i,J_i} \leftarrow \boldsymbol{C}_{i,J_i} \leftarrow \Lambda; \quad S_{i,J_i} \leftarrow \mathcal{E}_{K_i}.\text{init}(N)$
  return J_i

proc Enc.seg(i, j, A, M, b)   // $b \in \{0, 1\}$

  if $j \notin [1..J_i]$ or $S_{i,j} = \perp$, then return $\perp$
  if $(N_{i,j}, \boldsymbol{A}_{i,j} \| A, \boldsymbol{M}_{i,j} \| M', b) \in \mathcal{X}_i$, for some $M' \neq M$, then return $\perp$
  if $b = 0$, then $(C, S_{i,j}) \leftarrow \mathcal{E}_{K_i}.\text{next}(S_{i,j}, A, M)$, else $(C, S_{i,j}) \leftarrow \mathcal{E}_{K_i}.\text{last}(S_{i,j}, A, M)$
  $\boldsymbol{A}_{i,j} \leftarrow \boldsymbol{A}_{i,j} \| A; \quad \boldsymbol{M}_{i,j} \leftarrow \boldsymbol{M}_{i,j} \| M; \quad \boldsymbol{C}_{i,j} \leftarrow \boldsymbol{C}_{i,j} \| C;$
  $\mathcal{X}_i \leftarrow \mathcal{X}_i \cup \{(N_{i,j}, \boldsymbol{A}_{i,j}, \boldsymbol{M}_{i,j}, b)\}; \quad \mathcal{Y}_i \leftarrow \mathcal{Y}_i \cup \{(N_{i,j}, \boldsymbol{A}_{i,j}, \boldsymbol{C}_{i,j}, b)\}$
  return C

proc finalize $(i, N, \boldsymbol{A}, \boldsymbol{C}, b)$ // $b \in \{0, 1\}$

  if $(N, \boldsymbol{A}, \boldsymbol{C}, b) \in \mathcal{Y}_i$ or $|\boldsymbol{A}| \neq |\boldsymbol{C}|$ or $|\boldsymbol{A}| = 0$, then return false
  $S \leftarrow \mathcal{D}_{K_i}.\text{init}(N); \quad m \leftarrow |\boldsymbol{C}|$
  $j \leftarrow 1$ to $m - b$ do
    $(M, S) \leftarrow \mathcal{D}_{K_i}.\text{next}(S, \boldsymbol{A}[j], \boldsymbol{C}[j])$
    if $M = \perp$ then return false
  if $\mathcal{D}_{K_i}.\text{last}(S, \boldsymbol{A}[m], \boldsymbol{C}[m]) = \perp$ and $b = 1$, then return false
  return true

Fig. 2. Multi-user dOAE integrity experiment.

3 SpookChain Mode

The SpookChain mode is defined upon the TETSponge mode. For completeness, we recall the TETSponge mode of [7] in Fig. 3. We identity the first TBC call which produces B to feed the first permutation call as the "initial" part of TETSponge. The remaining part of the algorithm is named the "Duplex" part and it is denoted as DEnc (resp. DDec) for the encryption (resp. decryption). We stress that the last TBC call is included in these algorithms by convention.

Therefore, we can say that the TETSponge encryption consists of its initial part followed by an encryption of a single segment, processed by DEnc. The basic principle of SpookChain is to "chain" TETSponge by keeping in memory the capacity of the last permutation call which should have been erased after a careful execution of TETSponge. This capacity is denoted by R in Fig. 3. To process a second segment, we simply have to call DEnc again starting with input state $S = 0^r \| R$. This process can be repeated as many times as desired by keeping the next value R generated by DEnc in memory. In a chain, we thus save as many (initial) call to the TBC as the number of segments, and so TETSponge is not used in black-box. To get a fully OAE mode with dOAE security, we also have to treat the "last segment" in another way than the segments that can be further chained. For that purpose, we introduce nothing more than a separation

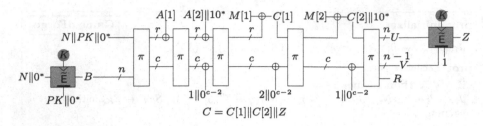

Fig. 3. TETSponge$[\pi, \widetilde{\mathsf{E}}]_{K,PK}$ AEAD with $\nu = 2$ and $\ell = 2$. Grey square indicates TBC call, where the input to the triangle denotes the key and the input to the dark rectangle denotes the tweak. The block $1\|0^{c-2}$ is inserted only if $|A[\nu]| < r$, resp. $|M[\ell]| < r$.

bit in the most significant bit of the input permutation when calling DEnc for the last time. To make the whole SpookChain mode working in all the cases, and so even when the first segment is also the last segment, we just re-order a bit the input permutation of the first call to DEnc, that is the initial part of SpookChain slightly differs from the one of TETSponge. We illustrate SpookChain in Fig. 4.

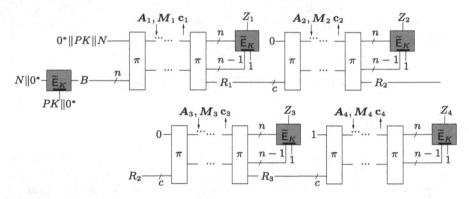

Fig. 4. SpookChain$[\pi, \widetilde{\mathsf{E}}]_{K,PK}$ with 4 segments, the final one being a *last* segment, then starting with 1. The TBC is in grey. See Fig. 3 for the details of each segment.

In the description of SpookChain, the input of the first permutation of DEnc corresponds to the state S in the sense of the segmented-AE definition, see Definition 1. Therefore, it also corresponds to the full input state of the permutation π. However, from a space complexity standpoint, only the c bits of the capacity must be stored (additionally to K) to process the next segments both in encryption and decryption. We now turn to the full specification of SpookChain.

Parameters. $\widetilde{\mathsf{E}}$ is an (n, n, n)-TBC and π is an $r + c$ bit keyless permutation. The encryption is made by r-bit block of the message. The key of SpookChain is $K\|PK$, where $|K| = n$ and $|PK| = n_p$. We stress that only K has to be kept *secret*, but PK can be public as in TETSponge. The secret key K is picked *uniformly* at random in $\{0,1\}^n$. The public key PK only needs to be *distinct* for each session (pair of users). For simplicity, in this paper we focus on uniform $PK \in \{0,1\}^{n_P}$. Moreover, we have $\mathcal{A} = \mathcal{M} = \mathcal{C} = \{0,1\}^*$ and $\mathcal{N} = \{0,1\}^{n_N}$, where the nonce length n_N is fixed. We require that $n_N, n_p + 1 \le n$ (initial $\widetilde{\mathsf{E}}$ input), $1 + n_p + n_N + n \le r + c$ (π input), and $2n \le r + c + 1$ (tag $\widetilde{\mathsf{E}}$ input). Yet, we recommend $n_p \approx n$ and $c \approx 2n$ and we actually choose $n_p = n - 1$ and $c = 2n$ as this leads to a security up to $2^n/n^2$ complexity. There is no recommendation for n_N, but when $n = 128$ one could take $n_N = 96$ which is a standard choice. The ciphertext expansion of SpookChain is $\tau = n$.

---

algorithm $\mathcal{E}_{K,PK}.\mathrm{init}(N)$

1. $B \leftarrow \widetilde{\mathsf{E}}_K^{PK\|0^{n-n_P}}(N\|0^{n-n_N})$
2. **return** $0^{r+c-n_P-n_N-n}\|PK\|N\|B$

algorithm $\mathcal{D}_{K,PK}.\mathrm{init}(N)$

1. $B \leftarrow \widetilde{\mathsf{E}}_K^{PK\|0^{n-n_P}}(N\|0^{n-n_N})$
2. **return** $0^{r+c-n_P-n_N-n}\|PK\|N\|B$

algorithm $\mathcal{E}_{K,PK}.\mathrm{next}(S,A,M)$

1. $(C, capa) \leftarrow \mathsf{DEnc}_K(S,A,M)$
2. **return** $(C, 0^r\|capa)$

algorithm $\mathcal{D}_{K,PK}.\mathrm{next}(S,A,M)$

1. $(M, capa) \leftarrow \mathsf{DDec}_K(S,A,M)$
2. **return** $(M, 0^r\|capa)$

algorithm $\mathcal{E}_{K,PK}.\mathrm{last}(S,A,M)$

1. $S \leftarrow S \oplus 10^{r+c-1}$ // i.e. $1\|\mathsf{lsb}_{r+c-1}(S)$
2. $(C, capa) \leftarrow \mathsf{DEnc}_K(S,A,M)$
3. **return** C

algorithm $\mathcal{D}_{K,PK}.\mathrm{last}(S,A,M)$

1. $S \leftarrow S \oplus 10^{r+c-1}$ // i.e. $1\|\mathsf{lsb}_{r+c-1}(S)$
2. $(M, capa) \leftarrow \mathsf{DDec}_K(S,A,M)$
3. **return** M

---

algorithm $\mathsf{DEnc}_K(S_0, A, M)$

1. $\ell \leftarrow \lceil |M|/r \rceil, \nu \leftarrow \lceil |A|/r \rceil$
2. $S_1 \leftarrow \pi(S_0)$
3. **if** $\nu \ge 1$ **then**
4. $\quad A[1]\|\ldots\|A[\nu] \xleftarrow{r} A$
5. $\quad$ **for** $i = 1$ to $\nu - 1$ **do**
6. $\quad\quad S_i \leftarrow S_i \oplus (A[i]\|0^c)$
7. $\quad\quad S_{i+1} \leftarrow \pi(S_i)$
8. $\quad$ **if** $|A[\nu]| < r$ **then**
9. $\quad\quad A[\nu] \leftarrow A[\nu]\|10^{r-|A[\nu]|-1}$
10. $\quad\quad S_\nu \leftarrow S_\nu \oplus (0^r\|[1]_2\|0^{c-2})$
11. $\quad S_\nu \leftarrow S_\nu \oplus (A[\nu]\|0^c)$
12. $\quad S_{\nu+1} \leftarrow \pi(S_\nu)$
13. **if** $\ell \ge 1$ **then**
14. $\quad M[1]\|\ldots\|M[\ell] \xleftarrow{r} M$
15. $\quad S_{\nu+1} \leftarrow S_{\nu+1} \oplus (0^r\|[2]_2\|0^{c-2})$
16. $\quad$ **for** $i = 1$ to $\ell - 1$ **do**
17. $\quad\quad j \leftarrow i + \nu$
18. $\quad\quad C[i] \leftarrow \mathsf{msb}_r(S_j) \oplus M[i]$
19. $\quad\quad S_j \leftarrow C[i]\|\mathsf{lsb}_c(S_j)$
20. $\quad\quad S_{j+1} \leftarrow \pi(S_j)$
21. $\quad C[\ell] \leftarrow \mathsf{msb}_{|M[\ell]|}(S_{\nu+\ell}) \oplus M[\ell]$
22. $\quad$ **if** $|C[\ell]| < r$ **then**
23. $\quad\quad S_{\nu+\ell} \leftarrow S_{\nu+\ell} \oplus (0^r\|[1]_2\|0^{c-2})$

24. $\quad\quad S_{\nu+\ell} \leftarrow C[\ell]\|10^{r-|C[\ell]|-1}\|\mathsf{lsb}_c(S_{\nu+\ell})$
25. $\quad$ **else** $S_{\nu+\ell} \leftarrow C[\ell]\|\mathsf{lsb}_c(S_{\nu+\ell})$
26. $\quad S_{\nu+\ell+1} \leftarrow \pi(S_{\nu+\ell})$
27. $\quad U\|V \xleftarrow{n} \mathsf{msb}_{2n-1}(S_{\nu+\ell+1})$
28. $\quad capa \leftarrow \mathsf{lsb}_c(S_{\nu+\ell+1})$
29. $\quad Z \leftarrow \widetilde{\mathsf{E}}_K^{V\|1}(U)$
30. **if** $\ell = 0$, **return** $(Z, capa)$
31. $\quad \mathbf{c} \leftarrow C[1]\|\ldots\|C[\ell], C \leftarrow \mathbf{c}\|Z$
32. **return** $(C, capa)$

algorithm $\mathsf{DDec}_K(S_0, A, C)$

1. Parse $\mathbf{c}\|Z \leftarrow C$, where $Z \leftarrow \mathsf{lsb}_n(C)$
2. $\ell \leftarrow \lceil |\mathbf{c}|/r \rceil, \nu \leftarrow \lceil |A|/r \rceil$
3. $S_1 \leftarrow \pi(S_0)$
4. **if** $\nu \ge 1$ **then**
5. $\quad A[1]\|\ldots\|A[\nu] \xleftarrow{r} A$
6. $\quad$ **for** $i = 1$ to $\nu - 1$ **do**
7. $\quad\quad S_i \leftarrow S_i \oplus (A[i]\|0^c)$
8. $\quad\quad S_{i+1} \leftarrow \pi(S_i)$
9. $\quad$ **if** $|A[\nu]| < r$ **then**
10. $\quad\quad A[\nu] \leftarrow A[\nu]\|10^{r-|A[\nu]|-1}$
11. $\quad\quad S_\nu \leftarrow S_\nu \oplus (0^r\|[1]_2\|0^{c-2})$
12. $\quad S_\nu \leftarrow S_\nu \oplus (A[\nu]\|0^c)$
13. $\quad S_{\nu+1} \leftarrow \pi(S_\nu)$
14. **if** $\ell \ge 1$ **then**

15. $C[1]\|\ldots\|C[\ell] \xleftarrow{r} \mathbf{c}$
16. $S_{\nu+1} \leftarrow S_{\nu+1} \oplus (0^r\|[2]_2\|0^{c-2})$
17. **for** $i = 1$ **to** $\ell - 1$ **do**
18. $\quad j \leftarrow i + \nu$
19. $\quad M[i] \leftarrow \mathsf{msb}_r(S_j) \oplus C[i]$
20. $\quad S_j \leftarrow C[i]\|\mathsf{lsb}_c(S_j)$
21. $\quad S_{j+1} \leftarrow \pi(S_j)$
22. $M[\ell] \leftarrow \mathsf{msb}_{|C[\ell]|}(S_{\nu+\ell}) \oplus C[\ell]$
23. **if** $|C[\ell]| < r$ **then**
24. $\quad S_{\nu+\ell} \leftarrow S_{\nu+\ell} \oplus (0^r\|[1]_2\|0^{c-2})$

25. $\quad S_{\nu+\ell} \leftarrow C[\ell]\|10^{r-|C[\ell]|-1}\|\mathsf{lsb}_c(S_{\nu+\ell})$
26. **else** $S_{\nu+\ell} \leftarrow C[\ell]\|\mathsf{lsb}_c(S_{\nu+\ell})$
27. $S_{\nu+\ell+1} \leftarrow \pi(S_{\nu+\ell})$
28. $U\|V \xleftarrow{n} \mathsf{msb}_{2n-1}(S_{\nu+\ell+1})$
29. $capa \leftarrow \mathsf{lsb}_c(S_{\nu+\ell+1})$
30. $U^* \leftarrow (\widetilde{\mathsf{E}}_K^{V\|1})^{-1}(Z)$
31. **if** $U \neq U^*$, **return** $(\perp, \perp)$
32. **if** $\ell \geq 1$, **return** $(M[1]\|\ldots\|M[\ell], capa)$
33. **return** $(\mathbf{true}, capa)$

Forward Secrecy Against Full State Recovery. As an interesting additional feature SpookChain provides forward secrecy if a full state of a permutation call is exposed. As a chain might be very long it is of great important to measure the degradation implied by the exposure of the rate and the capacity of a permutation call. Hopefully, if such an exposure occurs in a segment, its prefix in the chain is not affected. Indeed, by inverting the permutation calls, the adversary is able to compute backward the state of the segment, i.e. the first input of π in that segment containing the capacity value R, See Fig. 4, called *capa* in the specification. However, in order to carry on this backward process to adversary has to guess the output rate of the last permutation call of the previous segment (the rate which feeds the TBC call of the previous segment, resulting in Z). So, as long as r is long enough in $O(n)$, the adversary can no longer "rewind" the chain. In contrary, in the forward direction the adversary can easily breaks the privacy of all the next segments. Nevertheless, a full state exposure does not allow computing new valid authentication tags as the key (of the TBC) is still hidden.

Finally, it is worth noticing that the damage caused by a full state recovery in a session is only isolated in the chain where it happens. The security of the other chains of the same session is not impacted in any manner. Clearly, other sessions are neither impacted.

4   Security Analysis

We move on to show the beyond-birthday dOAE-security of SpookChain in the multi-user setting. In the dOAE experiments of privacy (Fig. 1) and integrity (Fig. 2) the adversary can make numerous calls to many different procedures. We say the adversary is $(\overrightarrow{q}, \sigma, \sigma_d)$-bounded, where $\overrightarrow{q} = (q_e, q_{\widetilde{\mathsf{IC}}}, q_\pi)$, q_e denotes the maximal number of adversarial queries to init, $q_{\widetilde{\mathsf{IC}}}$ and q_π denote the number of ideal TBC and permutation queries, σ denotes the total number of blocks in encrypted segments, and σ_d denotes the number of blocks in the decryption queries/adversarial forgery trial (for dOAE authenticity only).

Theorem 1. *Assuming that $u \leq 2^{n_p}$, $n_p \leq n$, $n \geq 5$, and $2\sigma + 2\sigma_d + q_\pi \leq \min\{2^n/4, 2^{r+c}/2\}$. Then, in the ideal TBC and permutation model, for any $(\vec{q}, \sigma)$-adversary $\mathscr{A}$ it holds*

$$\mathbf{Adv}_{\mathsf{SpookChain}}^{\mathsf{doae\text{-}priv}} \leq \frac{3u}{2^{n_p}} + \frac{4n(2\sigma + q_\pi) + nq_{\widetilde{\mathsf{IC}}} + n^2 q_e}{2^n} + \frac{17(2\sigma + q_\pi)^2}{2^c}, \tag{1}$$

$$\mathbf{Adv}_{\mathsf{SpookChain}}^{\mathsf{doae\text{-}auth}} \leq \frac{3u}{2^{n_p}} + \frac{4n(2\sigma + 2\sigma_d + q_\pi) + nq_{\widetilde{\mathsf{IC}}} + 2}{2^n} + \frac{16(2\sigma + 2\sigma_d + q_\pi)^2}{2^c}. \tag{2}$$

Intuition of the Proofs. We will consider the security game capturing the interaction between the adversary and the SpookChain mode. In a nutshell, our arguments proceed in two steps. First, we replace the ideal TBC $\widetilde{\mathsf{IC}}$ in SpookChain by another ideal TBC $\widetilde{\mathsf{IC}}^*$ that *cannot be queried* by the adversary. This modification is "invisible" to the adversary as long as certain types of collisions do not occur, and thus we are able to bound the difference. As the second step, we study the somewhat ideal game with SpookChain$[\pi, \widetilde{\mathsf{IC}}^*]$. For privacy, we further identify some bad collisions, and we are able to show that the outputs of SpookChain$[\pi, \widetilde{\mathsf{IC}}^*]$ are random as long as these collisions do not occur. Hence the collision probability, which can be bounded, cinches the privacy security bound. For integrity, we show that the probability to reach a forgery for SpookChain$[\pi, \widetilde{\mathsf{IC}}^*]$ is sufficiently small, and thus this forgery probability plus the already bounded gap between SpookChain$[\pi, \widetilde{\mathsf{IC}}^*]$ and SpookChain$[\pi, \widetilde{\mathsf{IC}}]$ gives the integrity security bound. See the two subsequent subsections for details.

4.1 Proof of dOAE Privacy

Proof (Sketch). We denote by G_0 the game capturing the interaction between $\mathscr{D}$ and **dReal**, and G_2 the game capturing $\mathscr{D}$'s interaction with **dRand**. We transit G_0 to G_2 via several hybrids.

Intermediate game G_1. First, we replace the ideal TBC used in SpookChain by another ideal TBC $\widetilde{\mathsf{IC}}^*$ that's independent from the $\widetilde{\mathsf{IC}}$ accessible to $\mathscr{D}$. This yields the game G_1. We formally describe G_1 in Fig. 5, in which we define four sets $\tau_{\widetilde{\mathsf{IC}}}, \tau_{\widetilde{\mathsf{IC}}}^*, \tau_\pi, \tau_\pi^*$ for subsequent arguments.

It can be seen that, as long as the following bad event does not happen in G_0, the behaviors of G_0 and G_1 are the same:

- (B-1) At any time, there exists $(i, N) \in \tau_{ie}$ such that $(K_i, PK_i \| 0^*, \star, \star) \in \tau_{\widetilde{\mathsf{IC}}}$, where τ_{ie} is the set of all earlier queries to $\mathsf{Enc.init}(i, N)$.

To analyze this event, we define

$$\mu_{PK} := \max_{pk \in \{0,1\}^{n_p}} \left| \{i \in \{1, \ldots, u\} : PK_i = pk\} \right|. \tag{3}$$

We consider the event $\mu_{PK} \geq n+1$. As $PK_1, \ldots, PK_u$ are uniformly distributed, it holds

$$\Pr[\mu_{PK} \geq n+1] \leq \binom{u}{n+1} \cdot \frac{1}{(2^{n_p})^n} \leq \left(\frac{u}{2^{n_p}}\right)^{n+1} \cdot \frac{2^{n_p}}{(n+1)!} \leq \left(\frac{u}{2^{n_p}}\right)^{n+1},$$

where the last inequality comes from $(n+1)! \geq \left(\frac{n+1}{e}\right)^{n+1} \geq 2^{n+1} \geq 2^{n_p}$ since $n+1 \geq 6 > 2e$. Furthermore, when $u \leq 2^{n_p}$ and $n_p \leq n$, we have

$$\Pr[\mu_{PK} \geq n+1] \leq \left(\frac{u}{2^{n_p}}\right)^{n+1} \leq \frac{u}{2^{n_p}}.$$

Conditioned on $\mu_{PK} \leq n$, we could bound $\Pr[\text{(B-1)}]$. Note that in G_1, for any $(i, N) \in \tau_{ie}$, the "user key" K_i is uniformly sampled. Then, using an auxiliary set

$$\tau_{\widetilde{\mathsf{IC}}}[T] := \left\{ K \in \{0,1\}^n : (K, T, \star, \star) \in \tau_{\widetilde{\mathsf{IC}}} \right\},$$

it holds

$$\Pr[\text{(B-1)}] \leq \sum_{(i,N) \in \tau_{ie}} \Pr\left[K_i \in \tau_{\widetilde{\mathsf{IC}}}[PK_i \| 0^*] \right]$$

$$\leq \mu_{PK} \cdot \sum_{PK \in \{0,1\}^{n_p}} \frac{\left| \tau_{\widetilde{\mathsf{IC}}}[PK \| 0^*] \right|}{2^n} \leq \frac{n q_{\widetilde{\mathsf{IC}}}}{2^n}.$$

Therefore,

$$\left| \Pr[\mathsf{G}_0 \Rightarrow 1] - \Pr[\mathsf{G}_1 \Rightarrow 1] \right| \leq \frac{u}{2^{n_p}} + \frac{n q_{\widetilde{\mathsf{IC}}}}{2^n}.$$

Gap between G_1 and G_2. Second, we define several bad conditions in G_1 that will trigger "abort". See Fig. 5 for details. Roughly speaking, they capture the following conditions:

- (C-1) When an initial key B is derived, it results in a $(r+c)$-bit initial state that collides with the adversarial π-queries nor the other earlier $(r+c)$-bit internal states;
- (C-2) When an internal $(r+c)$-bit state is derived, it collides with the adversarial π-queries nor the other earlier internal states in certain senses;
- (C-3) When a final $(r+c)$-bit state is derived for a query to $\mathcal{E}.\mathsf{next}$ or $\mathcal{E}.\mathsf{last}$, it collides with the earlier internal calls to $\widetilde{\mathsf{IC}}^*$ nor the π-queries in certain senses.

proc initialize

$\tau_{\widetilde{IC}}, \tau_{\widetilde{IC}}^*, \tau_\pi, \tau_\pi^* \leftarrow \emptyset; \quad J_1, \ldots, J_u \leftarrow 0;$
$\mathcal{X}_1, \ldots, \mathcal{X}_u \leftarrow \emptyset; \quad \mathcal{Y}_1, \ldots, \mathcal{Y}_u \leftarrow \emptyset$
$(K_1 \| PK_1, \ldots, K_u \| PK_u) \xleftarrow{\$} (\mathcal{K})^u$
if $\exists i \neq j : K_i \| PK_i = K_j \| PK_j$ then abort

proc Enc.init(i, N)

1. ...the same as Fig. 1 (Left).

proc Enc.seg(i, j, A, M, b)   // $b \in \{0,1\}$

1. ...the same as Fig. 1 (Left).

algorithm $\mathcal{E}_{K,PK}.\text{init}(N)$

1. $B \leftarrow (\widetilde{IC}^*)_K^{PK \| 0^{n-n_P}} (N \| 0^{n-n_N})$
2. **if** the query is new **and**
   $([0]\|PK\|N\|B, \star) \in (\tau_\pi \cup \tau_\pi^*)$
   then abort
3. **return** $[0]\|PK\|N\|B$

algorithm $\mathcal{E}_{K,PK}.\text{next}(S, A, M)$

1. ...the same as SpookChain

algorithm $\mathcal{E}_{K,PK}.\text{last}(S, A, M)$

1. ...the same as SpookChain

algorithm $\mathcal{D}_{K,PK}.\text{init}(N)$

1. $B \leftarrow (\widetilde{IC}^*)_K^{PK \| 0^{n-n_P}} (N \| 0^{n-n_N})$
2. **return** $[0]\|PK\|N\|B$

algorithm $\mathcal{D}_{K,PK}.\text{next}(S, A, M)$

1. ...the same as SpookChain

algorithm $\mathcal{D}_{K,PK}.\text{last}(S, A, M)$

1. ...the same as SpookChain

algorithm $\widetilde{IC}_K^T(X)$

1. **if** $(K, T, X, \star) \notin \tau_{\widetilde{IC}}$ **then**
2. $\quad Y \xleftarrow{\$} \{0,1\}^n$ s.t. $(K, T, \star, Y) \notin \tau_{\widetilde{IC}}$
3. $\quad \tau_{\widetilde{IC}} \leftarrow \tau_{\widetilde{IC}} \cup (K, T, X, Y)$

4. **return** Y s.t. $(K, T, X, Y) \in \tau_{\widetilde{IC}}$

algorithm $(\widetilde{IC}_K^T)^{-1}(Y)$

1. **if** $(K, T, \star, Y) \notin \tau_{\widetilde{IC}}$ **then**
2. $\quad X \xleftarrow{\$} \{0,1\}^n$ s.t. $(K, T, X, \star) \notin \tau_{\widetilde{IC}}$
3. $\quad \tau_{\widetilde{IC}} \leftarrow \tau_{\widetilde{IC}} \cup (K, T, X, Y)$
4. **return** X s.t. $(K, T, X, Y) \in \tau_{\widetilde{IC}}$

algorithm $(\widetilde{IC}^*)_K^T(X)$

if $(K, T, X, \star) \notin \tau_{\widetilde{IC}}^*$ **then**
$\quad Y \xleftarrow{\$} \{0,1\}^n$ s.t. $(K, T, \star, Y) \notin \tau_{\widetilde{IC}}^*$
$\quad \tau_{\widetilde{IC}}^* \leftarrow \tau_{\widetilde{IC}}^* \cup (K, T, X, Y)$
return Y s.t. $(K, T, X, Y) \in \tau_{\widetilde{IC}}^*$

algorithm $((\widetilde{IC}^*)_K^T)^{-1}(X)$

if $(K, T, \star, Y) \notin \tau_{\widetilde{IC}}^*$ **then**
$\quad X \xleftarrow{\$} \{0,1\}^n$ s.t. $(K, T, X, \star) \notin \tau_{\widetilde{IC}}^*$
$\quad \tau_{\widetilde{IC}}^* \leftarrow \tau_{\widetilde{IC}}^* \cup (K, T, X, Y)$
return X s.t. $(K, T, X, Y) \in \tau_{\widetilde{IC}}^*$

algorithm $\pi(S^{in})$

if $(S^{in}, \star) \notin \tau_\pi$ **then**
$\quad S^{out} \xleftarrow{\$} \{0,1\}^{r+c}$ s.t. $(S^{in}, S^{out}) \notin \tau_\pi$
$\quad$**if** $(\star \| \mathsf{lsb}_{c-2}(S^{out}), \star) \in \tau_\pi$ **then**
$\quad\quad$**abort**
$\quad$**if** $(\star, \star \| \mathsf{lsb}_{c-2}(S^{out})) \in \tau_\pi$ **then**
$\quad\quad$**abort**
$\quad U \| V \leftarrow \mathsf{msb}_{2n-1}(S^{out})$
$\quad$**if** $(\star, V \| 1, U, \star) \in (\tau_{\widetilde{IC}} \cup \tau_{\widetilde{IC}}^*)$ **then**
$\quad\quad$**abort**
$\quad \tau_\pi \leftarrow \tau_\pi \cup (S^{in}, S^{out})$
return S^{out} s.t. $(S^{in}, S^{out}) \in \tau_\pi$

algorithm $\pi^{-1}(S^{out})$

if $(\star, S^{out}) \notin \tau_\pi$ **then**
$\quad S^{in} \xleftarrow{\$} \{0,1\}^{r+c}$ s.t. $(S^{in}, S^{out}) \notin \tau_\pi$
$\quad \tau_\pi \leftarrow \tau_\pi \cup (S^{in}, S^{out})$
return S^{in} s.t. $(S^{in}, S^{out}) \in \tau_\pi$

Fig. 5. Game G_1 with abort conditions.

First, let us consider the condition (C-1). Consider the ℓ-th initializing call $\mathsf{Enc.init}(i_\ell, N_\ell)$ that internally results in the state $[0]\|PK\|N\|B_\ell$. Define

$$\tau_\pi[N_i, PK_i] := \{B \in \{0,1\}^n : (\star\|PK_i\|N_i\|B, \star) \in \tau_\pi\},$$

then this call causes abort if $B_\ell \in \tau_\pi[N_i, PK_i]$. We next argue that w.h.p., B_ℓ is uniform. For this, consider any earlier call $\mathsf{init}(i_{\ell'}, N_{\ell'})$ resulting in the n-bit seed $B_{\ell'}$ with $\ell' < \ell$. If $i_{\ell'} = i_\ell$, then $N_{\ell'} \neq N_\ell$ since abortion is only check in "new" calls, and thus B_ℓ is uniform in at least $2^n - q_e$ values given $B_{\ell'}$. Otherwise, conditioned on that the *key collision* event $\exists i \neq j : K_i\|PK_i = K_j\|PK_j$ in **initialize** did not happen, the two init-calls would induce two distinct TBC-calls $\widetilde{\mathsf{IC}}^{PK_{i_\ell}\|0^*}_{K_{i_\ell}}(N_\ell\|0^*) \to B_\ell$ and $\widetilde{\mathsf{IC}}^{PK_{i_{\ell'}}\|0^*}_{K_{i_{\ell'}}}(N_{\ell'}\|0^*) \to B_{\ell'}$, and thus B_ℓ is uniform given $B_{\ell'}$. By these, the probability of abortion in the call to $\mathsf{init}(i_\ell, N_\ell)$ is at most $|\tau_\pi[N_{i_\ell}, PK_{i_\ell}]|/(2^n - q_e)$. Summing over the q_e calls results in

$$
\begin{aligned}
\Pr[(\text{C-1}) \mid \neg key\ collision] &\leq \sum_{\ell=1}^{q_e} \frac{|\tau_\pi[N_{i_\ell}, PK_{i_\ell}]|}{2^n - q_e} \leq \sum_{\ell=1}^{q_e} \frac{2|\tau_\pi[N_{i_\ell}, PK_{i_\ell}]|}{2^n} \\
&\leq \mu_{PK} \cdot \sum_{N\|PK \in \{0,1\}^{n_N + n_P}} \frac{2|\tau_\pi[N, PK]|}{2^n} \\
&\leq \frac{2\mu_{PK}|\tau_\pi|}{2^n},
\end{aligned}
$$

where μ_{PK} is as defined in Eq. (3). Note that when the total number of queried blocks is σ, the number of internal π-calls can't exceed 2σ. Thus $|\tau_\pi| \leq 2\sigma + q_\pi$. Furthermore, as we've proved that $\Pr[\mu_{PK} \geq n+1] \leq \frac{u}{2^{n_p}}$, and clearly

$$\Pr[key\ collision] = \Pr[\exists i \neq j : K_i\|PK_i = K_j\|PK_j] \leq \frac{u^2}{2^{n+n_p}} \leq \frac{u}{2^{n_p}},$$

we obtain

$$\Pr[(\text{C-1})] \leq \frac{2n(2\sigma + q_\pi)}{2^n} + \frac{2u}{2^{n_p}}.$$

For (C-2), for each of the internal π-calls, the probability of colliding on the least significant $c-2$ bits is $\leq 2 \cdot 2|\tau_\pi|/2^{c-2} \leq 2(2\sigma + q_\pi)/2^{c-2}$. Thus we have

$$\Pr[(\text{C-2})] \leq \frac{16(2\sigma + q_\pi)^2}{2^c}.$$

Noticing that $|\tau_{\widetilde{\mathsf{IC}}}| + |\tau^*_{\mathsf{IC}}| \leq q_{\widetilde{\mathsf{IC}}} + 2q_e$. Thus a similar analysis gives rise to

$$\Pr[(\text{C-3})] \leq (2\sigma + q_\pi) \cdot \frac{2(q_{\widetilde{\mathsf{IC}}} + 2q_e)}{2^{2n-1}} \leq \frac{4(2\sigma + q_\pi)(q_{\widetilde{\mathsf{IC}}} + 2q_e)}{2^{2n}}.$$

Summing over the above, we obtain

$$\Pr[\mathsf{G}_1 \text{ aborts}] \leq \frac{2n(2\sigma + q_\pi)}{2^n} + \frac{2u}{2^{n_p}} + \frac{16(2\sigma + q_\pi)^2}{2^c} + \frac{4(2\sigma + q_\pi)(q_{\widetilde{\mathsf{IC}}} + 2q_e)}{2^{2n}}$$

$$\leq \frac{4n(2\sigma + q_\pi)}{2^n} + \frac{2u}{2^{n_p}} + \frac{16(2\sigma + q_\pi)^2}{2^c}.$$

The inequality leverages $4(2\sigma + q_\pi)(q_{\widetilde{\mathsf{IC}}} + 2q_e)/2^{2n} \leq 2(2\sigma + q_\pi)/2^n \leq 2n(2\sigma + q_\pi)/2^n$ assuming $q_{\widetilde{\mathsf{IC}}} + 2q_e \leq 2^n/2$.

To complete the analysis for $\mathbf{Adv}_{\mathsf{AEAD}}^{\mathsf{doae\text{-}priv}}$, we replace the freshly generated internal states with values uniformly distributed in $\{0,1\}^{r+c}$ and the tags Z with values uniformly distributed in $\{0,1\}^n$, to obtain the game $\mathsf{G}_2 = \mathbf{dRand}$. It is easy to see as long as G_1 does not abort, replacing internal states induces a gap of at most $\frac{\sigma^2}{2^{r+c}}$ (a somewhat standard RP-RF switch). On the other hand, replacing tags may cause a gap of $\frac{q_e^2}{2^n}$. However, define

$$\mu_V := \max_{v \in \{0,1\}^{n-1}} \left| \{\pi(S^{in}) \to S^{out}, \mathsf{msb}_{2n-1}(S^{out}) = \star \| V\} \right|,$$

then conditioned on $\mu_V \leq n$, replacing tags only induces a gap of $q_e \cdot \frac{n^2}{2^n}$ since the number of TBC-calls under each tweak $V\|1$ does not exceed n.

It remains to prove that the ciphertext blocks produced in G_1 are "as random as" those in G_2. This essentially requires to prove that in G_1, all new queries to $\mathcal{E}.\mathsf{next}$ and $\mathcal{E}.\mathsf{last}$ give rise to uniform output (as it is also the case in G_2). We show that it is the case in G_1 conditioned on the absence of abortion. For this, we first consider a new call to $\mathsf{Enc.seg}(i_\ell, j_\ell, A_\ell, M_\ell, 0)$, assume that its corresponding nonce is N_ℓ and initial key is B_ℓ, and distinguish two cases:

- Case 1: it is the first segment for the nonce N_ℓ. We show that all earlier queries to $\mathsf{Enc.seg}$ will not affect the randomness of the output. We only need to consider earlier calls of the form $\mathsf{Enc.seg}(i_\ell, j_\ell, \cdot, \cdot, \cdot)$, as the other calls must have a different 1st call to π, which give rise to completely independent computation flows. Earlier calls to $\mathsf{Enc.seg}(i_\ell, j_\ell, A_{\ell'}, M_{\ell'}, 1)$ will not affect $\mathsf{Enc.seg}(i_\ell, j_\ell, A_\ell, M_\ell, 0)$ either, as they only query $\pi(1\|\star)$ which does not affect $\pi([0]\|PK_{i_\ell}\|N_{i_\ell,j_\ell}\|\star)$. For earlier calls to $\mathsf{Enc.seg}(i_\ell, j_\ell, A_{\ell'}, M_{\ell'}, 0)$, it has to be $A_{\ell'} \neq A_\ell$ by the security definitions, and this necessarily make the two computation flows diverge after processing A_ℓ and $A_{\ell'}$. Since the abort conditions around queries to π were never fulfilled, this means all the π-calls made during processing M_ℓ and $M_{\ell'}$ are distinct. A similar argument applies to the resulted tag Z_ℓ. Therefore, the call $\mathsf{Enc.seg}(i_\ell, j_\ell, A_\ell, M_\ell, 0)$ gives rise to a ciphertext segment C_ℓ that is uniform and independent from all the previous ones, as well as a new state $capa_\ell$ that is fresh and not contained by any entries in τ_π.

- Case 2: it is not the first segment. Assume that the corresponding $2n$-bit chaining state is S. The subsequent discussion is similar: earlier calls to $\mathsf{Enc.seg}(i_\ell, j_\ell, A_{\ell'}, M_{\ell'}, 1)$ only query $\pi([1]\| \star \|S)$ and will not influence

$\pi([0]_{r+c-2n}\|S)$, while earlier calls to $\mathsf{Enc.seg}(i_\ell, j_\ell, A_{\ell'}, M_{\ell'}, 0)$ result in a computation flow that is distinct from $\mathsf{Enc.seg}(i_\ell, j_\ell, A_\ell, M_\ell, 0)$ after processing A_ℓ and $A_{\ell'}$. A similar argument applies to the resulted tag Z_ℓ, and thus the call to $\mathsf{Enc.seg}(i_\ell, j_\ell, A_\ell, M_\ell, 0)$ gives rise to a ciphertext segment C_ℓ that is uniform and independent from all the previous ones.

The analysis a new call to $\mathsf{Enc.seg}(i_\ell, j_\ell, A_\ell, M_\ell, 1)$ is similar. Therefore, the statistical distance between the ciphertext segments produced by G_1 and G_2 is the aforementioned gap $\frac{\sigma^2}{2^{r+c}} + \frac{n^2 q_e}{2^n} \le \frac{(2\sigma + q_\pi)^2}{2^c} + \frac{n^2 q_e}{2^n}$ plus the abort probability of G_1, i.e.,

$$\left| \Pr[\mathsf{G}_1 \Rightarrow 1] - \Pr[\mathsf{G}_2 \Rightarrow 1] \right| \le \frac{4n(2\sigma + q_\pi) + n^2 q_e}{2^n} + \frac{2u}{2^{n_p}} + \frac{17(2\sigma + q_\pi)^2}{2^c}.$$

This finally concludes with Eq. (1), i.e.,

$$\begin{aligned}
\mathbf{Adv}_{\mathsf{AEAD}}^{\mathsf{doae\text{-}priv}} &\le \frac{u}{2^{n_p}} + \frac{n q_{\widetilde{\mathsf{IC}}}}{2^n} + \frac{4n(2\sigma + q_\pi) + n^2 q_e}{2^n} + \frac{2u}{2^{n_p}} + \frac{17(2\sigma + q_\pi)^2}{2^c} \\
&\le \frac{3u}{2^{n_p}} + \frac{4n(2\sigma + q_\pi) + n q_{\widetilde{\mathsf{IC}}} + n^2 q_e}{2^n} + \frac{17(2\sigma + q_\pi)^2}{2^c}.
\end{aligned}$$

4.2　Proof of the dOAE Authenticity

Proof (Sketch). For authenticity, we follow the above proof flow and transit to the intermediate game G_1. However, with the additional blocks in the final decryption query, the technical results shall be updated as

$$\left| \Pr[\mathsf{G}_0 \Rightarrow 1] - \Pr[\mathsf{G}_1 \Rightarrow 1] \right| \le \frac{u}{2^{n_p}} + \frac{n q_{\widetilde{\mathsf{IC}}}}{2^n},$$

$$\Pr[\mathsf{G}_1 \text{ aborts}] \le \frac{4n(2\sigma + 2\sigma_d + q_\pi)}{2^n} + \frac{2u}{2^{n_p}} + \frac{16(2\sigma + 2\sigma_d + q_\pi)^2}{2^c}.$$

Then, assume that abortion never happens, we show that the final decryption of $(i, N, \boldsymbol{A}, \boldsymbol{C}, b)$ gives rise to $\bot$ except with a low probability. Assume that $\boldsymbol{A} = (A[1], \dots, A[m])$ and $\boldsymbol{C} = (C[1], \dots, C[m])$. Further assume that the tuple in $\mathcal{Y}_i$ that has the longest common prefix with $(\boldsymbol{A}, \boldsymbol{C})$ is $(N, \boldsymbol{A'}, \boldsymbol{C'}, b')$, where $\boldsymbol{A'} = (A'[1], \dots, A'[m])$ and $\boldsymbol{C'} = (C'[1], \dots, C'[m])$. We distinguish two cases:

– Case 1: $b = b'$. Then there must necessarily exist an index ℓ such that $(A[1], C[1]) \ne (A'[1], C'[1])$. This means the computation flows of processing $(A[1], C[1])$ and $(A'[1], C'[1])$ necessarily deviate at some point, and thus processing $(A[1], C[1])$ eventually gives rise to a fresh π-call at the end. This gives rise to a random $2n - 1$ bit value $U\|V$, which means the integrity checking condition $U = U^*$ (line 31 in DDec) is fulfilled with probability at most $\frac{2}{2^n}$. As such, with probability at least $1 - \frac{2}{2^n}$, the final decryption returns $\bot$.

- Case 2: $b \neq b'$. Regardless of the contents, the call to $\mathcal{D}.\mathsf{next}(S, \mathbf{A}[m], \mathbf{C}[m])$ (when $b = 0$) or $\mathcal{D}.\mathsf{last}(S, \mathbf{A}[m], \mathbf{C}[m])$ (when $b = 1$) necessarily started with a new state (similarly to that argued before). Similarly to Case 1, this gives rise to a random $2n - 1$ bit value $U \| V$, and thus the probability that it passes the integrity checking is at most $\frac{2}{2^n}$.

By the above, Eq. (2) is established:

$$
\begin{aligned}
\mathbf{Adv}_{\mathsf{SpookChain}}^{\mathsf{doae\text{-}auth}} &\leq \frac{u}{2^{n_p}} + \frac{nq_{\widetilde{IC}}}{2^n} + \frac{4n(2\sigma + 2\sigma_d + q_\pi)}{2^n} + \frac{2u}{2^{n_p}} + \frac{16(2\sigma + 2\sigma_d + q_\pi)^2}{2^c} + \frac{2}{2^n} \\
&\leq \frac{3u}{2^{n_p}} + \frac{4n(2\sigma + 2\sigma_d + q_\pi) + nq_{\widetilde{IC}} + 2}{2^n} + \frac{16(2\sigma + 2\sigma_d + q_\pi)^2}{2^c},
\end{aligned}
$$

which concludes the proof. $\qquad\qquad\qquad\qquad\qquad\qquad\qquad\qquad\qquad\qquad\qquad\square$

Acknowledgments. Gaëtan Cassiers is a Research Fellow and François-Xavier Standaert is a Senior Research Associate of the Belgian Fund for Scientific Research (FNRS-F.R.S.). This work has been funded in parts by the EU through the ERC project SWORD (Grant 724725), by the EU and the Walloon Region through the FEDER project USERMedia (convention number 501907-379156), and by the Walloon Region through the project DIGITRANS.

A   Original dOAE Definition

Formally, Hoang et al. define the dOAE privacy advantage $\mathbf{Adv}_{\mathsf{AEAD}}^{\mathsf{doae\text{-}priv}}(\mathscr{D}) = |\Pr[\mathscr{D}^{\mathbf{dReal}_{\mathsf{AEAD}}} \Rightarrow 1] - \Pr[\mathscr{D}^{\mathbf{dRand}_{\mathsf{AEAD}}} \Rightarrow 1]|$ and the dOAE authenticity advantage $\mathbf{Adv}_{\mathsf{AEAD}}^{\mathsf{doae\text{-}auth}}(\mathscr{D}) = \Pr[\mathbf{dForge}_{\mathsf{AEAD}}(\mathscr{D}) \Rightarrow \mathsf{true}]$, where the experiments dReal, dRand and dForge are given in Fig. 6.

proc initialize $\quad$ Game dReal	**proc initialize** $\quad$ Game dRand
$J \leftarrow 0;\ \mathcal{X}, \mathcal{Z} \leftarrow \emptyset;\ K \xleftarrow{\$} \mathcal{K};$	$J \leftarrow 0;\ \mathcal{X} \leftarrow \emptyset;$ $E(x) \leftarrow$ undef for all $x;$
proc Enc.init(N) $\quad$ **if** $N \notin \mathcal{N}$ **then return** $\perp$ $\quad J \leftarrow J+1;\ \boldsymbol{A}_J \leftarrow \boldsymbol{M}_J \leftarrow \boldsymbol{C}_J \leftarrow \Lambda;$ $\quad S_J \leftarrow \mathcal{E}_K.\mathrm{init}(N);\ N_J \leftarrow N;$ $\quad$ **return** J	**proc Enc.init**(N) $\quad$ **if** $N \notin \mathcal{N}$ **then return** $\perp$ $\quad J \leftarrow J+1;\ \boldsymbol{A}_J \leftarrow \boldsymbol{M}_J \leftarrow \Lambda;\ N_J \leftarrow N;$ $\quad$ **return** J
proc Enc.next(j, A, M) $\quad$ **if** $j \notin [1..J]$ **or** $S_j = \perp$, **then return** $\perp$ $\quad$ **if** $(N_j, \boldsymbol{A}_j\|A, \boldsymbol{M}_j\|M', 0) \in \mathcal{X}$, **for** $\qquad$ some $M' \neq M$, **then return** $\perp$ $\quad (C, S_j) \leftarrow \mathcal{E}_K.\mathrm{next}(S_j, A, M)$ $\quad \boldsymbol{A}_j \leftarrow \boldsymbol{A}_j\|A;\ \boldsymbol{M}_j \leftarrow \boldsymbol{M}_j\|M;\ \boldsymbol{C}_j \leftarrow \boldsymbol{C}_j\|C$ $\quad \mathcal{X} \leftarrow \mathcal{X} \cup \{(N_j, \boldsymbol{A}_j, \boldsymbol{M}_j, 0)\}$ $\quad \mathcal{Z} \leftarrow \mathcal{Z} \cup \{(N_j, \boldsymbol{A}_j, \boldsymbol{C}_j, 0)\}$ $\quad$ **return** C	**proc Enc.next**(j, A, M) $\quad$ **if** $j \notin [1..J]$ **or** $N_j = \perp$, **then return** $\perp$ $\quad$ **if** $(N_j, \boldsymbol{A}_j\|A, \boldsymbol{M}_j\|M', 0) \in \mathcal{X}$, **for** $\qquad$ some $M' \neq M$, **then return** $\perp$ $\quad \boldsymbol{A}_j \leftarrow \boldsymbol{A}_j\|A;\ \boldsymbol{M}_j \leftarrow \boldsymbol{M}_j\|M$ $\quad \mathcal{X} \leftarrow \mathcal{X} \cup \{(N_j, \boldsymbol{A}_j, \boldsymbol{M}_j, 0)\}$ $\quad$ **if** $E(N_j, \boldsymbol{A}_j, \boldsymbol{M}_j, 0) =$ undef, **then** $\qquad E(N_j, \boldsymbol{A}_j, \boldsymbol{M}_j, 0) \xleftarrow{\$} \{0,1\}^{|M|+\tau}$ $\quad C \leftarrow E(N_j, \boldsymbol{A}_j, \boldsymbol{M}_j, 0)$ $\quad$ **return** C
proc Enc.last(j, A, M) $\quad$ **if** $j \notin [1..J]$ **or** $S_j = \perp$, **then return** $\perp$ $\quad$ **if** $(N_j, \boldsymbol{A}_j\|A, \boldsymbol{M}_j\|M', 1) \in \mathcal{X}$, **for** $\qquad$ some $M' \neq M$, **then return** $\perp$ $\quad C \leftarrow \mathcal{E}_K.\mathrm{last}(S_j, A, M);\ S_j \leftarrow \perp$ $\quad \boldsymbol{A}_j \leftarrow \boldsymbol{A}_j\|A;\ \boldsymbol{M}_j \leftarrow \boldsymbol{M}_j\|M;\ \boldsymbol{C}_j \leftarrow \boldsymbol{C}_j\|C$ $\quad \mathcal{X} \leftarrow \mathcal{X} \cup \{(N_j, \boldsymbol{A}_j, \boldsymbol{M}_j, 1)\}$ $\quad \mathcal{Z} \leftarrow \mathcal{Z} \cup \{(N_j, \boldsymbol{A}_j, \boldsymbol{C}_j, 1)\}$ $\quad$ **return** C	**proc Enc.last**(j, A, M) $\quad$ **if** $j \notin [1..J]$ **or** $N_j = \perp$, **then return** $\perp$ $\quad$ **if** $(N_j, \boldsymbol{A}_j\|A, \boldsymbol{M}_j\|M', 1) \in \mathcal{X}$, **for** $\qquad$ some $M' \neq M$, **then return** $\perp$ $\quad \boldsymbol{A}_j \leftarrow \boldsymbol{A}_j\|A;\ \boldsymbol{M}_j \leftarrow \boldsymbol{M}_j\|M$ $\quad \mathcal{X} \leftarrow \mathcal{X} \cup \{(N_j, \boldsymbol{A}_j, \boldsymbol{M}_j, 1)\}$ $\quad$ **if** $E(i, N_j, \boldsymbol{A}_j, \boldsymbol{M}_j, 1) =$ undef, **then** $\qquad E(N_j, \boldsymbol{A}_j, \boldsymbol{M}_j, 1) \xleftarrow{\$} \{0,1\}^{|M|+\tau}$ $\quad C \leftarrow E(N_j, \boldsymbol{A}_j, \boldsymbol{M}_j, 1);\ N_j \leftarrow \perp$ $\quad$ **return** C
$- - - - - - - - - - - - - - - - - -$ **proc finalize** $(N, \boldsymbol{A}, \boldsymbol{C}, b)$ $\quad$ **if** $(N, \boldsymbol{A}, \boldsymbol{C}, b) \in \mathcal{Z}$ **or** $|\boldsymbol{A}| \neq |\boldsymbol{C}|$ $\qquad$ **or** $|\boldsymbol{A}| = 0$, **then return** false $\quad S \leftarrow \mathcal{D}_K.\mathrm{init}(N);\ m \leftarrow |\boldsymbol{C}|$ $\quad j \leftarrow 1$ **to** $m - b$ **do** $\qquad (M, S) \leftarrow \mathcal{D}_K.\mathrm{next}(S, \boldsymbol{A}[j], \boldsymbol{C}[j])$ $\qquad$ **if** $M = \perp$ **then return** false $\quad$ **if** $\mathcal{D}_K.\mathrm{last}(S, \boldsymbol{A}[m], \boldsymbol{C}[m]) = \perp$ **and** $\qquad b = 1$, **then return** false $\quad$ **return** true	

Fig. 6. (dOAE). First column: **dReal** experiment, finalize procedure excluded; **dForge** experiment includes all the procedures of the column. Second column: game **dRand**.

References

1. Bellare, M., Boldyreva, A., Knudsen, L., Namprempre, C.: Online ciphers and the Hash-CBC construction. In: Kilian, J. (ed.) CRYPTO 2001. LNCS, vol. 2139, pp. 292–309. Springer, Heidelberg (2001). https://doi.org/10.1007/3-540-44647-8_18

2. Bertoni, G., Daemen, J., Hoffert, S., Peeters, M., Assche, G.V., Keer, R.V.: Caesar submission: Keyak v2 (2015). https://keccak.team/obsolete/Keyak-2.0.pdf
3. Bertoni, G., Daemen, J., Peeters, M., Van Assche, G.: Duplexing the sponge: single-pass authenticated encryption and other applications. In: Miri, A., Vaudenay, S. (eds.) SAC 2011. LNCS, vol. 7118, pp. 320–337. Springer, Heidelberg (2012). https://doi.org/10.1007/978-3-642-28496-0_19
4. Böck, H., Zauner, A., Devlin, S., Somorovsky, J., Jovanovic, P.: Nonce-disrespecting adversaries: practical forgery attacks on GCM in TLS. In: 10th USENIX WOOT (2016)
5. Daemen, J., Mennink, B., Van Assche, G.: Full-state keyed duplex with built-in multi-user support. In: Takagi, T., Peyrin, T. (eds.) ASIACRYPT 2017, Part II. LNCS, vol. 10625, pp. 606–637. Springer, Cham (2017). https://doi.org/10.1007/978-3-319-70697-9_21
6. Fleischmann, E., Forler, C., Lucks, S.: McOE: a family of almost foolproof online authenticated encryption schemes. In: Canteaut, A. (ed.) FSE 2012. LNCS, vol. 7549, pp. 196–215. Springer, Heidelberg (2012). https://doi.org/10.1007/978-3-642-34047-5_12
7. Guo, C., Pereira, O., Peters, T., Standaert, F.: Towards lightweight side-channel security and the leakage-resilience of the duplex sponge. IACR Cryptology ePrint Archive 2019, 133 (2019). https://eprint.iacr.org/2019/133
8. Hoang, V.T., Reyhanitabar, R., Rogaway, P., Vizár, D.: Online authenticated-encryption and its nonce-reuse misuse-resistance. In: Gennaro, R., Robshaw, M. (eds.) CRYPTO 2015, Part I. LNCS, vol. 9215, pp. 493–517. Springer, Heidelberg (2015). https://doi.org/10.1007/978-3-662-47989-6_24
9. NIST: Lightweight cryptography. https://csrc.nist.gov/projects/lightweight-cryptography
10. Rescorla, E.: The transport layer security (TLS) protocol version 1.3. RFC 8446, 1–160 (2018). https://doi.org/10.17487/RFC8446
11. Vanhoef, M., Piessens, F.: Key reinstallation attacks: forcing nonce reuse in WPA2. In: Proceedings of ACM CCS 2017, pp. 1313–1328. ACM (2017)

One Trace Is All It Takes: Machine Learning-Based Side-Channel Attack on EdDSA

Léo Weissbart[1,2](✉), Stjepan Picek[1](✉), and Lejla Batina[2](✉)

[1] Delft University of Technology, Delft, The Netherlands
l.weissbart@cs.ru.nl, picek.stjepan@gmail.com
[2] Digital Security Group, Radboud University, Nijmegen, The Netherlands
lejla@cs.ru.nl

Abstract. Profiling attacks, especially those based on machine learning proved as very successful techniques in recent years when considering side-channel analysis of block ciphers implementations. At the same time, the results for implementations of public-key cryptosystems are very sparse. In this paper, we consider several machine learning techniques in order to mount a power analysis attack on EdDSA using the curve Curve25519 as implemented in WolfSSL. The results show all considered techniques to be viable and powerful options. Especially convolutional neural networks (CNNs) are effective as we can break the implementation with only a single measurement in the attack phase while requiring less than 500 measurements in the training phase. Interestingly, that same convolutional neural network was recently shown to perform extremely well for attacking the implementation of the AES cipher. Our results show that some common grounds can be established when using deep learning for profiling attacks on distinct cryptographic algorithms and their corresponding implementations.

1 Introduction

Cryptographic algorithms ensure the security of a system (e.g., communication on a network or payment with a smartcard), by providing security features (e.g., authenticity and non-repudiation). However, implementations of those algorithms can fail during the engineering process and present flaws, leaking secret information over side-channels, even for the strongest protocols. Side-channel analysis (SCA) designates a set of signal processing techniques targeting the execution of cryptographic implementations, evaluating a system's security.

Since Differential Power Analysis by Kocher et al. [16], many other powerful SCAs have been successfully used to break all cryptographic algorithms, including recent machine learning approaches, on both symmetric key cryptography [9, 14, 15, 18, 20, 27, 28, 31] and public-key cryptography [21, 30]. Among all SCAs, profiling attacks are the most powerful provided that the attacker has access to a clone device with full control that can be profiled offline, to later use this knowledge on another device during the attack phase. Template attack [9] has been the most popular instance of profiling attacks, but in recent years, new techniques based on machine learning were able to outperform template attack and break implementations protected with countermeasures. However, most of those results are obtained on block ciphers implementations (and more precisely on AES) and there are almost no results considering machine learning (deep learning) on public-key cryptography.

In this paper, we attack the digital signature algorithm Ed25519 as implemented in WolfSSL on an STM32F4 microcontroller and we also compare the results obtained from different profiling attacks. To that end, we consider several machine learning techniques (i.e., Random Forest, Support Vector Machines, and Convolutional Neural Network) that have been proved strong in related work (albeit mostly on block ciphers) and template attack, which we consider the standard technique and a baseline setting.

1.1 Related Work

Template attacks (TAs) have been introduced by Chari et al. in 2003 [9] as the most powerful SCA in the information-theoretic point of view and became a standard tool for profiling SCA. As straightforward implementations of TA can lead to computationally intensive computation, one option for more efficient computation is to use only a single covariance matrix, and is referred as the so-called pooled template attack presented by Choudary and Kuhn [10] where they were able to template a LOAD instruction and recover all 8 bits treated with a guessing entropy of 0. Several works applied machine learning methods to SCA of block ciphers because of their resemblance to general profiling techniques. Two methods stand out particularly in profiling SCA, namely Support Vector Machines (see, e.g., [18,20,28,33]) and Random Forest (see, e.g., [14,27,33]). With the general evolution in the field of deep learning, more and more works deal with neural networks for SCA and often show top performance. There, most of the research concentrated on either multilayer perceptron or convolutional neural networks [7,11,20,29].

There is a large portion of works considering profiling techniques for block ciphers but there is much less for public-key cryptography. Lerman et al. considered template attack and several machine learning techniques to attack RSA. However, the targeted implementation was not secure, which makes the comparison with non-machine learning techniques less favorable [18]. Nascimento et al. applied a horizontal attack on ECC implementation for AVR ATmega microcontroller targeting the side-channel leakage of cmov operation. Their approach to side-channel is similar to ours but they don't use deep learning in the analysis [23]. Poussier et al. used horizontal attacks and linear regression to conduct an attack on ECC implementations but their approach cannot be classified as deep learning [30]. Carbone et al. used deep learning to attack a secure implementation of RSA [8]. Previous work has shown TA to be efficient for attacking SPA-resistant ECDSA with P192 NIST curve on 32-bit microcontroller [21].

1.2 Contributions

There are two main contributions of this paper:

1. We present a comprehensive analysis of several profiling attacks by exploring different sets of hyper-parameters that permit to obtain the best results for each method. This evaluation can be helpful when deciding on an optimal strategy for machine learning and in particular, deep learning attacks on implementations of public-key cryptography.
2. We consider elliptic curve cryptography (actually EdDSA using curve Curve25519) and profiling attacks where we show that such techniques, and especially the convolutional neural networks can be extremely powerful attacks.

Besides those contributions, we also present a publicly available dataset we developed for this work. We aim to make our results more reproducible but also motivate other researchers to publish their datasets for public-key cryptography. Indeed, while the SCA community realizes the lack of publicly available datasets for block ciphers (and tries to improve it), the situation for public-key cryptography seems to attract less attention despite even worse availability of codes, testbeds, and datasets.

The rest of this paper is organized as follows. In Sect. 2, we give relevant background on elliptic curve scalar multiplication, Ed25519 algorithm, and profiling attack techniques. In Sect. 3, we explain the way an attacker can exploit this implementation of Ed25519. In Sect. 4, we present our testbed and data collection strategy. In Sect. 5, we give the results of the hyper-parameter tuning phase, dimensionality reduction, and profiling results. Finally, in Sect. 6, we conclude the paper and give some possible future research directions.

2 Background

In this section, we start by introducing the elliptic curve scalar multiplication operation and EdDSA algorithm. Afterward, we discuss profiling attacks that we use in our experiments.

2.1 EdDSA

In the context of public-key cryptography, one important feature is the authentication of a message between two parties. This feature ensures to party B that party A has indeed sent a message M and that this message is original and unaltered. Message authentication can be performed by Digital Signature Algorithms (DSA). DSA creates a signature pair (R, S) for proving that a message M was emitted by the known party A, unaltered and that A cannot repudiate. For security reasons and computational speed, public-key cryptography has turned toward Elliptic Curves based cryptography (ECC) as it tends to become the successor of RSA for public-key cryptography because it can meet higher security levels with smaller key lengths. ECC is based on the Elliptic Curve Discrete

Logarithm Problem (ECDLP), which states that it is easy and hence efficient to compute $Q = k \cdot P$, but it is difficult to find k knowing Q and P.

EdDSA [3] is a variant of the Schnorr digital signature scheme [34] using Twisted Edward Curves, a subgroup of elliptic curves that uses unified formulas, enabling speed-ups for specific curve parameters. This algorithm proposes a deterministic generation of the ephemeral key, different for every different message, to prevent flaws from a predictable random number generator. The ephemeral key r is made of the hash value of the message M and the auxiliary key b, generating a unique ephemeral public key R for every message.

EdDSA, when using parameters of Curve25519 is referred to as Ed25519 (domain parameters are given in Appendix A) [2]. EdDSA scheme for signature generation and verification is described in Algorithm 1, where the notation $(x, \ldots, y)$ denotes the concatenation of the elements. The notation used in Algorithm 1 is given in Table 1.

After the signature generation, party A sends (M, R, S), i.e., the message along with the signature pair (R, S) to B. The verification of the signature is done by B with Steps 10 to 11. If the last equation is verified, it represents a point on the elliptic curve and the signature is correct, ensuring that the message can be trusted as an authentic message from A.

Table 1. Notation for EdDSA

Name	Symbol
Private key	k
Private scalar	a (first part of $H(k)$)
Auxiliary key	b (last part of $H(k)$)
Ephemeral key	r
Message	M

Algorithm 1. EdDSA Signature generating and verification

Keypair Generation (k, P): (Used once, first time private key is used.)
1: Hash k such that $H(k) = (h_0, h_1, \ldots, h_{2u-1}) = (a, b)$
2: $a = (h_0, \ldots, h_{u-1})$, interpret as integer in little-endian notation
3: $b = (h_u, \ldots, h_{2u-1})$
4: Compute public key: $P = aB$.

Signature Generation:
5: Compute ephemeral private key $r = H(b, M)$.
6: Compute ephemeral public key $R = rB$.
7: Compute $h = H(R, P, M) \mod l$.
8: Compute: $S = (r + ha) \mod l$.
9: Signature pair (R, S)

Signature Verification:
10: Compute $h = H(R, P, M)$
11: Verify if $8SB = 8R + 8hP$ holds in E

2.2   Elliptic Curve Scalar Multiplication

The security of ECC algorithms depends on the ability to compute a point multiplication and the presumed inability to reverse the computation to retrieve the multiplicand given the original and product points. This security is strengthened with a greater prime order of the underlying finite field. In our attack, we aim to extract the ephemeral key r from its scalar multiplication with the Elliptic Curve base point B (see step 5 in Algorithm 1). To understand how this attack works, we decompose this computation as implemented in the case of WolfSSL Ed25519.

The implementation of Ed25519 in WolfSSL is based on the work of Bernstein et al. [3]. The implementation of elliptic curve scalar multiplication is a window-based method with radix-16, making use of a precomputed table containing results of the scalar multiplication of $16^i |r_i| \cdot B$, where $r_i \in [-8, 7] \cap \mathbb{Z}$ and B is the base point of Curve25519 (see Appendix B). This method is popular because of its trade-off between memory usage and computation speed, but also because the implementation is time-constant and does not feature any branch condition nor array indices and hence is presumably secure against timing attack. Leaking information from the corresponding value loaded from the memory with a function *ge_select* is used here to recover e and hence can be used to easily connect to the ephemeral key r. More details are given in the remainder of this paper.

2.3   Profiling Attacks

In this work, we consider several machine learning techniques that showed very good performance when considering side-channel attacks on block ciphers. Besides, we briefly introduce the template attack, which serves as a baseline to compare the performance of algorithms.

Random Forest. Random Forest (RF) is a well-known ensemble learning method consisting of a number of decision trees [6]. Decision trees consist of combinations of Boolean decisions on a different random subset of attributes of input data (called bootstrap sampling). For each node of each tree, the best split is taken among these randomly chosen attributes. RF is a stochastic algorithm because of its two sources of randomness: bootstrap sampling and attribute selection at node splitting. The most important hyper-parameter to tune is the number of trees in the forest (we do not limit the tree size nor use pruning methods).

Support Vector Machines. Support Vector Machines (denoted SVM) is a kernel-based machine learning family of methods that are used to accurately classify both linearly separable and linearly inseparable data [38]. The idea for linearly inseparable data is to transform them into a higher dimensional space using a kernel function, wherein the data can usually be classified with higher accuracy. The scikit-learn implementation we use considers libsvm's C-SVC classifier [25] that implements SMO-type algorithm [12]. The multi-class support is handled according to a one-vs-one scheme. We investigate two variations of SVM: with a linear kernel and with a radial kernel. Linear kernel-based SVM has the penalty hyper-parameter C of the error term. Radial kernel-based SVM has two significant hyper-parameters to tune: the cost of the margin C and the kernel γ.

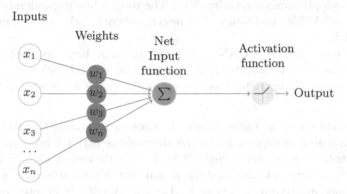

Fig. 1. Anatomy of a neuron.

Convolutional Neural Networks. Convolutional Neural Networks (CNNs) are a type of neural networks initially designed to mimic the biological process of animal's cortex to interpret visual data [17]. CNNs show excellent results for classifying images for various applications and have also proved to be a powerful tool to classify time series data such as music or speech [24]. The *VGG-16* architecture introduced in [35] for image recognition was also recently applied to the problem of side-channel analysis with very good results [15].

From the operational perspective, CNNs are similar to ordinary neural networks (e.g., multilayer perceptron): they consist of several layers where each layer is made up of neurons as depicted in Fig. 1. Every neuron in a layer computes a weighted combination of an input set by a net input function (e.g., the sum function in neurons of a fully-connected layer) from which a nonlinear activation function produces an output. When the output is different from zero, we say that the neuron activation feeds the next layer as its input. Layers with a convolution function as the Net Input Function are referred to as convolutional layers and are the core building blocks in a CNN.

CNNs use three main types of layers: convolutional layers, pooling layers, and fully-connected layers. Convolution layer computes the output of neurons from locally sparse combinations of initial raw input features, to reduce the space volume of information into smaller regions of interest. Pooling layers are used after a convolution layer to sample down local regions and create spatial regions of interest. The fully-connected layer at the end of a CNN behaves as a classifier for the extracted features from the inputs. The `ReLU` activation function will apply an element-wise activation function, such as the $max(0, x)$ thresholding at zero.

The architecture of CNN we choose in this paper makes use of some additional elements: batch normalization is used to normalize the input layer by applying standard scaling on the activations of the previous layer, using running mean and standard deviation. Flatten layer transforms input data of rank greater than two into a one-dimensional feature vector that is used in the fully-connected layer. Dropout is a regularization technique for reducing overfitting by preventing complex co-adaptations on training data. The term refers to randomly dropping out units (both hidden and visible) in a neural network with a certain probability at each batch.

The architecture of a CNN is dependent on a large number of hyper-parameters making the choice of hyper-parameters for each different application an engineering challenge. The choices made in this paper are discussed in Sect. 5.

Template Attack. The template attack relies on the Bayes theorem and considers the features as dependent. In the state-of-the-art, TA relies mostly on a normal distribution [9]. Accordingly, TA assumes that each $P(X = x|Y = y)$ follows a (multivariate) Gaussian distribution that is parameterized by its mean and covariance matrix for each class Y. The authors of [10] propose to use only one pooled covariance matrix averaged over all classes Y to cope with statistical difficulties and thus lower efficiency. In our experiments, we use the version of the attack with only one pooled covariance matrix.

3   Attacker Model

The general warning for implementations of ECDSA is to select different ephemeral private keys r for different signature. The flaw of using the same r for different messages happens since the two corresponding signatures would result in two signature pairs (R, S) and (R, S') for messages M and M', respectively. Then, an attacker can use this information to recover r as $r = (z - z')(S - S')^{-1}$ (with z and z', few bits of $H(M)$ and $H(M')$ interpreted as integers). Finally, to recover the private scalar a required to forge signatures, the attacker can trivially compute $a = R^{-1}(Sr - z)$.

Here, the aim of the attacker is the same as for every ECDSA attack: recover the secret scalar a. The difference is that the attacker cannot acquire two signatures with the same random r, but can still recover the secret scalar in two different ways. One method would consist of attacking the implementation of the hash function to recover b from the computation of ephemeral private key [32]. Another method (developed in this paper) attacks the implementation of the scalar multiplication during the computation of the ephemeral public key. With this method, the attacker collects side-channel traces of each computation since r is different in every message. This paper shows that even with a single attack trace, the attacker can recover private scalar with high confidence where we provide a comparison with different state-of-the-art profiling SCA.

4   Dataset Generation

In this section, we first present the measurement setup and explain the methodology for creating a dataset from the power traces obtained with our setup (see Fig. 2).

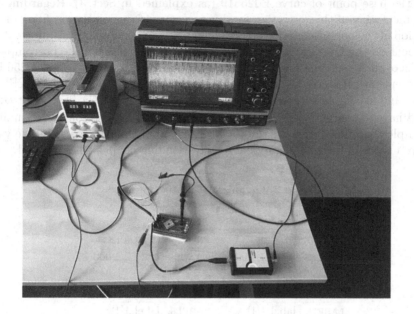

Fig. 2. The measurement setup

4.1   Measurement Setup

The device under attack is a Piñata development board developed by Riscure to perform SCA evaluations[1]. The board is based on a 32-bit STM32F4 microcontroller with an ARM-based architecture, running at the clock frequency of 168 MHz. The board is modified to perform SCA through power consumption. The target is Ed25519 implementation of WolfSSL 3.10.2. As WolfSSL is an open-source library written in C, we have a fully transparent and controllable implementation for the profiling phase.

Power consumption is measured with a current probe[2] placed between the power source and the board's power supply source. Power measurements are obtained with a Lecroy Waverunner z610i oscilloscope. The measures are performed with a sampling frequency of 1.025 GHz and the trigger is implemented with an I/O pin of the board around the *ge_select* function (see Algorithm 2) to retrieve a part of the key **e**.

---

[1] Pinata Board: https://www.riscure.com/product/pinata-training-target/
[2] Current Probe: https://www.riscure.com/product/current-probe/

4.2   Dataset

To evaluate the attack proposed in this paper and to facilitate reproducible experiments, we present the dataset we built for this purpose [1]. We follow the same format for the dataset as in recently presented ASCAD database [31]. For this attack, we profile the EC scalar multiplication with the ephemeral key with the base point of curve Ed25519 (as explained in Sect. 3). Regarding the implementation of this operation for our target, we focus on the profiling of one function of the operation as it is more challenging by exploiting less information. We focus on the Lookup Table (LUT) operation used to fetch the precomputed chunks of the result in a table stored in memory. For speed reasons, the 256 bits scalar/ephemeral secret key r is interpreted in slices of 4-bits (nibbles) $e[i], i \in [0, 63]$, and to compute $R = rB$, the field multiplication with the base point B, we would have to compute $\sum_{i=0}^{63} e[i]16^i B$. As multiplication is resource consuming, the implementation stores the results for every nibble number i and nibble value $e[i]$ in a precomputed LUT and loads corresponding chunks when needed.

Table 2. Organization of the database.

DATABASE			
ATTACK_TRACES		PROFILING_TRACES	
TRACES	trace_1[1 000]	TRACES	trace_1[1 000]
	...		...
	trace_n_a[1 000]		trace_n_p [1 000]
LABELS	label_1[1]	LABELS	label_1[1]
	...		...
	label_n_a[1]		label_n_p[1]

Each trace in the database is represented by a tuple composed of one power trace and its corresponding label (class). The database is composed of two groups: the first group is PROFILING_TRACES, which contains n_p tuples. The second group is ATTACK_TRACES, which contains n_a tuples (see Table 2). In total, there are 6 400 labeled traces. We divide the traces in 80/20 ratio for profiling/attacking groups, and consequently, have $n_p = 5\,120$ and $n_a = 1\,280$. The profiling group is additionally divided in 80/20 ratio for training and validation sets.

A group contains two datasets: TRACES and LABELS. The dataset TRACES contains the raw traces recorded from different nibbles during the encryption. Each trace contains 1 000 samples and represents the relevant information of one nibble encryption. The dataset LABELS contains the correct subkey candidate for the corresponding trace. In total, there are 16 classes since we consider all possible nibble values.

To the best of our knowledge, besides the dataset we presented here, there is only one publicly available dataset for SCA on public-key cryptography on elliptic curves. Tuveri et al. conducted a side-channel analysis of SM2 (a digital signature algorithm) public-key cryptography suite where they consider various side channels [37]. Additionally, the authors published EM side-channel measurements of elliptic curve point multiplication[3]. We note that due to the choice of the suite (SM2 is not an international standard), this dataset is difficult to compare with ours.

5 Experimental Setting and Results

To examine the feasibility and performance of our attack, we present different settings for power analysis and use two different metrics. We first compare the performance by using the accuracy metric since it is a standard metric in machine learning. The second metric we use is the success rate as it is an SCA metric that gives a more concrete idea on the power of the attacker [36]. Note that we assume the attacker who can collect as many power traces as she wants and that the profiling phase is nearly-perfect as also suggested by Lerman et al. [19].

5.1 Hyper-parameters Choice

Here we discuss the choice of hyper-parameters for each method we consider in this paper.

TA: Classical Template Attack is applied with pooled covariance [10]. Profiling phase is repeated for a different choice of points of interest (POI).

RF: Hyper-parameter optimization is applied to tune the number of decision trees used in Random Forest. We consider the following number of trees: 50, 100, 500. The best number of decision trees is 100 with no PCA and 500 when PCA is applied for 10 and 656 POI.

SVM: For the linear kernel, the hyper-parameter to optimize is the penalty parameter C. We search for the best C among a range of $[1, 10^5]$ in logarithmic space. In the case of the radial basis function (RBF) kernel, we have two hyper-parameters to tune: the penalty C and the kernel coefficient γ. The search for best hyper-parameters is done within $C = [1, 10^5]$ and $\gamma = [-5, 2]$ in logarithmic spaces. We consider only those hyper-parameters that give the best scores for each choice of POI (see Table 3).

CNN: The chosen hyper-parameters for *VGG-16* follows several rules that have been adapted for SCA in [15] or [31] and that we describe here:

1. The model is composed of several convolution blocks and ends with a dropout layer followed by a fully connected layer and an output layer with the Softmax activation function.

---

[3] Available at https://zenodo.org/record/1436828#.XRhmfY-xWrw.

Table 3. Chosen hyper-parameters for SVM

Number of features	Kernel	C	γ
1 000	linear	1 000	–
	rbf	1 000	1
656	linear	1 000	–
	rbf	1 000	1
10	linear	1 333	–
	rbf	1 000	1.23

Table 4. Architecture of the CNN

Hyper-parameter	Value
Input shape	$(1000, 1)$
Convolution layers	$(8, 16, 32, 64, 128, 256, 512, 512, 512)$
Pooling type	Max
Fully-connected layers	512
Dropout rate	0.5

2. Convolutional and fully-connected layers use the ReLU activation function.
3. A convolution block is composed of one convolution layer followed by a pooling layer.
4. An additional batch normalization layer is applied for every odd-numbered convolution block and is preceding the pooling layer.
5. The chosen filter size for convolution layers is fixed on size 3.
6. The number of filters $n_{filters,i}$ in a convolution block i keeps increasing according to the following rule: $n_{filters,i} = max(2^i \cdot n_{filters,1}, 512)$ for every layer $i \geq 0$ and we choose $n_{filters,1} = 8$
7. The stride of the pooling layers is of size 2 and halves the input data for each block.
8. Convolution blocks follow each other until the size of the input data is reduce to 1.

The resulting architecture is represented in Table 4 and Fig. 3.

5.2 Dimensionality Reduction

For computational reasons, one may want to select points of interest (POI) and consequently, we explore several different setting where we either use all the features in a trace or we conduct dimensionality reduction. Here, for dimensionality reduction, we use Principal Component Analysis (PCA) [5]. Principal component analysis (PCA) is a well-known linear dimensionality reduction method that may use Singular Value Decomposition (SVD) of the data matrix to project it

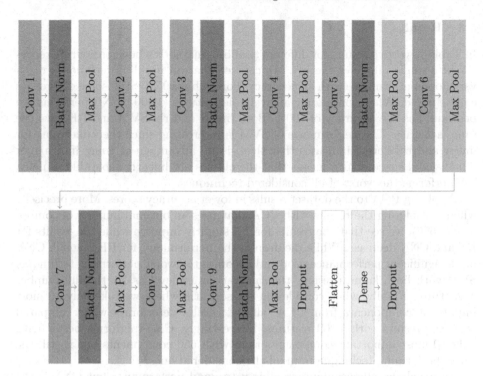

Fig. 3. CNN architecture as implemented in Keras. This architecture consists of 9 convolutional layers followed by max pooling layers. For each odd convolutional layer, there is a batch normalization layer before the pooling layer. At the end of the network, there is one fully connected layer.

to a lower dimensional space. PCA creates a new set of features (called principal components) that are linearly uncorrelated, orthogonal, and form a new coordinate system. The number of components equals the number of original features. The components are arranged in a way that the first component covers the largest variance by a projection of the original data and the subsequent components cover less and less of the remaining data variance. The projection contains (weighted) contributions from all the original features. Not all principal components need to be kept in the transformed dataset. Since the components are sorted by the variance covered, the number of kept components, designated with L, maximizes the variance in the original data and minimizes the reconstruction error of the data transformation.

Note, while PCA is meant to select the principal information from a data, there is no guarantee that the reduced data form will give better results for profiling attacks than its complete form. We apply PCA to have the least possible number of points of interest that maximize the score from TA (10 points of interest) and the number of POI using a Bayesian model selection that estimates the dimensionality of the data based on a heuristics (see [22]). After an automatic selection of the number of components to use, we have 656 points of interest.

5.3 Results

In Table 5, we give results for different profiling methods when considering recovery of a single nibble of the key. We can see that all profiling techniques reach very good performance with all accuracy scores above 95%. Still, some differences can be noted. When considering all available features (1 000), CNN performs the best and has the accuracy of 100%. Both linear and rbf SVM and RF have the same accuracy. The performance of SVM is interesting since the same value for linear and rbf kernel indicates that there is no advantage of going into higher dimensional space, which means that the classes are linearly separable. Finally, TA performs the worst of all considered techniques.

Applying PCA to the dataset results in lower accuracy scores. More precisely, when considering the results with PCA that uses an optimal number of components (656), we see that the results for TA slightly improve while the results for RF and CNN decrease. While the drop in the performance for RF is small, CNN has a significant performance drop and becomes the worst performing technique. SVM with both kernels retains the same accuracy level as for the full number of features. Finally, when considering the scenario where we take only 10 most important components from PCA, all the results deteriorate when compared with the results with 1 000 features. Interestingly, CNN performs better with only 10 most important components than with 656 components but is still the worst performing technique from all the considered ones.

To conclude, all techniques exhibit very good performance but CNN is the best if no dimensionality reduction is done. There, the maximum accuracy is obtained after only a few epochs (see Figs. 5 and 6). If there is dimensionality reduction, CNN shows a quick performance deterioration. This behavior should not come as a surprise since CNNs are usually used with the raw features (i.e., no pre-processing). In fact, applying such techniques could reduce the performance due to a loss of information and changes in the spatial representation of features. Interestingly, TA is never the best technique while SVM and RF show good and stable behavior for all feature set sizes.

In Fig. 4, we give the success rate with orders up to 10 for all profiling methods on the dataset without applying PCA. Note, a success rate of order o is the probability that the correct subkey is ranked among the firsts o candidates of the guessing vector. While CNN has a hundred percent success rate of order 1, other methods achieve the perfect score only for orders greater than 6.

The results for all methods are similar in the recovery of a single nibble from the key. If we want to have an idea of how good these methods are for the recovery of a full 256-bit key, we must apply the classification on the successive 64 nibbles. We can have an intuitive glimpse of the resulting accuracy P_c with the cumulative probability of the probability of one nibble $P_s : P_c = \Pi_{64} P_s$ (see Table 6). The cumulative accuracy obtained in such a way can be interpreted as the predictive first-order success rate of a full key for the different methods in terms of a security metric.

From these results, we can observe that the best result is obtained with CNN when there is no dimensionality reduction. Other machine learning methods and

Table 5. Accuracy for the different methods obtained on the attacking dataset.

Algorithm	1 000 features	656 PCA components	10 PCA components
TA	0.9977	0.9984	0.9830
RF	0.9992	0.9914	0.9937
SVM (linear)	0.9992	0.9992	0.995
SVM (rbf)	0.9992	0.9992	0.995
CNN	1.00	0.95	0.96

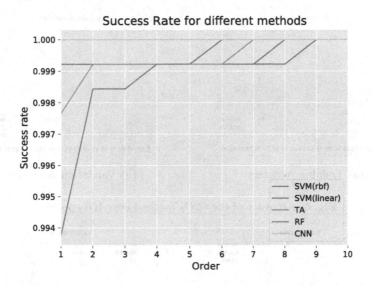

Fig. 4. Success rate results.

TA are nonetheless powerful profiling attacks with up to 95 and 90% performance to recover the full key on the first guess with the best choice of hyper-parameters and dimensionality reduction. Note the low accuracy value for CNN when using 656 PCA components: this result is obtained as the accuracy of CNN for a single nibble raised to the power of 64 (since now we consider 64 nibbles). When considering the results after dimensionality reduction, we see that SVM is the best performing technique, which is especially apparent when using only 10 PCA components. Finally, we observe again that TA is never the best performing technique.

As it can be observed from Figs. 5 and 6, both scenarios without dimensionality reduction and dimensionality reduction to 656 components, reach the maximal performance very fast. On the other hand, the scenario with 10 PCA components does not seem to reach the maximal performance within 100 epochs since we see that the validation accuracy does not start to decrease. Still, even longer experiments do not show further improvement in the performance, which indicates that the network simply learned all that is possible and that there is no more information that can be used to further increase the performance.

Table 6. Cumulative probabilities of the profiling methods.

Algorithm	1 000 features	656 PCA components	10 PCA components
TA	0.86	0.90	0.33
RF	0.95	0.57	0.66
SVM (linear)	0.95	0.95	0.72
SVM (rbf)	0.95	0.95	0.72
CNN	1.00	0.03	0.07

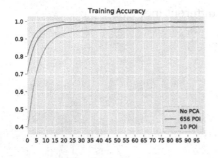

(a) Training Accuracy

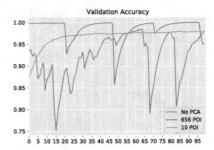

(b) Validation Accuracy

Fig. 5. Accuracy of the CNN method over 100 epochs

(a) Training Loss

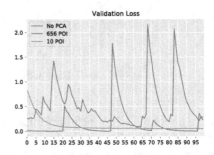

(b) Validation Loss

Fig. 6. Loss of the CNN method over 100 epochs.

Choosing the Minimum Number of Traces for Training on CNN. As it is possible to obtain a perfect profiling phase on our dataset using CNN, we focus here on finding the smallest training set that gives a success rate of 1. More precisely, we evaluate the attacker in a more restricted setting [26]. To do so, we first reduce the size of the training set to k number of traces per class (to always have a balanced distribution of the traces) and then we gradually increase it to find out when the success rate reaches 1. In Table 7, we give the results obtained after one hundred epochs.

Table 7. Validation and test accuracy of CNN with an increasing number of training traces.

Number of traces per class k	10	20	30	50	100	300
Validation accuracy	0.937	1.0	1.0	1.0	1.0	1.0
Testing accuracy	0.992	0.992	1.0	1.0	1.0	1.0

Interestingly, it turns out that 30 traces per class for training the CNN is enough to reach the perfect profiling of this dataset. At the same time, the additional experiments did not show good enough behavior with a lower number of traces per class. Note the scenario with only 10 traces per class where the validation accuracy is lower than the testing accuracy. This happens since we use only 20% of the training set for the validation, which results in an extremely small validation set and consequently, less reliable results.

6 Conclusions and Future Work

In this paper, we consider a number of profiling techniques to attack the Ed25519 implementation in WolfSSL. The results show that although several techniques perform well, convolutional neural networks are the best if no dimensionality reduction is done. In fact, in such a scenario, we can obtain the accuracy of 100%, which means that the attack is perfect in the sense that we obtain the full information with only a single trace in the attack phase. What is especially interesting is the fact that CNN used here is taken from related work (more precisely, CNN used for profiling SCA on AES) and is not further adapted to the scenario here. This indicates that CNNs can perform well over various scenarios in SCA. Finally, to obtain such results, we require only 30 measurements per class, which results in less than 500 measurements to reach a success rate of 1 with CNN.

The implementation of Ed25519 we attack in this work does not feature any countermeasure for SCA (that is, beyond constant-time implementation). In future work, we plan to evaluate CNN for SCA on Ed25519 with different countermeasures to test the limits of CNN in the side-channel analysis.

Appendix

A Ed25519 Domain Parameters

Ed25519 domain parameters:

– Finite field F_q, where $q = 2^{255} - 19$ is the prime.
– Elliptic curve $E(F_q)$, Curve25519

- Base point B
- Order of the point B, l
- Hash function H, SHA-512 [13]
- Key length $u = 256$ (also length of the prime)

For more details on other parameters of Curve25519 and the corresponding curve equations we refer to Bernstein [2].

B   EC Scalar Multiplication

Algorithm 2. Elliptic curve scalar multiplication with base point [4]

Input: R, a with $a = a[0] + 256 * a[1] + ... + 256^{31}a[31]$
Output: $H(a, s, m)$
1: **for** $i = 0; i < 32; + + i$ **do**
2:      $e[2i + 0] = (a[i] >> 0\&15)$;
3:      $e[2i + 1] = (a[i] >> 4)\&15$;
4: **end for**
5: $carry = 0$;
6: **for** $i = 0; i < 63; + + i$ **do**
7:      $e[i] + = carry$;
8:      $carry = (e[i] + 8)$;
9:      $carry >>= 4$;
10:      $e[i] - = carry << 4$;
11: **end for**
12: $e[63] + = carry$; $\triangleright \forall i < 64, -8 \leq e[i] \leq 8$
13: $ge\_p3\_0(h)$;
14: **for** $i = 1; i < 64; i+ = 2$ **do**
15:      $ge\_select(\&t, i/2, e[i])$; $\triangleright$ load from precomputed table $(e[i] \cdot 16^i) \cdot B$ in E.
16:      $ge\_madd(\&r, R, \&t)$; $ge\_p1p1\_to\_p3(R, \&r)$;
17: **end for**
18: $ge\_p3\_dbl(\&r, R)$; $ge\_p1p1\_to\_p2(\&s, \&r)$;
19: $ge\_p2\_dbl(\&r, \&s)$; $ge\_p1p1\_to\_p2(\&s, \&r)$;
20: $ge\_p2\_dbl(\&r, \&s)$; $ge\_p1p1\_to\_p2(\&s, \&r)$;
21: $ge\_p2\_dbl(\&r, \&s)$; $ge\_p1p1\_to\_p3(R, \&r)$;
22: **for** $i = 0; i < 64; i+ = 2$ **do**
23:      $ge\_select(\&t, i/2, e[i])$; $\triangleright$ load from precomputed table $(e[i] \cdot 16^i) \cdot B$ in E.
24:      $ge\_madd(\&r, R, \&t)$; $ge\_p1p1\_to\_p3(R, \&r)$;
25: **end for**

References

1. Database for EdDSA. https://github.com/leoweissbart/MachineLearningBased SideChannelAttackonEdDSA
2. Bernstein, D.J.: Curve25519: new Diffie-Hellman speed records (2006). http://cr. yp.to/papers.html#curve25519. Citations in this document 1(5) (2016)
3. Bernstein, D.J., Duif, N., Lange, T., Schwabe, P., Yang, B.Y.: High-speed high-security signatures. J. Cryptogr. Eng. **2**(2), 77–89 (2012)
4. Blake, I., Seroussi, G., Smart, N.: Elliptic Curves in Cryptography, vol. 265. Cambridge University Press, Cambridge (1999)
5. Bohy, L., Neve, M., Samyde, D., Quisquater, J.J.: Principal and independent component analysis for crypto-systems with hardware unmasked units. In: Proceedings of e-Smart 2003, Cannes, France, January 2003
6. Breiman, L.: Random forests. Mach. Learn. **45**(1), 5–32 (2001)
7. Cagli, E., Dumas, C., Prouff, E.: Convolutional neural networks with data augmentation against jitter-based countermeasures. In: Fischer, W., Homma, N. (eds.) CHES 2017. LNCS, vol. 10529, pp. 45–68. Springer, Cham (2017). https://doi.org/10.1007/978-3-319-66787-4_3
8. Carbone, M., et al.: Deep learning to evaluate secure RSA implementations. IACR Trans. Cryptogr. Hardw. Embed. Syst. **2019**(2), 132–161 (2019). https://doi.org/10.13154/tches.v2019.i2.132-161. https://tches.iacr.org/index.php/TCHES/article/view/7388
9. Chari, S., Rao, J.R., Rohatgi, P.: Template attacks. In: Kaliski, B.S., Koç, K., Paar, C. (eds.) CHES 2002. LNCS, vol. 2523, pp. 13–28. Springer, Heidelberg (2003). https://doi.org/10.1007/3-540-36400-5_3
10. Choudary, O., Kuhn, M.G.: Efficient template attacks. In: Francillon, A., Rohatgi, P. (eds.) CARDIS 2013. LNCS, vol. 8419, pp. 253–270. Springer, Cham (2014). https://doi.org/10.1007/978-3-319-08302-5_17
11. Cid, C., Jacobson Jr., M.J. (eds.): SAC 2018. LNCS, vol. 11349. Springer, Cham (2019). https://doi.org/10.1007/978-3-030-10970-7
12. Fan, R.E., Chen, P.H., Lin, C.J.: Working set selection using second order information for training support vector machines. J. Mach. Learn. Res. **6**, 1889–1918 (2005). http://dl.acm.org/citation.cfm?id=1046920.1194907
13. FIPS, PUB: 180–4. Secure hash standard (SHS), March 2012
14. Heuser, A., Picek, S., Guilley, S., Mentens, N.: Lightweight ciphers and their side-channel resilience. IEEE Trans. Comput. **PP**(99), 1 (2017). https://doi.org/10.1109/TC.2017.2757921
15. Kim, J., Picek, S., Heuser, A., Bhasin, S., Hanjalic, A.: Make some noise. Unleashing the power of convolutional neural networks for profiled side-channel analysis. IACR Trans. Cryptogr. Hardw. Embed. Syst. **2019**(3), 148–179 (2019). https://doi.org/10.13154/tches.v2019.i3.148-179. https://tches.iacr.org/index.php/TCHES/article/view/8292
16. Kocher, P., Jaffe, J., Jun, B.: Differential power analysis. In: Wiener, M. (ed.) CRYPTO 1999. LNCS, vol. 1666, pp. 388–397. Springer, Heidelberg (1999). https://doi.org/10.1007/3-540-48405-1_25
17. LeCun, Y., Bengio, Y., et al.: Convolutional networks for images, speech, and time series. In: The Handbook of Brain Theory and Neural Networks, vol. 3361, no. 10 (1995)
18. Lerman, L., Bontempi, G., Markowitch, O.: Power analysis attack: an approach based on machine learning. Int. J. Appl. Cryptol. **3**(2), 97–115 (2014). https://doi.org/10.1504/IJACT.2014.062722

19. Lerman, L., Poussier, R., Bontempi, G., Markowitch, O., Standaert, F.-X.: Template attacks vs. machine learning revisited (and the curse of dimensionality in side-channel analysis). In: Mangard, S., Poschmann, A.Y. (eds.) COSADE 2014. LNCS, vol. 9064, pp. 20–33. Springer, Cham (2015). https://doi.org/10.1007/978-3-319-21476-4_2

20. Maghrebi, H., Portigliatti, T., Prouff, E.: Breaking cryptographic implementations using deep learning techniques. In: Carlet, C., Hasan, M.A., Saraswat, V. (eds.) SPACE 2016. LNCS, vol. 10076, pp. 3–26. Springer, Cham (2016). https://doi.org/10.1007/978-3-319-49445-6_1

21. Medwed, M., Oswald, E.: Template attacks on ECDSA. In: Chung, K.-I., Sohn, K., Yung, M. (eds.) WISA 2008. LNCS, vol. 5379, pp. 14–27. Springer, Heidelberg (2009). https://doi.org/10.1007/978-3-642-00306-6_2

22. Minka, T.P.: Automatic choice of dimensionality for PCA. In: Advances in Neural Information Processing Systems, pp. 598–604 (2001)

23. Nascimento, E., Chmielewski, Ł., Oswald, D., Schwabe, P.: Attacking embedded ECC implementations through cmov side channels. In: Avanzi, R., Heys, H. (eds.) SAC 2016. LNCS, vol. 10532, pp. 99–119. Springer, Cham (2017). https://doi.org/10.1007/978-3-319-69453-5_6

24. van den Oord, A., et al.: WaveNet: a generative model for raw audio. arXiv preprint arXiv:1609.03499 (2016)

25. Pedregosa, F., et al.: Scikit-learn: machine learning in Python. J. Mach. Learn. Res. **12**, 2825–2830 (2011)

26. Picek, S., Heuser, A., Guilley, S.: Profiling side-channel analysis in the restricted attacker framework. Cryptology ePrint Archive, Report 2019/168 (2019). https://eprint.iacr.org/2019/168

27. Picek, S., Heuser, A., Jovic, A., Bhasin, S., Regazzoni, F.: The curse of class imbalance and conflicting metrics with machine learning for side-channel evaluations. IACR Trans. Cryptogr. Hardw. Embed. Syst. **2019**(1), 209–237 (2019). https://doi.org/10.13154/tches.v2019.i1.209-237

28. Picek, S., et al.: Side-channel analysis and machine learning: a practical perspective. In: 2017 International Joint Conference on Neural Networks, IJCNN 2017, Anchorage, AK, USA, 14–19 May 2017, pp. 4095–4102 (2017)

29. Picek, S., Samiotis, I.P., Kim, J., Heuser, A., Bhasin, S., Legay, A.: On the performance of convolutional neural networks for side-channel analysis. In: Chattopadhyay, A., Rebeiro, C., Yarom, Y. (eds.) SPACE 2018. LNCS, vol. 11348, pp. 157–176. Springer, Cham (2018). https://doi.org/10.1007/978-3-030-05072-6_10

30. Poussier, R., Zhou, Y., Standaert, F.-X.: A systematic approach to the side-channel analysis of ECC implementations with worst-case horizontal attacks. In: Fischer, W., Homma, N. (eds.) CHES 2017. LNCS, vol. 10529, pp. 534–554. Springer, Cham (2017). https://doi.org/10.1007/978-3-319-66787-4_26

31. Prouff, E., Strullu, R., Benadjila, R., Cagli, E., Dumas, C.: Study of deep learning techniques for side-channel analysis and introduction to ASCAD database. IACR Cryptology ePrint Archive **2018**, 53 (2018)

32. Samwel, N., Batina, L., Bertoni, G., Daemen, J., Susella, R.: Breaking Ed25519 in WolfSSL. In: Smart, N.P. (ed.) CT-RSA 2018. LNCS, vol. 10808, pp. 1–20. Springer, Cham (2018). https://doi.org/10.1007/978-3-319-76953-0_1

33. Schindler, W., Huss, S.A. (eds.): COSADE 2012. LNCS, vol. 7275. Springer, Heidelberg (2012). https://doi.org/10.1007/978-3-642-29912-4

34. Schnorr, C.P.: Efficient signature generation by smart cards. J. Cryptol. **4**(3), 161–174 (1991)

35. Simonyan, K., Zisserman, A.: Very deep convolutional networks for large-scale image recognition. arXiv preprint arXiv:1409.1556 (2014)
36. Standaert, F.-X., Malkin, T.G., Yung, M.: A unified framework for the analysis of side-channel key recovery attacks. In: Joux, A. (ed.) EUROCRYPT 2009. LNCS, vol. 5479, pp. 443–461. Springer, Heidelberg (2009). https://doi.org/10.1007/978-3-642-01001-9_26
37. Tuveri, N., Hassan, S.u., Garcia, C.P., Brumley, B.B.: Side-channel analysis of SM2: a late-stage featurization case study. In: Proceedings of the 34th Annual Computer Security Applications Conference, ACSAC 2018, pp. 147–160. ACM, New York (2018). https://doi.org/10.1145/3274694.3274725. http://doi.acm.org/10.1145/3274694.3274725
38. Vapnik, V.N.: The Nature of Statistical Learning Theory. Springer, New York (1995). https://doi.org/10.1007/978-1-4757-2440-0

An Efficient Parallel Implementation of Impossible-Differential Cryptanalysis for Five-Round AES-128

Debranjan Pal[✉], Dishank Agrawal, Abhijit Das,
and Dipanwita Roy Chowdhury

Crypto Research Lab, Department of Computer Science and Engineering,
IIT Kharagpur, Kharagpur, India
{debranjanpal,dishank,abhij,drc}@iitkgp.ac.in

Abstract. Impossible-differential cryptanalysis finds the correct round-key of a block cipher by eliminating wrong guesses which do not satisfy some impossible path(s). In this paper, we report our parallel implementation of the impossible-differential cryptanalysis of five-round AES-128, originally proposed by Biham and Keller [4]. In this attack, the time complexity is 2^{31} and the data complexity is $2^{29.5}$. But the primary memory requirement is very high, about 4 TB, making the attack somewhat impractical to implement. The first practical implementation of this attack appears in Kakarla et al. [11], where the primary memory requirement is reduced to 128.5 GB, and the running time achieved is 48 h. Here, we propose an improvement of the attack by exploiting data and task parallelism. We use a nine-node cluster (one master node and eight worker nodes) to implement the attack. In our attack, the time complexity and the data complexity remain the same as [11], but the primary memory requirement is reduced to 96.5 GB per node. This parallelism helps us retrieve the full key in only 6.5 mins.

Keywords: AES-128 · Impossible-differential Cryptanalysis · Precomputation · Parallel implementation · Distributed computation

1 Introduction

Rijndael is selected as the Advanced Encryption Standard (AES) [8] by the National Institute of Standards and Technology (NIST) in October 2000. Since then, AES is the most widely used symmetric-key block cipher used by the cryptographic community. Consequently, cryptanalysis of AES continues to be a very significant and active area of research in symmetric cryptology. The biclique attack [6] is the first key-recovery attack on full-round AES. The time complexity of this attack is too high: $2^{126.1}$ for AES-128, $2^{189.7}$ for AES-192, and $2^{254.4}$ for AES-256. Square attack [8] and impossible-differential cryptanalysis [3] are so far the most effective attacks on reduced-round AES. In this paper, we focus on the impossible-differential cryptanalysis of AES-128. Differential cryptanalysis [5]

© Springer Nature Switzerland AG 2019
S. Bhasin et al. (Eds.): SPACE 2019, LNCS 11947, pp. 106–122, 2019.
https://doi.org/10.1007/978-3-030-35869-3_9

is a type of chosen-plaintext attack which probabilistically correlates plaintext differences with last-round ciphertext differences. Impossible-differential cryptanalysis tries to exploit differentials in the cipher path, that can never occur, and the subkeys for which this incident occurs can be eliminated with impunity, thereby reducing the key-space.

Biham and Keller [4] introduce impossible-differential cryptanalysis (IDC) of five-round AES-128 in 2000. This attack requires $2^{29.5}$ chosen plaintexts, 2^{31} encryptions, 2^{42} bytes of memory, and 2^{37} one-round encryptions as precomputation. In 2001, Cheon et al. [7] apply IDC on six-round AES-128. They use about $2^{91.5}$ chosen plaintexts and 2^{122} encryptions of Rijndael. Another approach of the six-round attack is given by Zhang et al. [15] in 2007. The attack requires $2^{114.5}$ plaintexts and 2^{46} six-round encryptions, and the total memory requirement is 2^{45} bytes. In 2004, Phan [13] proposes an improved version of IDC on seven-round AES-192 and AES-256. Phan's attack on seven-round AES-192 uses 2^{92} chosen plaintexts, 2^{153} memory, and 2^{186} seven-round encryptions, whereas the attack on seven-round AES-256 requires $2^{92.5}$ chosen plaintexts, 2^{153} memory, and $2^{250.5}$ seven-round encryptions. Also, many other theoretically new attacks and improvements [1,9,12] are available for IDC in the literature.

Table 1. Key recovery attacks on 5-Round AES-128

Attack	Key	Data complexity	Memory	Time
Partial sum [14]	Partial key	2^8	Small	2^{38}
Square [8]	Partial key	2^{33}	64 GB	2^{34}
Improved square [9]	Partial Key	2^{33}	Small	2^{33}
MDC [10]	Partial key	2^{32}	64 GB	2^{32}
IDC [4]	Partial key	$2^{29.5}$	4 TB	2^{31}
IDC [11]	Full key	4×2^{32}	128.5 GB	2^{31}
MDC [2]	Partial key	$2^{21.5}$	45.25 MB	$2^{21.5}$

In Table 1, we summarize the major five-round key-recovery attacks on AES-128. Here, IDC and MDC stand for impossible-differential and mixture-differential cryptanalysis. Among these attacks, the only practically implemented attack on five-round AES-128 using IDC is reported by Kakarla et al. [11] in 2017. In what follows, we describe our improvement of this attack by adding parallelism in the implementation. In short, our contribution can be summarized as follows.

- We distribute the attack over multiple computing nodes not sharing any common memory. In each node, multiple cores run in parallel, and share memory among themselves.
- The precomputation time complexity is reduced from 2^{40} to 2^{37}.
- The total memory required is reduced from 128.5 GB to 96.5 GB per node.
- The total time required to get the full key is reduced from 48 h to 6.5 mins.

The rest of the paper is organized as follows. Section 2 provides the necessary background which includes a brief description of AES, the notations used in this paper, the four-round impossible-differential property of AES, and the original round-reduced attack of Biham [4]. Section 3 deals with our parallel implementation. Section 3.1 elaborates the data- and task-parallelism ideas used in our implementation. Section 3.2 gives a step-by-step procedure of the attack implementation. Our experimental results are presented in Sect. 4. Section 5 concludes the paper.

2   Differential Cryptanalysis of AES

2.1   A Brief Description of AES

AES has three variants. AES-128 uses 128-bit keys and has 10 rounds, AES-192 uses 192-bit keys and has 12 rounds, and AES-256 uses 256-bit keys and has 14 rounds. The block size is 128 bits in all these variants. The 128-bit input or output of any round of AES is a state matrix of size 4×4 as given in Fig. 1. Each element of the state matrix is a byte.

1	2	3	4
5	6	7	8
9	10	11	12
13	14	15	16

Fig. 1. Byte coordinates of an AES state

Each round of the AES encryption, except for the final one, performs the following operations. The last round is similar; only the MixColumn step is skipped. Moreover, before the first round, there is an XOR of the state with a 128-bit initial key.

- SubByte (SB): This is the only nonlinear operation of AES, and is applied byte-wise on the state matrix.
- ShiftRow (SR): This left shifts each row of the state matrix by a fixed number of bytes (except the first row).
- MixColumn (MC): This is a column-wise operation which multiplies each column of the state matrix with a constant MixColumn matrix.
- AddRoundKey (AK): The state matrix is XOR-ed with the 128-bit round key.

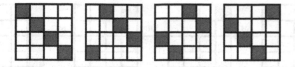

Fig. 2. Diagonal-wise byte positions of the plaintext

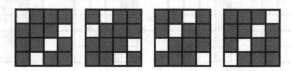

Fig. 3. Diagonal-wise byte positions of the ciphertext at the fifth-round output

The decryption process uses the inverse of each of the above operations. There is also a KeySchedule algorithm which generates the round keys. In this paper, we use the AES-128 variant, that is, all the keys are assumed to be of size 128 bits. In the rest of this paper, we use the following notations.

- P: Plaintext
- C: Ciphertext
- S_i: State matrix at the beginning of the i-th round.
- S_i^{SR}: State matrix after the ShiftRow operation of the i-th round.
- S_i^{BS}: State matrix after the SubBytes transformation of the i-th round.
- S_i^{MC}: State matrix after the MixColumn operation of the i-th round.
- S_i^{AK}: State matrix after the AddRoundKey step of the i-th round ($S_i^{AK} = S_{i+1}$).
- S^b: The b-th byte in the state for $b \in \{1, 2, \ldots, 16\}$ (see Fig. 1).
- K_0: The initial key.
- K_i: The round key in the i-th round ($i \geq 1$).
- P^D: The set of plaintext diagonals (given in Fig. 2 by filled boxes). This consists of four byte combinations:

$$P^D = \Big\{ (1, 6, 11, 16), (2, 7, 12, 13), (3, 8, 9, 14), (4, 5, 10, 15) \Big\}.$$

- C^D: The set of ciphertext diagonals (shown in Fig. 3 by unfilled or white boxes). This consists of four byte combinations:

$$C^D = \Big\{ (1, 8, 11, 14), (2, 5, 12, 15), (3, 6, 9, 16), (4, 7, 10, 13) \Big\}.$$

2.2 Four-Round Impossible-Differential Property of AES-128

In this section, we describe the four-round IDC property used by Biham and Keller [4]. Indeed, they use the four-round property to attack the five-round AES-128. Subsequently, this property is used in most of the higher-round attacks

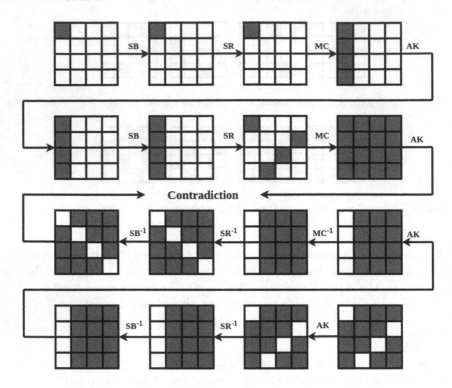

Fig. 4. Four-round Impossible-differential path

of this type. Here we take two chosen plaintexts as input. A byte in the state matrix, which is different(XOR difference is non-zero) in the encryptions of the two chosen plaintexts or after decryptions of the two generated ciphertexts, is called an active byte. A non-active byte is called passive. The position of the active bytes and passive bytes in chosen plaintexts are shown in Fig. 2. The active bytes are shown by filled boxes, and the passive bytes by white boxes.

Property 1 (MixColumn Property): In a state, if there is only one byte difference in a particular column, then after MixColumn the corresponding column will have all non zero differences.

In Fig. 4, let P_1 and P_2 be equal in all except one byte. The MixColumn property implies that after two round of encryption, all bytes become active. If C_1 and C_2 have zero difference in only one of the diagonals in C^D as in Fig. 3, then after two rounds of decryption, there will be zero difference only in one of the diagonal positions in P^D (with active and passive bytes switched in reference to Fig. 2). This observation leads to the following property.

Property 2 (Impossible-differential property): Let two plaintexts be equal in all bytes except one. Then after four rounds of encryption, the two ciphertexts cannot have zero differences in any one of the diagonals of C^D.

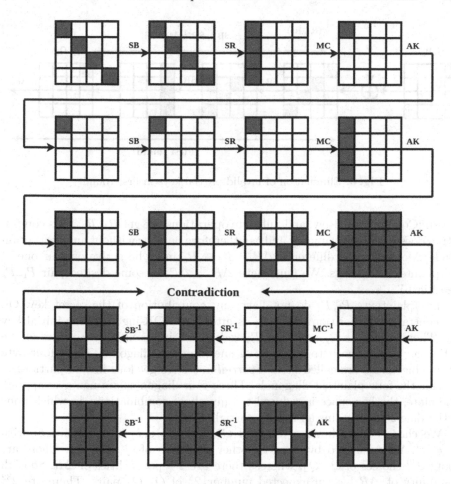

Fig. 5. Five-round Impossible-differential path

2.3   Five-Round Impossible-Differential Attack on AES-128

We now explain the five-round IDC on AES-128, as proposed by Biham and Keller [4]. To implement the five-round impossible-differential attack, an extra round is added at the top of the four-round impossible-differential path (see Fig. 5). Plaintext pairs which have active bytes in only any one of the diagonals from the set P^D are called *chosen pairs*. Those chosen pairs, for which the ciphertext pairs have passive bytes in any one of the diagonals from the set C^D, are called *desired pairs*.

Let P_1, P_2 be a desired pair. Let C_1, C_2 be the five-round encryptions of these plaintext messages, obtained by the encryption oracle. This means $\Delta C = C_1 \oplus C_2$ has passive bytes in one of the ciphertext diagonals. Also denote $\Delta P = P_1 \oplus P_2$.

Now, consider two states Q_1, Q_2 after the MixColumn operation of the first round such that their difference has only one active byte. Applying the inverses of

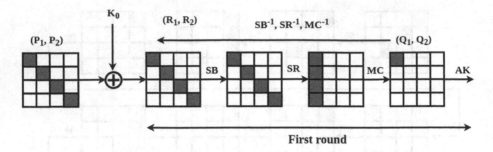

Fig. 6. Elimination of invalid partial keys in first round

the MixColumn, ShiftRow, and SubByte operations, we get R_1, R_2. This computation does not involve any key and can therefore be done without any decryption oracle. Moreover, the difference $\Delta R = R_1 \oplus R_2$ must be active only at one of the plaintext diagonals. We must have $\Delta R = \Delta P$ for some desired pair P_1, P_2 (see Fig. 6).

The plaintexts P_1, P_2 do not have any contribution of the secret key. On the contrary, the position of R_1, R_2 is after the XOR-ing with the initial key K_0. Therefore, $P_1 \oplus R_1$ and $P_2 \oplus R_1$ reveal two impossible byte values of the initial key K_0 in the byte positions of one plaintext diagonal. These four-byte impossible values are called *invalid partial keys*. We get four invalid partial-key sets for the four plaintext diagonals. These four diagonals are non-overlapping. Therefore, the key space is reduced to only those combinations, in which none of the diagonals contains an invalid partial key.

We choose one column of Q_1 and Q_2 as (w, x, y, z) and (w', x, y, z) with $w \neq w'$. We take zero bytes at all other positions of Q_1 and Q_2. There are about 2^{40} choices of Q_1, Q_2, whereas there are 2^{32} possibilities of ΔR. So each possibility of ΔR has an expected number 2^8 of Q_1, Q_2 pairs. There are 2^{32} plaintexts with one active diagonal, and the number of pairs of such plaintexts is $\binom{2^{32}}{2} \approx 2^{63}$. For each pair, the probability that one of the ciphertext diagonals is passive after five rounds of encryption is 2^{-32}. Since there are four ciphertext diagonals, the probability that any one of these is passive is 2^{-30}. So the expected number of desired pairs is $2^{63} \times 2^{-30} = 2^{33}$. Two invalid partial keys discovered in the process are the same with probability 2^{-32}. Finally, we work with 2^{32} chosen plaintexts. Therefore the expected number of wrong keys that remain after this filtering is about

$$2^{32} \left(1 - 2^{-32}\right)^{2^{33} \cdot 2^8} \approx 0 \tag{1}$$

Biham and Keller [4] argue that the working of the attack actually needs $2^{29.5}$ chosen plaintexts, yielding 2^{28} desired pairs. The precomputation cost is 2^{37} one-round decryptions. In the key elimination part, 2^{31} five-round encryptions are needed. The memory requirement is 4 TB.

This attack requires the maintenance of two tables. First, we need a table to identify all the desired pairs. To start with, we fix a plaintext diagonal and a ciphertext diagonal. Let P be a plaintext with active bytes only in the fixed plaintext diagonal. Let p be the 32-bit value in these active byte positions. We invoke the encryption oracle to obtain the five-round encryption C of P. We then extract from C the 32-bit value c from the position of the fixed ciphertext diagonal. The *desired pair table* stores p indexed by c. Multiple entries p_1, p_2 stored in the same index c corresponds to a plaintext pair (P_1, P_2) for which $\Delta C = C_1 \oplus C_2$ has passive bytes in the given ciphertext diagonal. These desired pairs allow us to eliminate invalid partial keys using the second table.

For constructing the second table, called the *hash table*, we generate all of the 2^{40} combinations of Q_1, Q_2, and compute the corresponding R_1, R_2 and subsequently $\Delta R = R_1 \oplus R_2$, as explained above. Let r_1 and δ_r be the 32-bit values extracted from the given plaintext diagonals of R_1 and ΔR, respectively. The hash table stores r_1 in the index δ_r. The expected size of the list at each hash-table index is 2^8.

3   Parallel Implementation of IDC for Five-Round AES-128

We implement the IDC algorithm on a cluster with one master node and eight worker nodes. The nodes do not share any memory, so some relevant data need to be copied to each of these. Each node runs 32 cores which can share data stored in the memory of that node.

Figure 7 gives the broad phases of the five-round IDC algorithm. In the precomputation phase, the hash table is generated by one-round decryption starting at S_1^{SM}. Also, by making five-round encryption requests to the oracle, the desired pair table is generated corresponding to each plaintext diagonal and each ciphertext diagonal. The precomputations proceed in the worker nodes in parallel. In the key elimination phase, all the invalid partial keys are identified for each plaintext diagonal. This stage uses both the hash table and the desired pair table, and is carried out in parallel at the eight worker nodes. The worker nodes eventually return four reduced valid partial-key sets. Finally, the full-key recovery phase is distributed to the eight working nodes which merge the partial key sets to a set of possible full keys, and identify the correct full key by making a brute force search over all these possibilities.

3.1   Task Distribution Across the Worker Nodes

As mentioned above, the phases that are parallelized across the eight worker nodes are hash-table generation, desired-pair table generation, and partial-key elimination. All these phases have data-parallelism possibilities in the sense that the different worker nodes perform the same task in parallel on different sets of data. The work of each node in these stages is broken down to 32 subtasks, each running on a single core. The final full-key recovery phase is likewise distributed to the eight worker nodes, each involving its 32 cores to complete its task.

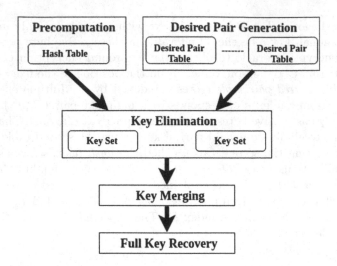

Fig. 7. Phases of the IDC implementation process

Parallelism in Hash-Table Generation. The hash table is generated by iterating over all of the 2^{40} values of (w, w', x, y, z), calculating the states R_1, R_2 by one-round decryption, and then storing $r_1 = \text{Extract}_{32}(R_1)$ in the index $\delta_r = \text{Extract}_{32}(\Delta R) = \text{Extract}_{32}(R_1 \oplus R_2)$. Here, the method "Extract$_{32}$" extracts the 32 bits of a plaintext diagonal. The procedure is elaborated in Algorithm 1. Since, we have eight worker nodes, we divide the set of 2^{40} calculations into eight sets of size $2^{40}/8 = 2^{37}$, one assigned to each worker node. The hash-table parts generated by the eight worker nodes can be merged.

Algorithm 1. Generation of the hash table

1: **procedure** FORMHASHTABLE( )
2:      $HashTable \leftarrow Empty$
3:      **for** tuples (w, w', x, y, z) assigned to the worker node, **do**
4:          $Q_1 \leftarrow$ InitializeColumn(w, x, y, z)
5:          $Q_2 \leftarrow$ InitializeColumn(w', x, y, z)
6:          $R_1 \leftarrow SB^{-1}(SR^{-1}(MC^{-1}(Q_1)))$
7:          $R_2 \leftarrow SB^{-1}(SR^{-1}(MC^{-1}(Q_2)))$
8:          $r_1 = \text{Extract}_{32}(R_1)$
9:          $\delta_r = \text{Extract}_{32}(R_1 \oplus R_2)$
10:         Append$(Hashtable[\delta_r], r_1)$
11:     **end for**
12:     **return**

Parallelism for Plaintext Diagonals. In our implementation, partial keys for one plaintext diagonal can be eliminated independently of the other three diagonals. So the partial-key elimination phase for the four diagonals can run in parallel

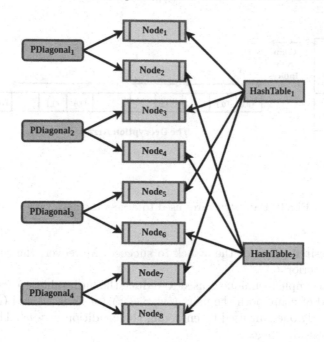

Fig. 8. Hash table and desired pair table mapping into worker nodes

without any dependency. Since, we have eight nodes in our cluster, we distribute the work for each diagonal to two nodes.

Hash Table Division. The hash table is divided into two parts to reduce the RAM requirements for this attack. The hash table contains 2^{32} rows indexed by the 32-bit value δ_r. We divide the table into two expectedly equal-sized halves H_0 and H_1 based on the most significant bit of δ_r. Along with the division of the work with respect to the plaintext diagonals, this creates a total of eight subtasks in the partial-key elimination phase. Eventually, the eight worker nodes produce eight valid partial-key sets, each corresponding to one plaintext diagonal and one half of the hash table. Figure 8 illustrates this division of work.

3.2   The Attack Procedure

In this subsection, we elaborate the different steps of our implementation.

Optimizing Memory Requirement. In our description given so far, the hash table stores an expected number 2^{40} of 4-byte entries distributed across 2^{32} indices. The memory requirement in bytes for this storage is four times 2^{40}, that is, 4 TB. This is a very high requirement for most modern machines. We propose ways of reducing the space occupied by the hash table. This requires a larger

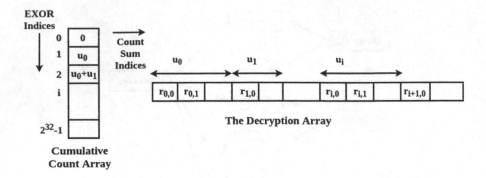

Fig. 9. Data structures used to access the hash table

number of desired pairs for the attack to succeed. Moreover, the running time should not deteriorate.

Initially, a simple technique is used to reduce the hash table size from 4 TB to 2 TB. Instead of using both the pairs $((w, x, y, z), (w', x, y, z))$ and $((w', x, y, z), (w, x, y, z))$, only one pair used by enforcing the condition $w > w'$. This memory is still impractically huge.

Biham and Keller [4] argue that instead of 2^{32} chosen plaintexts, one can work with only $2^{29.5}$ plaintexts. The hash-table size is kept at 2^{40} bytes. Kakarla et al. [11] propose a trade-off which uses all of the 2^{32} available plaintexts. They then throw away a part of the hash table.

Let the average number of entries per hash table index be 2^m, $0 \le m \le 7$. Then, for each desired pair, 2^{m+1} partial keys are expected to be discarded. If the number of desired pairs is 2^n, the number of potentially correct partial keys is given by

$$2^{32} \left(1 - 2^{-32}\right)^{2^{m+1} \cdot 2^n} \tag{2}$$

According to the probability calculations of [4], we should have

$$m + n + 1 = 36 \implies n = 35 - m \tag{3}$$

So, the total number of hash table entries is 2^{32+m}. For obtaining 2^n desired pairs, the number of chosen plaintexts required is $2^{(n+31)/2}$, that is, $2^{33-m/2}$ for $n = 35 - m$. Since we want to reduce m as much as possible, and we have the option of using at most 2^{32} chosen plaintexts, we set $33 - m/2 = 32$, that is, $m = 2$. This means that the hash table now contains $2^{32+m} = 2^{34}$ entries, and the memory requirement drops to 64 GB.

Hash Table Accessing. To access the hash table efficiently during the key-elimination phase, we maintain two arrays (see Fig. 9).

- The decryption array: This is used to store the r values generated after one round of decryption. The total no of r values is 2^{32}. For the choice $m = 2$

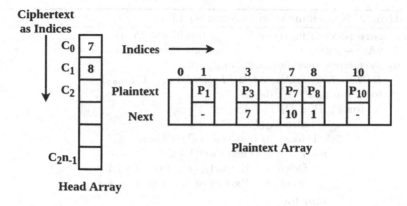

Fig. 10. List for storing plaintext-ciphertext pairs for identifying desired pairs

explained above, the expected number of entries per index is four, so a total of about 2^{34} entries are stored in the array.

- Cumulative count array: For an index r, let u_r denote the number of entries in the decryption array with the given r value. In the cumulative count array, we store the partial sums $0, u_0, u_0+u_1, u_0+u_1+u_2, \ldots, (u_0+u_1+u_2+\ldots+u_{2^{32}-2})$.

Desired Pair Table Generation. For each diagonal, 2^{32} plaintexts expectedly generate 2^{33} desired pairs before the key-elimination phase. We do not store the pairs explicitly. We instead store the extracted 32-bit plaintext p against the extracted 32-bit ciphertext c. The plaintext extractions p corresponding to the same ciphertext extraction c are stored as a linked list in an array called the plaintext array. The first index of each list is stored in a head array. Figure 10 illustrates this organization of the data. For example, the ciphertext c_0 arises from the plaintexts p_3, p_7, p_{10}, whereas the ciphertext c_1 originates from p_8, p_1.

Key Elimination. This phase runs in parallel at eight worker nodes. For invalidating the partial keys, we take a desired pair (P_1, P_2), and compute $\delta_r = \text{Extract}_{32}(P_1 \oplus P_2)$. If this index is not present in the part of the hash table assigned to the given node, nothing is done (this is processed by another node). Otherwise, for each r value stored at index δ_r of the hash table, the partial keys $r \oplus \text{Extract}_{32}(P_1)$ and $r \oplus \text{Extract}_{32}(P_2)$ are recorded as invalid. The key-elimination procedure for a particular node is given as Algorithm 2. Each node takes a plaintext diagonal and one of the two parts of the hash table as input.

Key-Set Merging and Full Key Recovery. To recover the correct full key, we perform the following steps.

- **Key-Set Merging:** Take the intersection of the two key arrays calculated by a pair of nodes for a single plaintext diagonal. The hash table is divided

---

Algorithm 2. Key elimination at a worker node

1: **procedure** KEYELIMINATION(PT_{Diag}, $HashTablePart$)
2:     $KeyArr \leftarrow$ AllKeys   ▷ Initially mark all possible 4-byte keys as valid
3:     **for** each ciphertext diagonal CT_{Diag}, **do**
4:         $DPT \leftarrow CreateDesiredPairTable(PT_{Diag}, CT_{Diag})$
5:         **for** $c = 0$ to $2^{32} - 1$ **do**
6:             **for** $P_1, P_2 \in DPT[c]$ **do**
7:                 $\delta_r \leftarrow$ Extract$_{32}(P_1 \oplus P_2)$
8:                 **if** δ_r belongs to $HashTablePart$ **then**
9:                     **for** $r \in HashTablePart[\delta_r]$ **do**
10:                         Delete $r \oplus$ Extract$_{32}(P_1)$ from $KeyArr$
11:                         Delete $r \oplus$ Extract$_{32}(P_2)$ from $KeyArr$
12:                     **end for**
13:                 **end if**
14:             **end for**
15:         **end for**
16:     **end for**
17:     **return**($KeyArr$)

---

in two parts, and two nodes for a given plaintext diagonal handle these two parts independently. Only the keys not eliminated by both the nodes are kept for further consideration.

- **Full Key Recovery:** Finally, we have around 480–500 partial keys for each of the diagonals. We combine them, and make a brute-force search on the reduced key-space to recover the correct full key.

4   Implementation and Results

Our code is executed on a cluster with one master node (working as the coordinator), eight worker nodes, connected by InfiniBand switch. Each node has 32 cores clocked at 2.1 GHz. Each worker node has 128 GB RAM. The gcc compiler version 4.8.5 is used along with the POSIX threads (Pthread) API. We have compiled our prgrams with the -O2 optimization flag.

We now work out the exact space usage and report the running time achieved by our implementation.

- **Space Usage:** The total space required for the entire hash table is $2^{34} \times 4 + 2^{32} \times 8 = 96$ GB. With the splitting of the hash table, each plaintext diagonal involves two nodes, each of which works on its part of the hash table. This reduces the space usage of the Count and Decryption arrays per node to 48 GB. To access the desired pair table, the Head array takes $2^{32} \times 4 = 16$ GB space, and the Plaintext array takes $2^{32} \times 8 = 32$ GB. Finally, the boolean array $KeyArr$ takes only 0.5 GB, bringing the total RAM requirement in each worker node to about 96.5 GB. Table 2 summarizes these space-usage figures. It is to be noted that our implementation does not reduce the overall space complexity of the attack. Since our program runs on multiple nodes having no shared memory, we have to replicate the hash-table data across nodes. However, different desired-pair tables are used in different nodes.

- **Running Time:** The precomputation of the hash table incurs only a one-time cost of 2^{36} one-round decryptions and is independent of any key. Our implementation needs 2^{32} chosen plaintexts for each plaintext diagonal, so the total data complexity is $4 \times 2^{32} = 2^{34}$ (oracle encryptions). For each desired pair in the key-elimination phase, we need to check an average of four entries from the hash table at the relevant hash index, so the expected number of XOR calculations is $2^{33} \times 2^3 = 2^{36}$, which is roughly equivalent to the time of 2^{31} five-round encryptions [4].

We have implemented the attack on the distributed platform with one thread running in each node. The running time of our implementation is about two hours for each worker node. This time pertains to the key-elimination phase (Algorithm 2), and does not include the time for the generation of the hash table and the desired-pair tables. Traditionally, these are treated as precomputation stages. In the full-key recovery phase, the brute-force search is distributed to the eight worker nodes resulting in a further reduction in the parallel running time. It requires about 10 min to retrieve the correct key using brute-force search. So, the total time required for the key-elimination and the full-key recovery phases is 2 h 10 min.

Table 2. Memory requirement at each worker node

Data structure	Memory requirement
Hash table	48 GB
Head array	16 GB
Plaintext array	32 GB
Key array	0.5 GB
Total	96.5 GB

If the tasks done by the eight worker nodes are sequentially carried out in a single node (like the master node), the total sequential time achieved by our implementation would be 8×2 h $+ 8 \times 10$ mins ≈ 17.33 h. We have not implemented this sequential version. Table 3 reports the projected running time.

We have also carried out a multi-threaded implementation. Each node of our cluster has 32 cores, so the computation at each node can be shared by these available cores. Both the key-elimination stage and the brute-force key-merging stage have parallelization potentials. We face some synchronization and critical-section issues during the key-elimination phase. As the threads invalidate the wrong subkeys in $KeyArr$ in parallel, we need to handle concurrent writes by multiple threads. If the entire $KeyArr$ is guarded by a mutex (semaphore), then all the writes proceed sequentially, thereby leading to a significant loss of parallelization. On the other hand, if we guard each element of *KeyArr* by a mutex, the number of mutexes will be astronomically large. As a practical compromise, the *KeyArr* is divided into 1024 equal-sized blocks. One mutex is used to guard each block, so we need a total of 1024 mutexes. When a thread updates the status of a key in a block, it locks the mutex pertaining to that block only. This ensures mutual exclusion of concurrent write requests to the same block. Since 32 threads run in parallel, and there are 1024 mutexes, the probability of a collision is no more than $1/2$ by the birthday paradox. That is, the event that a thread has to wait for acquiring its lock is rather infrequent.

After effectively handling the concurrent-write problem, the running time we get is 6.5 min (6 min for key elimination and 30 s for full key recovery using brute-force search).

Performance Comparison

A comparison of the theoretical performance of our approach with those of Biham and Keller [4] and Kakarla et al. [11] is given in Table 3. Also, the comparison for implementation with respect to running time is given in Table 4.

Table 3. Comparison of performance for full key recovery of five-round AES-128 using IDC

Attack	Data complexity	Memory used
Biham and Keller [4]	$4 \times 2^{29.5}$	4 TB
Kakarla et al. [11]	4×2^{32}	128.5 GB
This work	4×2^{32}	96.5 GB per node

Table 4. Comparison with respect to time required for full key recovery

Implementation	Type	System used	Time taken
Kakarla et al. [11]	Sequential	Centralized Server	48 h
This work	Sequential	Single node, one thread	17 h 20 min
	Distributed	Eight worker and one master nodes, one thread per node	2 h 10 min
	Distributed	Eight worker and one master nodes, 32 threads per node	6.5 min

Communication Complexity

The running times reported above do not include the time needed for distributing data (hash-table parts and desired-pair tables) to the worker nodes. We use a 56 Gbps InfiniBand switch to speed up this data transmission. We experience a communication delay of about 10–12 min in our implementation. Ironically, this is larger than the best computation times achieved. This overhead can however be completely eliminated by storing the relevant data in the local hard disk of each worker node. Indeed, these data are generated by the precomputation phase, and their distribution can be considered as a part of precomputation.

5   Conclusion

In this paper, we report our parallel implementation of impossible-differential cryptanalysis of five-rounds AES. We propose a way to distribute the data and the tasks to eight working nodes. This results in practical memory usage in each node, and a sizeable reduction in the running time over a previous implementation. Indeed, to the best of our knowledge, ours is the fastest implementation of this attack.

Extensions of this attack to work for more than five rounds of AES increase data and time complexities almost unmanageably. While theoretical estimates for six-round and seven-round AES are available in the literature, effective implementations of these attacks are never attempted, and remain as challenging open problems to the cryptology community.

References

1. Bahrak, B., Aref, M.R.: Impossible differential attack on seven-round AES-128. IET Inf. Secur. **2**(2), 28–32 (2008). https://doi.org/10.1049/iet-ifs:20070078
2. Bar-On, A., Dunkelman, O., Keller, N., Ronen, E., Shamir, A.: Improved key recovery attacks on reduced-round AES with practical data and memory complexities. In: Advances in Cryptology - CRYPTO 2018–38th Annual International Cryptology Conference, Santa Barbara, CA, USA, August 19–23, 2018, Proceedings, Part II, pp. 185–212 (2018). https://doi.org/10.1007/978-3-319-96881-0_7
3. Biham, Eli, Biryukov, Alex, Shamir, Adi: Cryptanalysis of skipjack reduced to 31 rounds using impossible differentials. In: Stern, Jacques (ed.) EUROCRYPT 1999. LNCS, vol. 1592, pp. 12–23. Springer, Heidelberg (1999). https://doi.org/10.1007/3-540-48910-X_2
4. Biham, E., Keller, N.: Cryptanalysis of reduced variants of rijndael. In: 3rd AES Conference, vol. 230 (2000)
5. Biham, E., Shamir, A.: Differential Cryptanalysis of the Data Encryption Standard. Springer-Verlag, Berlin (1993)
6. Bogdanov, A., Khovratovich, D., Rechberger, C.: Biclique cryptanalysis of the full AES. In: Advances in Cryptology - ASIACRYPT 2011–17th International Conference on the Theory and Application of Cryptology and Information Security, Seoul, South Korea, December 4–8, 2011. Proceedings, pp. 344–371 (2011). https://doi.org/10.1007/978-3-642-25385-0_19

7. Cheon, Jung Hee, Kim, MunJu, Kim, Kwangjo, Jung-Yeun, Lee, Kang, Sung-Woo: Improved impossible differential cryptanalysis of rijndael and crypton. In: Kim, Kwangjo (ed.) ICISC 2001. LNCS, vol. 2288, pp. 39–49. Springer, Heidelberg (2002). https://doi.org/10.1007/3-540-45861-1_4

8. Daemen, J., Rijmen, V.: The Design of Rijndael: AES - The Advanced Encryption Standard. Information Security and Cryptography, Springer, Berlin (2002). https://doi.org/10.1007/978-3-662-04722-4

9. Ferguson, Niels, Kelsey, John, Lucks, Stefan, Schneier, Bruce, Stay, Mike, Wagner, David, Whiting, Doug: Improved cryptanalysis of rijndael. In: Goos, Gerhard, Hartmanis, Juris, van Leeuwen, Jan, Schneier, Bruce (eds.) FSE 2000. LNCS, vol. 1978, pp. 213–230. Springer, Heidelberg (2001). https://doi.org/10.1007/3-540-44706-7_15

10. Grassi, L.: Mixture differential cryptanalysis: a new approach to distinguishers and attacks on round-reduced AES. IACR Trans. Symmetric Cryptol. **2018**(2), 133–160 (2018). https://doi.org/10.13154/tosc.v2018.i2.133-160

11. Kakarla, S., Mandava, S., Saha, D., Roy Chowdhury, D.: On the practical implementation of impossible differential cryptanalysis on reduced-round AES. In: Applications and Techniques in Information Security - 8th International Conference, ATIS 2017, Auckland, New Zealand, July 6–7, 2017, Proceedings, pp. 58–72 (2017). https://doi.org/10.1007/978-981-10-5421-1_6

12. Mala, H., Dakhilalian, M., Rijmen, V., Modarres-Hashemi, M.: Improved impossible differential cryptanalysis of 7-round AES-128. In: Progress in Cryptology - INDOCRYPT 2010–11th International Conference on Cryptology in India, Hyderabad, India, December 12–15 2010, Proceedings, pp. 282–291 (2010). https://doi.org/10.1007/978-3-642-17401-8_20

13. Phan, R.C.: Impossible differential cryptanalysis of 7-round advanced encryption standard (AES). Inf. Process. Lett. **91**(1), 33–38 (2004). https://doi.org/10.1016/j.ipl.2004.02.018

14. Tunstall, M.: Improved "partial sums"-based square attack on AES. IACR Cryptology ePrint Archive 2012, 280 (2012). http://eprint.iacr.org/2012/280

15. Zhang, W., Wu, W., Feng, D.: New results on impossible differential cryptanalysis of reduced AES. In: Information Security and Cryptology - ICISC 2007, 10th International Conference, Seoul, Korea, November 29–30, 2007, Proceedings, pp. 239–250 (2007). https://doi.org/10.1007/978-3-540-76788-6_19

Automated Classification
of Web-Application Attacks
for Intrusion Detection

Harsh Bhagwani, Rohit Negi, Aneet Kumar Dutta, Anand Handa[✉],
Nitesh Kumar, and Sandeep Kumar Shukla

C3I Center, Department of CSE, Indian Institute of Technology, Kanpur, India
harshbhagwani@ymail.com,
{rohit,aneet,ahanda,niteshkr,sandeeps}@cse.iitk.ac.in

Abstract. In today's information driven society and economy, web facing applications are most common way to run information dissemination, banking, e-commerce etc. Web applications are frequently targeted by attackers through intelligently crafted http requests to exploit vulnerabilities existing in the application, front-end, and the web-clients. Some of the most frequent such attacks are SQL Injection, Cross-Site Scripting, Path-traversal, Command Injection, Cross-site request forgery etc. Detecting these attacks up front and blocking them, or redirecting the request to a honey-pot could be a way to prevent web applications from being exploited. In this work, we developed a number of machine learning models for detecting and classifying http requests into normal, and various types of attacks. Currently, the models are applied as an ensemble on the http server logs, to classify and build data analytics on the http requests received by any web server in order to garner threat intelligence, and threat landscape. We also implemented an online log-analysis version that analyzes logs every 15 s to classify http requests in the recent 15 s. However, it can also be used as a web application firewall to block the http requests based on the classification results. We also have implemented an intrusion protection mechanism by redirecting http requests classified upfront as malicious towards a web honeypot. We compare various existing signature based, regular expression based, and machine learning based techniques against our models for detection and classification of http based attacks, and show that our methods achieve better performance over existing techniques.

Keywords: Intrusion detection system · Web security · Machine learning

1 Introduction

In the last few years, there has been a tremendous growth in the use of the Internet. According to the Internet World statistics, the number of Internet users has increased by 30% within a decade [10]. From booking an appointment for

© Springer Nature Switzerland AG 2019
S. Bhasin et al. (Eds.): SPACE 2019, LNCS 11947, pp. 123–141, 2019.
https://doi.org/10.1007/978-3-030-35869-3_10

health check-ups to online purchasing, the Internet is becoming part and parcel of our lives. With the introduction of these web facing services, there has been a huge growth in the web-application attacks which necessitates timely detection of attacks and prevention. Malicious users are exploiting the vulnerabilities of these services to obtain the personal data of other users, and affecting the quality of service. According to the survey done by Sophos, India is ranked third in the world, in the number of cyber attacks in 2018 and around 76% of the Indian organizations faced cyber attacks in 2018 [9]. In another survey done by Small Business Trends, hackers have targeted 43% of the start-ups, and around 60% of them have gone out of business within a few months of the attacks [24].

According to the ENISA Threat Landscape report (ETL) of 2018 [18], web application attack is ranked 3rd, consecutively for two years, among other attacks in the cyber domain. Among the various types of web application attacks, there are different techniques of different levels of difficulties, and different damages they cause. In ETL 2018 report, SQL injection [5] dominates the web application attacks with a share of 51%. Local File Inclusion and Cross-Site Scripting (XSS) [7] come 2nd and 3rd in the attack ranking respectively. Attacks like injection (mainly including SQL, Lightweight Directory Access Protocol (LDAP) [29], XML Path (XPath) [2], etc.) and XSS come under one of the categories in the OWASP Top 10 list of the most common attacks [28]. According to a report published by Positive Technologies in 2017 [35], SQL injection and Cross-site Scripting together have contributed about 50% of the attacks.

Intrusion Detection Systems (IDS) are security applications that monitor a computer network or hosts therein, to detect any malicious activities or threats. On detection, they alert the system administrators [17,23,32]. Alerting may vary from logging the attacks in log files or alerting an administrator on security dashboards to take necessary actions. Ideally, an Intrusion Detection System should be simple, fast and precise. But it is impossible for an IDS to provide complete protection as no detection method is 100% accurate. They make two types of errors: False Positive - this is generally when a normal access is falsely considered as a threat and False Negative - when a real attack goes undetected by the IDS systems. Although, false positives are acceptable because they are passed to the administrator for reviews, too many false positives can be a burden for them as well. However, false negatives are never reviewed by the administrator as they are mistaken as non-malicious threats. Hence, most of the organizations tune their IDS from time to time to ensure close to zero false negatives, and close to tolerance level of false positives.

One could use many different techniques to implement an IDS. Signature based techniques use existing database of patterns for malicious access which are matched against incoming activities (in web-application case, http requests). Regular expression based signature schemes generalize the static patterns for such detection. However, in this work, we show that these methods are often not very effective in reducing false negatives or false positives. Also, as attackers apply more intelligent encoding schemes to hide their malicious payload, static or regular expression based patterns can be easily bypassed. Rule based techniques are another generalization of pattern matching. Dynamic learning of rules for attack detection with reinforcement learning could be one way to mitigate these problems – however, that requires complex training process, and requires administrators to be interactive. Customers of IDS often want out-of-the-box solutions rather than those requiring training on-site. Machine learning based on past attack payloads therefore have been proposed by a number of researchers. However, most prior work seem to be focused on detection of SQL injection, and Cross-site scripting attacks. Our goal in this work has been to build a tool that uses an ensemble of models trained to detect a larger variety of attacks, and use the ensemble to classify the http requests into different attack types. We also target offline detection from log files, and online detection from incremental log files of http servers. Further, we are in the process of applying the same ensemble of models to detect attacks even before the request has been executed by the web application – thereby creating a web-application firewall. However, in this paper, we only discuss the log file based detection. One might question the need for classification/detection after the request has been processed – by analyzing after the fact, from log files. This is useful when one has a web application that is highly secure with all vulnerabilities patched, hence the malicious requests have no effect even when processed, but after the fact analysis provides system administrators with statistics of various kinds of attack attempts, the payload structures, and thereby the threat landscape.

Therefore, the models presented in this paper feeds on the log files of the web applications to detect attacks like SQLi, XSS, path traversal [11, 26], OS command [30], Server Side Includes (SSI) [34], LDAP, CRLF [6], and XPath. It is able to detect the mentioned eight most popular attacks along with any other anomalies which cannot be classified in one of the above classes of attacks. The same machine learning based tool can be turned into a firewall by intercepting http requests before it is delivered to the web application.

It is to be noted that a web server provides two different log files - access log and error log. The access log maintains the history of all the requests a web server receives and the error log maintains the records of all the error a web server encountered while processing the requests. This work focuses more on 'access.log' because it contains all the necessary information required to monitor the server. In Table 1 the various fields in a typical log file entry are shown.

Due to lack of space, we do not provide the definitions of the eight different web application attacks considered in this paper. Readers unfamiliar with the definitions of these attacks are referred to [2, 6, 11, 12, 29, 30, 34, 36].

The rest of the paper is organized as: In Sect. 2, we discuss the existing regular expression based approaches and machine learning based approaches to detect or classify web application attacks. Section 3 discusses our proposed framework. In Sect. 4, we evaluate our proposed framework and discuss the results. Section 5 compares our framework with the existing approaches, and finally, we conclude the paper in Sect. 6 with some discussion on future work.

Table 1. Definition of different log fields

Fields	Definition
122.172.41.188	Client's IP address
–	The identity of the client on client's machine
–	Username of the client if the request was authenticated
$[24/Jun/2018{:}08{:}12{:}12 + 0000]$	Time at which the request was received
"GET /main.php HTTP/1.1"	This contains HTTP method, path of the requested resource and HTTP protocol version used by client
200	It is a status code send by the server to the client after processing the request
203	Size of the resources requested by client
–	Referrer - Indicates from where did the request arrived
"Mozilla/5.0 (Macintosh; Intel Mac OS X 10_10_5) Gecko/ 20100101 Firefox/45.0"	Gives information about the user making requests like web browser, OS used, website source etc

2   Related Work

In this section we outline the different existing approaches to detect or classify web application attacks.

2.1   Regular Expression Based Approaches

Regular Expression or Regex is a set of strings represented in an algebraic format which is used to describe the search pattern of a string [26]. This makes regex fit for text processing, data validation and searching of strings. Searching strings using regular expression is fast. A proposed method of detection of web application attacks from entries in http server log files using regular expressions, can be found in [26]. The paper proposes regular expressions to match http requests formed by attackers in cases of XSS, code injection attacks (such as SQLi, LDAPi, XPath and OS Command) and Path Traversal attack. The regular expressions may be able to detect both obfuscated and non-obfuscated version of attacks. They search for keywords like scripts, update, insert,../, etc. (which are found in these attacks) in the received requests. Although they do not provide any analysis of accuracy or precision of applying these regular expression on log files, still their prescribed regular expressions are widely used in many web application IDS. Table 2 shows the attack types and their corresponding regular expressions provided in [26] for SQLi, XSS, and Path Traversal. The regular expressions for other attacks are missing in [26]. Later in this paper, we measure the accuracy of detection using these regular expressions on test data to check their accuracy.

Table 2. Regular expressions used in [26].

Attack type	Regular expression
XSS	$1./((\backslash\%3C)\,\vert<)(\backslash\%2F)\,\vert\,\backslash/)*[az09\backslash\%]+((\backslash\%3E)\,\vert>)/ix$
	$2./((\backslash\%3C)\,\vert<)((\backslash\%69)\,\vert\,i\,\vert\,(\backslash\%49))((\backslash\%6D)\,\vert\,m\,\vert\,(\backslash\%4D))$
	$((\backslash\%67)\,\vert\,g\,\vert\,(\backslash\%47))[\wedge\backslash n]+((\backslash\%3E)\,\vert>)/I$
	$3.\backslash(javascript\,\vert\,vbscript\,\vert\,expression\,\vert\,applet\,\vert\,script\,\vert\,embed\,\vert$
	$object\,\vert\,iframe\,\vert\,frame\,\vert\,frameset)/i$
SQLi	$1./(\backslash')\,\vert\,(\backslash\%27)\,\vert\,(\backslash\backslash)\,\vert\,(\#)\,\vert\,(\backslash\%23)/ix$
	$2./((\backslash\%3D)\,\vert\,(=))[\wedge\backslash n]*((\backslash\%27)\,\vert\,(\backslash')\,\vert\,(\backslash\backslash)\,\vert\,(\backslash\%3B)\,\vert\,(;))/i$
	$3./\backslash w*((\backslash\%27)\,\vert\,(\backslash'))(\backslash s\,\vert\,\backslash+\,\vert\,\backslash\%20)*((\backslash\%6F)\,\vert\,o\,\vert$
	$(\backslash\%4F))((\backslash\%72)\,\vert\,r\,\vert\,(\backslash\%52))/ix$
	$4./((\backslash\%27)\,\vert\,(\backslash'))(select\,\vert\,union\,\vert\,insert\,\vert\,update\,\vert\,delete\,\vert$
	$replace\,\vert\,truncate)/ix$
	$5./exec(\backslash s\,\vert\,\backslash+)+(s\,\vert\,x)p\backslash w+/ix$
Path Traversal	$/(\backslash.\,\vert\,(\%\,\vert\,\%25)2E)(\backslash.\,\vert\,(\%\,\vert\,\%25)2E)(\backslash/(\%\,\vert\,\%25)2F\,\vert\,\backslash\backslash\,\vert\,(\%\,\vert$
	$\%25)5C)/i$
SSI	Not Provided
OS Command	Not Provided
XPath	Not Provided
CRLF	Not Provided
LDAP	Not Provided

Table 3. Regular expressions used by [27]

Attack type	Regular expressions used by OWASP ModSecurity
XSS	$http:\backslash/\backslash/[\backslash w\backslash.]+?\backslash/.*?\backslash.pdf\backslash b[\wedge\backslash x0d\backslash x0a]*\#$
SQLi	No Regular Expression provided
Path Traversal	No Regular Expression provided
SSI	$<!--\backslash W*?\#\backslash W*?(?:e(?:cho\,\vert\,xec)\,\vert\,printenv\,\vert\,include\,\vert$
	$cmd)$
OS Command	$(?i:(?:[\backslash;\backslash\,\vert\,\backslash']\backslash W*?\backslash bcc\,\vert\,\backslash b(wget\,\vert\,curl))\backslash b\,\vert\,\backslash/(?:[\backslash'\backslash"\backslash\,\vert$
	$\backslash;\backslash'\backslash-\backslash s]\,\vert\,\$))$
XPath	No Regular Expression provided
CRLF	No Regular Expression provided
LDAP	$(?:\backslash((?:W*?(?:objectc(?:ategory\,\vert\,lass)\,\vert\,homedirectory\,\vert$
	$[gu]idnumber\,\vert\,cn)\backslash$
	$b\backslash W*?=\vert\,[\wedge\backslash w\backslash x80-\backslash xFF]*?[\backslash!\backslash\&\backslash\,\vert$
	$][\wedge\backslash w\backslash x80-\backslash xFF]*?\backslash()\backslash)[\wedge\backslash w\backslash x80-\backslash xFF]$
	$*?\backslash[\wedge\backslash w\backslash x80-\backslash xFF]*?[\backslash!\backslash\&\backslash\,\vert])$

OWASP ModSecurity Core Rule Set (CRS)[27] gives the regular expressions to most of the attacks. They use the rule sets in ModSecurity, a firewall used to provide securities from web app attacks. Table 3 depicts the types of attacks and their corresponding regular expressions used to detect the attacks. In this work, we also measure the accuracy obtainable by these regular expression based matching in detecting different attack types. As we find in Sect. 4, we obtain better results in the detection of web application attacks using machine learning based approaches than regex based ones.

Now, we discuss some of the most well known approaches in web attack detection using the concept of machine learning.

2.2   Machine Learning Based Approaches

In [13], authors propose a machine learning method to detect anomalous web traffic. They perform their experiments on CSIC 2010 HTTP dataset. The dataset consists of 25065 anomalous requests and 36000 normal requests. In CSIC 2010 dataset, the anomalous request is a collection of various attacks like XSS, SQLi, CSRF, etc. Using Weka analysis, they obtain five best features from a set of 9 features based on their relevance and their impact on accuracy. The best five features are request length, arguments length, number of arguments, path length and number of special characters in the path. For classification of requests into normal and anomalous, they have used various machine learning techniques like Random Forest, Logistic Regression, Decision Tree, AdaBoost Classifier, Stochastic Gradient Descent Classifier, and Naive Bayes. With all the mentioned classifiers, they have achieved an accuracy of 99.94% except with Stochastic Gradient Descent for which they obtain 99.88% and with Naive Bayes they obtain 88.83%. Although they got good accuracy, they do not further classify the attacks into individual categories. We implement their model and applied to our dataset. The highest accuracy using Random Forest classifier came out to be 88.84%. This indicates that the model might not generalize well beyond the CSIC 2010 dataset.

In [25], the authors discuss the detection of Cross-site Scripting attacks using machine learning techniques. They dealt with both normal and obfuscation version of XSS attacks. For training, they collected 4000 requests from many different sites consisting of 2000 benign samples from Dmoz and ClueWeb09 and 2000 XSS attack samples from [21]. Their testing dataset includes 13000 each of benign and XSS samples. They prepare the data by removing duplicates, removing extra new lines and blank spaces and at last, changing all the characters of the request to lowercase. To get a good result, they select two types of features namely structural features and behavioral features. The structural features deals with punctuation like $\&, \%, /, \backslash, +, @, space, |, \#$ and combinations of different punctuation like $><,'" ><, [], ==, \&\#$. Behavioural features contain a list of selected commands and functions like `eval()`, `Onload`, `Onerror`, `createelement`, `String.fromCharCode`, `Search` which are usually found in an XSS attack. Together, they form a total of 38 structural features and 21 behavioral features. These features have been used to create binary feature vectors indicating the presence or absence of individual features in a request. To classify the attacks into XSS and benign samples, they used four classifiers: Random Forest, K-Nearest Neighbor and two variations of Support Vector Machine (Linear Kernel and Polynomial Kernel). After tuning the classifiers using 5-fold cross-validation, they tested the classifiers with test data and achieve an accuracy of 99.5% with Random Forest, 99.75% with K-NN, 99.6% with Polynomial Kernel SVM and 96.32% with Linear Kernel SVM. When we implement machine learning models with their feature set, we get the best accuracy of 89.81% with Random Forest.

Cheon et al. [20] propose a method to prevent SQL injection in web applications. They detect the SQLi attacks using Bayesian Classifier, a machine learning classifier using only two features which are the length of the parameters and the number of keywords of parameters. The keywords are the commands and symbols found in SQL statements like commas, quotation marks, "UNION," "SELECT", etc., but they do not specify the full set of keywords used in second feature set. They form their training dataset of size 2142 containing a mix of both SQL injection patterns and benign samples by using a python script and a test dataset of 4070 different patterns. After training the Bayesian Classifier with full training dataset, upon testing they achieve an accuracy of 99.61%. Also, they detect different patterns of SQL injection attacks. We are not able to reproduce their model due to lack of enough details in [20].

These most recent machine learning based approaches supersede a few other previous approaches, and hence not discussed here. In summary, our observations on the past approaches are as follows:

- We found no substantial amount of work to detect attacks like XPath injection, CRLF, LDAP Injection, OS Command, SSI attack and Path traversal attack using machine learning techniques so far.
- Only after the fact analysis is done in the detection of attacks on web application from http log files.
- Although, the above mentioned approaches have achieved high accuracy, but none of them has implemented the sub-classification of attacks.

3   Proposed Framework

In this section, we explain the architecture of our proposed log-based attack detection and classification methods to achieve better detection accuracy. We also discuss the implementation of our solution for a live website. We divide this section into two phases offline log based detection and classification, and online implementation.

3.1   Offline Log Based Detection and Classification

This step include dataset collection, data processing, feature extraction and modeling of processed data as shown in Fig. 1.

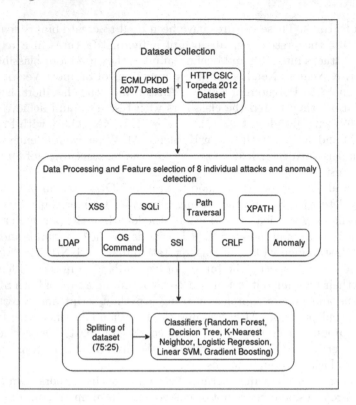

Fig. 1. Architecture for Phase 1

Dataset Collection. We use a combination of two different datasets ECML/PKDD 2007 Discovery Challenge dataset [1] and HTTP CSIC Torpeda 2012 dataset [15].

1. **ECML/PKDD 2007 Dataset**
   ECML/PKDD 2007 Discovery Challenge aims to address the classification of malicious HTTP requests received by a web application and identification of the attack requests. They provide the real-time traffic of HTTP requests in XML format stored in .txt file. The dataset consists of a total of 50116 samples, out of which 35006 are valid requests and 15110 are different types of attack request.

2. **HTTP CSIC Torpeda 2012 Dataset**
   This dataset is created using Torpeda framework [16]. Torpeda framework is used to develop labeled web traffic. The motive of Torpeda is to generate a dataset of HTTP requests for the purpose of evaluating the effectiveness of a Web Application Firewall. The torpeda dataset is given in XML document.

The statistics of the final dataset used for our work is shown in Table 4. In an HTTP request, there are many fields like URL, Query, Protocol, Method, Path,

Table 4. Dataset used for detection of each attack.

Attack types	Attack requests	Bengin requests	Total requests	Training set	Testing set
XSS	5310	5138	10448	7836	2612
SQL	4418	4801	9219	6914	2305
Path Traversal	1933	2000	3933	2949	984
OS Command	2094	2200	4294	3220	1074
CRLF	319	337	656	492	164
SSI	1889	1999	3888	2916	972
LDAP	1791	1945	3736	2802	934
XPath	1913	2035	3948	2961	987
Anomaly	22258	28033	50291	37718	12573

etc. In this work, we focus only on Path and Query part of the HTTP request because payload of the attacks are encoded in these parts [22,37]. Figure 2 explains both the Path and Query parts of the HTTP requests.

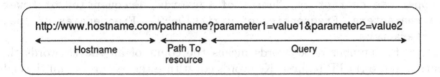

Fig. 2. Structure of an HTTP request

Data Processing. This section explains the data processing required to extract the necessary features. Data processing involves the following steps:

- URL decoding of the requests
- Converting the request to lowercase (except CRLF where we change the request to uppercase)
- Replacement of characters

These steps are almost same for all the attacks. The only variation is in the number of decoding of URLs and characters to be replaced for each attack. After data processing, we pass the processed data for feature extraction. Table 5 shows operations involved in data processing.

Feature Engineering. A feature is a measurable attribute based on which machine learning classifiers predict the results. For each malicious attack, features are described as a set of punctuation and keywords (commands or functions) present in that attack. These features are labeled as 0/1 showing whether a particular keyword or punctuation is present or not in the HTTP request. We extract these features manually using the technique as explained in [25].

Table 5. Data processing

Attack types	Number of URL decoding	Characters removed and replaced
XSS	2	\n and whitespace removed
SQLi	2	\n removed
Path Traversal	4	\n removed
LDAP	1	\n removed
XPath	1	\n removed
SSI	1	\n removed and whitespaces replaced with +
OS Command	2	\n and + replaced with single whitespace
CRLFi	1	-

Table 6 shows the features used for each attack. For anomaly detection, we have considered the following features. They are **Request length, Argument's length, Number of arguments, Path length, Frequencies of Uppercase characters, Number of keywords, Frequencies of Lower case characters, Frequencies of digits[0--9], Frequencies of special characters**.

Here, the number of keywords means the count of all the keywords that occurred in the HTTP request. Keywords constitute the features of all the eight attacks. The features are extracted directly from the HTTP requests. But for the calculation of the last feature, some data processing has been done which includes 'URL decoding', lowercasing of all the characters, removal of newline characters and replacement of '+' with a single whitespace. For feature selection, information gain algorithm is applied to select the most prominent features.

Classification. For the classification of the web application attacks, we use six different machine learning classifiers namely Logistic Regression [4], K-Nearest Neighbour (KNN) [8], Support Vector Machine (SVM) [33], Decision Tree [31], Random Forest [14], Gradient Boosting Algorithm [3]. We use Python's Sckit-learn library to implement these machine learning algorithms. We carry out our experiments on Ubuntu 18.04 LTS having 32 GB RAM and Intel i7 octa-core processor. We add approximately the same number of valid requests as the number of attack requests to balance the dataset. Each attack dataset has been randomly split into 75% training and 25% testing set and the results are shown in Tables 8 and 9.

3.2 Online Implementation

In this phase, we describe the implementation of our models obtained from offline log based analysis for a live website. These models read HTTP requests in real time from the log file of a website ''security.cse.iitk.ac.in'' to detect

Table 6. Features used for different attacks

Attack types	Features used
XSS	'&', '%', '/', '\\', '+', '""', '?', '!', ';', '#', '=', '[', ']', '$', '(', ')', '∧', '*', ',', '-', '<', '>', '@', '_', ':', '{', '}', ' ', '.', ' ', '|', '"', '<>', '"', '<>', '[]', "==", '&#', 'document', 'window', 'iframe', 'location', 'this', 'onload', 'onerror', 'createelement', 'string.fromcharcode', 'search', 'div', 'img', '<script', 'src', 'href', 'cookie', 'var', 'eval()', 'http', '.js'
SQLi	'-', '/**/', '%', '+', '""', ';', '#', '=', '[', ']', '(', ')', '∧', '*', 'char', ',', '-', '<', '>', ' ', '.', '|', '"', '<>', '<=', '>=', '&&', '||', ':', '!=', '', 'count', 'into', 'or', 'and', 'not', 'null', 'select', 'union', '#', 'insert', 'update', 'delete', 'drop', 'replace', 'all', 'any', 'from', 'count', 'user', 'where', 'sp', 'xp', 'like', 'exec', 'admin', 'table', 'sleep', 'commit', '()', 'between'
Path Traversal	'../', '..\\', 'etc', 'passwd', '\\.', '\\/', './', '/', ':', '//', ':/', 'system', 'ini', '..', 'exec', ':\\', '%00', '.bat', 'file', 'windows', 'boot', 'winnt', '.conf', 'access', 'log', ',,'
LDAP	'\\', '*', ,'(', ')', '/', '+', '<', '>', ';', '"', '&', '|', '(&', '(|', ')(', ',', '!', '=', ')&', ' ', '*)', '))', '&(', '+)', '=)','cn=', 'sn=', '=*', '(|','mail', 'objectclass', 'name'
XPath	'/*', '%', '+', '', ';', '#', '=', '[', ']', '(', ')', '∧', '*', '()', '//', ',', '-', '<', '>', ':', '|', '"', '<>', '<=', '>=', '&&', '||', '::', '((', '< --', ' ', 'or', 'count', 'path/', 'and', 'not', 'text()', 'child', 'position()', 'node()', 'name', 'user', 'comment'
SSI	'<!-', '-->', '#', '+', ',', '"', 'etc/', '/passwd', 'dir', '#exec', 'cmd', 'fromhost', 'email', 'odbc', '#include', 'virtual', 'bin/', 'toaddress', 'message', 'replyto', 'sender', '#echo', 'httpd', 'access.log', 'var', '+connect', 'date_gmt', '+statement', 'log/', '/mail', '"mail', '"id', '+id', '.bat', 'ls+', 'home/', 'winnt\\', 'system.ini', '.conf', '+-l', 'windows', '.conf', '.com', ':\\'
OS Command	'../', '..\\', 'etc', 'passwd', '\\.', '\\/', './', ':', ':/', '.','system32', 'display', '.exe', 'cmd', 'dir', ';', 'tmp/', 'etc/passwd', 'wget', 'cat', 'ping', 'bash', 'ftp', '|', '..', 'exec', ':\\', '.bat', 'file', 'script', 'rm ', 'c:', 'winnt', 'access', 'log', '', 'www.', 'http', ' ', 'bin/', 'telnet', 'echo', 'root', '-aux', 'shell', 'uname', 'IP'
CRLFi	'%0A', '%0D', '%0D%0A', 'SET', 'COOKIE', ':', '+', 'TAMPER'

different attacks. The same log file is fed to each attack model consecutively for detection of attacks. Figure 3 shows the architecture of our implementation.

Here, the models continuously read new requests from the log file every 15 s. Once the new requests are received, they are passed to the parser for formatting. The formatted traffic is then passed to each attack model sequentially, as shown in the Fig. 3. The attack detection models are arranged sequentially from most dangerous to least dangerous attacks [35]. Each model detects its corresponding attack and passes the rest of the traffic to the subsequent attack models for detection. Each detection process carries out its own data processing, and

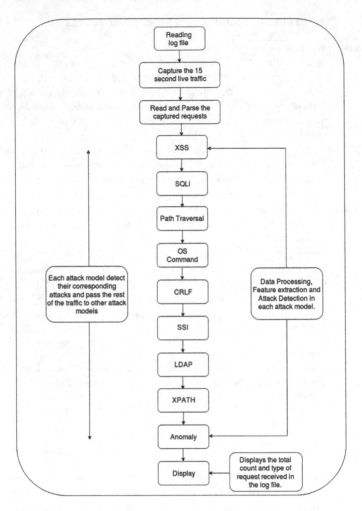

Fig. 3. Architecture for Phase 2

feature extraction as both the steps are different for each attack model. After the detection of all the attacks, we display the count of attacks received and types of requests detected in the last 15 s. This procedure for detection of attack is repeated in every 15 s. Figures 4 and 5 displays screen shots of the implemented tool for our real website and the corresponding dashboard.

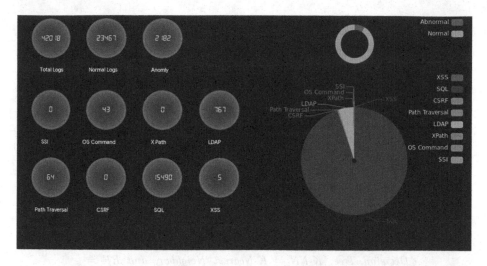

Fig. 4. IDS System showing the count of each attacks

Latest log							
		/2019:17:07:30		ZC3vRntFIHTIzWhoH3BGj5D36mpPgPw w.js			
172.27.20.117	Unknown	15/May /2019:17:07:30	GET	/sites/default/files/css/css_mNCu73iX1 bhA4nFy7P0ZaBxoGpgA8V4bsqBErV1m w8l.css?prhe9c	200		Normal
172.27.20.117	Unknown	15/May /2019:17:07:30	GET	/sites/default/files/css/css_PXKyJUac5 CjOsyl7xA6aCmq51JomRky41Sc9wSdnk NM.css?prhe9c	200		Normal
172.27.20.117	Unknown	15/May /2019:17:07:30	GET	/%3cscript%3ealert(1)%3c/script%3e	404		xss
172.27.20.117	Unknown	15/May	GET	/%3Cscript%3Ealert(1)%3C/script%3E	301		xss

Fig. 5. IDS System showing the types of request received

4   Evaluation of the Proposed Framework

To evaluate the performance of our models, we use ten-fold cross-validation
on each attack dataset. Table 7 shows the results of 10-fold cross-validation for
different machine learning classifiers on the features selected for each attack.
Tables 8 and 9 shows the performance in terms of accuracy, precision, recall, F1-
score, TPR, FPR, TNR, and FNR for all the classifiers on each attack dataset.
On the basis of these metrics, we select a model which performs better.

Table 8 shows the results for XSS, SQLi, Path Traversal, and LDAP attacks.
For XSS attacks, Random Forest achieves the highest accuracy of 99.38% with
a low FPR. Also for SQLi attacks, Random Forest performs better with an
accuracy of 97.91%. Random Forest and Gradient Boosting classifiers achieve the
highest accuracy of 99.28% for Path Traversal attacks. In case of LDAP attacks,

Table 7. 10-fold cross-validation results in %

Attacks\Classifiers	LR	LSVM	GB	DT	K-NN	RF
XSS	98	99	99	99	98	99
SQL	96	96	97	97	97	98
Path Traversal	97	98	98	98	95	98
OS Command	98	98	98	97	96	98
CRLF	100	100	100	100	100	100
SSI	100	100	100	100	100	100
LDAP	100	100	100	100	99	100
XPath	100	100	100	100	100	100
Anomaly	89	85	95	95	93	97

where *LR = Logistic Regression, LSVM = Linear Support Vector Machine, GB = Gradient Boosting Classifier, DT = Decision Tree, K-NN = K-Nearest Neighbor, and RF = Random Forest*

Table 8. XSS, SQLi, path traversal, and LDAP detection test results in %

Classifiers	XSS results							SQLi results						
	Acc.	Pre.	FS	TPR	FPR	TNR	FNR	Acc.	Pre.	FS	TPR	FPR	TNR	FNR
LR	98.04	98.4	97.98	97.55	1.4	98.6	2.45	95.7	95.16	95.84	96.53	5.1	94.9	3.47
LSVM	98.66	98.32	98.6	98.88	1.5	98.5	1.12	95.57	95	95.71	96.44	5.3	94.7	3.56
GB	98.88	98.64	98.84	99.04	1.2	98.8	0.96	96.52	95.16	96.61	98.1	5.1	94.9	1.9
DT	99.15	99.2	99.12	99.04	0.7	99.3	0.96	96.78	95.83	96.88	97.95	4.4	95.6	2.05
K-NN	99.27	99.36	99.24	99.12	0.5	99.5	0.88	96.39	95.75	96.51	97.29	4.5	95.5	2.71
RF	**99.38**	99.6	99.36	99.12	0.3	99.7	0.88	**97.91**	97	97.97	98.97	3.1	96.9	1.03
Classifiers	Path traversal results							LDAP results						
	Acc.	Pre.	FS	TPR	FPR	TNR	FNR	Acc.	Pre.	FS	TPR	FPR	TNR	FNR
LR	98.27	98.15	98.25	98.35	1.8	98.2	1.65	99.67	99.77	99.66	99.55	0.2	99.8	0.45
LSVM	98.88	99.79	98.88	97.98	0.2	99.8	2.02	99.89	100	99.88	99.77	0	100	0.23
GB	99.28	100	99.28	98.58	0	100	1.42	99.89	100	99.88	99.77	0	100	0.23
DT	99.18	100	99.18	98.38	0	100	1.62	99.89	100	99.88	99.77	0	100	0.23
K-NN	96.23	93.63	96.1	98.7	5.9	94.1	1.3	99.89	100	99.88	99.77	0	100	0.23
RF	**99.28**	100	99.28	98.58	0	100	1.42	**99.89**	100	99.88	99.77	0	100	0.23

where *Acc. = Accuracy, Pre. = Precision, FS = F1-Score, TPR = True Positive Rate, FPR = False Positive Rate, TNR = True Negative Rate, FNR = False Negative Rate*

except Logistic Regression all other classifiers achieve an highest accuracy of 99.89% having zero FPR.

The results for XPath, OS command, SSI, and anomaly detection are shown in Table 9. Random Forest classifier achieves the highest accuracy of 99.94% for detection of XPath attack with zero FPR. The highest detection accuracy for OS command attacks is 98.13% using Gradient Boosting classifier with low FPR. All the classifiers achieve the highest detection accuracy of 99.89% with zero FPR for the SSI attack. For the detection of anomaly Random Forest achieves the highest accuracy of 96.92%.

Table 9. XPath, OS command, SSI and anomaly detection test results in %

Classifiers	XPath results							OS command results						
	Acc.	Pre.	FS	TPR	FPR	TNR	FNR	Acc.	Pre.	FS	TPR	FPR	TNR	FNR
LR	99.89	100	99.9	99.8	0	100	0.2	97.85	99.01	97.75	96.53	0.9	99.1	3.47
LSVM	99.84	99.9	99.85	99.8	0.1	99.9	0.2	97.95	99.4	97.85	96.36	0.5	99.5	3.64
GB	99.89	99.9	99.9	99.9	0.1	99.9	0.1	**98.13**	99.8	98.05	96.37	0.1	99.9	3.63
DT	99.84	99.8	99.84	99.89	0.2	99.8	0.11	97.39	98.61	97.27	95.96	1.2	98.8	4.04
K-NN	99.89	99.9	99.9	99.9	0.1	99.9	0.1	96.55	98.61	96.42	94.32	1.2	98.8	5.68
RF	**99.94**	100	99.95	99.9	0	100	0.1	97.57	98.61	97.46	96.33	1.2	98.8	3.67
Classifiers	SSI results							Anomaly results						
	Acc.	Pre.	FS	TPR	FPR	TNR	FNR	Acc.	Pre.	FS	TPR	FPR	TNR	FNR
LR	99.89	100	99.89	99.79	0	100	0.21	89.13	94.43	90.58	87.03	7.7	92.3	12.97
LSVM	99.89	100	99.89	99.79	0	100	0.21	86.53	99.33	89.09	80.76	1.1	98.9	19.24
GB	99.89	100	99.89	99.79	0	100	0.21	94.96	97.54	95.54	93.62	3.2	96.8	6.38
DT	99.89	100	99.89	99.79	0	100	0.21	94.73	94.95	95.23	95.5	6.2	93.8	4.5
K-NN	99.89	100	99.89	99.79	0	100	0.21	93.2	95.14	93.94	92.77	6.2	93.8	7.23
RF	99.89	100	99.89	99.79	0	100	0.21	**96.92**	97.94	97.24	96.55	2.5	97.5	3.45

In CRLF, all the classifiers give 100% accuracy in the detection of CRLF because of the same kind of pattern among the data points.

We also check the performance of some of the attack detection models based on the data that were not used in the training, validation, and testing. For their performance comparison, we train all the classifiers on the full training dataset and test on the data which we collected from different sources [19,21] having 81804 (Attack requests: 40637 + Valid requests: 41167) requests for XSS attack detection and 9120 (Attack requests: 4824 + Valid requests: 4296) requests for anomaly detection. This experimental analysis is performed to check whether the models generalize or not, and the selected features which are used to train the model are independent of the dataset. Table 10 shows the result of the detection of XSS attacks and anomaly using all the considered machine learning classifiers, and the results show that the model performs best on the previously unseen dataset using Random Forest classifier.

Table 10. Test results of some of the attacks on new test data.

Classifiers	XSS results							Anomaly results						
	Acc.	Pre.	FS	TPR	FPR	TNR	FNR	Acc.	Pre.	FS	TPR	FPR	TNR	FNR
LR	94.03	91.34	93.9	96.62	8.3	91.7	3.38	95.42	95.11	95.14	95.17	4.3	95.7	4.83
LSVM	83.27	69.68	80.74	95.96	24	76	4.04	95.06	95.5	94.8	94.1	4	96	5.9
GB	96.79	98.01	96.85	95.73	2	98	4.27	88.27	88.26	87.64	87.03	10.5	89.5	12.97
DT	95.41	95.65	95.45	95.25	4.4	95.6	4.75	86.14	79.21	84.33	90.16	16.7	83.3	9.84
K-NN	97.19	98.86	97.25	95.7	1.1	98.9	4.3	96.99	99.33	96.88	94.57	0.6	99.4	5.43
RF	**97.53**	98.87	97.58	96.33	1.1	98.9	3.67	**97.23**	99.46	97.13	94.91	0.4	99.6	5.09

5   Analyzing the Existing Approaches

In this section, we compare our work with existing work on the detection of web attacks. In previous work, most of the attacks have been detected using regular expressions. Some of the attacks, like SQL injection, XSS, etc. are identified using Machine Learning, but they are tested on a small amount of data. To compare our approach against these, we implement the models in the earlier papers and test on our dataset. The results show that our approach performs better as compared to their approach. Table 11 summarises the results reported in their paper and the ones obtained by using their approach on our dataset.

In [26] and [27], the authors do not report their dataset details and accuracy. They provide the regular expressions used for the detection of attacks. We consider their regular expressions and apply them on our dataset and report the accuracy in Table 11. In [37], they detect many different web attacks, but the common to our approach are XSS, SQL, and Path Traversal, for which we analyse their approach on our dataset. We want to mention here that we did not implement Path Traversal attack as the corresponding regular expressions are not provided. Note that the regular expressions used to detect these attacks have become dated, and multiple rounds of encoding schemes are being used by attackers often to disguise the attack signatures. As a result, the accuracy numbers for regex based detection seems to be low compared to models trained with latest attack requests.

Table 11. Comparison with existing approaches

Authors	Approach	Reported dataset	Author's reported accuracy (%) on their dataset	Accuracy (%) on our dataset
Meyer et al. [26]	Regular expression	Not provided	Not provided	XSS: 78.44 SQL: 93.06 Path Traversal: 73.19
OWASP [27]	Regular expression	Not provided	Not provided	XSS: 49.17 SSI: 55.78 OS Command: 74.5 LDAP: 56.29
Yu et al. [37]	Regular expression	297 - XSS 113 - SQL 127 - Path Traversal	XSS - 97.98 SQL - 98.23 Path Traversal - 90.55	XSS: 78.44 SQL: 91.64 Path Traversal: Regex not provided
Althubiti et al. [13]	Machine learning	25000 - Anomaly 360000 - Normal	RF - 99.94	RF: 88.84
Mereani et al. [25]	Machine learning	13000 - XSS 13000 - Normal	K-NN - 99.75	RF: 89.81
Proposed method	Learning machine	Dataset Sect. 3.1	XSS - 99.34, SQL - 97.91 Path Traversal - 99.28, SSI - 99.89 LDAP - 99.89, XPath - 99.79 OS Command - 98.13, CRLF - 100 Anomaly - 96.92	XSS - 99.34, SQL - 97.91 Path Traversal - 99.28, SSI - 99.89 LDAP - 99.89, XPath - 99.79 OS Command - 98.13, CRLF - 100 Anomaly - 96.92

In [13] and [25] authors use machine learning approaches to detect the anomaly and XSS attack, respectively. We implement their approach to our dataset and achieve less accuracy as compared to their reported accuracy. The reason may be that the authors in [13] used a highly imbalanced dataset, but we used balanced dataset. Another reason may be that the feature set used is dependent on the dataset. This is the reason why we also implement our app-roach for the unseen dataset, and the results are discussed in Table 10 to test for generalization.

6   Conclusion

Web application attacks are significant threats to most of the organizations, and attacks like XSS, injections, etc. are on the rise. Hence, to detect these attacks, we implement a two-phase approach i.e. offline log-based analysis using various machine learning models and an online implementation of the log-analysis ver-sion. Here, the online log-analysis system reads HTTP requests from the log files every 15 s for the classification of these requests into corresponding attacks or normal requests. For this, the system parses those requests and then passes them to different machine learning models for detection of attacks. In this work, we found features and machine learning classifiers which are effective for high accuracy detection of attacks. Lastly, we also analyse the XSS and anomaly detection models for unseen requests. Since we use supervised machine learning algorithm; hence, we can detect only those attack requests for which we perform the analysis.

Various improvements can be done to this work. In this work, we perform the detection of web application attacks using HTTP requests, which contain only Query and Path field. This can be extended to all the other aspects such as 'Accept-Encoding,' 'Cookie,' 'Referrer', etc. We can also implement the clas-sification of attacks into its sub-categories, e.g., XSS can be sub-classified into Stored, Reflected and DOM-based XSS. Similarly, other attacks can also be sub-categorized. In future, we plan to detect the attacks that use HTTP POST method to deliver the attack payload. As of now, we do not have any ground truth to validate live data results. Hence, in future, we shall validate these results. We also plan to develop a web application firewall using our models which would intercept HTTP requests before they are processed at the web servers.

Acknowledgement. This work has been partially supported by grants from the Sci-ence and Engineering Research Board (SERB), and Department of Science and Tech-nology (DST), Government of India.

References

1. ECML/PKDD 2007 Dataset (2007). http://www.lirmm.fr/pkdd2007-challenge/
2. Xpath injection (2015). https://www.owasp.org/index.php/XPATH_Injection
3. Gradient boosting (2016). https://machinelearningmastery.com/gentle-introd-uction-gradient-boosting-algorithm-machine-learning/

4. Logistic regression (2016). https://machinelearningmastery.com/logistic-regression-for-machine-learning/
5. Sql injection (2016). https://www.owasp.org/index.php/SQL_Injection
6. Crlf injection (2018). https://www.owasp.org/index.php/CRLF_Injection
7. Cross-site scripting (xss) (2018). https://www.owasp.org/index.php/Cross-site_Scripting_(XSS)
8. Nearest neighbors (2018). http://scikit-learn.org/stable/modules/neighbors.html
9. Sophos India (2018).https://www.businesstoday.in/current/economy-politics/76-per-cent-indian-businesses-hit-by-cyber-attacks-in-2018-finds-survey/story/327389.html
10. World Internet Users and 2019 Population Stats (2019). https://www.internetworldstats.com/stats.htm
11. acunetix: Path traversal (2017). https://www.acunetix.com/blog/articles/path-traversal/
12. acunetix: Cross-site scripting (2019). https://www.acunetix.com/websitesecurity/cross-site-scripting/
13. Althubiti, S., Yuan, X., Esterline, A.: Analyzing http requests for web intrusion detection. KSU Proceedings on Cybersecurity Education, Research and Practice (2017)
14. Breiman, L.: Random forests. Mach. Learn. **45**(1), 5–32 (2001)
15. Carmen Torrano, A.P., Álvarez, G.: Http csic torpeda 2012 (2012). http://www.tic.itefi.csic.es/torpeda/datasets.html
16. Carmen Torrano, A.P., Álvarez, G.: Http csic torpeda 2012 (2012). http://www.tic.itefi.csic.es/torpeda
17. Elprocus: Basic intrusion detection system (2019). https://www.elprocus.com/basic-intrusion-detection-system/
18. ENISA: Enisa threat landscape report 2018 (2019). https://www.enisa.europa.eu/publications/enisa-threat-landscape-report-2018
19. Giménez, C.T., Villegas, A.P., Marañón, G.Á.: Http data set csic 2010. Information Security Institute of CSIC (Spanish Research National Council) (2010)
20. Hong Cheon, E., Huang, Z., Lee, Y.S.: Preventing sql injection attack based on machine learning. Int. J. Advancements Comput. Technol. **5**, 967–974 (2013). https://doi.org/10.4156/ijact.vol5.issue9.115
21. KF, DP: Xssed dataset (2007). http://www.xssed.com/
22. Kozik, R., Choraś, M., Renk, R., Hołubowicz, W.: Modelling http requests with regular expressions for detection of cyber attacks targeted at web applications. In: International Joint Conference SOCO 2014-CISIS 2014-ICEUTE 2014, pp. 527–535. Springer, Switzerland (2014). 10.1007/978-3-319-07995-0_52
23. Kumar, B.S., Ch, T., Raju, R.S.P., Ratnakar, M., Baba, S.D., Sudhakar, N.: Intrusion detection system-types and prevention. Int. J. Comput. Sci. Info. Tech. (IJCSIT) **4**(1), 77–82 (2013)
24. Mansfield, M.: General small business cyber security statistics (2018). https://smallbiztrends.com/2017/01/cyber-security-statistics-small-business.html
25. Mereani, F.A., Howe, J.M.: Detecting cross-site scripting attacks using machine learning. In: Hassanien, A.E., Tolba, M.F., Elhoseny, M., Mostafa, M. (eds.) AMLTA 2018. AISC, vol. 723, pp. 200–210. Springer, Cham (2018). https://doi.org/10.1007/978-3-319-74690-6_20
26. Meyer, R.: Detecting attacks on web applications from log files (2008). https://www.sans.org/reading-room/whitepapers/logging/detecting-attacks-web-applications-log-files-2074

27. OWASP: Owasp modsecurity core rule set (2014). https://github.com/SpiderLabs/ owasp-modsecurity-crs/blob/master/base_rules/modsecurity_crs_40_generic_ attacks.conf
28. OWASP: Owasp top 10–2017 (2017). https://www.owasp.org/images/7/72/ OWASP_Top_10-2017_%28en%29.pdf.pdf
29. OWASP: Testing for ldap injection (2017). https://www.owasp.org/index.php/ Testing_for_LDAP_Injection_(OTG-INPVAL-006)
30. OWASP: Command injection (2018). https://www.owasp.org/index.php/ Command_Injection
31. Quinlan, R.: C4.5: Programs for Machine Learning. Morgan Kaufmann Publishers, San Mateo (1993)
32. Sarmah, A.: Intrusion detection systems: definition, need and challenges (2019). https://www.sans.org/reading-room/whitepapers/detection/intrusion-detection-systems-definition-challenges-343
33. Scholkopf, B., Smola, A.J.: Learning with Kernels: Support Vector Machines, Regularization, Optimization, and Beyond. MIT press, Cambridge (2001)
34. Shatabda: Ssi injection (2018). https://medium.com/@shatabda/security-ssi-injection-what-how-fbce1dc232b9
35. Technologies, P.: Web application attack statistics (2018). https://www.ptsecurity. com/upload/corporate/ww-en/analytics/Web-application-attacks-2018-eng.pdf
36. W3Schools: SQL Injection (2019). https://www.w3schools.com/sql/sql_injection. asp
37. Yu, J., Tao, D., Lin, Z.: A hybrid web log based intrusion detection model. In: 2016 4th International Conference on Cloud Computing and Intelligence Systems (CCIS), pp. 356–360. IEEE (2016)

Formal Analysis of PUF Instances Leveraging Correlation-Spectra in Boolean Functions

Durba Chatterjee$^{(\boxtimes)}$ ⓘ, Aritra Hazra, and Debdeep Mukhopadhyay

Indian Institute of Technology Kharagpur, Kharagpur, India
durba@iitkgp.ac.in, {aritrah,debdeep}@cse.iitkgp.ac.in

Abstract. In this paper, we present a novel formal analysis scheme considering that the fabrication of a batch of $N > 1$ PUFs is equivalent to drawing random instances of Boolean mappings. We model PUFs as black-box Boolean functions of dimension $m \times 1$ and show combinatorially that random designs of such $m \times 1$ functions exhibit correlation-spectra which can be used to characterize random and thus *good* designs of PUFs. We first develop theoretical results to quantize the correlation values and subsequently find the expected number of pairs of such Boolean functions which should belong in different regions of the spectra. We extend the concept of correlation to PUFs and theoretically prove that a randomly chosen sample of PUFs and Boolean functions follow the same distribution. In addition to this, we show through extensive experimental results that a randomly chosen sample of such PUFs also resembles the correlation-spectra property of the overall PUF population. We finally propose a formal analysis tool for evaluation of PUFs by observing the correlation-spectra of the PUF instances under test. We show through experimental results on 50 FPGAs that when the PUFs are infected by faults the usual randomness tests for the PUF outputs such as uniformity, fail to detect any aberration. However, the spectral-pattern is clearly shown to get affected, which we demonstrate by standard statistical measure like KL Divergence.

Keywords: Physically Unclonable Functions · Formal analysis · Boolean functions

1 Introduction

Due to the inherent challenge of producing clones physically or characterizing mathematical models, Physically Unclonable Functions (PUFs) are widely adopted to act primarily as the fingerprint in devices [7]. Typically, a PUF (first proposed in [16]) is built over the notion of a one-way function embedded in a physical device and has been an active topic of research for many years. PUF is a physical mapping that maps an input, also known as the *challenge* to a unique and random output, also known as the *response*. The challenge

© Springer Nature Switzerland AG 2019
S. Bhasin et al. (Eds.): SPACE 2019, LNCS 11947, pp. 142–158, 2019.
https://doi.org/10.1007/978-3-030-35869-3_11

response combination defines the functional behaviour of a PUF instance and is known as challenge response pair (CRP). Ideally, such challenge-response mapping is unique for every PUF instance and is independent of each other. The uncontrollable manufacturing varieties bring in random variations in its internal properties, which forms the unique relationship. PUFs are designed leveraging such random internal properties of the device. For instance, in delay-based PUFs [7], the propagation delay of a signal through various paths in the circuit is a source of randomness and is used to generate responses subject to different challenges. The role of the challenge is to select which path the signal will travel through. Many security solutions have been developed leveraging the uniqueness property of PUFs, such as PUF based RFID [1], authentication of devices [22], cryptographic key generation [13]. Besides, the unique nature of PUF has also been exploited in various security protocols [18,19]. Delvaux *et al.* [3] provides a detailed overview of all protocols using strong PUFs.

To develop highly secure and reliable PUF variants, a lot of research has been conducted on various aspects of PUFs ranging from creating metrics for quality evaluation to understanding the intricacies of its internal circuit structure [8,14]. Despite the enormous work on the application of PUFs in various security applications, the area for formal analysis of this primitive lacks depth. Unlike other conventional cryptographic primitives, PUFs do not have a defined functionality; thus it does not have a golden instance against which new instances can be compared. Due to the widespread use of PUFs as a promising security measure, it becomes imperative to understand this entity from a theoretical perspective. There is a dearth of formal methods which uses statistical tests to yield metrics which can be used to estimate a PUFs quality.

The CRP behaviour of a PUF can be thought of as a Boolean mapping, $f_{PUF} : \mathscr{C} \rightarrow \mathscr{R}$, where $\mathscr{C} = \{0,1\}^n$ is a n-bit challenge and $\mathscr{R} = \{0,1\}^m$ is a m-bit response. A set of challenge response pairs or CRPs uniquely define the behaviour of an instance. PUFs can be classified into two broad categories, Strong PUFs, and Weak PUFs, based on the number of CRPs it admits. Strong PUFs such as Arbiter PUF, XOR PUF have an exponential number of challenges with respect to some system parameter. On the other hand, weak PUFs such as SRAM PUFs have a limited challenge space. Depending on the number of challenges a PUF allows the applications of PUF changes. Strong PUFs are mostly used in applications like authentication based protocols and identification. On the other hand, weak PUFs are mainly used in key generation.

PUFs can be considered to be black-box Boolean functions [5,6], which implies that all properties of Boolean functions become inherent to PUFs. It is well established that Boolean functions exhibit correlation, indicating the inter-relationship among Boolean functions [15]. Due to such correlation properties of Boolean functions, random choices of Boolean functions, which are realized as PUFs also should ideally manifest such correlations. Such characteristics may form a basis for the analysis of a given sample of PUFs, which otherwise may be infeasible to evaluate individually as PUFs ideally have no describable functionality (as then we have a mathematical model!). Furthermore, faults or any defect inside a PUF circuitry may not be detected by the standard metrics like uniformity or other randomness tests, while correlation analysis may form a novel basis for evaluating the *goodness* of a given sample of PUFs. Our work articulates the idea of PUF analysis based on correlation properties of Boolean functions.

There are some well-defined functions [25] to measure correlations of Boolean functions, such as Pearson correlation function, auto-correlation function etc. There are some works which explore similarity among PUFs. In [9], analysis of PUF responses has been done using Welch's t-test and PUF responses are categorized based on its first order and second order moments. Other existing approaches explore the uniqueness and quality of PUFs based on querying the identifiers generated by the PUFs either by computing the entropy of the identifiers [17] (high entropy reveals better randomness) or by determining the number of collisions among the identifiers [14] (fewer the collisions better the randomness). In [24], theoretical analysis of PUFs using distribution of delay difference is presented. Our paper presents a new approach for formal analysis of PUFs leveraging the spectral properties of Boolean functions. The primary contributions of this work are summarized as follows:

- We define PUFs as random black-box Boolean functions and formally present a correlation-spectra of PUFs.
- We theoretically quantize the correlation values and the expected number of pairs of Boolean functions which will belong to a specified correlation-spectra.
- We present a novel Formal Correlation and Spectral Analysis Tool (FCSA) for PUFs which utilizes the correlation properties of PUFs.
- Finally we test our FCSA tool using two samples of PUF instances, one consisting of good instances another sample consisting of faulty instances. We also employ statistical method like KL-Divergence to verify the results.

The rest of the paper is organized as follows. Section 2 presents a brief background of PUF and properties of Boolean functions along with necessary statistical tests. Section 3 starts with an explanation of correlation properties of Boolean functions in-depth, followed by formally defining the correlation between PUFs. It is followed by a detailed description of our proposed analysis tool leveraging these properties. Section 4 presents the experimental setup and results and Sect. 5 concludes the paper.

2   Background

In this section, we present an introduction to PUFs and its properties, followed by a few relevant properties of Boolean functions. We also provide a brief description of the statistical tests used in our analysis.

2.1   Physically Unclonable Function (PUF)

Physically Unclonable Function (PUF) is a hardware based cryptographic primitive that exploits the uncontrollable imperfections of the underlying circuit to create unique and unclonable functional behaviour. This makes it a promising candidate in multiple security applications. A PUF is attributed with properties mentioned below.

Properties of PUF. An ideal PUF, $f_{PUF} : \mathscr{C} \to \mathscr{R}$, exhibits certain properties which are as follows:

- *Evaluable:* f_{PUF} evaluates in polynomial time.
- *Unique:* f_{PUF} mapping is instance-specific.
- *Reproducible:* If $c_i = c_j$ ($\forall\ c_i, c_j \in \mathscr{C}$), then $|f_{PUF}(c_i) - f_{PUF}(c_j)| < \Delta$ (distance).
- *Unclonable:* It is impossible to construct another $g_{PUF} : \mathscr{C} \to \mathscr{R}$, where $g_{PUF} \approx f_{PUF}$.
- *Unpredictable:* Given $U = \{(c_i, r_i) \mid r_i = f_{PUF}(c_i)\}$, it is impossible to predict a response $r_z = f_{PUF}(c_z)$, where c_z is a random challenge and $(c_z, r_z) \notin U$.
- *One-way:* Applying a challenge c, drawn from a uniform distribution on $\{0,1\}^n$, we obtain $r = f_{PUF}(c)$ so that $\text{Prob}[A(f_{PUF}(c)) = c] < \frac{1}{p(n)}$, where $p(\cdot)$ is any positive polynomial. The probability that any probabilistic polynomial time algorithm or physical procedure A can output c itself is negligible.

An Example PUF (5-4 DAPUF). 5-4 DAPUF (5-4 Double Arbiter PUF) [2] is a variant of a Double Arbiter PUF proposed in [12]. It is a delay-based PUF consisting of five equal length delay chains, followed by twenty arbiters and four XOR gates, as shown in Fig. 1. An input challenge c is applied to each chain. The outcome of these five chains is then fed into arbiters which results in twenty intermediate outcomes. Each XOR gate takes 5 of these outcomes and produces 1-bit output as shown in equations of Fig. 1 to produce a 4-bit response r.

5-4 DAPUF, being a delay based PUF, exploits the difference of propagation delay accumulated over all switches in each chain. The XOR gates at the last level make the circuit non-linear. Hardware implementation of 5-4 DAPUF on Artix-7 FPGA reveals the uniformity for the four response bits to be 44.6%, 54.9%, 43.4% and 40.9%, respectively. 5-4 DAPUF is a strong PUF, admitting a large set of challenges, making it resistant to model building attacks. As per our knowledge, there is only one work which has modelled a DAPUF [10], but that requires about a million challenges. This makes it a good candidate for analysis.

Faults in Physically Unclonable Functions. A fault is defined as an aberration in a circuit caused due to manufacturing defects or intentional changes made from external sources. Faults cause a deviation from the normal execution of the circuit. Faults can be of various types such as stuck-at faults, glitches, transient faults. The process of introducing a fault in device or circuit is known as fault injection and attacks involving such injections are known as fault attacks. The objective behind a fault attack on a cryptographic implementation is to reveal some secret information. In the case of PUFs, since the secret lies embedded in device randomness, a fault attack on PUF tries to reduce the randomness or

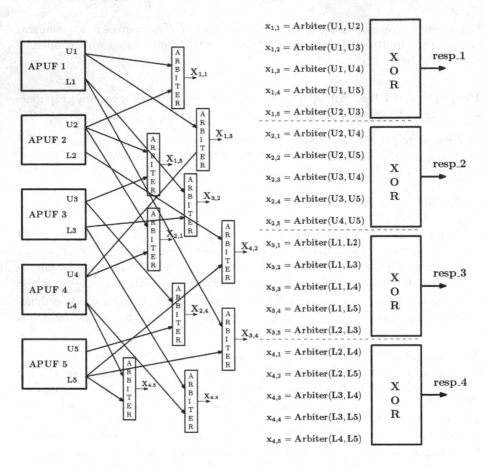

Fig. 1. Schematic representation of a 5-4 DAPUF

entropy. Such a PUF instance tends to become biased, making it vulnerable to modelling attacks [4,20,23] and is referred to as a *faulty* PUF or a *biased* PUF. In this work, we introduce a stuck-at fault at an intermediate switch in all the delay chains of DAPUF.[1]

2.2 Boolean Functions and Its Properties

In this section, we represent Boolean functions formally and provide the formal notion of correlation between two Boolean functions.

---

[1] It may be noted that while there are potential methods of introducing faults in PUF circuits, the objective of the paper is to study the effects of faults on the Boolean spectrum of PUF instances.

Boolean Function and Its Representation. A Boolean function f: $\{0,1\}^m \rightarrow \{0,1\}$ of m variables a mapping of m input variables to $\{0,1\}$. It can be represented by a Boolean row vector $\mathbf{f} = \langle f_0, f_1, \ldots f_{2^m-1} \rangle$ of length 2^m. This is known as the truth table representation of f. The value at the ith index of $\mathbf{f}$ stores the output of f, when the binary equivalent of i is given as input. Another way to represent a Boolean function is by a vector of the form $\{-1,1\}^{2^m} = \langle (-1)^{f_0}, (-1)^{f_1}, \ldots (-1)^{f_{2^m-1}} \rangle$, also known as polarity truth table or sequence of a function.

Correlation Properties of Boolean Functions. There are various measures to assess similarity among Boolean functions, correlation being one of them. One of the well known correlation functions is cross-correlation function [21] which measures the statistical *closeness* between two functions f and g $(f \neq g)$ with one of them shifted by α, denoted by $\mathcal{C}_{f,g}(\alpha)$ is given by,

$$\mathcal{C}_{f,g}(\alpha) = \sum_{x \in \{0,1\}^m} (-1)^{f(x) \oplus g(x+\alpha)} \tag{1}$$

A modified version of the cross-correlation is shown below. This equation computes the *closeness* between functions f and g without any shift $(\alpha = 0)$ and the correlation coefficient is normalized with the size of the input space. This can be written in terms of the truth table representation of the functions involved, as follows

$$\mathcal{C}_{f,g} = \frac{\sum_{x \in \{0,1\}^m} (-1)^{\mathbf{f}(x) \oplus \mathbf{g}(x)}}{2^m} \tag{2}$$

The output of the cross-correlation function is called the correlation coefficient and is denoted by $\mathcal{C}_{f,g} \in [-1,1]$. A cross-correlation value of 0 $(\mathcal{C}_{f,g} = 0)$ implies that f and g are completely uncorrelated or independent. Positive values of $\mathcal{C}_{f,g}$ imply that f and g are positively correlated, on the other hand, negative values of $\mathcal{C}_{f,g}$ imply that their functional behaviours are rather complementary. Given a set of N random Boolean functions, we get a $N \times N$ correlation matrix by applying Eq. 2 for all possible pairs. The frequency distribution of the correlation matrix is called the **correlation spectrum**. Note that, in the correlation spectrum, we do not count the self pairs, as we are solely concerned with the cross-correlation between function pairs. Moreover, each pair (f,g) is counted only once. The pie representation of correlation spectrum for all 3-input and 4-input Boolean functions is shown in Fig. 2[2]. From Fig. 2 it is evident that total number of pairs can be partitioned into $(2^m + 1)$ bins, each corresponding to a unique correlation value. Each correlation value is in turn dependent on the number of mismatches between the truth tables of functions in the pair. The relationship between the number of bit mismatches, correlation coefficient and the number of function pairs has been elaborated in Sect. 3.2. For small values of m, we get discrete correlation segments as shown in Fig. 3. As the size of the input will increase, the spectra will start to resemble a continuous spectrum.

---

[2] We have omitted the bin for correlation value 1, as these correspond to the self pairs.

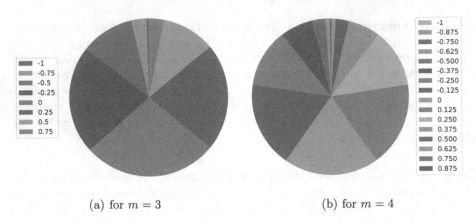

(a) for $m = 3$ (b) for $m = 4$

Fig. 2. Correlation-spectra of m-variable Boolean functions

2.3   Statistical Tests

Given two samples of data, statistical tests enable us to differentiate between the samples. One of the well known statistical measures is Kullback-Leibler (KL) Divergence which quantitatively determines the difference between two distributions.

Kullback-Leibler Divergence: Kullback-Leibler (KL) Divergence [11] is a statistical measure of divergence of one distribution from a reference distribution. The divergence value is directly proportional to the similarity of the distribution under test to the reference distribution. A value of 0 implies that the distributions are identical. KL Divergence is an asymmetric measure and thus changes with the swap of the test and reference distribution. For discrete distributions $\mathcal{P}$ and $\mathcal{Q}$, KL-Divergence from $\mathcal{Q}$ to $\mathcal{P}$ is given by,

$$D_{KL}(\mathcal{Q}||\mathcal{P}) = \sum_i \mathcal{Q}(i) ln\left(\frac{\mathcal{Q}(i)}{\mathcal{P}(i)}\right) \tag{3}$$

Here, $\mathcal{Q}$ is the reference distribution and $\mathcal{P}$ is the distribution under test.

3   Theoretical Analysis of PUFs

In this section, we formalize an analysis mechanism for PUFs using spectral properties of Boolean functions. In the first part, we elaborate on the correlation properties of Boolean functions which form the base of our PUF analysis tool. We proceed to provide the theoretical basis for the analysis of correlation among PUF instances.

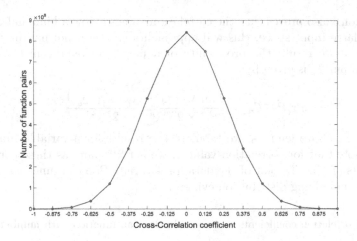

Fig. 3. Frequency distribution of 4-variable Boolean function

3.1 Correlation Properties of Boolean Function

In this part we continue the discussion on correlation properties of Boolean functions from Sect. 2.2. The relationships are formulated as lemmas as follows. These lemmas highlight some necessary relations needed for our analysis.

Lemma 1. *Let f and g be two m-variable Boolean functions with i bit mismatches $(0 \leq i \leq 2^m)$. The cross-correlation coefficient between f and g is*

$$\mathcal{C}_{f,g} = 1 - \frac{i}{2^{m-1}} \tag{4}$$

Proof: *For m-variate Boolean function, truth table contains 2^m values.*
    Simplifying the exponent in Eq. 2, we get,

$$\mathcal{C}_{f,g} = \frac{(-1)i + (1)(2^m - i)}{2^m} = \frac{2^m - 2i}{2^m} = 1 - \frac{i}{2^{m-1}}$$

which completes the proof. □

Lemma 2. *Let $\mathcal{C}_\alpha$ be a given correlation value. The number of unordered $m \times 1$ function pairs with this cross-correlation value is given by,*

$$\text{Pair Count} = (2^{2^m - 1})\binom{2^m}{2^{m-1}(1 - \mathcal{C}_\alpha)} \tag{5}$$

Proof: *Number of unordered function pairs having i bit differences (mismatches) in their truth table is*

$$\text{Pair Count} = \frac{2^{2^m}}{2}\binom{2^m}{i} \tag{6}$$

Substituting the value of i from Eq. 4 completes the proof. □

Equation 6 also proves that the correlation values follow a binomial distribution. For large input space, this will approach a standard normal distribution. Using the above result, the probability of a pair P belonging in a particular correlation bin $\mathcal{C}_\alpha$ is given by:

$$\Pr[P \in \mathcal{C}_\alpha] = \frac{\text{Pair Count}}{2^{2m} \times 2^{2m}} = \frac{\binom{2^m}{2^{m-1}(1-\mathcal{C}_\alpha)}}{2^{2m+1}} \tag{7}$$

Using the above lemmas, we tabulate the results for 4-variable function in Table 1. Note that for correlation value 1, we get 2^{16} pairs as these correspond to self pairs (f, f). The plot of the data for 4-variate Boolean functions in Fig. 3 makes the underlying distribution evident.

Table 1. Correlation coefficients of 4-variable Boolean function with number of function pairs

Coefficient	Mismatch count	Pair count
−1.000	16	32768
−0.875	15	524288
−0.750	14	3932160
−0.625	13	18350080
−0.500	12	59637760
−0.375	11	143130624
−0.250	10	262406143
−0.125	9	374865919
0	8	421724159
0.125	7	374865919
0.250	6	262406143
0.375	5	143130624
0.500	4	59637760
0.625	3	18350080
0.750	2	3932160
0.875	1	524288
1.00	0	65536

In the next subsection, we extend the correlation properties to PUFs. Finally, we use the correlation-spectra as the fundamental tool for analysis of a sample of randomly picked PUF instances.

3.2   Formalization of PUFs Correlation

PUFs can be defined as physical mapping from the set of *challenges* ($\mathscr{C}$) to corresponding *responses* ($\mathscr{R}$). Let us represent the mapping by $f_{PUF} : \mathscr{C} \to \mathscr{R}$

where $f_{PUF}(\mathbf{c}) = \mathbf{r}, \mathbf{c} \in \mathscr{C}$ and $\mathbf{r} \in \mathscr{R}$. This representation is striking similar to the representation of Boolean functions and is frequently used in the literature [5,6]. Thus, we represent PUFs as random instances of Boolean function over $\mathbb{F}_2$. Let us represent a challenge as a vector $\mathbf{c} = <c_1, c_2, \ldots, c_n>$. According to the PUF to Boolean function mapping, each element c_i of $\mathbf{c}$ corresponds to a Boolean variable which can be either $1(true)$ or $0(false)$ and $\mathbf{c}$ corresponds to an n-bit binary string. This implies that fabrication of a batch of $N > 1$ PUFs is equivalent to drawing N random instances of Boolean mappings over $\mathbb{F}_2$.

In this part, we formally define the correlation between PUF instances. Given n-bit input and m-bit output, the total number of unique PUF instances enumerate to $2^{m \times 2^n}$ which encompass the PUF space. Sampling of N random instances from the PUF space is equivalent to drawing N random Boolean functions. In the previous section we have established that for large input size n, frequency of cross-correlation values between pairs of Boolean functions follow a Gaussian distribution. This distribution is often referred to as the correlation spectra. We show that PUFs correlation spectra follows a Gaussian distribution, owing to the previously established analogy between PUFs and Boolean Functions. This provides us with a template which we subsequently use as a guide to identifying *good* PUFs. For a multibit response, each response bit is considered to be the outcome of an independent function over the challenge bits. Thus, for correlation analysis, we treat each response bit independently.

Consider two random $n \times m$ PUF instances PUF_A and PUF_B and let $\mathbf{r}_{A,i}$ and $\mathbf{r}_{B,i}$ be their respective responses to a challenge $\mathbf{c}_i$. Each response can be expressed as a tuple given by,

$$\mathbf{r}_{A,i} = \left(r_{A,i,1}, r_{A,i,2}, \ldots, r_{A,i,m}\right) \qquad \mathbf{r}_{B,i} = \left(r_{B,i,1}, r_{B,i,2}, \ldots, r_{B,i,m}\right)$$

For K challenges $\{\mathbf{c}_1, \mathbf{c}_2, \ldots, \mathbf{c}_K\}$, we get K responses from both PUF_A and PUF_B given by $\{\mathbf{r}_{A,1}, \mathbf{r}_{A,2}, \ldots, \mathbf{r}_{A,K}\}$ and $\{\mathbf{r}_{B,1}, \mathbf{r}_{B,2}, \ldots, \mathbf{r}_{B,K}\}$ respectively. Each response tuple (for one PUF) can be split into m vectors, each corresponding to one response bit. Thus, for K challenges, we get m vectors each of size K, given by:

$$\mathbf{r}_{A|1} = \left(r_{A,1,1}, r_{A,2,1}, \ldots, r_{A,K,1}\right)^T \qquad \mathbf{r}_{B|1} = \left(r_{B,1,1}, r_{B,2,1}, \ldots, r_{B,K,1}\right)^T$$

$$\mathbf{r}_{A|2} = \left(r_{A,1,2}, r_{A,2,2}, \ldots, r_{A,K,2}\right)^T \qquad \mathbf{r}_{B|2} = \left(r_{B,1,2}, r_{B,2,2}, \ldots, r_{B,K,2}\right)^T$$

$$\vdots \qquad\qquad\qquad\qquad\qquad \vdots$$

$$\mathbf{r}_{A|m} = \left(r_{A,1,m}, r_{A,2,m}, \ldots, r_{A,K,m}\right)^T \qquad \mathbf{r}_{B|m} = \left(r_{A,1,m}, r_{B,2,m}, \ldots, r_{B,K,m}\right)^T$$

The correlation between PUF_A and PUF_B is computed for each response bit independently. The cross-correlation between PUF_A and PUF_B for the pth response bit is calculated as follows

$$\mathcal{C}_{A,B}(p) = \frac{\sum_{j=1}^{K}(-1)^{\mathbf{r}_{A|p} \oplus \mathbf{r}_{B|p}}}{K} \tag{8}$$

Thus, for one pair of PUFs (PUF_A, PUF_B), we get m independent values of correlation, which form the tuple $\mathcal{C}_{A,B} = (\mathcal{C}_{A,B}(1), \mathcal{C}_{A,B}(2), \ldots, \mathcal{C}_{A,B}(m))$. This calculation is done for all possible PUF pairs in the PUF space. Given N PUFs, we have $N' = \binom{N}{2}$ possible pairs. For ease of representation, let us denote pairs by $(P_1, P_2, \ldots P_{N'})$. Finally, we get a $N' \times m$ matrix combining all pair tuples. Let the matrix be denoted by $\mathcal{M}$.

$$\mathcal{M} = \begin{bmatrix} \mathcal{C}_{P_1}(1) & \mathcal{C}_{P_1}(2) & \mathcal{C}_{P_1}(3) & \ldots & \mathcal{C}_{P_1}(m) \\ \mathcal{C}_{P_2}(1) & \mathcal{C}_{P_2}(2) & \mathcal{C}_{P_2}(3) & \ldots & \mathcal{C}_{P_2}(m) \\ \vdots & \vdots & \vdots & \ddots & \vdots \\ \mathcal{C}_{P_{N'}}(1) & \mathcal{C}_{P_{N'}}(2) & \mathcal{C}_{P_{N'}}(3) & \ldots & \mathcal{C}_{P_{N'}}(m) \end{bmatrix} \tag{9}$$

The correlation spectra for each response bit is obtained by picking the corresponding column from $\mathcal{M}$ and generating its frequency distribution. This distribution is similar to the correlation spectrum of Boolean functions. From Lemma 2 it follows that the spectrum is Gaussian in nature. Equation 6 enumerates the number of function pairs having i mismatches in their truth table representation. Varying the value of i from 0 to 2^m, and adding the pair counts, we get a binomial series. As the size of the input increases, it approximates a normal distribution. This proves that individual response bit pairs of PUF instances also follow a Gaussian distribution. Thus, we can theoretically estimate the number of PUF instances that lie in a region of the spectrum. This is precisely the information that we leverage in our analysis tool. We would like to stress on the generality of the described methodology. This spectrum generation method is solely dependent on the challenge response system making it architecture independent.

3.3   Spectral Analysis of PUFs

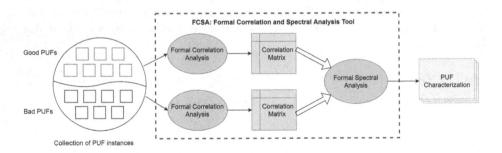

Fig. 4. Flowchart description for analysis of PUF instances

In the above subsection, we theoretically proved that for a collection of PUFs, each response bit exhibits a correlation spectra analogous to Boolean Functions. This property is leveraged in the correlation analysis of PUFs. The fundamental property of a good PUF design is that it exhibits randomness and uniqueness. In the previous section, we defined the correlation between two PUF instances for individual bits, using the correlation concepts from Boolean theory. Since PUFs can be represented as random black-box Boolean functions, a given sample of such good designs is anticipated to exhibit the correlation-spectra of Boolean functions.

Figure 4 schematically represents our analysis tool flow which includes correlation analysis of PUF responses followed by the tests conducted on PUF responses leveraging its correlation properties. For spectral analysis of PUFs, we have used KL divergence over correlation spectra of two collections (*good* and *faulty*) of multiple instances of 64-bit 5-4 DAPUF.

4   Experimental Setup and Results

We have divided our experiment into two parts:

1. Correlation Analysis: Evaluation of correlation among PUF instances using the correlation-spectrum
2. Spectral Analysis: Applying KL divergence on correlation spectra of correct and faulty PUF to analyse the difference

4.1   Implementation Setup

We have used 64-bit 5-4 DAPUF[3] for implementation of the proposed methodology. The setup includes 50 instances of hardware implementation of 5-4 DAPUF implemented on Xilinx Artix-7 FPGA. The challenge set $\mathscr{C}$ consisting of 10000 randomly generated challenges. Each PUF takes a 64-bit challenge from $\mathscr{C}$ and returns a 4-bit response. To account for reliability, we have taken 5 measurements for each challenge and PUF instance and selected a reference response using majority voting from the generated responses. We have also generated a collection of faulty PUF instances by inducing a stuck-at-fault at an input of 10th switch of delay chains in the hardware implementation of PUF. The same data collection process was done for the faulty PUFs as well.

4.2   Experiments and Correlation Results for PUFs

Experiment: The first step is to generate responses of each PUF instance for the challenge set $\mathscr{C}$ and compute the correlation matrix for all PUF instances. We obtain the correlation spectrum by plotting the frequency of the correlation values. We then compute the correlation matrix for all the faulty pairs and generate the corresponding correlation spectra. We compute the correlation coefficient for all four response bits individually for the set of 50 instances. Since there are a large number of distinct real-valued correlation coefficients spanning from -1 to $+1$, we have grouped the coefficients into 256 bins. For each response bit, we count the number of PUF pairs having the same correlation value. This gives the frequency distribution of the cross-correlation coefficient. For 64-bit 5-4 DAPUF, all possible input realizations amount to 2^{64}, which makes the truth table of a

---

[3] From here on, we will refer it as 5-4 DAPUF.

single instance of DAPUF extremely large and unmanageable. Since it is not possible to compute the outcome of 2^{64} challenges, we have used a challenge subset comprising of 10000 randomly picked challenges. The plots in Fig. 5 show the frequency distribution of the correlation coefficient for each response bit for a set of non faulty (*good*) PUF instances. In the second part of the experiment, we induce a *stuck-at-1 fault* at the 10th switch from the beginning of the delay chain, for all five chains in the hardware implementation of DAPUF. This introduces a bias in responses. We repeat the above steps to obtain correlation-spectra for each response bit, as shown in Fig. 6. Note that, even with a small challenge subset, we get a correlation-spectra similar to Boolean functions.

The key point to be noted is that after injecting the fault, there were negligible changes in the uniformity measure of the response bits, as can be found from the high similarity percentages in Table 2. In this table, we have listed some PUF instances along with its uniformity measure before and after fault injection. However, it can be observed that for each bit, there is a change in the mean and standard deviation of the frequency distribution which can be observed from Fig. 7. This shows that the key properties of a PUF are insufficient to detect if the PUF is being tampered with. Thus, analysing the correlation spectra helps us to judge the quality of PUFs.

In Fig. 7, we can see the change in the mean and standard deviation of the distributions for correct and faulty instances. Specifically, there is a decrease in the standard deviation in case of faulty PUFs in comparison to the good PUFs.

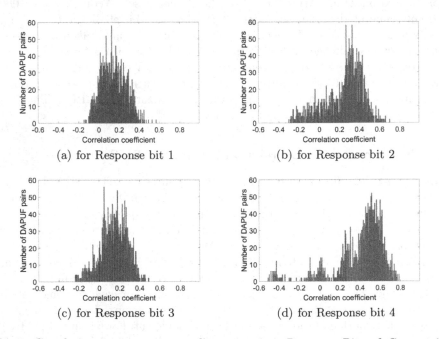

(a) for Response bit 1

(b) for Response bit 2

(c) for Response bit 3

(d) for Response bit 4

Fig. 5. Correlation-spectra corresponding to various Response Bits of *Correct* 5-4 DAPUF (for $N = 50$)

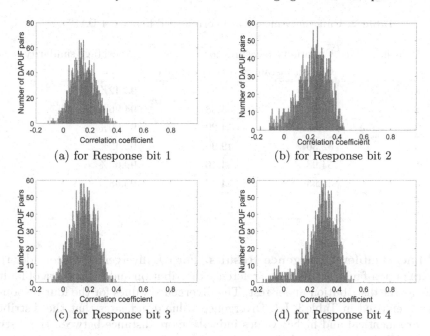

(a) for Response bit 1   (b) for Response bit 2

(c) for Response bit 3   (d) for Response bit 4

Fig. 6. Correlation-spectra corresponding to various response bits of *Faulty* 5-4 DAPUF (for $N = 50$)

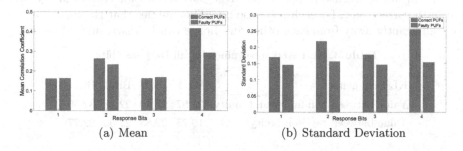

(a) Mean   (b) Standard Deviation

Fig. 7. Mean and standard deviation of *Correct* and *Faulty* PUFs

Smaller standard deviation values can be explained by a decrease in the range of correlation values. One plausible reason for the narrowing of the correlation range could be an introduction of bias in the responses.

4.3 Spectral Analysis Results for PUFs

Correlation analysis provides an essence of the change in the spectra with a change in circuit, but it fails to give a quantitative metric. Statistical tools gives a quantitative metric, which helps to understand the difference better. Given two correlation spectra, one for good PUF instances and one for faulty PUF instances, we use Kullback-Leibler Divergence to understand the statistical difference better.

Table 2. Uniformity measure of correct and faulty 5-4 DAPUFs

PUF instances	Uniformity measures for		Percentage similarity
	Correct instances	Faulty instances	
1	57.10	53.34	93.42%
2	56.74	53.88	94.96%
3	59.66	54.29	91.00%
4	52.36	49.96	95.42%
5	54.98	54.46	99.05%
6	56.93	54.47	95.68%
⋮	⋮	⋮	⋮

Kullback-Leibler Divergence Results. For KL divergence, we consider the spectra of non-faulty PUFs as the reference distribution and the spectra of faulty PUFs as the distribution under test. The divergence values for the four response bits are enlisted in Table 3. KL Divergence value 0 indicates that the distributions are identical and higher values indicate more distance between the distributions. We have compared the values with the divergence values for a pair of correct distributions (over different challenge sets), as shown in Table 3. There is a significant difference between the divergence values for correct-faulty pair and both correct pair, for each response bit. This implies that the distributions are significantly away from each other and hence can be distinguished easily.

Table 3. KL Divergence values for all Response bits

KL Divergence	Bit 1	Bit 2	Bit 3	Bit 4
Value between non faulty and faulty	21.97	27.10	22.18	32.50
Value between two non faulty	19.75	22.83	22.06	22.77

5 Conclusion

In this paper, we present a novel approach for formal analysis of PUF instances from the perspective of Boolean functions. Extending the Boolean function representation of PUFs, this work leverages the correlation properties of Boolean functions. From this work, we conclude that correlation of a sample of PUFs obeys Gaussian distribution, similar to a sample of randomly selected Boolean functions. Thus, for ideal PUFs, the probability distribution of both the samples should coincide. This forms a concrete base for analysis of PUF instances. We have also presented an overview of formal analysis tool (FCSA) to evaluate the *goodness* of PUFs. Our theoretical claims are well supported by the statistical test of a collection of good and faulty PUF instances. Thus, a combination of correlation analysis and statistical test provide a complete analytical picture and can be used as an aid during a new PUF characterization.

References

1. Bolotnyy, L., Robins, G.: Physically unclonable function-based security and privacy in RFID systems. In: Fifth Annual IEEE International Conference on Pervasive Computing and Communications, PerCom 2007, pp. 211–220. IEEE (2007)
2. Chatterjee, U., Sahoo, D.P., Mukhopadhyay, D., Chakraborty, R.S.: Trustworthy proofs for sensor data using FPGA based physically unclonable functions. In: Design, Automation and Test in Europe Conference and Exhibition (DATE), pp. 1504–1507. IEEE (2018)
3. Delvaux, J., Peeters, R., Gu, D., Verbauwhede, I.: A survey on lightweight entity authentication with strong PUFs. ACM Comput. Surv. (CSUR) **48**(2), 26 (2015)
4. Delvaux, J., Verbauwhede, I.: Fault injection modeling attacks on 65 nm arbiter and RO sum PUFs via environmental changes. IEEE Trans. Circuits Syst. I Regul. Pap. **61**(6), 1701–1713 (2014)
5. Ganji, F.: On the Learnability of Physically Unclonable Functions. Springer, Cham (2018). https://doi.org/10.1007/978-3-319-76717-8
6. Ganji, F., Tajik, S., Fäßler, F., Seifert, J.-P.: Strong machine learning attack against PUFs with no mathematical model. In: Gierlichs, B., Poschmann, A.Y. (eds.) CHES 2016. LNCS, vol. 9813, pp. 391–411. Springer, Heidelberg (2016). https://doi.org/10.1007/978-3-662-53140-2_19
7. Herder, C., Yu, M., Koushanfar, F., Devadas, S.: Physical unclonable functions and applications: a tutorial. Proc. IEEE **102**(8), 1126–1141 (2014)
8. Hori, Y., Yoshida, T., Katashita, T., Satoh, A.: Quantitative and statistical performance evaluation of arbiter physical unclonable functions on FPGAs. In: International Conference on Reconfigurable Computing and FPGAs, pp. 298–303, December 2010
9. Immler, V., Hiller, M., Obermaier, J., Sigl, G.: Take a moment and have some t: hypothesis testing on raw PUF data. In: 2017 IEEE International Symposium on Hardware Oriented Security and Trust (HOST), pp. 128–129. IEEE (2017)
10. Khalafalla, M., Gebotys, C.: PUFs deep attacks: enhanced modeling attacks using deep learning techniques to break the security of double arbiter PUFs. In: 2019 Design, Automation and Test in Europe Conference and Exhibition (DATE), pp. 204–209. IEEE (2019)
11. Kullback, S., Leibler, R.A.: On information and sufficiency. Ann. Math. Stat. **22**(1), 79–86 (1951)
12. Machida, T., Yamamoto, D., Iwamoto, M., Sakiyama, K.: A new mode of operation for arbiter PUF to improve uniqueness on FPGA. In: 2014 Federated Conference on Computer Science and Information Systems, pp. 871–878. IEEE (2014)
13. Maes, R., Van Herrewege, A., Verbauwhede, I.: PUFKY: a fully functional PUF-based cryptographic key generator. In: Prouff, E., Schaumont, P. (eds.) CHES 2012. LNCS, vol. 7428, pp. 302–319. Springer, Heidelberg (2012). https://doi.org/10.1007/978-3-642-33027-8_18
14. Maiti, A., Gunreddy, V., Schaumont, P.: A systematic method to evaluate and compare the performance of physical unclonable functions. In: Athanas, P., Pnevmatikatos, D., Sklavos, N. (eds.) Embedded Systems Design with FPGAs, pp. 245–267. Springer, New York (2013). https://doi.org/10.1007/978-1-4614-1362-2_11
15. O'Donnell, R.: Analysis of Boolean Functions. Cambridge University Press, New York (2014)
16. Ravikanth, P.S.: Physical one-way functions. Ph.D. thesis, Massachusetts (2001)

17. Rioul, O., Solé, P., Guilley, S., Danger, J.: On the entropy of physically unclonable functions. In: IEEE International Symposium on Information Theory (ISIT), pp. 2928–2932, July 2016
18. Rührmair, U.: Oblivious transfer based on physical unclonable functions. In: Acquisti, A., Smith, S.W., Sadeghi, A.-R. (eds.) Trust 2010. LNCS, vol. 6101, pp. 430–440. Springer, Heidelberg (2010). https://doi.org/10.1007/978-3-642-13869-0_31
19. Rührmair, U., Busch, H., Katzenbeisser, S.: Strong PUFs: models, constructions, and security proofs. In: Sadeghi, A.R., Naccache, D. (eds.) Towards Hardware-Intrinsic Security, pp. 79–96. Springer, Heidelberg (2010). https://doi.org/10.1007/978-3-642-14452-3_4
20. Sahoo, D.P., Bag, A., Patranabis, S., Mukhopadhyay, D., Chakraborty, R.S.: Fault-tolerant implementations of physically unclonable functions on FPGA. In: Chakraborty, R., Mathew, J., Vasilakos, A. (eds.) Security and Fault Tolerance in Internet of Things, pp. 129–153. Springer, Cham (2019). https://doi.org/10.1007/978-3-030-02807-7_7
21. Sarkar, P., Maitra, S.: Cross-correlation analysis of cryptographically useful boolean functions and S-boxes. Theory Comput. Syst. 35(1), 39–57 (2002)
22. Suh, G.E., Devadas, S.: Physical unclonable functions for device authentication and secret key generation. In: 44th ACM/IEEE Design Automation Conference, pp. 9–14, June 2007
23. Tajik, S., Lohrke, H., Ganji, F., Seifert, J.P., Boit, C.: Laser fault attack on physically unclonable functions. In: 2015 Workshop on Fault Diagnosis and Tolerance in Cryptography (FDTC), pp. 85–96. IEEE (2015)
24. Wang, Y., Wang, C., Gu, C., Cui, Y., O'Neill, M., Liu, W.: Theoretical analysis of delay-based PUFs and design strategies for improvement. In: 2019 IEEE International Symposium on Circuits and Systems (ISCAS), pp. 1–5. IEEE (2019)
25. Zhang, B., Srihari, S.N.: Properties of binary vector dissimilarity measures. In: Proceedings of JCIS International Conference on Computer Vision, Pattern Recognition, and Image Processing, vol. 1 (2003)

ProTro: A Probabilistic Counter Based Hardware Trojan Attack on FPGA Based MACSec Enabled Ethernet Switch

Vidya Govindan[1]([✉]), Sandhya Koteshwara[2], Amitabh Das[3], Keshab K. Parhi[2],
and Rajat Subhra Chakraborty[1]

[1] Department of Computer Science and Engineering,
Indian Institute of Technology Kharagpur, Kharagpur, West Bengal, India
vidya.mazhur@gmail.com, vidya.govindan@iitkgp.ac.in,
rschakraborty@gmail.com, rschakraborty@cse.iitkgp.ernet.in
[2] Department of Electrical and Computer Engineering,
University of Minnesota, Minneapolis, MN 55455, USA
{kotes001,parhi}@umn.edu
[3] Austin, TX, USA
dashamitabh@gmail.com

Abstract. Over the past decades, the exponentially high rate of growth in number of connected devices has been accompanied by the discovery of new security loopholes, vulnerabilities and attacks in the network infrastructure. The original ethernet protocol was not designed considering the security aspect of the network architecture. In order to improve the security of the ethernet, many solutions and standards have been proposed. The IEEE 802.1AE Media Access Control Security (MACSec) standard is one of the most recent link layer security protocols which provides encryption and authentication between two network interfaces for secure next-generation deployments. In this paper we present a network packet redirection attack on a MACSec enabled NetFPGA-SUME based ethernet switch, by means of a Hardware Trojan (HT). The HT design is based on a *probabilistic counter update mechanism* with multiple triggers which eventually affects the way in which a network packet flows through the switch. In particular, an activated HT redirects a packet to an incorrect port, and in turn to a malicious eavesdropper. The proposed HT evades most of the recent hardware trust verification schemes. We present the complete architecture of the proposed MACSec enabled ethernet switch, followed by the design and mode of operation of the HT with promising experimental results.

Keywords: FPGA · Hardware Trojan · AXI4-Stream · NetFPGA · MACSec · Network security · AES-GCM

1 Introduction

A steep increase in growth and demand of the internet bandwidth has forced the networking industry to continuously innovate the ethernet architecture. The

© Springer Nature Switzerland AG 2019
S. Bhasin et al. (Eds.): SPACE 2019, LNCS 11947, pp. 159–175, 2019.
https://doi.org/10.1007/978-3-030-35869-3_12

advent of Internet of Things has opened a whole new world – be it data centers hosting cloud services, in-car automotive networks or a smart grid infrastructure. The success of the Internet has left it unprotected and defenseless at the hands of resourceful malicious attackers [18]. In view of this scenario, there is great necessity of a very stable security mechanism to protect data integrity, authenticity and confidentiality. The IEEE 802.1AE MACSec standard is one step towards securing the current ethernet architecture at Layer 2 of the Open Systems Interconnection (OSI) network model [14]. In [2], the authors have presented a hardware implementation of the MACSec protocol suitable for automotive applications on Altera Stratix V FPGA. The paper [16] proposes MACSec based Layer 2 security for Smart Grid Communication networks.

A Hardware Trojan (HT) is defined as a malicious, intentional modification of a circuit design that results in undesired behavior when the circuit is deployed [30]. Designs that are infected by a HT may experience changes to their functionality or specification, may leak sensitive information, or may experience degraded or unreliable performance. Designing a stealthy yet powerful HT has been the goal of many researchers. There are a plethora of sophisticated methods available in the literature, which have been proposed to detect different types of HTs. Some of these HT detection techniques include formal and functional verification schemes [8,10,23], Unused Circuit Identification (UCI) [13], Functional Analysis for Nearly-unused Circuit Identification (FANCI) [29], Verification for Hardware Trust (VeriTrust), and Hardware Trojan Catcher (HaTCh) [11]. However, side-by-side techniques to defeat many of the above mentioned state-of-the-art HT detection techniques have also been proposed, e.g., those targeting Unused Circuit Identification (UCI) [26], Hardware Trust Verification [34], malicious LUT [20] and XOR-LFSR [12] (please refer to Sect. 2 for more details).

This paper presents a HT attack on a MACSec enabled ethernet switch implemented on NetFPGA-SUME board. To the best of our understanding this is the first work which targets a MACSec enabled ethernet switch architecture using a multi-level probabilistic counter based HT that redirects the data packets to incorrect ports, possibly to malicious eavesdroppers. Given its probabilistic mode of operation, we have named our designed HT as **Pro**babilistic **Tro**jan (ProTro). The ProTro HT when implemented has negligible overhead, and severely interferes with the proper functionality of the ethernet switch. This HT also evades most of the hardware trust verification techniques like UCI, VeriTrust and HaTCh with the help of a non-deterministic element in its construction. The major contributions of this paper are the following: (a) a hardware implementation of MACSec standard on NetFPGA-SUME platform, and, (b) an implementation of a highly disruptive but stealthy and low-overhead HT, targeting this FPGA implementation, that affects the confidentiality of the data processed by this switch.

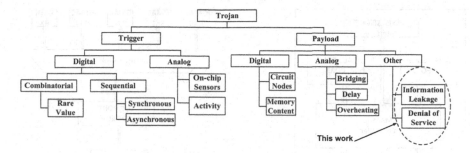

Fig. 1. Trojan designs: a structural classification [3] (adapted with modifications).

2 Background

2.1 Hardware Trojan

Hardware Trojans can be classified in many ways. We describe one of the most widely accepted classifications based on HT structure and impact. Generally, HTs comprises of two sections: a *trigger* for its initiation and a *payload* to cause the undesired function. But few types of HTs exists without trigger [21]. The triggers can be launched from the internals of circuits such as the output of on-chip sensor [1], as well as external such as particular input. However, it is reasonable to assume that the attacker will retain some control over the HT, and in the process she will make it externally triggered. To be undetectable during the test phase and most of the deployment phase, HTs are designed to get activated at extremely rare conditions [4]. Based on structure, classification of HTs was mentioned in [3] (please refer to Fig. 1). This classification considers digital, analog and hybrid (combination of digital and analog) HTs, e.g., analog trigger mechanism with digital payload [6]. Digital HTs constitute the most common threats. **The HT proposed in this paper is digitally triggered which causes both information leakage and denial-of-service.** An important recent alternative classification of HTs has been presented in [11], by dividing them into S_t and S_i groups, where S_t refers to the HTs which leverage the standard I/O channels to deliver the payload, while S_i represents the HTs which use side-channels to deliver the payload. S_t class of HTs are further classified into deterministic (H_D) and non-deterministic (H_{ND}) types, where H_D represents the HTs which are embedded in a digital IP core whose output is a function of only its input, and the algorithmic specification of the IP core can exactly predict the IP core behavior. In this work we present a H_{ND} type HT whose details are described in Sect. 4.

2.2 FPGA Based Secured Ethernet Switch

MACSec is a security standard which provides secure communication between stations that are attached to the same Local Area Network (LAN). It comprises of two standards, namely IEEE 802.1AE [15] and IEEE 802.1X [14].

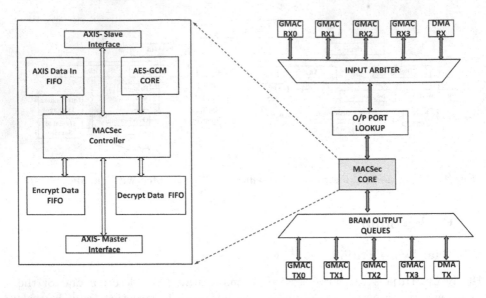

Fig. 2. Proposed MACSec-enabled ethernet switch architecture. This is a combination of the FPGA-SUME ethernet switch with the MACSec core.

IEEE 802.1AE specifies provisions for connectionless user data confidentiality, frame data integrity, and data origin authenticity by media access independent protocols and entities that communicate transparently with MAC clients [15]. IEEE 802.1X specifies a general method for port-based network access control. It also defines protocols such as MACSec Key Agreement (MKA) that establishes secure associations and facilitates the use of industry standard authentication and authorization protocols [14]. MACSec uses keys derived from MKA protocol to encrypt data of authenticated users and perform integrity check on the data, using the Advanced Encryption Standard-Galois Counter Mode (AES-GCM 128/256 bit) as the cipher suite for cryptographic functions. In brief, the MACSec security architecture comprises of a control plane that provides the keys using an authenticated key agreement protocol, and a data plane for secure transport of payloads in order to protect the upper protocol data.

In this paper we have implemented the MACSec protocol at the ethernet switch level which behaves as one of the connected devices in a point-to-point MACSec secure network architecture. We assume that the keys required for the cryptographic operations have been already installed after the successful completion of the MKA protocol using a software. The full-fledged implementation of the control plane services are beyond the scope of this paper. Figure 2 shows the overall architecture of the MACSec-enabled ethernet, details of which, including the implementation details of the data plane provisions are discussed in Sect. 3.

Applying reconfigurable hardware for network infrastructure security has drawn plenty of attention recently in the network security community [5]. The increasing number and sophistication of attacks, the performance limitations

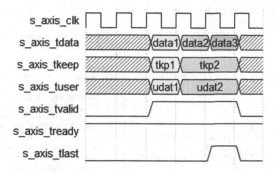

Fig. 3. AXI4-Stream slave interface bus signals.

of sequential software execution, and the increase in network throughput all contribute to a huge gap between the requirements and implementations. NetF-PGA [35], an open-source platform for rapid prototyping and deployment of networking devices with I/O capabilities up to 100 Gbps, can be used to reduce this gap. The NetFPGA project [28] currently supports three platforms, of which NetFPGA-SUME is the most recent platform. The NetFPGA-SUME board is based on the *Xilinx Virtex-7* Field Programmable Gate Array (FPGA), along with peripherals such as 3rd generation PCI Express (PCIe), multiple memory interfaces, and high-speed expansion interfaces. In this work we propose a hardware implementation of the basic MACSec protocol over the NetFPGA-SUME's reference switch design [22]. The AXI4-Stream protocol [31] is one of the data interfacing protocols added in the ARM AMBA4 specifications to support low resource, high bandwidth unidirectional data transfers. It is well-suited for FPGA implementation because the transfer protocol allows for high frequency versus clock latency trade-offs to help meet design goals. An ethernet packet flows through data plane of the reference switch design on the NetFPGA-SUME platform through AXI4-Stream interface [32]. The protocol interface consists of a master interface and a slave interface. The two interfaces are symmetric and point-to-point, such that master interface output signals can connect directly to the slave interface input signals. Typical signals at the AXI4-Stream slave interface are depicted in Fig. 3 where a valid data transfer takes place whenever s_axis_tvalid and s_axis_tready signals are asserted. An asserted s_axis_tlast signal indicates that the last word has been transmitted. The signal s_axis_tkeep is a byte identifier in the s_axis_tdata and the signal s_axis_tuser consists of user defined information. Next, we describe the system architecture of the MACSec enabled ethernet switch, as adopted by us on the NetFPGA-SUME platform.

3 System Architecture

As mentioned in the previous section, the system architecture is based on NetFPGA-SUME's reference switch design [22]. The reference switch design has

Table 1. Verilog code snippets from MAC CAM Lookup Module

MAC Address learning	Destination Port Lookup Update
```//MAC Address learning always @ (posedge clk) begin if (reset) lut[i] <= {(56){1'b0}}; else if (lookup_req) begin if ((lut[i][47:0] == src_mac) || (~lut_learn_hit[15] && (lut_wr_addr == i))) // lut[i] <= {(src_port), src_mac}; lut[i] <= {src_port[7:3],src_port[0],src_port[1] ,src_port[2], src_mac}; end end```	```//Destination Port Lookup Update always (posedge clk) begin if(reset) dst_ports <= {8{1'b0}}; else begin if (lookup_req) begin //dst_ports <= (lut_lookup_hit[15]) ? // (rd_oq[15][7:0] & ~(src_port)) : // (DEFAULT_MISS_OUTPUT_PORTS & ~src_port); case ({llh_m,llh}) 2'b00: begin dst_ports <= d1; end 2'b01: begin dst_ports <= r1; end 2'b10: begin dst_ports <= d1; end 2'b11: begin dst_ports <= r2; end endcase end end end```

a pipelined architecture, with three main stages, namely the Input Arbiter, the Output Port Lookup and the Block RAM (BRAM) Output queues, as depicted in Fig. 2. However, the architecture is flexible enough to allow an user to insert his/her own module as part of the pipeline, for additional functionality. In our case, we have introduced a MACSec core module into the reference data pipeline which makes the switch design MACSec-enabled. The ethernet packet is received by the board through one of the four SFP+ interfaces, which is accepted by the design's 10 Gigabit ethernet MAC (GMAC) IP.

The data pipeline follows packet based module interfaces according to the AXI4-Stream protocol. The input arbiter has five input interfaces: four GMAC RX modules and one Direct Memory Access (DMA) RX module. Each input to the arbiter connects to an input queue, which is in fact a small fall-through FIFO. The simple arbiter is time-multiplexed between all the input queues in a round-robin manner, each time selecting a non-empty queue and writing one full packet from it to the next stage in the data-path. The Output Port Lookup module is responsible for deciding the packet output port with the help of the destination MAC address (dMAC) register. After that decision is made, the packet is then handed to the output queues module. The lookup module implements a simple learning Content Addressable Memory (CAM) implemented using Xilinx's CAM core. Packets with unknown destination MAC address are broadcasted. Once a packet arrives to the BRAM Output Queues module, it already has a marked destination (provided on the TUSER field of the stream interface). According to the destination it enters a dedicated output queue. There are five such output queues: one per each 10 Gbps port and one to the DMA block. The DMA module includes Xilinx's PCIe core, a DMA engine and AXI4 Interconnect module. To the other NetFPGA modules it exposes AXI4-Stream (master+slave) interfaces for sending/receiving packets, as well as a AXI4-LITE master interface through which all AXI registers can be accessed from the host (over PCIe). The reference switch design also implements a Xilinx Microblaze 32-bit RISC processor subsystem, including a BRAM block and its controller.

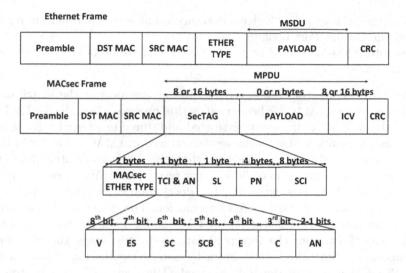

Fig. 4. Ethernet and MACSec-secured ethernet data format [15].

The MACSec protocol as described in [15] provides secure communication between stations that are attached to the same LAN by forming a set of trusted entities. Every station can receive both encrypted or unencrypted messages depending on the configuration of the system policy. Every node capable of participating in an instance of the secure MAC Service comprises both a MAC Security Key Agreement Entity (KaY) and a MAC Security Entity (SecY). A secure Connectivity Association (CA) is created between the communicating nodes which may have multiple Secure Channels (SCs) supporting secure transmission of frames through the use of symmetric key cryptography. Each SC supports multiple Security Associations (SAs), each of which uses a fresh Secure Association Key (SAK) to provide the MACSec security services for a sequence of transmitted frames. The protocol modifies the traditional ethernet frame structure to include MACSec specific functions by adding a Security TAG (SecTAG) and an Integrity Check Value (ICV) along with the secure data. The ethernet frame and its modified MACSec-enabled version is shown in Fig. 4. The MACSec core implemented by us consists of a MACSec controller, an AES-GCM core and three data FIFOs to facilitate the encryption and decryption functions. The controller along with AES-GCM core is the central part of the design. The controller core controls and synchronizes the following operations:

1. Receive inbound ("Ingress") ethernet packet with MACSec header at an input port.
2. Extract MACSec header from Ingress packet.
3. Decrypt user data and perform secure frame verification, with credentials of process bound to Ingress port.
4. Encrypt user data and generate secure frame for outbound ("Egress") ethernet packet, with credentials of process bound to Outgress port.

5. Route the packet to the Outgress port, according to the information received from the Output Port Lookup module.
6. Generate AXI4-Stream Master Interface signal to announce completion of operation.

The MACSec ethernet frame arrives through one port of the switch design and first undergoes a MACSec header extraction process, where the SecTAG field along with the MAC addresses are extracted and stored in internal registers. The source and destination MAC addresses are stored in sMACSec and dMACSec registers, respectively. We assume here that the SAKs associated with every frame are already updated into the key registers of the MACSec core. Once the incoming frame header is extracted, the decryption of the data is performed using the obtained Key and SecTAG information. The symmetric key algorithm used in this core is the efficient AES-GCM 128-bit implementation described in [19]. Before forwarding the decrypted data to the next stage, the receive path performs an integrity check verification by comparing the tag generated from the AES-GCM core with the ICV received. The decrypted data is stored in the Decrypt data FIFO if the frame verification is successful. As soon as the Decrypt data FIFO receives first word of data, the frame encryption process is initiated with a different key associated with the Egress port (port that forwards network traffic or the exiting port) of the switch. The ethernet switch model considered in this work operates as follows. The incoming encrypted data arriving at the incoming port ("Ingress port") is decrypted using a key ("key-1"), and is encrypted again using a different key ("key-2") for the outgoing port ("Egress port") of the switch. The encrypted data received from the AES-GCM core is stored in the Encrypt data FIFO before being sent out through the AXI4-master interface, after performing the frame encapsulation using the new SecTAG and key information. **This method of operation makes it vulnerable to HT attacks in which the HT infects the ethernet switch itself, because inside the switch the data traffic is available in an unencrypted form between the abovementioned decryption and the encryption steps. This observation is the main motivation behind the method of working of the HT designed by us, as described in the next section.**

4   Mode of Operation of Inserted Hardware Trojan

4.1   Threat Model

Our threat model is based on the model discussed in [25,34]. We assume that a hardware design can be covertly compromised by HTs inserted into Register Transfer Level (RTL) source code or the gate-level netlist. These HTs are introduced by one or more rogue designers in the in-house design team, or integrated into the design with third-party IP (3PIP) cores. An attacker having physical access to the board or an attacker who can reconfigure the FPGA bitstream remotely through partial reconfiguration during a design update [17] could introduce the proposed HT.

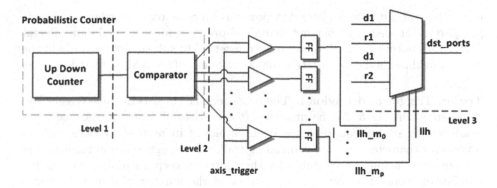

Fig. 5. Proposed Hardware Trojan circuit.

Consider a scenario that the simple ethernet switch is deployed in a data center. In order to support higher speed and better security policies, data centers are moving towards Layer-2 secure connectivity inside the center [7]. The Layer-2 security policy facilitates updating the ethernet switch core with MAC-Sec functionality. While adding the MACSec functionality, the new design also opens up the possibility of a HT being introduced that can modify the flow of packets through the switch. Once the HT is activated, data which needs to be secured using the MACSec protocol is no longer secure, as it is delivered to an incorrect port, possibly being accessed by a malicious user. **From a network perspective, this can be viewed as an example of a network packet interception and removal, or network traffic redirection attack leading to Denial of Service (DoS), while from a security perspective, this is an information leakage attack.**

4.2 Hardware Trojan Design

Trojan Premise. Our attack is based on a HT which is embedded in the Output Port Lookup module of the reference switch design discussed in Sect. 3. The Output Port Lookup module consists of two main submodules: ethernet parser and learning CAM. The ethernet parser module first extracts the source and destination MAC address and the source port from the input packet. The fields are next looked up in the CAM, implementing a lookup table (LUT). If the result is a hit, the packet is sent to the destination ports indicated by the lookup (except for the source port), if the result is a miss, the destination ports are set to broadcast to all output ports (except for the source port). If the source MAC is not found in the LUT, it is learned for future lookups.

Table 1 shows Verilog code snippets from the learning CAM switch module (`mac_cam_lut.v`). The register `lut` represents the lookup table (LUT) which stores the source address and the corresponding port. Each entry in this memory is 56 bits wide (8 bits for the port and 48 bits for the address). At the end of each lookup the register `dst_ports` consists of the information as to which ports the input packet has to be sent out. The register dst_ports is an 8-bit register, where each output port is encoded in an one-hot manner supporting up to a maximum of eight ports. This output port information is transferred to subsequent modules in the data plane through the meta-data signal axis_tuser of the AXI4 stream interface.

Trojan Trigger and Payload. The proposed HT consists of three trigger levels as shown in Fig. 5. At the first level it comprises of a probabilistic counter. Traditionally packet counting has been employed in network devices such as routers for characterizing and controlling traffic. For diagnostic and record keeping purposes, it may be desirable for the router to keep a running total of the number of dropped packets. Keeping track of the number of dropped packets may require large hardware registers that can be time consuming to update. Thus, there is a need to efficiently maintain a counter capable of counting a large number of items. We assume that one such counter pre-existed in the network switch design, and has been replaced by a malicious probabilistic counter (as part of the inserted HT). Probabilistic counters have been used widely in processor architectures to improve predictability [9,24]. In this design, the probabilistic counter is enabled whenever an incoming packet has one of the following EtherType field values:

- MACSec packet - 0x88E5
- IPv4 packet - 0x0800
- IPv6 packet - 0x86DD
- ARP packet - 0x0806

The counter update mechanism is based on a hardware pseudo-random number generator (PRNG) to increment or decrement counter value, as described in [24]. A generalized counter is represented as 4-tuple (n, I, D, T): an n-bit counter's value is incremented by I or decremented by D on the basis of two different values of an *up_down* signal, with T being a pre-determined threshold value.

In our HT design the counter value is incremented whenever the switch receives an IPv4 or IPv6 packet, and it is decremented when the switch receives a MACSec or ARP packet. The counter is updated only when the PRNG output value is greater than the threshold value T, which we also term as the HT "trigger value". The resulting counter value is then passed through a complex combinational and flip-flop based circuit, which forms the second-level trigger. In our implementation we used an 8-bit counter with $I = D = 1$, and $T = 0x7C1FE0$ represented as $(8, 1, 1, 0x7C1FE0)$. The PRNG used in this work is a 23-bit Fibonacci linear feedback shift register (LFSR) with a primitive polynomial $x^{23} + x^{18} + 1$. Because we use a probabilistic counter in the design of our HT, we term our HT **Pro**babilistic **Tro**jan (ProTro). The second level of the trigger also consists of the signal axis_trigger, which is defined by the combination of AXI4 stream slave signals of Output Port Lookup module as:

$$\text{axis\_trigger} = \text{s\_axis\_tvalid} \& \text{s\_axis\_tready} \& (\sim\text{s\_axis\_tlast}) \qquad (1)$$

The signal llh_m, i.e., the malicious LUT lookup hit signal forms the third level of the trigger mechanism. This signal, when active, affects the Trojan payload. The

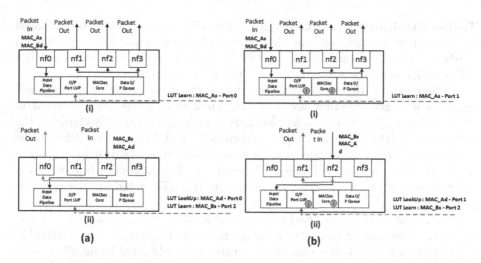

Fig. 6. Ethernet packet flow in a switch design with and without inserted HT.

HT payload comprises of the registers `lut` and `dst_ports` as shown in Table 1. It can be observed that when the HT is inactive only the `lut_lookup_hit` (`llh`) signal is used to update the `dst_ports` register, while when the HT is active the `llh_m` signal also contributes to the `dst_ports` output value. The signals `d1`, `r1` and `r2` are defined as follows:

$$d1 = \text{DEFAULT\_OUTPUT\_PORTS} \,\&\, (\sim \text{src\_port}) \tag{2}$$

$$r1 = \text{rd\_oq}[15][7:0] \,\&\, \sim \text{src\_port} \tag{3}$$

$$r2 = \text{rd\_oq}[15][7:0] \,\&\, (\sim (\text{src\_port} << 2)) \tag{4}$$

The `rd_oq` register acts as an intermediate register which stores the addresses looked up and the associated ports. It is the value of this register which finally updates `dst_ports` and the `axis_tuser` signal of AXI4-Stream bus. Note that the MAC address learning mechanism is also slightly altered during writing in the `lut` register by swapping the input `src_port` bits. This modification is crucial for the HT operation as it changes the port associated to a particular MAC address. **More specifically, by multiplication of the `src_port` signal by 4, as shown in Eq. (4), only the input `src_port` values of 0x01 and 0x04 are changed by swapping one with the other. This means a packet arriving at the physical port-0 is learned in the switch to be associated with the physical port-1, and vice versa, leading to passing packets to incorrect ports. If these ports are being currently accessed by malicious eavesdropper process, the possibly confidential data to the process of port-0 is accessed by an unintended receiver at port-1. As a result, the process at port-0 will be experiencing simultaneously a DoS attack and confidentiality violation.**

Trojan Stealthiness and Detection. The effectiveness of any HT is based on its ability to evade existing detection techniques, while having minimum hardware area overhead. In this section we discuss about how our proposed HT is unaffected by state-of-the art HT detection techniques.

Hicks et al. in [13] proposed to detect rare event triggering using data flow graph of a design. Multiple levels of functional simulations are performed in order to flag a signal or circuit as malicious or unused. By carefully changing the code writing style and trigger inputs, an circuit which has been identified to be "unused" by the UCI technique, can be transformed to a useful circuit as shown in [26,33]. Our proposed HT inherently evades UCI technique by implementing the comparator and multiplexer circuit in the HT RTL, following the methods proposed in [26].

Walksman et al. in [29] tried to statically identify "weakly affecting inputs" which are wires having the potential of operating as HT trigger. This method of HT detection is based on computing a control value obtained by building truth tables of intermediate outputs in the suspicious circuit. Here, a signal is deemed suspicious when the control value remains under a threshold value. The authors of [34] have shown that FANCI can be defeated by making control values of Trojan related signals comparable to those of normal signals. This can be done by introducing multiple sequential levels in the HT trigger logic. We propose similar modification in our HT design in order to evade FANCI.

Also in [34], a method to overcome the VeriTrust detection technique is also proposed which makes the Trojan affected signals driven by only non-redundant inputs under non-trigger condition. The authors also provide well-explained observation on how most of the Trust-Hub [27] benchmark HTs are all explicitly triggered, and hence detectable by VeriTrust. To counteract detection techniques, they implemented HTs which are implicitly triggered which means the HT generated output is indistinguishable from the normal output. There are other papers such as [20] which evades all the above mentioned detection techniques and proposed an effective HT design. It should be noted that most of these Trojan design and detection techniques are centered around RTL design modification and very few of them are directed towards FPGA application only. In this work, we launch an attack on FPGA based Ethernet switch through the means of a HT inserted through partial reconfiguration.

Recently, in [11], Haider et al. proposed a HT detection algorithm, namely Hardware Trojan Catcher (HaTCh) which claims to detect a large and complex class of deterministic HTs. The HaTCh tool consists of two phases. The first phase is the "learning phase" which performs functional testing on an IP core under test, and produces a blacklist of all the unactivated potentially harmful transitions of internal wires. The second phase is the "tagging phase" which adds additional logic to the core to track the previously listed malicious behavior. The main claim of this work is that it can detect a larger class of HTs with much less computational complexity and false positives when compared to other existing works.

Also, considering the classification of HTs by [11] as presented in Sect. 2, one can easily observe that the HT proposed in our work falls under H_{ND} class, since the IP core here is the switch design whose behavior is largely dependent on the

Table 2. Design overhead for ProTro

Resource	Without HT	With HT	HT insertion overhead (%)
LUT	48650	48744	0.19
LUTRAM	1880	1880	0.00
FF	70264	70376	0.16
BRAM (kbit)	213.50	213.50	0.00
BUFG	22	22	0.00
MMCM	3	3	0.00
PCIe	1	1	0.00
Power (watt)	6.90	6.90	0.00

traffic that the switch is subjected to. Even if we consider that there exists a deterministic algorithmic specification of the design implemented in this work, the detection of our HT is very difficult, firstly because it has multiple trigger levels, and secondly it involves a probabilistic counter.

5 Experimental Results

The HT described in the previous section was designed using Verilog HDL, and the HT-free and HT-infected ethernet switches were implemented on Xilinx's Virtex-7 based NetFPGA-SUME board, using Xilinx Vivado (v. 2016.4) design platform. A Python based testing framework is part of the NetFPGA reference switch project, which was modified to include then MACSec module, to verify the functionality of the design. Packet stimuli and verification scripts were built using the scapy Python module, which was also used to construct MACSec packets.

In the Python testing infrastructure, first a packet is sent with pre-defined source and destination MAC addresses through the nf0 port of the board as shown in Fig. 6(a)(i). We assume that the switch's CAM table is initially empty. As an incoming packet is received at an Ingress port, the switch collects the source address of the packet and adds that source address to a lookup table of addresses that the switch maintains. So the first packet received is broadcast to other ports of the switch, while it learns the MAC address associated to the port (we indicate this as LUT Learn). For example, here MAC_A_s is the source address associated with port-0 of the switch. Second, another packet with MAC_A_d as the destination address is sent through the nf2 port as shown in Fig. 6(a)(ii). Under normal condition as the switch has learned the port associated with MAC_A_d earlier, the packet is correctly directed out of the port-0 of the switch by looking up the port from the CAM table (we indicate this as LUT Lookup). The switch also learns the port associated with the new source address MAC_B_s.

When the proposed HT is active, during the learning phase of source MAC address, the associated port linked to this address is modified and then stored

Table 3. TrustHub benchmark overhead

Trust-Hub Trojans	Resource overhead (%)			
	LUT	LUTRAM	FF	BRAM
MC8051T200	0.80	0	0	0
MC8051T300	0.19	0	0	0
MC8051T400	15.30	0	1.45	0
MC8051T500	2.82	0	0	0
MC8051T600	0.50	0	0	0
MC8051T700	3.74	0	0	0
MC8051T800	0.32	0	0	0
Average	3.38	0	0.20	0
PIC16F84T100	6.25	0	0	0
PIC16F84T200	1.30	38.40	3.10	0
PIC16F84T300	1.32	38.40	0.37	0
PIC16F84T400	1.20	38.40	37.00	0
Average	2.51	28.80	10.12	0

in the CAM table, as indicated in Fig. 6(b)(i). Now, instead of storing the nf0 port with MAC_A$_s$, the switch saves nf1 port with MAC_A$_s$. As a result of this malicious hardware modification, one can observe that a packet destined to be sent out of the nf0 port is actually directed out of nf1 port (Fig. 6(b)(ii)). The highlighted yellow marking in Fig. 6(b) indicates the presence of HT in these particular modules of the switch. Table 2 shows the resource overhead of the proposed design, with and without HT. The HT circuit only incurs 0.19% and 0.16% overhead for the number of LUTs and flip-flop (FF) elements respectively. The number of FF elements can be reduced or eliminated altogether if we use the pre-exiting counters in the switch design to characterize the traffic, and one such counter is reconfigured to behave differently in this case as an HT. In Table 3 we have compared ProTro with similar TrustHub Benchmarks which fall under the H$_{ND}$ category. We can observe that our proposed Trojan is comparable or even better than state-of-the-art Trojan designs, in terms of resource overhead. Also the inserted HT did not incur any delay and power overhead.

6   Conclusion

In this paper we have presented a hardware implementation of the MACSec protocol over an ethernet switch reference design targeting the NetFPGA-SUME platform. We have also proposed a HT attack on this MACSec enabled switch, whereby the normal functionality of the switch is altered such that an eavesdropper user attached to one of the ports of the switch can receive the ethernet traffic intended for another user. Our proposed HT circuitry is based on a probabilistic counter. The proposed HT's resource overhead is negligible, and since it is based on a multi-level trigger mechanism, detection of such a HT is extremely difficult using the state-of-the-art detection techniques. Our future work will involve integrating the MKA protocol to develop a complete hardware-software co-design for FPGA based ethernet security, and development of advanced HT detection techniques to detect HTs of the type proposed in the paper.

References

1. Bhunia, S., et al.: Protection against hardware Trojan attacks: towards a comprehensive solution. IEEE Des. Test **30**(3), 6–17 (2013)
2. Carnevale, B., Falaschi, F., Crocetti, L., Hunjan, H., Bisase, S., Fanucci, L.: An implementation of the 802.1AE MAC security standard for in-car networks. In: 2015 IEEE 2nd World Forum on Internet of Things (WF-IoT), pp. 24–28 (2015)
3. Chakraborty, R.S., Narasimhan, S., Bhunia, S.: Hardware Trojan: threats and emerging solutions. In: Proceedings of the IEEE International High Level Design Validation and Test Workshop (HLDVT 2009), pp. 166–171. IEEE (2009)
4. Chakraborty, R.S., Wolff, F., Paul, S., Papachristou, C., Bhunia, S.: *MERO*: a statistical approach for hardware Trojan detection. In: Clavier, C., Gaj, K. (eds.) CHES 2009. LNCS, vol. 5747, pp. 396–410. Springer, Heidelberg (2009). https://doi.org/10.1007/978-3-642-04138-9_28
5. Chen, H., Chen, Y., Summerville, D.H.: A survey on the application of FPGAs for network infrastructure security (2011)
6. Chen, Z., Guo, X., Nagesh, R., Reddy, A., Gora, M., Maiti, A.: Hardware Trojan designs on BASYS FPGA board. In: Embedded System Challenge Contest in Cyber Security Awareness Week-CSAW (2008)
7. CISCO Ethernet Encryption for High Speed WAN deployments (2018). https://www.cisco.com/c/dam/en/us/td/docs/solutions/Enterprise/Security/MACsec/WP-High-Speed-WAN-Encrypt-MACsec.pdf
8. Cruz, J., Farahmandi, F., Ahmed, A., Mishra, P.: Hardware Trojan detection using ATPG and model checking. In: 2018 31st International Conference on VLSI Design and 2018 17th International Conference on Embedded Systems (VLSID), pp. 91–96, January 2018. https://doi.org/10.1109/VLSID.2018.43
9. Dice, D., Lev, Y., Moir, M.: Scalable statistics counters. In: Proceedings of the Twenty-Fifth Annual ACM Symposium on Parallelism in Algorithms and Architectures, SPAA 2013, pp. 43–52. ACM, New York (2013). https://doi.org/10.1145/2486159.2486182. http://doi.acm.org/10.1145/2486159.2486182
10. Guo, X., Dutta, R.G., Jin, Y., Farahmandi, F., Mishra, P.: Pre-silicon security verification and validation: a formal perspective. In: 2015 52nd ACM/EDAC/IEEE Design Automation Conference (DAC), pp. 1–6, June 2015. https://doi.org/10.1145/2744769.2747939
11. Haider, S.K., Jin, C., Ahmad, M., Shila, D.M., Khan, O., van Dijk, M.: Advancing the State-of-the-Art in Hardware Trojans Detection. IEEE Trans. Dependable Secur. Comput. **16**(1), 18–32 (2019). https://doi.org/10.1109/TDSC.2017.2654352
12. Haider, S.K., Jin, C., van Dijk, M.: Advancing the state-of-the-art in hardware Trojans design. CoRR abs/1605.08413 (2016). http://arxiv.org/abs/1605.08413
13. Hicks, M., Finnicum, M., King, S.T., Martin, M.M.K., Smith, J.M.: Overcoming an untrusted computing base: detecting and removing malicious hardware automatically. In: 2010 IEEE Symposium on Security and Privacy, pp. 159–172, May 2010. https://doi.org/10.1109/SP.2010.18

14. IEEE Standard for Local and metropolitan area networks–Port-Based Network Access Control (2010)
15. IEEE Standard for Local and Metropolitan Area Networks: Media Access Control (MAC) Security (2006)
16. Indukuri, N.R.: Layer 2 security for smart grid networks. In: 2012 IEEE International Conference on Advanced Networks and Telecommunciations Systems (ANTS), pp. 99–104 (2012)
17. Johnson, A.P., Saha, S., Chakraborty, R.S., Mukhopadhyay, D., Gören, S.: Fault attack on AES via hardware Trojan insertion by dynamic partial reconfiguration of FPGA over ethernet. In: Proceedings of the 9th Workshop on Embedded Systems Security, WESS 2014, pp. 1:1–1:8 (2014)
18. Kiravuo, T., Sarela, M., Manner, J.: A survey of ethernet LAN security. IEEE Commun. Surv. Tutor. 15(3), 1477–1491 (2013)
19. Koteshwara, S., Das, A., Parhi, K.K.: FPGA implementation and comparison of AES-GCM and Deoxys authenticated encryption schemes. In: 2017 IEEE International Symposium on Circuits and Systems (ISCAS), pp. 1–4 (2017)
20. Krieg, C., Wolf, C., Jantsch, A.: Malicious LUT: a stealthy FPGA Trojan injected and triggered by the design flow. In: 2016 IEEE/ACM International Conference on Computer-Aided Design (ICCAD), pp. 1–8, November 2016. https://doi.org/10.1145/2966986.2967054
21. Lin, L., Burleson, W., Paar, C.: MOLES: malicious off-chip leakage enabled by side-channels. In: Proceedings of the 2009 International Conference on Computer-Aided Design, pp. 117–122. ACM (2009)
22. NetFPGA SUME's Reference Switch Design (2018). https://github.com/NetFPGA/NetFPGA-SUME-public/wiki/NetFPGA-SUME-Reference-Learning-Switch
23. Rajendran, J., Dhandayuthapany, A.M., Vedula, V., Karri, R.: Formal security verification of third party intellectual property cores for information leakage. In: 2016 29th International Conference on VLSI Design and 2016 15th International Conference on Embedded Systems (VLSID), pp. 547–552, January 2016. https://doi.org/10.1109/VLSID.2016.143
24. Riley, N., Zilles, C.: Probabilistic counter updates for predictor hysteresis and bias. IEEE Comput. Archit. Lett. 5(1), 18–21 (2006)
25. Rostami, M., Koushanfar, F., Karri, R.: A primer on hardware security: models, methods, and metrics. Proc. IEEE 102(8), 1283–1295 (2014)
26. Sturton, C., Hicks, M., Wagner, D., King, S.T.: Defeating UCI: building stealthy and malicious hardware. In: 2011 IEEE Symposium on Security and Privacy, pp. 64–77, May 2011
27. Tehranipoor, M., Karri, R., Koushanfar, F., Potkonjak, M.: Trust-Hub (2019). http://trust-hub.org
28. The NetFPGA Project (2018). https://netfpga.org/
29. Waksman, A., Suozzo, S., Sethumadhavan, S.: FANCI: identification of stealthy malicious logic using Boolean functional analysis. In: Proceedings of the 2013 ACM SIGSAC Conference on Computer and Communications Security, CCS 2013, pp. 697–708 (2013). https://doi.org/10.1145/2508859.2516654
30. Xiao, K., Forte, D., Jin, Y., Karri, R., Bhunia, S., Tehranipoor, M.: Hardware Trojans: lessons learned after one decade of research. ACM Trans. Des. Autom. Electron. Syst. 22(1), 6:1–6:23 (2016)
31. Xilinx AXI Protocol Reference Guide (2018). https://www.xilinx.com/support/documentation/ip_documentation/ug761_axi_reference_guide.pdf

32. Xilinx AXI4-Stream Infrastructure IP Suite (2018). https://www.xilinx.com/support/documentation/ip_documentation/axis_infrastructure_ip_suite/v1_1/pg085-axi4stream-infrastructure.pdf
33. Zhang, J., Xu, Q.: On hardware Trojan design and implementation at register-transfer level. In: 2013 IEEE International Symposium on Hardware-Oriented Security and Trust (HOST), pp. 107–112, June 2013. https://doi.org/10.1109/HST.2013.6581574
34. Zhang, J., Yuan, F., Xu, Q.: DeTrust: defeating hardware trust verification with stealthy implicitly-triggered hardware trojans. In: Proceedings of the 2014 ACM SIGSAC Conference on Computer and Communications Security, CCS 2014, pp. 153–166. ACM (2014)
35. Zilberman, N., Audzevich, Y., Kalogeridou, G., Manihatty-Bojan, N., Zhang, J., Moore, A.: NetFPGA: rapid prototyping of networking devices in open source. SIGCOMM Comput. Commun. Rev. 45(4), 363–364 (2015)

Encrypted Classification Using Secure K-Nearest Neighbour Computation

B. Praeep Kumar Reddy$^{(\boxtimes)}$ and Ayantika Chatterjee

Indian Institute of Technology Kharagpur, Kharagpur, India
pradeepkumarreddy.bukka@gmail.com, cayantika@gmail.com

Abstract. Machine learning (ML) is one of the growing areas of engineering with sweeping applications. Executing machine learning algorithms on vast amount of data raises demand of huge resources and large data set handling. Thus, machine learning was too costly for many enterprise budgets. However, cloud service suppliers are making this technology reasonable to enterprises by offering massive shared resources. Machine learning as a service (MlaaS) is a category of cloud computing services that provides machine learning tools to allow customers to run, develop and manage applications in cloud without the complexity of building and maintaining. However, ascent of machine learning as a service procreates scenarios where one faces concealment dilemma, where the model must be revealed to the outsourced platform. Hence, cloud data security is an important issue where users can fancy the ability of executing applications by outsourcing sensitive data. Fully Homomorphic Encryption (FHE) offers a refined way to accommodate these conflicting interests in the cloud scenario by preserving data confidentiality as well as applying Mlaas in secure domain. However, processing on FHE data can not be directly performed on traditional instruction execution flow, but requires special circuit based representation of algorithms. In this paper, we focus on realizing K-Nearest Neighbour (KNN) computation on encrypted data, where data is stored using a generalized encrypted representation. Such representation will be suitable for easily extending to encrypted ensemble learning framework supporting multiple encrypted learners for higher accuracy. Extensive performance studies are carried out to evaluate the timing overhead of the encrypted KNN computation.

Keywords: Cloud · FHE · Machine learning · KNN

1 Introduction

Along with traditional cloud services like Infrastructure as a service (IaaS), Platform as a service (PaaS) and Software as a service (SaaS), Machine learning as a service (MLaaS) is also gaining attention with an array of machine learning tools provided by different cloud service providers. Clouds' pay-per-use model allows organizations to avail intelligent machine learning options as and when required without much need of advanced skills and individual resource requirements.

© Springer Nature Switzerland AG 2019
S. Bhasin et al. (Eds.): SPACE 2019, LNCS 11947, pp. 176–194, 2019.
https://doi.org/10.1007/978-3-030-35869-3_13

Table 1. Famous cloud/server data hacks

Organization	Impact
Yahoo 2013–14	3 billion user accounts were compromised with names, dates of birth, email addresses and passwords
Marriott International 2014–18	Attackers were able to take some combination of contact info, passport number and other personal information of 500 million customers from internal server
eBay May 2014	145 million users compromised when attackers got access to company network for 229 days using the credentials of three corporate employees
Equifax 2017	Personal information and Credit card data hacking of 143 million consumers of this one of the largest credit bureaus in the U.S.
Heartland Payment Systems 2008	134 million credit cards exposed through SQL injection, company paid out an estimated 145 million in compensation
Uber 2016	Personal information of 57 million Uber users and 600,000 drivers exposed along with driver license numbers
Home Depot 2014	Theft of credit/debit card information of 56 million customers, company agreed to pay at least 19.5 million to compensate US consumers
Microsoft 2010	Experienced breach due to configuration issue within Business Productivity Online Suite, allowed non-authorized users of the cloud service to access employee contact info
Dropbox 2014	Hackers tapped more than 68 million user accounts and passwords, disclosed after four years
LinkedIn 2012	6 million user passwords were stolen then published on a Russian forum
LinkedIn 2016	Hackers stole and posted for sale on the dark web an estimated 167 million LiknedIn email addresses and passwords
Apple iCloud 2014	High-profile cloud security breach, the iCloud service for personal storage of celebrities had been compromised, private photos leaked online

Leading public cloud platforms like AWS, Microsoft Azure, Google Cloud hence broken the barriers of scaling issues faced by organizations' in-house machine learning model generation attempts which require large computation clusters.

In spite of lots of promises from cloud computing, security is a major bottleneck to adapt cloud for world-wide applications. Due to incomplete control over who can access sensitive data and limited monitoring capability of data in transit to and from cloud applications, theft of data from cloud domain is very common. Starting from big names for cloud computing services like Apple-iCloud, Google,

Microsoft Azure and several other organizations are concerned about this data security issue in cloud. Table 1 [37] has listed some of the major data breaches which shows that data security is not only a concern when data is outsourced to cloud platform, critical data should also be protected in internal organization specific servers.

That raises a pertinent question in what form critical data should be stored in cloud without leaking sensitive information to untrusted cloud service providers. One immediate solution is to upload the data encrypting with traditional encryption schemes. That may conform data security, but processing on that encrypted form of data is not possible. That defeats the purpose of cloud computing as huge computing resources of cloud can not be utilized and encrypted data in cloud need to be taken back in repeatedly for decryption to process further. FHE [34] is an aid to such problems which supports direct processing on encrypted data in the cloud domain without the need of intermediate decryption. However, for developing suitable tools to execute algorithms operating on FHE data on general purpose computers, suitable translations of algorithms should be designed [28]. This requirement derives from the fact that all the existing FHE schemes (for example: libraries like HElib [36], TFHE [35]) are by design circuit-based and are not easily amenable to non-circuit representations of traditional algorithms. Thus, to perform classification or regression analysis on encrypted form of data, it is essential to translate suitable algorithms to their equivalent encrypted counterpart.

In this work, we focus on realizing classification over encrypted data. Considering classification to be performed on sensitive information related to healthcare, financial credit evaluation and many more, it is important to investigate how to execute such algorithms over encrypted data. Data classification in general includes two-step machine learning approach. The first training step involves determining the parameters for the classification algorithm, which is termed as "training phase' of sample data. The second prediction step classifies the data using the trained parameters, termed as 'model'. Therefore, it is essential to perform classification without exposing the sensitive information used as input for the classification algorithm or the test data set [1]. There are different classification algorithms in literature. In this work, we specifically concentrate on KNN classification algorithm due to its simplicity. It is also easy to understand and implement and does not make much assumptions as compared to other parametric models. Different efforts have been made to design secure KNN [6]. Most of these works are either based on underlying order preserving scheme, somewhat homomorphic schemes or bounded polynomial based vector homomorphic schemes [6,14,16], suitable for particular analytic scenario. Stored data in cloud particularly encrypted with such restricted encryption schemes are not general to support further complex ML algorithms on that same dataset. Thus, such restricted form of representation may not be suitable in real world applications specially in case of applying ensemble learning with multiple models combined to solve a particular computational intelligence problem to achieve higher accuracy. In this work, we consider a more general representation of FHE data outsourced in cloud. Such representation will keep the provision of applying multiple models on same form of encrypted dataset to handle encrypted ensemble learning framework in future.

The overall paper is organized as follows: Sect. 2 highlights few related works in this direction. Section 3 explains few basics of homomorphic encryption and Sect. 4 justifies why we choose KNN over other ML classification algorithms. Section 5 provides the details of KNN implementation over encrypted data along with required submodules. Section 6 includes extensive experimental results and analysis. Finally, Sect. 7 states the conclusion and possible future extension of this work.

2   Related Works

Realizing machine learning over encrypted data is an active area of research for last few years. In the work mentioned in [3], three major classification protocols: hyperplane decision, Naïve Bayes, and decision trees are constructed to be combined with AdaBoost. However, building blocks of these classifiers are developed based on multiple encryption techniques and that intermediate switching incurs added security overhead. Authors in [1] implemented Naive Bayes (NB) classifier for encrypted dataset which has inherent limitation due to the underlying classification scheme. Among different encrypted analytic algorithms, few explored on Logistic regression [4,8,9] and few other works analyze encrypted support vector machines [10,11].

Authors in [13] revisit the secure nearest neighbour problem with a design analysis based on new partition-based secure Voronoi diagram (SVD) method. Work in [15] proposes particular KNN Queries implementation with Location privacy useful for mobile communication. In [14], authors proposed a secure KNN query processing based on mutable order preserving encoding (mOPE). An effort has been made to design compact privacy-preserving KNN search using garbled circuits (GC) in [25]. The work [16] performs only the secure nearest neighbour search over encrypted data on untrusted clouds with underlying searchable encryption scheme. In [26], authors proposed secure KNN design with restricted homomorphic property, not suitable to extend for further complex ML algorithms. Secure KNN Classification in [7] using Vector Homomorphic Encryption is suitable for low dimensional representations of the encrypted data. Recent work in [6] demonstrates secure KNN computing in two-party federated cloud setting, with two non-colluding public cloud servers, which also requires one round of communication between the two.

Overall, all these existing works are based on limited homomorphic property or specific representation of data optimized for KNN implementation. In the subsequent sections, we highlight how to implement KNN with a generalized encrypted representation suitable for further complex multiple classification algorithms working over encrypted data.

3   Preliminaries

A homomorphism is a structure-preserving transformation between two sets, where an operation on two members in the first set is preserved in the second set on the corresponding members. Let P and C be sets with members $p_1, p_2 \in P$ and $c_1, c_2 \in C$. Let a transformation, $T : P \rightarrow C$ such that $T(P_1) = C_1$ and $T(P_2) = C_2$. Let us define an operator $\oplus$ on the elements of P and $\ominus$ an operator on those of C, T is said to define an homomorphism if,

$$T(P_1 \oplus P_2) = T(C_1) \ominus T(C_2) \tag{1}$$

Homomorphism may be valid for multiple operators and it is termed as algebraic cryptosystem. Note that, the operators on P (say, $\oplus$) may be same or different with operators on C (say, $\ominus$). Further, an algebraically homomorphic cryptosystem can be described as a 6-tuple $H_1 = (P, C, E, D, \oplus, \otimes)$ where P and C denote the plaintext space and the ciphertext space, respectively, whereas E and D denote the encryption and decryption functions. $\oplus$ and $\otimes$ tag the two algebraic operations. Gentry's approach [34] of bootstrapping is to develop a fully homomorphic from a somewhat homomorphic system and provide addition and multiplication plus a normalization procedure that is supposed to allow unlimited chaining of operations in ciphertext space. This technique of reducing noise in the cipher-text space requires for an additional formal descriptive item, extending H_1 to $H_2 = (P, C, E, D, \oplus, \otimes, r)$, introducing a reduction-function r, which takes a noisy cipher-text and transforms it into an equivalent with reduced noise.

An encryption scheme ε consists of three algorithms: $KeyGen_\varepsilon$, $Encrypt_\varepsilon$ and $Decrypt_\varepsilon$. Each of these algorithms must be efficient, i.e. they must all run in polynomial time (λ), where λ is the security parameter which specifies the bit-length of the keys. $KeyGen_\varepsilon$ generates a key, which is used in both $Encrypt_\varepsilon$ and $Decrypt_\varepsilon$. In the next subsections, we shall discuss about two main homomorphic schemes: Somewhat homomorphic scheme and fully homomorphic scheme.

3.1   Fully Homomorphic Scheme

Consider the following encryption scheme. Here λ is the security parameter. We set $N = \lambda$, $P = \lambda^2$ and $Q = \lambda^5$.

- $KeyGen_\varepsilon(\lambda)$: Generate a random P-bit odd integer p, which acts as the key.
- $Encrypt_\varepsilon(p, m)$: Output a ciphertext $c \leftarrow m' + p * q$, where m' is a random N-bit number such that $m' = m$ mod 2 and q is any random Q-bit number.
- $Decrypt_\varepsilon(p, c)$: Output $(c \mod p) \mod 2$.
- $Evaluate_\varepsilon(f, c_1, \ldots c_t)$: The boolean function f is first converted to an equivalent function f' with only AND and XOR gates. Then the AND and XOR operators are replaced with multiplication and addition operators respectively to generate the function f''. Compute and return $f''(c_1, \ldots, c_t)$.

One can observe that the ciphertexts from ε are near-multiples of p. ($c \bmod p$) is referred to as the noise associated with the cipher-text. It is the difference from the nearest multiple of p. Since the noise has the same parity as the message encrypted. Operations like $Add\_\varepsilon(c_1, c_2)$, $Sub\_\varepsilon(c_1, c_2)$ and $Mult\_\varepsilon(c_1, c_2)$ are computed as $(c_1 + c_2)$, $(c_1 - c_2)$ and $(c_1 * c_2)$ respectively.

In order to make it more convincing, an example is presented. For the computation of $Mult\_\varepsilon(c_1, c_2)$, where $c_1 \leftarrow Encrypt_\varepsilon(p, m_1) = m_1' + p * q_1$, and $c_2 \leftarrow Encrypt_\varepsilon(p, m_2) = m_2' + p * q_2$. The cipher-text output by $Evaluate\_\varepsilon$ is $c = c_1 * c_2$. So,

$$c = m_1' * m_2' + p * q' \tag{2}$$

where q' is some integer. As long as the noise $m_1' * m_2'$ is small, and not comparable to p, we have:

$$c \bmod p = m_1' * m_2' \tag{3}$$

Therefore, $(c \bmod p) \bmod 2 = m_1 * m_2$. This scheme works as long as the noise does not blow up too much and start affecting the result. It is clear that this scheme is incomplete and somewhat homomorphic, because if the result of an operation between the two operands a and b exceeds the prime modulus p, the decryption fails. So starting with two clean plain-text items, the intermediate result grows towards the modulus with every operation and in this sense is polluted. To compensate for this, a fully homomorphic encryption scheme must define normalization (as mentioned reencryption procedure in [34] of the intermediate result. In the case of the system shown here, a normalization would be any function that can minimize the remainder mod p of the result while preserving the parity mod p. Gentry addresses this problem by generating a public key that contains a decryption hint. This hint allows to homomorphically decrypt the intermediate result in the encrypted domain, which means that the plain-text of the argument remains unknown. With the plain-text at hand in cipherspace, it is possible to reencrypt the plaintext which generates a new cipher of the plain-text with reduced noise.

In this paper, we consider TFHE library [35] as the underlying homomorphic scheme where the normalization process is defined in a different way as expressed in [41]. We are mostly interested in the library due to the fact that it provides fastest gate-by-gate bootstrapping and not constrained in case of supported set of efficient operations as previous BGV based FHE schemes [40].

4   Choice of KNN over Other ML Algorithms

As defined by Arthur Samuel "machine learning is the field of study that gives computers the ability to learn without being explicitly programmed." Machine learning algorithms are either parametric or non-parametric. Parametric algorithms incorporate a mounted range of parameters. A parametric algorithm is computationally quicker, however, makes stronger assumptions concerned to data, the algorithmic program may match well if the assumptions prove to be correct. However, it's going to perform poorly if the assumptions go wrong. In distinction, a non-parametric algorithm uses a versatile range of parameters, and also the variety of settings typically grow because it learns from additional information. A non-parametric algorithm is computationally slower, however, makes fewer assumptions related to the information. A typical example of a non-parametric algorithm is KNN, which is inherently slow but robust to noisy training data.

Overall, machine learning algorithms are grossly classified as:supervised learning and unsupervised learning. Supervised learning is based on the idea of learning with known quantities to support future judgment whereas, in case of unsupervised learning, the algorithm learns by itself. "Supervise" means to observe and direct the execution of the task. Supervised learning is a method in which machine infer from labeled data, which indicates group of samples that have been tagged with one or more labels identifying certain properties or characteristics. After learning, new set of data without labels are provided. Test algorithms analyze labels of the given data based on the labeled data. Under Supervised ML, few notable techniques for classification are as follows:

- **Linear regression** creates a relationship between target scalar and one or more predictors [19]. Simple regression is of one predictor where as multiple regression is associated with more than one predictor [20]. Predictor function estimates parameters from the data. Linear regression is applied if the target scalar is continuous. Linear regression is widely utilized in biological, behavioral, and social sciences to explain doable relationships between variables [22].
- **Logistic Regression** Logistic regression applies a logistic function to a linear combination of features to predict the outcome of a categorical dependent variable based on predictor variables [22]. Logistic regression is a commonly used tools for discrete data analysis and applied statistics [21].
- **Decision trees** are tree-like structure which use branching methodology to illustrate possible outcomes of the decision based on the specific boundary condition. Each node represents a condition on the attribute, a branch of the test corresponds to the outcome of the trial, and leaf nodes represent labels. The classification rules described through the path from the root to the leaf node [23].
- **Naive Bayes algorithm** belongs to the family of the probabilistic classifier. Naive Bayes parameter estimation uses Bayesian methods or maximum likelihood in the domain of document, news article classification, sentiment analysis etc [24].
- **Support Vector Machine** (SVM) involves linear algebra to realize hyperplanes to classify among different data sets to be classified.
- **Neural Networks (NN)** classification technique is inspired by biological network composed of massively parallel interconnections, where the system consists of processing elements connected using weights. NN is trained using the algorithm for estimation of parameters to do one or more classification tasks.

Implementation of all these above mentioned ML classification algorithms in encrypted domain either requires costly probability computation with encrypted division (for Naive Bayes classification and Logistic regression), numerous encrypted decision making (for Decision trees), encrypted complex mathematical sub-operation module implementation (for SVM classifier) or huge parameter estimation (for NN based approaches). Due to all these issues, in this paper. We focus on the implementation of comparatively simpler K Nearest Neighbour (kNN), which has the following advantages:

- KNN is simple, easy to understand, and implement. To classify the new datum KNN reads through the whole dataset to search out K nearest neighbours.
- No assumptions need to make to implement kNN. Parametric models have a lot of assumptions.
- KNN does not explicitly build any model, merely tags the new data entry based learning from historical data.
- The classifier at once adapts as we tend to collect new coaching knowledge. KNN is an instance-based learning and memory-based approach.
- KNN complies with multi-class with none additional efforts. Classification algorithms are easy to apply for binary classifications, needs the effort to implement for multiclass.
- KNN might take some time while selecting the first hyper-parameter but after that rest of the parameters are aligned to it.

In the next section, we discuss how to realize KNN in encrypted domain.

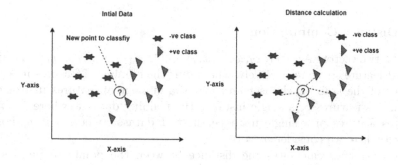

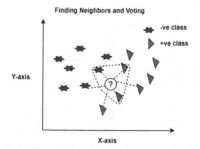

Fig. 1. KNN classification.

5   Encrypted KNN Computation

KNN based classification is a non-parametric method, where the input is the K (number of neighbours) closest training data in the feature space[1] [39]. KNN classifies an object by analyzing fixed number of plurality voting of neighbours as shown in Fig. 1a. Number of neighbours are involved in voting depend on the amount of K, a positive integer, with the object being assigned to the class most common among its K nearest neighbours [2,26].

Figure 2 outlines the major steps of implementing KNN algorithm on unencrypted data. The algorithm considers input as n point training data set P = $\{p_1, p_2, p_3, \ldots p_n\}$ with m dimensional features and associated class labels, number of nearest neighbours integer value K and a test data T_i. The training phase of the algorithm only requires storing the feature vectors and class labels of the training samples. Main challenge of realizing this classification model computation in the encrypted domain ultimately boils down to the realization of the following submodules in encrypted domain:

1. Encrypted distance computation between the points p_i and T_i.
2. Sorting of the computed distances.
3. K-Nearest Neighbours Voting based on the class label of the neighbours.
4. Class Label Assignment of test input T_i.

In the subsequent sections, we highlight the realization of the encrypted counterpart of above operations.

5.1   Distance Computation

Consider two vectors A $= \{x_1, x_2, x_3 \ldots x_m\}$ and B $= \{y_1, y_2, y_3 \ldots y_n\}$ in training and test feature space respectively, where m is the number of features in a single instance of the training dataset and n is the number of features in test data, x_i indicates features of a single instance the training dataset, where $i \in m$, y_j indicates features of a single instance the test dataset, where $j \in n$. For the simplicity, here we consider $m = n$.

KNN classifier calculates the distance between the points to be classified and training instances in feature space. KNN offers the flexibility to decide on a distance, whereas building the KNN model requires any one of the following distance metrics:

1. Euclidean Distance:

$$EuclideanDistance(A, B) = \sqrt{\sum_{i=1}^{m}(x_i - y_i)^2} \qquad (4)$$

---

[1] Feature vectors are used to represent numeric or symbolic characteristics, called features, of an object in a mathematical, easily analyzable way.

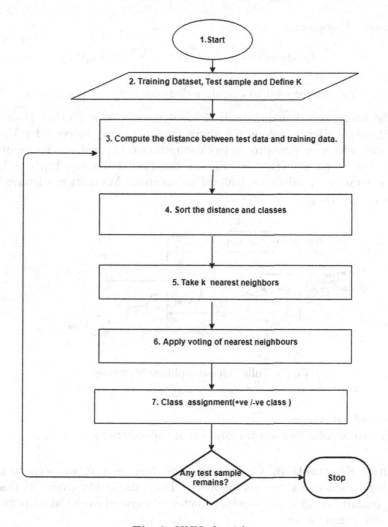

Fig. 2. KNN algorithm

2. Hamming Distance:

$$HammingDistance(A, B) = \sum_{i=1}^{m}(x_i, y_i) \tag{5}$$

where, $(x_i, y_i) = \{0 \; x_i = y_i \; 1, \; x_i \neq y_i\}$

3. Manhattan Distance:

$$ManhattanDistance(A, B) = (\sum_{i=1}^{m}|x_i - y_i|) \tag{6}$$

4. Minkowski Distance:

$$MinskowiDistance(A, B) = (\sum_{i=1}^{m} |x_i - y_i|^r)^{\frac{1}{r}} \qquad (7)$$

where r = Parameter used to calculate distance between the points

In the encrypted domain, multiplication operation is costlier than addition/subtraction. Hence, among the above four distances, we consider Manhattan distance which promises to be less computation expensive. The input data has been encrypted bit wise with Enc_pk function. Following Eq. 6, following two sub-operations need to be realized to compute Manhattan distance with encrypted homomorphic primitives:

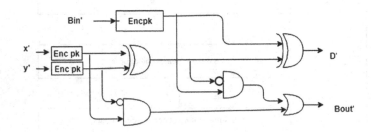

Fig. 3. Fully Homomorphic subtraction

– Encrypted subtraction
– Encrypted absolute value computation of the subtraction result

Encrypted Subtraction. Considering b-bit feature size, we need to design b-bit subtractor for distance computation. The subtraction circuit is designed bit-wise initially and the bit-wise subtractor is iterated over the loop for b-bit subtraction computation.

For the bit-wise subtraction, half subtractor is designed between two single bits (X_i and Y_i). If any borrow (B_{in}) occurs to the next bit then we need to complete a subtraction between three bits. Thus, this full subtractor with two input bits and borrow input generates two outputs, difference (D) and borrow out (B_{out}) based on the following equations:

$$B_{out} = Bin \cdot \overline{(X_i \, XOR \, B_{in})} + \overline{X_i} \cdot Y_i$$
$$D = (X_i \, XOR \, Y_i) \, XOR \, Bin \qquad (8)$$

As shown in Fig. 3, FHE subtraction between two encrypted operands x' and y' with borrow B'_{in} is computed with this logic (as explained in Eq. 8) and implemented using FHE primitive gates provided underlying TFHE library. In the next subsection, we explain how to compute the absolute value of the subtraction result.

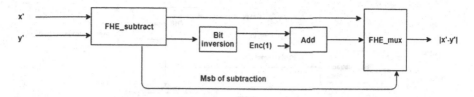

Fig. 4. Encrypted absolute value computation

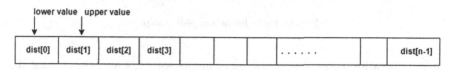

Fig. 5. Distance array

Absolute Value Computation. For two encrypted operands x' and y', absolute value of the subtraction result $x' - y'$ will be $|x' - y'|$, non-negative value of $x' - y'$ irrespective of its sign. In this implementation, we are considering two's complement notation where negative number. According to this notation, $-num'$, negation of a positive encrypted number num' can be computed by complementing the bits of num' and subsequently adding encrypted one ($Enc(1)$) to the result [28]. Again, num' can be obtained back from $-num'$ by same way.

Hence, while absolute value computation of any subtraction result $x' - y'$, it is important to check whether $x' - y'$ is already positive or negative. If $x' - y'$ is positive, then $|x' - y'| = x' - y'$. Else, $|x' - y'| = -(x' - y')$. Such encrypted conditional assignment or encrypted decision making can be done with encrypted multiplexer (FHE_mux) [28]. For two encrypted inputs A'_i and B'_i and encrypted selection line s', the encrypted multiplexer output (Z') will be $A'_i.\overline{s'} + B'_i.s'$. Depending on the values of selection line (either $Enc(0)$ or $Enc(1)$), B'_i or A'_i will be selected as the value of Z'.

Figure 4 shows $|x' - y'|$ Computation, where MSB of the subtraction result is fed as selection of FHE_mux. If the $x' - y'$ value is positive, MSB is $Enc(0)$ and direct $x' - y'$ value is selected. Otherwise, if the subtraction result is negative, MSB is $Enc(1)$ and $-(x' - y')$ is selected as the final absolute value. Further, summing up these absolute subtraction values with encrypted adder [28] final encrypted distances ($dist'[i]$) between p_i and test input T_i are computed. Next step of KNN computation is the sorting of these computed distances which will be detailed in the subsequent section.

5.2   Distance Sorting

Sorting of computed distances requires implementation of encrypted sorting with $dist'[i]$ values. As discussed in [29]. Bubble sort has been proven to be promising sorting technique while considering encrypted data. Bubble sort repeatedly compares adjacent elements and based on the result of the comparison,

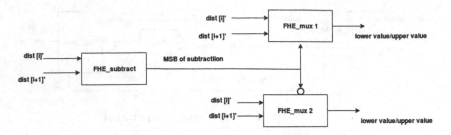

Fig. 6. Fully homomorphic swap

swapping operation takes place until the elements sorted. Thus, the sorting algorithm involves comparison, decision making and swapping operation. In case of sorting of the Manhattan distance, the main operation is the swap of two distances based on their greater-lesser relationship. Hence, considering two consecutive encrypted distances $dist[i]'$ followed by $dist[i+1]'$ in sorting input array, their positions will be changed during the sorting process if $dist[i]' > dist[i+1]'$. That decision making involves subtraction of two operands and MSB of subtraction outcome to be fed to encrypted multiplexers as shown in Figs. 5 and 6. While $dist[i]' > dist[i+1]'$, value of encrypted MSB will be $Enc(0)$. Thus, lower value position of sorted array will hold $dist[i+1]'$ as output of FHE_mux1. Similarly, the selection value of FHE_mux2 will be $Enc(1)$ and that will give output $dist[i]'$ as upper value position of sorted array.

From the final sorted distance array, K nearest neighbours are selected and final assignment of test input's class label will be done by KNN Voting, which will be detailed in the next section.

5.3   KNN Voting and Class Label Assignment

By KNN Voting, we mean predicting the class label of test input based on the existing class labels (as assigned and stored in the training phase) of the nearest neighbours. Training phase class labels are assigned either as positive (+) class or negative (−) class marked as label (L_i) and encrypted as $Enc(1)$ or $Enc(0)$ respectively. Thus, voting involves the following sub-operations:

– Equality comparison of nearest neighbours class labels with $Enc(1)$ or $Enc(0)$ and summing up the equality check results to get the total positive (posCount') and negative counts (negCount').
– Subtraction of encrypted posCount' and negCount' to get the higher count and predict the final label of test input.

Figure 7 performs equality comparison between L_i and $Enc(1)$ and the equality check result ($Enc(1)$ if values are equal [28]) is fed to two multiplexers FHE_mux1 and FHE_mux2. If L_i equals to $Enc(1)$, $posCount'$ increases else $negCount$ value increases.

Finally, as shown in Fig. 8, $negCount'$ and $posCount'$ are fed as input of FHE subtraction module and MSB of the subtraction result provides the final

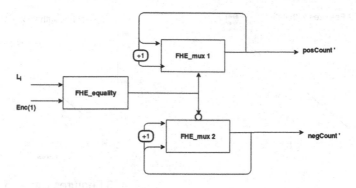

Fig. 7. Fully homomorphic prediction

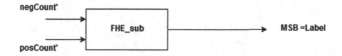

Fig. 8. Fully homomorphic label assignment

predicted label. If $negCount' > posCount'$, MSB turns to be $Enc(0)$ and that predicts the negative class.

Here 8-bits, 10-bits and 16-bits represent the number of bits used to store input data and output.

6   Result

The real world multivariate Iris data set from UCI machine learning repository [33] is used to verify our encrypted kNN classification. The Iris data set has 150 rows, and each row contains single label and four features. Based on these features, flowers are classified into three categories namely Iris setosa, Iris Versicolor, and Iris Virginia. To implement binary classification, we are considering two classes of Iris data set such as positive class and negative class. The positive class and the negative class are represented by Iris versicolor and Iris setosa respectively, where each category of flower has 50 rows of positive and negative classes. Our implemented algorithm had been estimated on Linux Ubuntu 64-bit machine with i7700 with the 3.6 GHz processor using FHE module of TFHE library. Due to the RAM limitation, we managed to process partial blocks of values at a time.

We implement KNN over encrypted form of Iris data, where encryption is done using underlying TFHE library. Our extensive experimental results show how the timing requirement varies with the change of dataset size (Fig. 9), varying numbers of features (Fig. 11) and the selection of number of neighbours K (Fig. 10). With increase in number of bits of the input data, the time for computation increases too. The library used here, TFHE supports symmetric

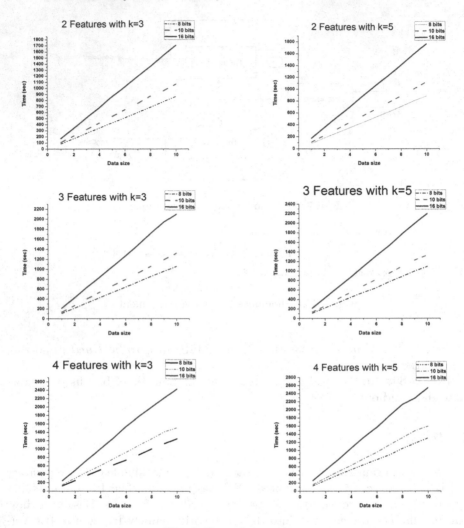

Fig. 9. Data size vs. time

encryption, decryption, and evaluation of a boolean circuit in Gate bootstrapping mode only (one bootstrapping per binary gate), and in single threaded mode. Unsupervised ML algorithm implementations, as shown in the work [2] are even more costly in comparison to our results. In the paper [2], authors considered K-means algorithm over encrypted data with Lsun dataset [38] of 400 data instances, and every single instance has two features (32 bits each) and the execution time is 0.85 months approximately for 3 clusters. However, the scope of comparison with other secure KNN results is very limited since most of the previous implementations are either based on some specific assumptions or with limited homomorphic property.

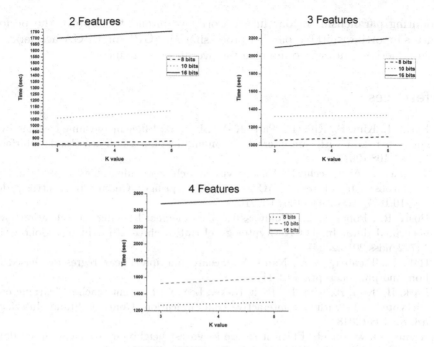

Fig. 10. K value vs. time

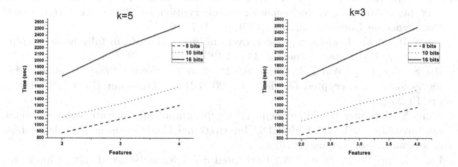

Fig. 11. Features vs. time

7   Conclusion

To preserve privacy in machine learning, applying algorithms over encrypted data can be an optimal solution. Our proposed implementation provides accurate privacy-preserving training and classification in this direction by utilizing a state of the art approach based on encrypted KNN algorithm. This encrypted classification can be used for some specific medical or financial long term decision making scenario, but not for real time critical applications due to its performance bottleneck. The reason may be the present algorithm uses underlying TFHE library which solely operates on the single thread computation without accounting parallelism. In our future work, we intend to improve the performance supporting suitable parallel processing and GPU or FPGA acceleration of the underlying library to improve the overall performance.

References

1. Park, H., Kim, P., Kim, H., Park, K.-W., Lee, Y.: Efficient machine learning over encrypted data with non-interactive communication. Comput. Stand. Interfaces **58**, 87–108 (2017)
2. Jäschke, A., Armknecht, F.: Unsupervised machine learning on encrypted. In: Cid, C., Jacobson Jr., M. (eds.) SAC 2018. LNCS. Springer, Cham (2018). https://doi.org/10.1007/978-3-030-10970-7_21
3. Bost, R., Popa, R.A., Goldwasser, S.: Machine learning classification over encrypted data. In: IACR Cryptology ePrint Archive 2014. https://doi.org/10.14722/ndss.2015.23241
4. Hall, R., Fienberg, S.E., Nardi, Y.: Secure multiple linear regression based on homomorphic encryption (2011)
5. Park, H., Kim, P., Kim, H., Park, K.-W., Lee, Y.: Efficient machine learning over encrypted data with non-interactive communication. Comput. Stand. Interfaces **58**, 87–108 (2018)
6. Kesarwani, M., et al.: Efficient secure k-nearest neighbours over encrypted data. In: EDBT (2018). https://doi.org/10.5441/002/edbt.2018.67
7. Yang, H., He, W., Li, J., Li, H.: Efficient and secure kNN classification over encrypted data using vector homomorphic encryption. In: 2018 IEEE International Conference on Communications (ICC), pp. 1–7 (2018)
8. Chen, H., et al.: Logistic regression over encrypted data from fully homomorphic encryption. BMC Med. Genomics **11**, 81 (2018)
9. Hu, S., Wang, Q., Wang, J., Chow, S.S.M., Zou, Q.: Securing fast learning! Ridge regression over encrypted big data. In: 2016 IEEE Trustcom/BigDataSE/ISPA, pp. 19–26 (2016)
10. Laur, S., Lipmaa, H., Mielikinen, T.: Cryptographically private support vector machines. In: 12th ACM SIGKDD International Conference on Knowledge Discovery and Data Mining (2016)
11. Liu, F., Ng, W.K., Zhang, W.: Encrypted SVM for outsourced data mining. In: IEEE 8th International Conference on Cloud Computing (2015). https://doi.org/10.1109/CLOUD.2015.158
12. Hesamifard, E., Takabi, H., Ghasemi, M.: CryptoDL: deep neural networks over encrypted data. CoRR abs/1711.05189 (2017)
13. Yao, B., Li, F., Xiao, X.: Secure nearest neighbor revisited. In: 2013 IEEE 29th International Conference on Data Engineering (ICDE), pp. 733–744 (2013)
14. Elmehdwi, Y., Samanthula, B.K., Jiang, W.: Secure k-nearest neighbor query over encrypted data in outsourced environments. In: IEEE 30th International Conference on Data Engineering, pp. 664–675 (2014)
15. Yi, X., Paulet, R., Bertino, E., Varadharajan, V.: Practical k nearest neighbor queries with location privacy. In: IEEE 30th International Conference on Data Engineering, pp. 640–651 (2014)

16. Wang, B., Hou, Y., Li, M.: Practical and secure nearest neighbor search on encrypted large-scale data. In: IEEE INFOCOM 2016 - The 35th Annual IEEE International Conference on Computer Communications, pp. 1–9 (2016)
17. Thosar, D.S., Thosar, R.D., Gadakh, P.J.: Secure kNN Query Processing in Untrusted Cloud Environments (2015)
18. Wong, W.K., Cheung, D.W.-L., Kao, B., Mamoulis, N.: Secure kNN computation on encrypted databases. In: SIGMOD Conference (2009)
19. Freedman, D.A.: Statistical Models: Theory and Practice. Cambridge University Press, Cambridge (2009)
20. Rencher, A.C., Christensen, W.F.: Multivariate regression, Chap. 10 (2012)
21. Introduction. In: Methods of Multivariate Analysis. Wiley Series in Probability and Statistics, vol. 709, 3rd edn., p. 19. Wiley. ISBN 9781118391679
22. Harrell, F.E.: Regression Modeling Strategies, 2nd edn. Springer, Cham (2001). https://doi.org/10.1007/978-3-319-19425-7. ISBN 978-0-387-95232-1
23. Caruana, R., Niculescu-Mizil, A.: An empirical comparison of supervised learning algorithms. In: 23rd International Conference on Machine Learning. CiteSeerX (2006)
24. Pagel, J.F., Kirshtein, P.: Machine Dreaming and Consciousness (2017)
25. Songhori, E.M., Hussain, S.U., Sadeghi, A.-R., Koushanfar, F.: Compacting privacy-preserving k-nearest neighbor search using logic synthesis. In: 52nd ACM/EDAC/IEEE Design Automation Conference (DAC), pp. 1–6 (2015)
26. Zhu, Y., Huang, Z., Takagi, T.: Secure and controllable k-NN query over encrypted cloud data with key confidentiality. Parallel Distrib. Comput. **89**, 1–12 (2016)
27. Kaur, G., Pandey, P.S.: Emotion recognition system using IOT and machine learning-a healthcare application. In: 23rd Conference of Open Innovations Association FRUCT, p. 63. FRUCT Oy (2018)
28. Chatterjee, A., Sengupta, I.: Translating algorithms to handle fully homomorphic encrypted data on the cloud. IEEE Trans. Cloud Comput. **6**, 287–300 (2018)
29. Chatterjee, A., Sengupta, I.: Searching and sorting of fully homomorphic encrypted data on cloud. IACR Cryptology ePrint Archive 2015: 981 (2015)
30. Chillotti, I., Gama, N., Georgieva, M., Izabachène, M.: TFHE: fast fully homomorphic encryption over the torus. J. Cryptol. 1–58 (2018)
31. Carpov, S., Gama, N., Georgieva, M., Troncoso-Pastoriza, J.R.: Privacy-preserving semi-parallel logistic regression training with Fully Homomorphic Encryption. IACR Cryptology ePrint Archive 2019: 101 (2019)
32. Bourse, F., Minelli, M., Minihold, M., Paillier, P.: Fast homomorphic evaluation of deep discretized neural networks. In: Shacham, H., Boldyreva, A. (eds.) CRYPTO 2018, Part III. LNCS, vol. 10993, pp. 483–512. Springer, Cham (2018). https://doi.org/10.1007/978-3-319-96878-0_17
33. Dua, D., Graff, C.: UCI Machine Learning Repository (2017). http://archive.ics.uci.edu/ml
34. Gentry, C.: Computing arbitrary functions of encrypted data. Commun. ACM **53**(3), 97–105 (2010)
35. https://tfhe.github.io/tfhe/
36. https://github.com/homenc/HElib
37. https://www.csoonline.com/article/2130877/the-biggest-data-breaches-of-the-21st-century.html
38. Ultsch, A.: Clustering with SOM: U*C. In: Proceedings of Workshop on Self-Organizing Maps (2005)
39. Bishop, C.M.: Pattern Recognition and Machine Learning. Springer, New York (2006)

40. Chillotti, I., Gama, N., Georgieva, M., Izabachène, M.: Faster packed homomorphic operations and efficient circuit bootstrapping for TFHE. In: Takagi, T., Peyrin, T. (eds.) ASIACRYPT 2017. LNCS, vol. 10624, pp. 377–408. Springer, Cham (2017). https://doi.org/10.1007/978-3-319-70694-8_14
41. Chillotti, I., Gama, N., Georgieva, M., Izabachène, M.: Faster fully homomorphic encryption: bootstrapping in less than 0.1 seconds. In: Cheon, J.H., Takagi, T. (eds.) ASIACRYPT 2016. LNCS, vol. 10031, pp. 3–33. Springer, Heidelberg (2016). https://doi.org/10.1007/978-3-662-53887-6_1

A Few Negative Results on Constructions of MDS Matrices Using Low XOR Matrices

Kishan Chand Gupta[1], Sumit Kumar Pandey[2], and Susanta Samanta[1(✉)]

[1] Applied Statistics Unit, Indian Statistical Institute,
203, B.T. Road, Kolkata 700108, India
kishan@isical.ac.in, susanta.math94@gmail.com
[2] Computer Science and Engineering, Indian Institute of Technology Jammu,
Jagti, PO Nagrota, Jammu 181221, India
emailpandey@gmail.com

Abstract. This paper studies some low XOR matrices systematically. Some known low XOR matrices are companion, DSI and sparse DSI matrices. Companion matrices have been well studied now whereas DSI and sparse DSI are newly proposed matrices. There are very few results on these matrices. This paper presents some new mathematical results and rediscovers some existing results on DSI and sparse DSI matrices. Furthermore, we start from a matrix with the minimum number of fixed XORs required, which is one, to construct any recursive MDS matrix. We call such matrices 1-XOR matrices. No family of low XOR matrices can have lesser fixed XORs than 1-XOR matrices. We then move on to 2-XOR and provide some impossibility results for matrices of order 5 and 6 to compute recursive MDS matrices. Finally, this paper shows the non-existence of 8-MDS sparse DSI matrix of order 8 over the field $\mathbb{F}_{2^8}$.

Keywords: MDS matrix · DSI matrix · Sparse DSI matrix · Permutation matrix

1 Introduction

Consider an 8×8 matrix

$$
M = \begin{bmatrix}
b_1 & 0 & 0 & 0 & 0 & 0 & 0 & a_1 \\
a_2 & 0 & 0 & 0 & 0 & 0 & 0 & 0 \\
0 & a_3 & b_3 & 0 & 0 & 0 & 0 & 0 \\
0 & 0 & a_4 & 0 & 0 & 0 & 0 & 0 \\
0 & 0 & 0 & a_5 & b_5 & 0 & 0 & 0 \\
0 & 0 & 0 & 0 & a_6 & 0 & 0 & 0 \\
0 & 0 & 0 & 0 & 0 & a_7 & b_7 & 0 \\
0 & 0 & 0 & 0 & 0 & 0 & a_8 & 0
\end{bmatrix}
$$

where a_i's and b_i's are from the field $\mathbb{F}_{2^8}$. The question is - does there exist any M over the field $\mathbb{F}_{2^8}$ such that M^8 becomes MDS? One special case is when all

S. Bhasin et al. (Eds.): SPACE 2019, LNCS 11947, pp. 195–213, 2019.
https://doi.org/10.1007/978-3-030-35869-3_14

a_i's are 1 (the multiplicative identity in the field $\mathbb{F}_{2^8}$). An obvious way is to try all possible values of b_i's, considering all a_i's are 1, which is $(2^8)^4 = 2^{32}$ possible values. It can be easily checked from existing computational resources, but what if we do not fix a_i's to 1? The total possible values will be $(2^8)^{12} = 2^{96}$ which is now infeasible to explore considering the current computational resources. In [15], the main reason for not providing any 8×8 sparse DSI matrix (see Definition 8 in this paper) was a large search space which is 2^{96} matrix checking for MDS property. This paper settles this answer by reducing the search space of 2^{96} elements to a search space of 2^{32} elements. It can be verified by exhaustive search that there does not exist any such M over $\mathbb{F}_{2^8}$ whose power raised to 8 yields an MDS matrix.

The structure of M like matrices was first studied in [15] and such matrices are called sparse DSI matrices. The motivation behind the introduction of sparse DSI matrices was to achieve the optimal diffusion along with a low hardware area. The study on achieving optimal diffusion with low hardware area is not a recent activity; in fact, in recent years, a lot of research has been done to achieve so - notably using circulant, variants of circulant, Hadamard, variants of Hadamard, Cauchy, Vandermonde, companion matrices etc [1–5,7,8,10,12–14]. One can find a very nice account of the recent advances in obtaining MDS matrices using different kinds of matrices in [6].

The DSI and sparse DSI matrices were first introduced and studied in [15]. The motivation behind this study was to provide an optimal cryptographically significant diffusion layer in terms of the hardware area. The authors showed the existence of $n \times n$ sparse DSI matrices for $n \leq 7$ along with some mathematical results. But, the paper could not settle the answer for 8×8 sparse DSI matrices because of a huge search space. Needless to say, that paper [15] lacked sufficient mathematical results to conclude the impossibility of 8-MDS sparse DSI matrices of order 8 over the field $\mathbb{F}_{2^8}$ which has been finally settled in this paper.

Our Contribution: In this paper, we make an attempt to formalize the low XOR matrices and study their properties systematically. Our study starts with the minimum number of fixed XORs required in low XOR matrices which could yield recursive MDS matrices. The minimum number of fixed XORs required is one. We call such matrices 1-XOR matrices (for definition of t-XOR see Sect. 3.1). We provide an upper bound on the number of nonzero elements of an $n \times n$ 1-XOR matrices when raised to power n. Toh et al. [15] proved that 1-XOR matrices of order 4 are not k-MDS for $k \leq 8$. In this paper, we provide a similar but more generic result for any $n \times n$ 1-XOR matrices with some constraints in Theorem 3. Moreover, we have provided some results for 2-XOR matrices of order up to 6 in Sect. 3.3. We have shown that there does not exist 2-XOR matrices of order 5 and 6 whose 5-th and 6-th power respectively yield MDS matrices. These results are significant because they give a lower bound on the number of fixed XORs required for k-MDS lower XOR matrices of order n for $n \leq 6$. Finally, this paper shows the non-existence of 8-MDS sparse DSI matrix of order 8 over the field $\mathbb{F}_{2^8}$ which was remain unsolved in [15] due to huge search space. The drastic reduction in the search space comes from the result in the paper which shows that checking sparse DSI matrices with a_i's equal to 1 to obtain recursive MDS matrices is sufficient.

2   Definition and Preliminaries

Let $\sum$ be a set of variables. We assume that 0 (zero) and 1 (one) belong to $\sum$. Now we define binary operations $+ : \sum \times \sum \mapsto \sum$ and $\cdot \sum \times \sum \mapsto \sum$ such that

1. $a + b = b + a, \forall\, a, b \in \sum$,
2. $a \cdot b = b \cdot a, \forall\, a, b \in \sum$,
3. $0 + a = a, \forall\, a \in \sum$,
4. $0 \cdot a = 0, \forall\, a \in \sum$,
5. $1 \cdot a = a, \forall\, a \in \sum$,
6. $a + (b + c) = (a + b) + c, \forall\, a, b, c \in \sum$,
7. $a \cdot (b \cdot c) = (a \cdot b) \cdot c, \forall\, a, b, c \in \sum$,
8. $a \cdot (b + c) = a \cdot b + a \cdot c, \forall\, a, b, c \in \sum$,
9. $a \cdot b$ is nonzero if and only if both a and b are nonzero,
10. $a + b$ is zero if and only if both of a and b are zero.

0 is called the "zero" and rest are nonzero. For simplicity, we may denote $a \cdot b$ as ab only.

An integral domain satisfies all properties except the last one. In an integral domain, the additive inverse exists for all elements whereas it is not true in $\sum$ because the sum of zeros only can produce zero (the last property).

Let $A(S)$ denotes a matrix A, whose entries are from the set S. The row (and column) index of a matrix starts from 1. The (i, j)-th entry of a matrix A is denoted by $(A)_{i,j}$. An $n \times n$ matrix is called a matrix of order n. Suppose $A(\sum)$ and $B(\sum)$ are two matrices, then $A + B$ and $A \cdot B$ are defined as usual matrix addition and multiplication whose entries operations are done as defined above. For simplicity, we may denote $A \cdot B$ as AB only. We denote by $|A|$ for the number of nonzero entries in the matrix A. We denote a commutative ring with unity by $\mathcal{R}$ and a field by $\mathbb{F}$. If there are $q = p^r$ elements for some prime p and $r > 0$ in a field, we denote the field by $\mathbb{F}_q$. The algebraic closure and multiplicative group of $\mathbb{F}_q$ are denoted by $\bar{\mathbb{F}}_q$ and $\mathbb{F}_q^*$ respectively. For two $m \times n$ matrices A and B, we symbolize $A(\sum) \leqq B(\sum)$ if $(A)_{i,j} \neq 0$ implies $(B)_{i,j} \neq 0$. It is not hard to observe the following:

1. $|A_1(\sum) + A_2(\sum)| \leq |A_1(\sum)| + |A_2(\sum)|$ for any two matrices A_1 and A_2 over $\sum$.
2. If $A_1(\sum) \leqq B_1(\sum)$ and $A_2(\sum) \leqq B_2(\sum)$, then $A_1(\sum) + A_2(\sum) \leqq B_1(\sum) + B_2(\sum)$ and $A_1(\sum)A_2(\sum) \leqq B_1(\sum)B_2(\sum)$.

The second observation is true because of the last property of $\sum$ which allows the sum of two elements be zero only when both of them are zero. Furthermore, the motivation behind the introduction of $\sum$ is the fact that the second observation happens only over $\sum$; it is not true in any arbitrary ring or field. In general, the number of nonzero elements in the resultant matrix keeps varying (sometimes goes up, sometimes goes down) when the matrix operations are done over a ring or a field, and it is very difficult to find an upper bound on the number of nonzero elements. But it is not very difficult to obtain the same over $\sum$.

Definition 1. *A matrix D is said to be diagonal if $(D)_{i,j} = 0$ for $i \neq j$. By setting $d_i = (D)_{i,i}$, we denote the diagonal matrix D as $diag(d_1, d_2, \ldots, d_n)$. The diagonal matrix D is non-singular if and only if $d_i \neq 0$ for $1 \leq i \leq n$.*

Theorem 1 *[9]. A square matrix A is an MDS matrix if and only if every square submatrices of A are nonsingular.*

An MDS matrix must have all its entries nonzero. Therefore, any $n \times n$ matrix cannot be MDS if the number of nonzero entries is less than n^2. In this paper, we are using this fact to obtain some negative results. The upper bound on the nonzero elements in the resultant matrix over $\sum$ ensures the upper bound over any ring or a field also. And that is why the structure $\sum$ becomes very significant.

MDS matrices provide maximal diffusion which is useful in cryptographic applications, but they are not sparse resulting in costly implementations. Several techniques have been proposed to construct efficiently implementable MDS matrices. In this direction, recursive MDS matrices are proposed which are more suited for lightweight applications.

Definition 2. *A recursive MDS matrix is an MDS matrix which can be expressed as a power of some matrix, i.e. an MDS matrix $M = B^k$ for some matrix B and some integer $k > 0$. We say that the B yields a recursive MDS matrix M.*

In [5], B was a companion matrix; in [15], B was any one of companion, DSI or sparse DSI matrix, but in this paper we will consider only low XOR matrices for B.

Definition 3 *[15]. A matrix of order n is k-MDS if it is MDS when raised to the k-th power.*

Example 1. For example, the matrix

$$M = \begin{bmatrix} 0 & 1 & 0 & 0 \\ 0 & 0 & 1 & 0 \\ 0 & 0 & 0 & 1 \\ 1 & 1 & \alpha & 1 \end{bmatrix}$$

yields an MDS matrix when raised to power 8, where α is a primitive element of $\mathbb{F}_{2^4}$ whose constructing polynomial is $x^4 + x + 1$.

Definition 4. *A permutation matrix P is a binary matrix which is obtained from the identity matrix by permuting the rows (or columns).*

Note that a permutation matrix is invertible and the inverse of P is the transpose of P, i.e. $P^{-1} = P^T$. The product of two permutation matrices is a permutation matrix.

Definition 5. *Let ρ be an element of the symmetric group S_n (set of all permutations over the set $\{1, 2, \ldots, n\}$). Then ρ is called a k length cycle permutation, written $(i_1\ i_2\ i_3\ \cdots\ i_k)$, if*

$$\rho = \begin{pmatrix} i_1\ i_2\ i_3\ \ldots\ i_k \\ i_2\ i_3\ i_4\ \ldots\ i_1 \end{pmatrix}$$

i.e. $i_1 \mapsto i_2$, $i_2 \mapsto i_3$, $\ldots$, $i_k \mapsto i_1$.

Lemma 1 *[6, Corollary 4]. If M is an MDS matrix, then for any permutation matrices P and Q, PMQ is an MDS matrix.*

Definition 6. *Two matrices M and M' are called permutation-equivalent if there exists a permutation matrix P such that $M' = PMP^{-1}$.*

Remark 1. Therefore by Lemma 1, permutation equivalent of an MDS matrix is again an MDS matrix.

Definition 7 *[15, Definition 5]. Let $\mathbf{a} = [a_1\ a_2\ \cdots\ a_n]$ and $\mathbf{b} = [b_1\ b_2\ \cdots\ b_{n-1}]$ where $a_i, b_j \in \sum$ for $1 \leq i \leq n$ and $1 \leq j \leq n-1$. A Diagonal-Serial-Invertible (DSI) matrix $D(\sum)$ is determined by two vectors $\mathbf{a}$ and $\mathbf{b}$ defined as follows:*

$$(D)_{i,j} = \begin{cases} a_1, & i = 1, j = n \\ a_i, & i = j+1 \\ b_i, & i = j \leq n-1 \\ 0, & otherwise. \end{cases}$$

We would like to mention here that the Definition 7 is slightly different than the definition (5) of [15]. Here, all a_i's and b_i's are being assumed from $\sum$ whereas in [15], these are from the field $\mathbb{F}_{2^r}$ for some $r \geq 1$. Note that by choosing $\sum$ instead of the field $\mathbb{F}_{2^r}$, the results proved in this paper are also valid for arbitrary fields $\mathbb{F}_{p^r}$ and arbitrary rings.

Definition 8 *[15, Definition 6]. A DSI matrix $D = DSI(a_1, a_2, \ldots, a_n; b_1, b_2, \ldots, b_{n-1})$ of order n is sparse if it satisfies:*

$$\begin{cases} b_2 = b_4 = \ldots = b_{n-2} = 0, & \text{if } n \text{ is even} \\ b_2 = b_4 = \ldots = b_{n-3} = 0, & \text{if } n \text{ is odd.} \end{cases}$$

Example 2. An example of a sparse DSI matrix of order 4 and 5 are given below:

$$\begin{bmatrix} b_1 & 0 & 0 & a_1 \\ a_2 & 0 & 0 & 0 \\ 0 & a_3 & b_3 & 0 \\ 0 & 0 & a_4 & 0 \end{bmatrix}, \qquad \begin{bmatrix} b_1 & 0 & 0 & 0 & a_1 \\ a_2 & 0 & 0 & 0 & 0 \\ 0 & a_3 & b_3 & 0 & 0 \\ 0 & 0 & a_4 & b_4 & 0 \\ 0 & 0 & 0 & a_5 & 0 \end{bmatrix}.$$

3   Low XOR Matrices

Low XOR matrices have great importance in lightweight constructions of diffusion layers as they are sparse. We will consider an $n \times n$ matrix of the form $M = PD_1 + D_2$, where D_1 and D_2 are two diagonal matrices and P is a permutation matrix. We consider that all matrices have entries from $\sum$, unless specified.

3.1   t-XOR Matrices

To yield a recursive MDS matrix, a matrix must have at least one nonzero element in each row and each column. So, we consider an $n \times n$ matrix M of the form $P(D + A') = PD + A$, where P is a permutation matrix, D is a nonsingular diagonal matrix and A' contains t $(t \geq 1)$ nonzero elements in some non-diagonal position. Moreover, A also has t nonzero elements. We will call such matrix t-XOR matrix.

The reason for calling t-XOR matrix can be explained through an example. Consider

$$M = \begin{bmatrix} 0 & 0 & 1 & 0 \\ 1 & 0 & 0 & 0 \\ 0 & 1 & 0 & 0 \\ 0 & 0 & 0 & 1 \end{bmatrix} \begin{bmatrix} a & 0 & 0 & 0 \\ 0 & b & 0 & 0 \\ 0 & 0 & c & 0 \\ 0 & 0 & 0 & d \end{bmatrix} + \begin{bmatrix} 0 & e & 0 & f \\ 0 & 0 & 0 & 0 \\ g & 0 & 0 & 0 \\ 0 & 0 & 0 & 0 \end{bmatrix} = \begin{bmatrix} 0 & e & c & f \\ a & 0 & 0 & 0 \\ g & b & 0 & 0 \\ 0 & 0 & 0 & d \end{bmatrix}$$

If $\mathbf{y} = [y_1 \; y_2 \; y_3 \; y_4]^T$ (a column vector), then $M\mathbf{y} = [ey_2 + cy_3 + fy_4 \; ay_1 \; gy_1 + by_2 \; dy_4]^T$. The number of total additions in $M\mathbf{y}$, which is 3 in this example, is equal to the number of nonzero elements in A. In a field or a ring of characteristic 2, these additions are implemented using XORs and that's why the name t-XOR. These XORs are referred as fixed XORs. In this paper, we will assume $t \leq n-1$ which is a reasonable assumption otherwise there is no point of calling these matrices low XOR matrices.

Some known t-XOR matrices are companion [5], DSI and sparse DSI matrices. For an $n \times n$ companion and DSI matrix, t is $n-1$ whereas for sparse DSI matrix, t is $\lceil n/2 \rceil$. Since a sparse DSI matrix has the least t value among companion, DSI and sparse DSI, that is why it is more suited for the lightweight diffusion layer. Lesser the value of t, more suited for implementation.

In the following lemma, we study an equivalence relation between the t-XOR matrices.

Lemma 2. *Let M_1 be a t-XOR matrix of order $n \geq 2$. Then M_1 is permutation equivalent to some t-XOR matrix $M_2 = QD' + A'$, where Q is a permutation matrix, D' is a nonsingular diagonal matrix and A' has t nonzero elements in its first t rows.*

Proof. Let $M_1 = PD + A$ be a t-XOR matrix, where A has $r_1, r_2, \ldots, r_k$ nonzero elements in the $i_1, i_2, \ldots, i_k$-th row respectively such that $r_1 + r_2 + \ldots + r_k = t$ and $k \leq t$.

Now consider the permutation matrix P_1 obtained from the identity matrix by permuting the row i_1 to row 1, row i_2 to row 2, ..., row i_k to row k. Now

$$P_1 M_1 P_1^{-1} = P_1(PD + A)P_1^{-1}$$
$$= P_1 PDP_1^{-1} + P_1 AP_1^{-1}$$

Since $DP_1^{-1} = P_1^{-1}D'$ for some diagonal matrix D', we have

$$P_1 M_1 P_1^{-1} = P_1 PP_1^{-1}D' + P_1 AP_1^{-1}$$
$$= QD' + A',$$

where $Q = P_1 PP_1^{-1}$ and $A' = P_1 AP_1^{-1}$. Also note that A' has altogether t nonzero elements in its 1st, 2nd, ..., k-th row. Let $M_2 = QD' + A'$. Therefore M_1 is permutation equivalent to M_2.   □

Remark 2. For example, consider a 1-XOR matrix of order 4

$$M_1 = \begin{bmatrix} b & 0 & 0 & 0 \\ 0 & c & d & 0 \\ 0 & 0 & e & 0 \\ 0 & 0 & 0 & f \end{bmatrix} \text{ and } P_1 = \begin{bmatrix} 0 & 1 & 0 & 0 \\ 1 & 0 & 0 & 0 \\ 0 & 0 & 1 & 0 \\ 0 & 0 & 0 & 1 \end{bmatrix}.$$

Then $P_1 M_1 P_1^{-1} = M_2$, where M_2 is a 1-XOR matrix given by

$$M_2 = \begin{bmatrix} c & 0 & d & 0 \\ 0 & b & 0 & 0 \\ 0 & 0 & e & 0 \\ 0 & 0 & 0 & f \end{bmatrix}.$$

Therefore, to construct MDS matrices from t-XOR matrices, we need to check only for t-XOR matrices whose nonzero elements (for A) are in the first t rows. This reduces the search space. For example, to construct recursive MDS matrices from 2-XOR matrices of order 5 and 6, we need to check only $5! \times {}^8C_2 = 3360$ and $6! \times {}^{10}C_2 = 32400$ 2-XOR matrices respectively.

3.2   1-XOR Matrices

We try to minimize the number of nonzero elements in a matrix which will yield a recursive MDS matrix. Also note that to yield a recursive MDS, an $n \times n$ matrix should have at least $n+1$ nonzero elements. Therefore, we start with the 1-XOR matrices. Because of Lemma 2, we are considering those A only whose first row has exactly one nonzero element.

In Theorem 2, we prove that for $n \geq 3$, there exists no $n \times n$ 1-XOR matrix which is n-MDS. For this, we need the following lemma.

Lemma 3. *Let $M = (P + A)$ be a 1-XOR matrix. Then, there exists some A_i's such that $M^r \leq P^r + P^{r-1}A_1 + P^{r-2}A_2 + P^{r-3}A_3 + \ldots + PA_{r-1} + A_r$ for $1 \leq r \leq n$, where A_i are the matrices whose first row contain exactly i nonzero elements and rest rows zero.*

Proof. We will prove this result by mathematical induction. When $r = 1$, $M \leq P + A_1 = P + PA_0 + A_1$. Therefore the result is true for $r = 1$. Now assume that the result is true for $r = k < n$. Now we show that the result is true for $r = k + 1$. Now $M^{k+1} = (P + A_1)^k (P + A_1)$. Therefore

$$M^{k+1} \leq (P^k + P^{k-1}A_1 + P^{k-2}A_2 + P^{k-3}A_3 + \ldots + PA_{k-1} + A_k)(P + A_1)$$
$$= (P^{k+1} + P^{k-1}A_1 P + P^{k-2}A_2 P + P^{k-3}A_3 P + \ldots + PA_{k-1}P + A_k P)$$
$$+ (P^k A_1 + P^{k-1}A_1^2 + P^{k-2}A_2 A_1 + P^{k-3}A_3 A_1 + \ldots + PA_{k-1}A_1 + A_k A_1)$$

Note that $A_i A_1 \leq A_1$ and $A_i P = A_i'$ for some A_i', where A_i' are the matrices whose first row contain exactly i nonzero elements and rest rows zero. Therefore,

$$M^{k+1} \leq (P^{k+1} + P^{k-1}A_1' + P^{k-2}A_2' + P^{k-3}A_3' + \ldots + PA_{k-1}' + A_k')$$
$$+ (P^k A_1 + P^{k-1}A_1 + P^{k-2}A_1 + P^{k-3}A_1 + \ldots + PA_{k-1}A_1 + A_1)$$
$$\leq P^{k+1} + P^k A_1 + P^{k-1}(A_1' + A_1) + P^{k-2}(A_2' + A_1)$$
$$+ \ldots + P(A_{k-1}' + A_1) + (A_k' + A_1).$$

Note that $A_i' + A_1 \leq A_{i+1}''$, where A_i'' are the matrices whose first row contain exactly i nonzero elements and rest rows zero. Therefore,

$$M^{k+1} \leq P^{k+1} + P^k A_1'' + P^{k-1}A_2'' + P^{k-2}A_3'' + \ldots + PA_k'' + A_{k+1}''.$$

Hence the result.   □

Theorem 2. *For $n \geq 3$, there does not exist any 1-XOR matrix of order n which is n-MDS.*

Proof. From Lemma 3, we have

$$M^n \leq (P + A)^n$$
$$\leq P^n + P^{n-1}A_1 + P^{n-2}A_2 + P^{n-3}A_3 + \ldots PA_{n-1} + A_n.$$

Thus

$$|M^n| \leq |P^n| + |P^{n-1}A_1| + |P^{n-2}A_2| + |P^{n-3}A_3| + \ldots + |PA_{n-1}| + |A_n|$$
$$= |P^n| + |A_1| + |A_2| + |A_3| + \ldots + |A_{n-1}| + |A_n|$$

Note that P^n and A_n have a common element. Therefore

$$|M^n| \leq n + (1 + 2 + 3 + \ldots + n) - 1 = \frac{n(n+3)}{2} - 1.$$

Therefore for $n \geq 3$, $|M^n| < n^2$. Hence the theorem.   □

In the following theorem, we prove that that some specific type of 1-XOR matrices of order n are not k-MDS for $k \leq 3n - 5$.

Theorem 3. *For $n \geq 4$, let $M = PD + A$ be an $n \times n$ 1-XOR matrix over a field of characteristic 2, where P is a permutation matrix corresponding to an n length cycle permutation and A has a nonzero entry in $(1,1)$-th position. Then M is not k-MDS for $k \leq 3n - 5$.*

Proof. Let P_i be the permutation matrix corresponding to the n length cycle permutation σ_i of the symmetric group S_n for $i = 1, 2, \ldots, (n-1)!$. Suppose P_i and P_j be two permutation matrices corresponding to the n length cycle $\sigma_i = (i_1 = 1 \ i_2 \ i_3 \ \ldots \ i_n)$ and $\sigma_j = (j_1 = 1 \ j_2 \ j_3 \ \ldots \ j_n)$ respectively. Now consider the permutation $\lambda = \begin{pmatrix} j_1 & j_2 & j_3 & \cdots & j_n \\ i_1 & i_2 & i_3 & \cdots & i_n \end{pmatrix}$. Therefore $\lambda \sigma_j \lambda^{-1} = (\lambda(j_1) \ \lambda(j_2) \ \lambda(j_3) \ \ldots \ \lambda(j_n)) = (i_1 \ i_2 \ i_3 \ \ldots \ i_n) = \sigma_i$. Let Q be the permutation matrix corresponding to λ. Therefore we have $Q P_j Q^{-1} = P_i$. Hence all P_i's for $i = 1, 2, \ldots, (n-1)!$ are permutation equivalent to each other. Therefore for all $i, j \in \{1, 2, \ldots, (n-1)!\}$, $P_i = Q P_j Q^{-1}$ for some permutation matrix Q, where the first row of Q is the first row the identity matrix. Now

$$Q(P_j D + A)Q^{-1} = Q P_j D Q^{-1} + Q A Q^{-1}$$

Since $DQ^{-1} = Q^{-1} D'$, for some diagonal matrix D' and A has the nonzero entry in $(1,1)$-th position, we have

$$Q(P_j D + A)Q^{-1} = Q P_j Q^{-1} D' + A$$
$$= P_i D' + A$$

Therefore all $P_i D + A$ for $i \in \{1, 2, \ldots, (n-1)!\}$ are permutation equivalent. Therefore to check whether all such $M = PD + A$, P is the permutation matrix corresponding to a full length cycle permutation and A has the nonzero entry in the $(1,1)$-th position, is k-MDS, where $k \leq 3n - 5$, we need to check only one such M. Consider the matrix

$$M = \begin{bmatrix} a & 0 & 0 & \cdots & 0 & x_n \\ x_1 & 0 & 0 & \cdots & 0 & 0 \\ 0 & x_2 & 0 & \cdots & 0 & 0 \\ 0 & 0 & x_3 & \cdots & 0 & 0 \\ \vdots & \vdots & \vdots & \cdots & \vdots & \vdots \\ 0 & 0 & 0 & \cdots & x_{n-1} & 0 \end{bmatrix}.$$

Now consider the input vector $(0, 1, y, 0, \ldots, 0)^T$. The resultant vector after each iteration are

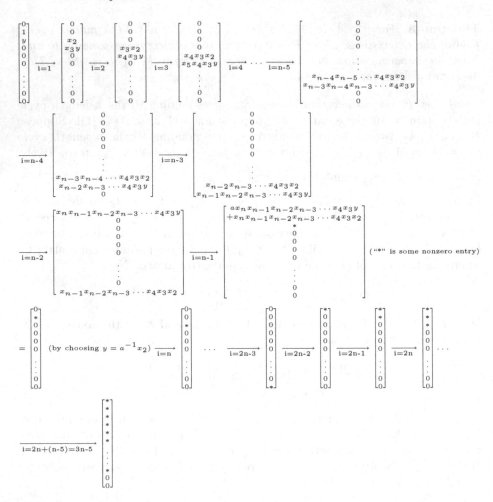

The sum of nonzero elements of input vector and output vector in each iteration is $< n + 1$. Therefore M is not k-MDS, where $k \leq 3n - 5$.   □

Remark 3. For $n = 3$, choose the input vector $y = (0, ax_2^{-1}, 1)^T$ and it can be easily checked that the sum of nonzero elements of input vector and output vector in $i = 2, 3$ and 4 is less than $n + 1$. Also for the input vector $(0, 1, 0)^T$, the sum of nonzero elements of input vector and output vector in iteration $i = 1$ is less than $n + 1$. Therefore the above result is also true for $n = 3$. Again for $n = 2$, the result is trivially true. Therefore the above result is true for all $n \geq 2$.

Remark 4. For $n = 3$ and the input vector $y = (1, a^2 x_2^{-1} x_3^{-1}, 0)$ it is easy to check that the above result is true for $i = 5, 6$. Therefore the above result is true for up to $k = 6$.

Remark 5. For $n = 4$ and the input vector $y = (0, a^2 x_2^{-1} x_3^{-1}, 0, 1)$ it is easy check that the above result is true for $i = 1, 3, 4, 5, 6, 7, 8, 9, 10$. Therefore the above result is true up to $k = 10$.

Experimental Observation: We have also observed that if in a 1-XOR matrix $M = PD + A$ of order n (for $n \leq 8$), if P is not a permutation matrix corresponding to a n length cycle permutation or A has a nonzero entry in some different position other than $(1,1)$-th position, then M^k contains at least one zero entry for $k \leq 3n - 5$. Therefore by Theorem 3, 1-XOR matrices of order n (for $n \leq 8$) are not k-MDS for $k \leq 3n - 5$ over a field of characteristic 2.

1-XOR Matrix of Order 2: There exists a 1-XOR matrix of order 2 which is 2-MDS. For example, consider the matrix

$$M = \begin{bmatrix} 0 & 1 \\ 1 & 0 \end{bmatrix} \begin{bmatrix} \alpha & 0 \\ 0 & 1 \end{bmatrix} + \begin{bmatrix} 1 & 0 \\ 0 & 0 \end{bmatrix} = \begin{bmatrix} 1 & 1 \\ \alpha & 0 \end{bmatrix}$$

over the field $\mathbb{F}_{2^4}$, where α is a root of the constructing polynomial $x^4 + x + 1$. It is easy to check that M^2 is an MDS matrix.

3.3   2-XOR Matrices

Now we are considering two nonzero elements in A for the study of recursive MDS matrices. In this section, most of the results are experimental.

2-XOR Matrix of Order 3: There exists a 2-XOR matrix of order 3 which is 3-MDS. For example, consider the matrix

$$M = \begin{bmatrix} 1 & 0 & 1 \\ 1 & \alpha & 0 \\ 0 & \alpha^3 + 1 & 0 \end{bmatrix}$$

over the field $\mathbb{F}_{2^4}$, where α is a root of the constructing polynomial $x^4 + x + 1$. It is easy to check that M^3 is an MDS matrix.

2-XOR Matrix of Order 4: There exists a 2-XOR matrix of order 4 which is 4-MDS. For example, consider the matrix

$$M = \begin{bmatrix} 0 & 1 & \alpha^3 + 1 & 0 \\ 0 & 0 & \alpha & 0 \\ 1 & 0 & 0 & 1 \\ 1 & 0 & 0 & 0 \end{bmatrix}$$

over the field $\mathbb{F}_{2^4}$, where α is a root of the constructing polynomial $x^4 + x + 1$. It is easy to check that M^4 is an MDS matrix.

2-XOR Matrix of Order 5: We have observed that among 3360 2-XOR matrices of order 5 (Remark 2), 12 matrices provide all nonzero element, when raised to power 5 but in a ring of characteristic 2 these matrices have zero elements when it raised to power 5. Therefore over a ring of characteristic 2, there exist no 5-MDS 2-XOR matrix of order 5. Thus for 5×5 low XOR matrices, the minimum number of fixed XOR required is 3 to get a 5-MDS matrices. In other words, for a 5-MDS, the minimum number of nonzero elements needed in a 5×5 matrix is $5 + 3 = 8$.

Remark 6. Note that there may exist 2-XOR matrices M of order 5 such that M is q-MDS where $5 < q \le 10$. For example, consider the matrix

$$M = \begin{bmatrix} 0 & 0 & 0 & 0 & 1 \\ 1 & 1 & 0 & 0 & 0 \\ 0 & 1 & 0 & 0 & 0 \\ 0 & 0 & 1 & \alpha & 0 \\ 0 & 0 & 0 & 1 & 0 \end{bmatrix}$$

over the field $\mathbb{F}_{2^8}$ where α is a root of the constructing polynomial $x^8 + x^7 + x^6 + x + 1$. It is easy to check that M^9 is a MDS matrix.

2-XOR Matrix of Order 6: We have observed that among the 32400 2-XOR matrix of order 6, there exist no such matrix that gives all nonzero element when raised to power 6. Therefore for 6×6 low XOR matrices, the minimum number of fixed XOR needed is 3 to get 6-MDS matrices. In other words for a 6-MDS, the minimum number of nonzero elements in a 6×6 matrix is $6 + 3 = 9$.

4   Some (Negative) Results on the Constructions of MDS Matrices from DSI Matrices

In the structure $M = PD_1 + D_2$, if

$$P = \begin{bmatrix} 0 & 0 & 0 & \dots & 0 & 1 \\ 1 & 0 & 0 & \dots & 0 & 0 \\ 0 & 1 & 0 & \dots & 0 & 0 \\ \vdots & \vdots & \vdots & \ddots & & 0 \\ 0 & 0 & 0 & \ddots & 1 & 0 \end{bmatrix}, \ D_2 = \begin{bmatrix} b_1 & 0 & 0 & \dots & 0 & 0 \\ 0 & b_2 & 0 & \dots & 0 & 0 \\ \vdots & \vdots & \vdots & \ddots & \vdots & \vdots \\ 0 & 0 & 0 & \dots & b_{n-1} & 0 \\ 0 & 0 & 0 & \ddots & 0 & 0 \end{bmatrix} \quad (1)$$

and D_1 is a nonsingular diagonal matrix, then M is called a DSI matrix.

In [15, Theorem 2], authors proved that given a DSI matrix M of order n, M^r contains at least one zero for $0 \le r < n$ and $n \ge 2$. In Theorem 4, we prove this by providing a combinatorial argument. For this, we need the following lemma.

Lemma 4. *Let $M = P + D_2$ be an $n \times n$ matrix, where D_2 is a diagonal matrix having zero in the n-th diagonal position and P is the permutation matrix defined in 1. Then $M^r \le P^r + P^{r-1}D + P^{r-2}D + \dots + PD + D_{n=0}$ for $r \ge 2$, where D denotes some nonsingular diagonal matrix and $D_{j=0}$ be some diagonal matrix with 0 only at the j-th diagonal position.*

Proof. We will prove this result using mathematical induction. We have

$$\begin{aligned} M^2 &= (P + D_2)(P + D_2) \\ &= P^2 + PD_2 + D_2P + D_2^2 \\ &\le P^2 + PD_{n=0} + D_{n=0}P + D_{n=0} \\ &\le P^2 + PD_{n=0} + PD_{n-1=0} + D_{n=0} \end{aligned}$$

Therefore

$$M^2 \leqq P^2 + PD + D_{n=0}$$

Therefore the result is true for $r = 2$. Assume that the result is true for $r = k$. Now, $M^{k+1} = M^k(P + D_2)$. Therefore we have

$$
\begin{aligned}
M^{k+1} &\leqq (P^k + P^{k-1}D + P^{k-2}D + \ldots + PD + D_{n=0})(P + D_{n=0}) \\
&\leqq P^{k+1} + P^k D D_{n=0} + P^{k-1}DP + P^{k-1}D D_{n=0} + P^{k-2}DP \\
&\quad + P^{k-2}D D_{n=0} + \ldots + PDP + PD_{n=0} + D_{n=0}P + D_{n=0} \\
&\leqq P^{k+1} + P^k D_{n=0} + P^k D + P^{k-1}D_{n=0} + P^{k-1}D + \ldots \\
&\quad + P^2 D + PD_{n=0} + PD_{n-1=0} + D_{n=0} \\
&= P^{k+1} + P^k(D_{n=0} + D) + P^{k-1}(D_{n=0} + D) + \ldots + P(D_{n=0} + D_{n-1=0}) \\
&\quad + D_{n=0} \\
&\leqq P^{k+1} + P^k D + P^{k-1}D + \ldots + PD + D_{n=0}
\end{aligned}
$$

Thus the lemma. $\qquad\qquad\square$

Theorem 4. *Given a DSI matrix M of order $n \geq 2$, M^k is not MDS for $k < n$.*

Proof. From Lemma 4, we have

$$
\begin{aligned}
|M^k| &\leq |P^k D + P^{k-1}D + \ldots + PD + D_{n=0}| \\
&\leq |P^k D| + |P^{k-1}D| + \ldots + |PD| + |D_{n=0}|
\end{aligned}
$$

Therefore $|M^k| \leq \underbrace{|D| + |D| + \ldots + |D|}_{k \text{ times}} + |D_{n=0}| \leq kn + n - 1$. Now for $k \leq n-1$, we have $|M^k| \leq (n-1)n + n - 1 = n^2 - 1$. $\qquad\square$

Recall that in the DSI matrix structure $M = PD_1 + D_2$ of order n, if $D_2 = diag(b_1, 0, b_3, \ldots, 0, b_{n-1}, 0)$ (when n is even) or $D_2 = diag(b_1, 0, b_3, \ldots, b_{n-2}, b_{n-1}, 0)$ (when n is odd), then M is called a sparse DSI matrix of order n.

Lemma 5. *Suppose $n \geq 2$. Let $M = P + D_2$ be an $n \times n$ matrix, where D_2 have zeros in the i-th and $(i \bmod n+1)$-th diagonal position and P is the permutation matrix defined in 1. Then $M^r \leqq P^r + P^{r-1}D + P^{r-2}D + \ldots + PD_{i=0} + D_{i,i+1=0}$ for $r \geq 2$, where D denotes some nonsingular diagonal matrix and $D_{j,k=0}$ be some diagonal matrix with 0 only at the j-th and k-th diagonal position.*

Proof. We will prove this result using mathematical induction. We simply denote $(i + 1)$ for $(i \bmod n + 1)$. We have

$$
\begin{aligned}
M^2 &= (P + D_2)(P + D_2) \\
&= P^2 + PD_2 + D_2 P + D_2^2 \\
&\leqq P^2 + PD_{i,i+1=0} + PD_{i-1,i=0} + D_{i,i+1=0} \\
&= P^2 + P(D_{i,i+1=0} + D_{i-1,i=0}) + D_{i,i+1=0}
\end{aligned}
$$

Therefore

$$M^2 \leqq P^2 + PD_{i=0} + D_{i,i+1=0}$$

Therefore the result is true for $r = 2$. Assume that the result is true for $r = k$.
Now, $M^{k+1} = M^k(P + D_2)$. Therefore we have

$$
\begin{aligned}
M^{k+1} &\leqq (P^k + P^{k-1}D + P^{k-2}D + \ldots + PD_{i=0} + D_{i,i+1=0})(P + D_{i,i+1=0}) \\
&\leqq P^{k+1} + P^k D_{i,i+1=0} + P^{k-1}DP + P^{k-1}DD_{i,i+1=0} + \cdots \\
&\quad + PD_{i=0}P + PD_{i=0}D_{i,i+1=0} + D_{i,i+1=0}P + D_{i,i+1=0} \\
&\leqq P^{k+1} + P^k D_{i,i+1=0} + P^k D + P^{k-1}D_{i,i+1=0} + \cdots \\
&\quad + P^2 D_{i-1=0} + PD_{i,i+1=0} + PD_{i-1,i=0} + D_{i,i+1=0} \\
&= P^{k+1} + P^k(D_{i,i+1=0} + D) + \ldots + P(D_{i,i+1=0} + D_{i-1,i=0}) + D_{i,i+1=0} \\
&\leqq P^{k+1} + P^k D + \ldots + PD_{i=0} + D_{i,i+1=0}
\end{aligned}
$$

Thus the lemma.   □

Theorem 5. *Let $M = PD_1 + D_2$ be an $n \times n$ matrix, where P be the permutation matrix defined in 1, D_1 is a nonsingular diagonal matrix and D_2 has any two consecutive zero entries in the diagonal position, then M^r must contain a zero entry for $2 \leq r \leq n$.*

Proof. From Lemma 5, we have

$$
\begin{aligned}
M^r &\leqq (P + D_2)^r \\
&\leqq P^r + P^{r-1}D + P^{r-2}D + \ldots + PD_{i=0} + D_{i,i+1=0}.
\end{aligned}
$$

Therefore, we have

$$
\begin{aligned}
|M^r| &\leq |P^r + P^{r-1}D + P^{r-2}D + \ldots + PD_{i=0} + D_{i,i+1=0}| \\
&\leq |P^r| + |P^{r-1}D| + |P^{r-2}D| + \ldots + |PD_{i=0}| + |D_{i,i+1=0}| \\
&\leq (r-1)n + (n-1) + (n-2) \\
&= (r-1)n + 2n - 3
\end{aligned}
$$

When $r \leq n - 1$, we have $|M^r| \leq (n-2)n + 2n - 3 = n^2 - 3 < n^2$. It is easy to check that $P^n = I$, where I is the identity matrix. Thus for $r = n$, we have

$$
\begin{aligned}
|M^r| &\leq |I + P^{n-1}D + P^{n-2}D + \ldots + PD_{i=0} + D_{i,i+1=0}| \\
&\leq |I + D_{i,i+1=0}| + |P^{n-1}D| + |P^{n-2}D| + \ldots + |PD_{i=0}|
\end{aligned}
$$

Note that $|I + D_{i,i+1=0}| = n$ and $|PD_{i=0}| = n - 1$. Hence
$$|M^n| \leq \underbrace{n + n + \ldots + n}_{n\text{-1 times}} + n - 1 = (n-1)n + (n-1) = n^2 - 1 < n^2. \qquad \square$$

The authors in [15], could not find a sparse DSI matrix of order 8 which is 8-MDS, over the field $\mathbb{F}_{2^8}$ due to large search space. In the following lemma and theorem, we have provided an equivalence criteria for checking a $n \times n$ sparse DSI matrix to be a n-MDS. Through these results, we reduce the large search space into a small search space and show that there exists no 8×8 sparse DSI matrix over $\mathbb{F}_{2^8}$ which is 8-MDS.

Lemma 6. *Let $a \in \mathbb{F}_q^*$ and P is an $n \times n$ permutation matrix. Given any $n \times n$ diagonal matrix D, there exists an $n \times n$ diagonal matrix D' such that $(P+D)^r$ is MDS if and only if $(aP+D')^r$ is MDS for $r \geq 1$.*

Proof. Note that $(P+D)^r$ is MDS if and only if $a^r(P+D)^r$ because $a \neq 0$. Now we have

$$a^r(P+D)^r = (a(P+D))^r$$
$$= (aP+aD)^r = (aP+D')^r,$$

where $D' = aD$. $\qquad\square$

Note that in the above lemma as $D' = aD$, D and D' have nonzeros in the same position.

Theorem 6. *Let $a_1, a_2, \ldots, a_n \in \mathbb{F}_q^*$, $D_1 = diag(a_1, a_2, \ldots, a_n)$ and*

$$P = \begin{bmatrix} 0 & 0 & 0 & \ldots & 0 & 1 \\ 1 & 0 & 0 & \ldots & 0 & 0 \\ 0 & 1 & 0 & \ldots & 0 & 0 \\ \vdots & \vdots & \vdots & \ddots & \vdots & \vdots \\ 0 & 0 & 0 & \ddots & 1 & 0 \end{bmatrix}.$$

Given any diagonal matrix D_2, there exists $a \in \bar{\mathbb{F}}_q$ satisfying $a^n = a_1 a_2 \ldots a_n$ such that $(PD_1 + D_2)^r$ is MDS if and only if $(aP + D')^r$ is MDS for $r \geq 1$.

Proof. Consider a nonsingular diagonal matrix $D_d = diag(d_1, d_2, \ldots, d_n)$. Let $D_{d,a} = diag(ad_2^{-1}, ad_3^{-1}, \ldots, ad_n^{-1}, ad_1^{-1})$. Then, we have

$$aP + D_2 = aD_d D_d^{-1} P D_d D_d^{-1} + D_d D_2 D_d^{-1}$$
$$= D_d(aD_d^{-1}PD_d + D_2)D_d^{-1}$$
$$= D_d(PD_{d,a}D_d + D_2)D_d^{-1} \qquad\qquad (2)$$
$$= D_d(PD_1 + D_2)D_d^{-1}.$$

where $D_1 = D_{d,a}D_d$. Now we will show that there exists $D_{d,a}$ such that $D_1 = D_{d,a}D_d$.

If $D_1 = D_{d,a}D_d$, we have

$$a_1 = ad_2^{-1}d_1$$
$$a_2 = ad_3^{-1}d_2$$
$$a_3 = ad_4^{-1}d_3$$
$$\cdots$$
$$a_{n-1} = ad_n^{-1}d_{n-1}$$
$$a_n = ad_1^{-1}d_n.$$

Therefore, we have

$$d_2 = aa_1^{-1}d_1$$
$$d_3 = a^2a_1^{-1}a_2^{-1}d_1$$
$$d_4 = a^3a_1^{-1}a_2^{-1}a_3^{-1}d_1$$
$$\cdots$$
$$d_{n-1} = a^{n-2}a_1^{-1}a_2^{-1}a_3^{-1}\ldots a_{n-2}^{-1}d_1$$
$$d_n = a^{n-1}a_1^{-1}a_2^{-1}a_3^{-1}\ldots a_{n-2}^{-1}a_{n-1}^{-1}d_1$$
$$d_1 = a^n(a_1^{-1}a_2^{-1}a_3^{-1}\ldots a_{n-2}^{-1}a_n^{-1})d_1.$$

Thus, $a^n = a_1a_2a_3\ldots a_n$, for $a_1, a_2, \ldots, a_n \in \mathbb{F}_q^*$ and such a exists in $\bar{\mathbb{F}}_q$. Therefore from Eq. 2, we can say that $(PD_1 + D_2)^r$ is MDS if and only if $(aP + D_2)^r$ is MDS. $\qquad\square$

Corollary 1. *Let $a_i \in \mathbb{F}_q^*$ for $1 \le i \le n$ and $a \in \bar{\mathbb{F}}_q$ satisfying $a^n = a_1a_2\ldots a_n$. Let $b_j \in \mathbb{F}_q$ and $b_j' = a^{-1}b_j$ for $1 \le j \le n-1$. Suppose $M = DSI(a_1, a_2, \ldots, a_n; b_1, b_2, \ldots, b_{n-1})$ and $M' = DSI(1, 1, \ldots, 1; b_1', b_2', \ldots, b_{n-1}')$. Then M^r is MDS if and only if M'^r is MDS for $r \ge 1$.*

Proof. Let $\bar{M} = DSI(a, a, \ldots, a; b_1, b_2, \ldots, b_{n-1})$. From Theorem 6, M^r is MDS if and only if $\bar{M}^r$ is MDS for $r \ge 1$.

From Lemma 6, $\bar{M}^r$ is MDS if and only if M'^r is MDS. Hence the corollary. $\square$

4.1   Non Existence of 8-MDS Sparse DSI Matrix of Order 8 over $\mathbb{F}_{2^8}$

Now we show that there does not exist any sparse DSI matrix of order 8 over $\mathbb{F}_{2^8}$. From Corollary 1, any sparse DSI matrix $M' = DSI(a_1, a_2, a_3, a_4, a_5, a_6, a_7, a_8; b_1', 0, b_3', 0, b_5', 0, b_7', 0)$ over $\mathbb{F}_{2^8}$ is permutation equivalent to a sparse DSI matrix $M = DSI(1,1,1,1,1,1,1,1; b_1, 0, b_3, 0, b_5, 0, b_7, 0)$ where $b_i = a^{-1}b_i'$ for $i = 1, 3, 5, 7$ and $a^n = a_1a_2\ldots a_8$.

Since $x \mapsto x^8$ is an isomorphism over $\mathbb{F}_{2^8}$, such a exists in the field $\mathbb{F}_{2^8}$ only. Therefore it is sufficient to check only those M whose b_i's belong to $\mathbb{F}_{2^8}$ which has $(2^8)^4 = 2^{32}$ choices. Otherwise, the total choices would be $(2^8)^{12} = 2^{96}$ considering $a_1, a_2, \cdots, a_8, b_1', b_3', b_5', b_7'$ all belong to $\mathbb{F}_{2^8}$. This was perhaps the reason why the authors in [15] could not provide the answer for either the possibility or impossibility of 8-MDS sparse DSI matrix of order 8 over $\mathbb{F}_{2^8}$.

After reducing the search space from 2^{96} candidates to 2^{32} candidates only, we experimentally observed that M^8 over a field of characteristic 2 will not be MDS if the following conditions are satisfied.

1. If $b_1 + b_3 + b_5 + b_7 = 0$
2. If $b_1 b_3 + b_1 b_5 + b_1 b_7 + b_3 b_5 + b_3 b_7 + b_5 b_7 = 0$
3. If $b_1 b_3 b_5 + b_1 b_3 b_7 + b_1 b_5 b_7 + b_3 b_5 b_7 = 0$
4. If $b_1 b_3 b_5 b_7 = 0$
5. If $b_1 = b_3$ or $b_1 = b_7$ or $b_3 = b_5$ or $b_5 = b_7$.

One can get the above conditions by (i) looking at some of the entries of M^8 and M^{-8} and (ii) computing the determinants of some of the 2×2 matrices in M^8 and M^{-8}. We want to emphasize that these are not the only conditions we got from (i) and (ii); these are only a few. One can get many more such conditions and can further enhance the search time. We considered only five because the first four conditions are symmetric in b_1, b_3, b_5 and b_7 and the fifth one appears very simple.

We ran an experiment over all choices of $b_1, b_3, b_5, b_7 \in \mathbb{F}_{2^8}$ except which satisfy at least one of the above five conditions. Our experiment could not find any 8-MDS matrix of order 8. Thus, we conclude that there does not exist any sparse DSI matrix of order 8 over the field $\mathbb{F}_{2^8}$ which is 8-MDS.

Remark 7. An 8-MDS sparse DSI matrix of order 8 exists over the higher order field. For example, consider the matrix

$$
M = \begin{bmatrix}
1 & 0 & 0 & 0 & 0 & 0 & 0 & 1 \\
1 & 0 & 0 & 0 & 0 & 0 & 0 & 0 \\
0 & 1 & \alpha & 0 & 0 & 0 & 0 & 0 \\
0 & 0 & 1 & 0 & 0 & 0 & 0 & 0 \\
0 & 0 & 0 & 1 & \alpha^{12} & 0 & 0 & 0 \\
0 & 0 & 0 & 0 & 1 & 0 & 0 & 0 \\
0 & 0 & 0 & 0 & 0 & 1 & \alpha^{30} & 0 \\
0 & 0 & 0 & 0 & 0 & 0 & \alpha^{30} & 0
\end{bmatrix}
$$

over $\mathbb{F}_{2^{10}}$, where α is a root of the constructing polynomial $x^{10} + x^3 + 1$. It can be verified that M^8 is MDS.

5   Conclusion and Future Work

Our investigations in this paper open up some possibilities for future work.

1. We have provided an upper bound on nonzero elements in 1-XOR matrices of order n when raised to power n. But we could not find similar results for any arbitrary t-XOR matrices. So it can be a future work to find an upper bound on nonzero elements in t-XOR matrices of order n when raised to power n.

2. There are many direct constructions of recursive MDS matrices from companion matrices. So it can be a problem for further research to find a direct construction of recursive MDS matrices from sparse DSI matrices.

Acknowledgments. We are thankful to the anonymous reviewers for their valuable comments. We also wish to thank Prof. Rana Barua for providing several useful and valuable suggestions.

References

1. Augot, D., Finiasz, M.: Direct construction of recursive MDS diffusion layers using shortened BCH codes. In: Cid, C., Rechberger, C. (eds.) FSE 2014. LNCS, vol. 8540, pp. 3–17. Springer, Heidelberg (2015). https://doi.org/10.1007/978-3-662-46706-0_1. http://eprint.iacr.org/2014/566.pdf
2. Berger, T.P.: Construction of recursive MDS diffusion layers from Gabidulin codes. In: Paul, G., Vaudenay, S. (eds.) INDOCRYPT 2013. LNCS, vol. 8250, pp. 274–285. Springer, Cham (2013). https://doi.org/10.1007/978-3-319-03515-4_18
3. Gupta, K.C., Ray, I.G.: On constructions of involutory MDS matrices. In: Youssef, A., Nitaj, A., Hassanien, A.E. (eds.) AFRICACRYPT 2013. LNCS, vol. 7918, pp. 43–60. Springer, Heidelberg (2013). https://doi.org/10.1007/978-3-642-38553-7_3
4. Gupta, K.C., Ray, I.G.: Cryptographically significant MDS matrices based on circulant and circulant-like matrices for lightweight applications. Cryptogr. Commun. **7**, 257–287 (2015)
5. Gupta, K.C., Pandey, S.K., Venkateswarlu, A.: Towards a general construction of recursive MDS diffusion layers. Des. Codes Cryptogr. **82**, 179–195 (2017)
6. Gupta, K.C., Pandey, S.K., Ray, I.G., Samanta, S.: Cryptographically significant MDS matrices over finite fields: a brief survey and some generalized results. Adv. Math. Commun. **13**(4), 779–843 (2019)
7. Lacan, J., Fimes, J.: Systematic MDS erasure codes based on vandermonde matrices. IEEE Trans. Commun. Lett. **8**, 570–572 (2004)
8. Liu, M., Sim, S.M.: Lightweight MDS generalized circulant matrices. In: Peyrin, T. (ed.) FSE 2016. LNCS, vol. 9783, pp. 101–120. Springer, Heidelberg (2016). https://doi.org/10.1007/978-3-662-52993-5_6
9. MacWilliams, F.J., Sloane, N.J.A.: The Theory of Error Correcting Codes. North Holland, Amsterdam (1986)
10. Pehlivanoğlu, M.K., Sakalli, M.T., Akleylek, S., Duru, N., Rijmen, V.: Generalisation of Hadamard matrix to generate involutory MDS matrices for lightweight cryptography. IET Inf. Secur. **12**, 348–355 (2018)
11. Sajadieh, M., Dakhilalian, M., Mala, H., Omoomi, B.: On construction of involutory MDS matrices from Vandermonde Matrices in $GF(2^q)$. Des. Codes Cryptogr. **64**, 287–308 (2012)
12. Sarkar, S., Syed, H.: Lightweight diffusion layer: importance of Toeplitz matrices. IACR Trans. Symmetric Cryptol. **2016**, 95–113 (2016)
13. Sarkar, S., Syed, H.: Analysis of Toeplitz MDS matrices. In: Pieprzyk, J., Suriadi, S. (eds.) ACISP 2017. LNCS, vol. 10343, pp. 3–18. Springer, Cham (2017). https://doi.org/10.1007/978-3-319-59870-3_1

14. Sim, S.M., Khoo, K., Oggier, F., Peyrin, T.: Lightweight MDS involution matrices. In: Leander, G. (ed.) FSE 2015. LNCS, vol. 9054, pp. 471–493. Springer, Heidelberg (2015). https://doi.org/10.1007/978-3-662-48116-5_23

15. Toh, D., Teo, J., Khoo, K., Sim, S.M.: Lightweight MDS serial-type matrices with minimal fixed XOR count. In: Joux, A., Nitaj, A., Rachidi, T. (eds.) AFRICACRYPT 2018. LNCS, vol. 10831, pp. 51–71. Springer, Cham (2018). https://doi.org/10.1007/978-3-319-89339-6_4

Revisiting the Security of LPN Based RFID Authentication Protocol and Potential Exploits in Hardware Implementations

Krishna Bagadia, Urbi Chatterjee[(✉)] [ID], Debapriya Basu Roy [ID],
Debdeep Mukhopadhyay, and Rajat Subhra Chakraborty [ID]

Secured Embedded Architecture Laboratory (SEAL), Department of Computer
Science and Engineering, Indian Institute of Technology Kharagpur, Kharagpur, India
krishna.bagadia2@gmail.com,
{urbi.chatterjee,deb.basu.roy,debdeep,rajat}@cse.iitkgp.ac.in

Abstract. Lightweight, computationally efficient HB-like protocol family has been used for privacy-preserving authentication mechanisms of Radio-Frequency Identification (RFID) tags in recent past. Most of these protocols are proved to be provably secure using the hardness assumption of Learning Parity with Noise (LPN) problem, but failed to resist against man-in-the-middle attack. Li et al. extended this concept and proposed a scheme called *LCMQ protocol* which was based on Learning Parity with Noise, Circulant Matrix, and Multivariate Quadratic problems. It was proved to be secure against man-in-the-middle attack and ciphertext only attacks. Execution of LCMQ protocol requires involvement of two secret m bit keys: $\mathbf{K_1}$ and $\mathbf{K_2}$. In this paper, we first make a critical observation that though the LCMQ based authentication protocol requires two keys, knowledge of $\mathbf{K_2}$ is sufficient to launch an impersonation attack. Next, since the value of $\mathbf{K_2}$ can be revealed by a precise fault attack, we have developed a hardware Trojan horse based fault attack methodology on the hardware implementation of the LCMQ protocol to retrieve $\mathbf{K_2}$. To validate our proposed attack methodology, we have developed and implemented an optimized hardware architecture of the LCMQ on a FPGA platform. To the best of our knowledge, this is the first FPGA based hardware implementation of the LCMQ protocol. We have then augmented our developed hardware design with a stealthy and lightweight hardware Trojan horse (requiring only 4 Look Up Tables) for precise fault injection, to corroborate the proposed attack methodology.

Keywords: RFID · Learning parity with noise · Circulant matrix · Multivariate quadratic · LCMQ · Lightweight entity authentication · HB · Fault attack · Impersonation attack

Abstract of the present work [1] has appeared in International Symposium on Hardware Oriented Security and Trust (HOST-2017), titled as "Exploiting safe error based leakage of (RFID) authentication protocol using hardware Trojan horse".

S. Bhasin et al. (Eds.): SPACE 2019, LNCS 11947, pp. 214–230, 2019.
https://doi.org/10.1007/978-3-030-35869-3_15

1   Introduction

From supply chain to anti-counterfeiting, RFID tags have been a vital component for solving range of problems in recent years. E-passports and RFID enabled bank notes are mere examples of such a set of authentication and tracking applications. As more government and multinational corporations have accepted it as an integral part of almost every possible household gadgets, they have started occupying a substantial part in this framework. Therefore several lightweight authentication protocols and algorithms have been proposed for these low-cost, strictly resource-constrained devices.

One of the most significant family of protocols that has been widely discussed and analysed in this broad area of research was designed by Hopper and Blum (HB) [2] based on *Learning Parity with Noise* (LPN) problem. Subsequently several HB-like protocols such as HB$^+$ [3], HB^{++} [4], HB$^{\#}$ [5,6], HB-MP [7], HB-MP$^+$ [8], HB-MAC [9], PUF-HB [10], HB+PUF [11], Tree-LSHB++ [12], Trusted-HB [13], GHB$^{\#}$ [14], LAPIN [15] have been proposed in the literature. However several cryptanalysis techniques and man-in-the middle attacks have been proposed in [16–18] for most of these HB-family protocols. Finally Li et al. [19] presented a novel entity authentication protocol titled LCMQ which is not direct descendant of HB protocol, rather a consolidation of *LPN*, *Circulant Matrix* and *Multivariate Quadratic* (MQ) problem that has been proved to be secure against mathematical cryptanalysis, ciphertext only attacks and man-in-the-middle attacks.

Fault attacks [20] have been introduced in the literature to leak information from a system by forcing spurious computations in the hardware and software implementations of cryptographic schemes. Several authors have shown how such fault injections can result in leakage of secret keys in block ciphers such as AES and DES [21–23]. Static faults that set a register bit to 0/1 for a particular round of execution are called *Safe errors*. It gets reset once the next execution begins. These safe errors were also exploited [24] in modular exponentiation to break constant time simple power attack resistant RSA algorithm. Similarly many researchers have also started to realize the impact of SCA on the physical implementation of HB family protocols. In [25], Gaspar et al. illustrated a DPA-like attack on the hardware implementation of masked Lapin algorithm. Carrijo et al. proposed a fault analytic model [26] which can lead to a cogent attack against HB-like protocols. But Berti and Standaert presented a security analysis [27] of LPN based implementations against fault attacks and showed that it inherently possess an algebraic structure that can resist such attacks. They have shown thatt flipping of intermediate variable of LPN algorithm through the fault attack does not provide any information leakage. Moreover, when we use external sources like clock glitch, EM wave radiation or laser for fault injection, precise fault injection may not happen. In [27], the authors have shown that such inaccuracy in fault injection makes the key retrieval significantly hard.

On the other hand, the opportunity of a fault attack can still be exploited by potential hardware trojan horses (HTHs) which can be inserted by malicious entities in the distributed IC design cycle. To execute accurate fault insertion in the circuit or for side channel, HTHs have been leveraged in multiple works in the past [28–34], both in IC and PCB level. Manufacturing of ICs is usually outsourced to potentially untrusted remote electronic manufacturing facilities. HTHs are surreptitious-by-design, malicious modifications to ICs which have the capability to evade traditional post-manufacturing testing, and once deployed, can cause disastrous functional failure or information. Once a HTH-infected circuit is deployed, usually they cannot be neutralized by any hardware or software updates. Hence, they are regarded as one of the foremost threats to security and privacy. Notably, in [35], it was shown how a tiny chip on PCB was used to create stealth doorway to any network on which the altered machines were deployed. Radio-Frequency Identification tags are used for several applications requiring authentication mechanisms, which if subverted by any of the above mentioned attacks can lead to unauthorized access, clandestine scanning and tracking, skimming and cloning.

With this regard, the major contributions in this work are as follows:

- First we give a security evaluation of the protocol and show that although the authentication uses two keys, **knowledge of only one key is sufficient to impersonate as a legitimate tag.** This shows that all three mathematical building blocks used in the scheme might provide some security features independently. But all together, they fail to provide the level of security to the protocol it actually claims.
- Next we present a lightweight hardware architecture of LCMQ authentication protocol on an FPGA platform. To the best of our knowledge, no hardware implementation based analysis of LCMQ protocol, especially a lightweight one targeting resource-constrained applications such as RFIDs, has been reported so far.
- To investigate the above mentioned weakness in the LCMQ protocol further, we propose a HTH based fault attack methodology which leaks one of the authentication keys ($\mathbf{K}_2$) when triggered. The usage of HTH is motivated by the fact that inaccuracy in the fault injection will increase the complexity of the attack.
- We demonstrate the use of HTH to induce precise fault attack on the protocol. We also design a hardware implementation of HTH and demonstrate that when triggered, it requires less than 2^8 rounds of protocol run to guess the key and forge the authentication. Finally, we propose a subtle modification of the LCMQ protocol to eliminate the threat of impersonation attack with the knowledge of only one key.

This paper is organized as follows. In Sect. 2, we briefly present the mathematical background necessary to understand the LCMQ protocol. Then we illustrate the tag impersonation attack in Sect. 3. Its hardware architecture have been described in Sect. 4. Next, in Sect. 5, we have presented the methodology behind the proposed HTH along with the description of the payload and triggering modules. Section 6 provides the overhead of the proposed HTH module and present a possible modification of the LCMQ protocol to circumvent this threat. Finally the paper has been concluded in Sect. 7.

2   Background

In this section we provide the basics of the LPN problem, circulant matrices, multivariate quadratic polynomials and finally, the LCMQ protocol.

2.1   LPN Problem

Suppose both the tag and the reader share an already agreed m-bit key $\mathcal{K}$ for the successive authentication rounds. Initially, the reader randomly selects l number of m-bit binary vectors $\mathbf{a_0},\mathbf{a_1},...,\mathbf{a_{l-1}}$ and sends them as a challenge to the tag. To generate the response, the tag computes $z_i = <\mathbf{a_i},\mathcal{K}>$ for all $i \in \{0,\cdots,l-1\}$, where $<\mathbf{a_i},\mathcal{K}>$ denotes the dot product modulo-2 of $\mathbf{a_i}$ and $\mathcal{K}$. Now, the reader will only accepts the tag if $<\mathbf{a_i},\mathcal{K}> = z_i$. But this scheme is simply vulnerable as an adversary can eavesdrop m linearly independent challenge-response pairs $(\mathbf{a_i}, z_i)$ and retrieve the secret key $\mathcal{K}$ by solving a linear system of equations modulo-2. But the determination of the key becomes difficult in the presence of noise. Hence the LPN problem can be defined as:

Definition 1 (LPN Problem): Let A be a random $(l \times m)$-binary matrix, $\mathcal{K}$ be a random m-bit vector, $\epsilon \in (0,\frac{1}{2})$ be a noise parameter, and $\mathcal{V}$ be a random l-bit vector such that $\text{Hwt}(\mathcal{V}) \le \epsilon \times l$. where $\text{Hwt}(\mathcal{V})$ denotes the *Hamming Weight* of a binary vector $\mathcal{V}$, i.e., the number of bits which are 1 in a binary vector $\mathcal{V}$. Given A, ϵ, and $\mathbf{z} = <A \cdot \mathcal{K}^t> \oplus \mathcal{V}^t$, find a k-bit vector $\mathbf{y^t}$ such that $\text{Hwt}(<A \cdot \mathbf{y^t}> \oplus \mathbf{z}) \le \epsilon \times l$.

This problem is proven to be NP-Hard [36] and the key length m and the noise level ϵ decides the security of the problem instances. As stated in [19], for 80-bit security, m and ϵ are set to 512 and 0.25.

2.2   Circulant-P2 Matrix

Now, as given in [19], we will provide the definition of square circulant matrix and circulant-P2 matrix.

Definition 2 (Square Circulant Matrix): A square circulant matrix M of order $(m \times m)$ is a matrix with first row $= [\alpha_0\ \alpha_1\ \dots\ \alpha_{m-1}]$ and the next rows are generated by right circular rotation of the previous row.

Definition 3 (Circulant-P2 Matrix): Given $n < m$, a circulant-P2 matrix is an $(m \times m)$ square circulant matrix, or an $(n \times m)$ landscape circulant matrix, or an $(m \times n)$ portrait circulant matrix, satisfying the below criteria.

1. It must be a binary matrix.
2. m is a prime number such that 2 is a primitive element of the finite field $\mathbb{F}_m$. Here, m is defined as a *P2 number*.
3. No row vector and column vector of a Circulant-P2 matrix can be all zeroes or all ones.

It is to be noted that all row vectors in a landscape circulant matrix are linearly independent to each other. Similarly, all column vectors in a portrait circulant matrix are linearly independent.

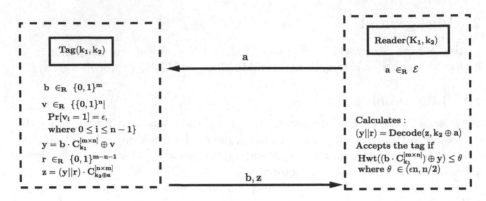

Fig. 1. The LCMQ protocol.

2.3   LCMQ Problem

Let $\mathcal{E} = \{\mathbf{a} | \mathbf{a} \in \{\{0,1\}^m \setminus \{\{0\}^m, \{1\}^m\}\}$ and $\mathrm{Hwt}(\mathbf{a})$ is even$\}$ and given an m-bit binary vector α, C_α denotes the square circulant matrix of order $m \times m$ with first row as α. Then we can define LCMQ problem as follows.

Definition 4 (LCMQ problem): Let m be a P2 number, $n < m$, $\epsilon \in (0, \frac{1}{2})$ be the noise parameter, $\mathbf{K_1} \in_R \{0,1\}^m$, parity of Hamming weight of $\mathbf{K_1}$ is publicly known and $\mathbf{K_2} \in_R \mathcal{E}$. Given l pairs of $(\mathbf{b_i}, \mathbf{z_i} = (((\mathbf{b_i} \cdot C_{\mathbf{K_1}}^{[m \times n]}) \oplus \mathbf{v_i}) || \mathbf{r_i}) \cdot C_{\mathbf{K_2}}^{[(m-1) \times m]})$, $\forall i \in \{0, \cdots, l-1\}$, where $\mathbf{b_i} \in_R \{0,1\}^m$, $\Pr[\mathbf{v_i}[j] = 1] = \epsilon$, $\Pr[\mathbf{v_i}[j] = 0] = (1 - \epsilon)$ $\forall 0 \le j \le n-1$ and $\mathbf{r_i} \in_R \{0,1\}^{m-n-1}$, determine $\mathbf{K_1}$ and $\mathbf{K_2}$.

If we consider $n = m - 1$ and there is no noise in the system, then this problem reduces to finding K_1 and K_2 such that:

$$(\mathbf{b_i} \in_R \{0,1\}^m, \mathbf{z_i'} = (\mathbf{b_i} \cdot C_{\mathbf{K_1}}^{[m \times n]}) \cdot C_{\mathbf{K_2}}^{[(m-1) \times m]})$$

As shown in [19], this problem is an instance of the multivariate quadratic (MQ) problem in $2(m - 1)$ variants. This is another problem known to be NP-complete [37] and stated as below:

Definition 5 (MQ Problem): Given a system of d multivariate quadratic equations in t variables over a finite field, find a valid solution satisfying all equations.

Next we describe the LCMQ protocol in details.

2.4   The LCMQ Protocol

Let parameter $\theta \in (\epsilon \times n, \frac{n}{2})$ be a threshold value, similar to the LPN problem. The steps for the LCMQ protocol are as follows:

– Both tag and the reader share two m-bit secret keys $\mathbf{K_1}$ and $\mathbf{K_2}$. For 80-bit security, the authors proposed m to be 163 bit in [19].

- First the reader selects an m-bit random binary vector $\mathbf{a}$ from the set $\mathcal{E}$ and sends it to the tag.
- The tag randomly selects an m-bit binary vector $\mathbf{b}$ and also selects another random n-bit vector $\mathbf{v}$ based on the noise parameter ϵ. Typically $n = m - 1$.
- Then it generates the circulant matrix $C_{\mathbf{K_1}}^{[m \times n]}$ using $\mathbf{K_1}$ as the first row and multiplies with $\mathbf{b}$. The final n-bit output is XOR-ed with $\mathbf{v}$ and thus $\mathbf{y}$ is generated.
- Next, it chooses another random variable $\mathbf{r}$ of length $(m - n - 1)$ and appends it to $\mathbf{y}$. This is finally multiplied with the matrix $C_{\mathbf{K_2} \oplus \mathbf{a}}^{[(m-1) \times m]}$ to produce $\mathbf{z}$.
- The tag then sends $(\mathbf{b}, \mathbf{z})$ to the reader.
- The reader first decodes $(\mathbf{y} \| \mathbf{r})$ from $\mathbf{z}$ and $(\mathbf{K_2} \oplus \mathbf{a})$ using the algorithm described in [19]. Finally it checks whether the Hamming weight of $((\mathbf{b} \cdot C_{\mathbf{K_1}}) \oplus \mathbf{y})$ is less than or equal to the threshold θ or not. If yes, then it accepts the tag.

Keeping this in mind, we will next describe how tag impersonation attack can be launched in the subsequent sections.

3   Tag Impersonation Attack on the Protocol

In this paper, we make a major observation about a weakness of the LCMQ protocol, which to the best of our knowledge was not reported earlier: the recovery of $\mathbf{K_2}$ is sufficient for the adversary to enable successful authentication! The basic intuition behind the attack is: the adversary initially captures a transcript $(\mathbf{a_c}, \mathbf{b_c}, \mathbf{z_c})$ of the authentication protocol exchanged between the reader and the tag. Now, if the adversary has the knowledge of $\mathbf{K_2}$, it can successfully execute Decode algorithm and retrieve the value of $\mathbf{y_c}$ using $\mathbf{K_2}, \mathbf{a_c}, \mathbf{z_c}$. Once she gets a valid $\mathbf{y_c}$, she can calculate $\mathbf{z}$'s for new values of $\mathbf{a}$'s and replay previously captured $\mathbf{b_c}$ everytime with new $\mathbf{z}$'s. To understand the vulnerability and the associated attack, consider the scenario as follows.

- Suppose that the adversary is able to monitor the communication network between a tag and a reader. She eavesdrops to obtain a triplet $\mathbf{a_c}, \mathbf{b_c}, \mathbf{z_c}$ that leads to a successful authentication as shown in Fig. 1.
- We consider that she also knows the correct key $\mathbf{K_2}$.
- Using this, she can calculate $\mathbf{y_c} = \text{Decode}(\mathbf{z_c}, \mathbf{K_2} \oplus \mathbf{a_c})$. The Decode algorithm corresponds to polynomial multiplication of $\mathbf{z_c}$ and $(\mathbf{K_2} \oplus \mathbf{a_c})^{-1}$ modulo $(\mathbf{x^m} + 1)$ leading to the calculation of $\mathbf{y_c}$ as mentioned in [19].
- Now, the adversary interacts with the reader.
- Let us assume that the reader sends the adversary a new challenge $\mathbf{a_w}$.
- Adversary reuses $\mathbf{y_c}$ and calculates $\mathbf{z_w} = \mathbf{y_c} \cdot C_{\mathbf{K_2} \oplus \mathbf{a_w}}$ and sends $\mathbf{z_w}, \mathbf{b_c}$ over the network.
- The reader executes decode algorithm with $\mathbf{z_w}$ and $\mathbf{K_2} \oplus \mathbf{a_w}$ and obtains $\mathbf{y_c}$ which was already authenticated by the reader for $\mathbf{b_c}$.
- Hence, if the adversary obtains the key $\mathbf{K_2}$, it can impersonate as a valid tag, without even having the knowledge of key $\mathbf{K_1}$.

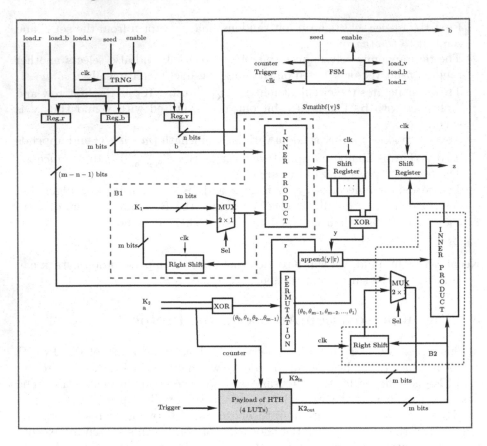

Fig. 2. Architecture of LCMQ - Tag.

In the subsequent sections, we present the first reported hardware architecture of the RFID tag executing the LCMQ protocol. Please note that the dimension of circulant matrix is $m \times n$. Hence the hardware architecture needs $m \times n$ number of registers to store the matrix in the tag. However this approach would have made the design more resource-hungry. So, we implement the circulant matrix in a $1 \times m$ register. The idea is to do a circular right shift in each clock cycle when we multiply a n-bit vector with the matrix. Next we try to induce accurate stuck at one fault in the $1 \times m$ register that holds the first row of the matrix. The proposed HTH flips the first bit of the register and this fault propagates in all of the m bits of the matrix in subsequent clock cycles. This eventually leaks K_2 depending on whether the authentication passes or fails.

4   Architecture of the LCMQ Hardware Implementation

As shown in Fig. 2, the components involved in the hardware architecture of the tag are m-bit random number generator (RNG), $(m - n - 1)$-bit register Reg_r,

m-bit register Reg_b, n-bit register Reg_v for the variables r, b, v respectively. The two blocks $B1$, $B2$, each consists of an Inner Product Module (IP), a 2:1 multiplexer, one right shift module (RS) and one shift register (SR). Block $B2$, also contains a permutation module which is used to convert the initial input key $\mathbf{K_2} \oplus \mathbf{a}$ into the first column of circulant matrix $C_{\mathbf{K_2}}^{[(m-1)\times m]}$. Since, the random numbers are needed at different stages in an authentication round, control signals $load\_r, load\_b, load\_v$ are provided to load values into Reg_r, Reg_b, Reg_v respectively. An Finite State Machine (FSM) is also designed to control the clock and other control signals. The components are discussed in details as follows.

4.1 RNG Module

The RNG module produces an m-bit random number using an 32-bit LFSR. This LFSR is run for $\lceil [m/32] \rceil$ cycles to produce an m-bit output. An LFSR-based RNG might not provide sufficient entropy in a practical situation; however, as our attack is not based on the source of randomness, we use an LFSR as a source of entropy required to imitate the tag.

4.2 Generate_v Module

Generation of n-bit $\mathbf{v}$ is based on Bernoulli trials with parameter η. An 7-bit binary random number simulates 1-bit of v. If this number is less than $\eta * 128/100$, then the corresponding bit is 1, otherwise 0. Therefore, an m-bit random number can generate $\lceil m/7 \rceil$ bits of v. Hence, total number of random numbers required are $\left\lceil \frac{n}{\lceil m/7 \rceil} \right\rceil$.

4.3 Matrix Multiplication Module

Typical matrix multiplication requires us to store the whole matrix, but it is impractical for a RFID tag because of severe area constraints. According to [18], an RFID protocol must not take more than 1000 Lookup Tables (LUTs) for a Field Programmable Gate Array (FPGA) implementation. To solve this problem, we exploit the property of circulant matrices to perform the matrix multiplication with less memory and a relatively small computational overhead. Recall from Sect. 2, there are two multiplication operations in the tag. We name these two multiplication blocks as $B1$ and $B2$. The first multiplication block $B1$, is for the multiplication of a portrait circulant matrix with a vector, ($\mathbf{b} \cdot C_{\mathbf{K_1}}^{[m \times n]}$). Similarly, the second block $B2$, is used to calculate the multiplication of a landscape circulant matrix with a vector, $((\mathbf{y} \| \mathbf{r} \cdot C_{\mathbf{K_2} \oplus \mathbf{a}}^{[(m-1)\times m]}))$. In $B1$, $\mathbf{b}$ along with secret key $\mathbf{K_1}$ are inputs. Multiplexer along with the right shift module imitates i^{th} column in i^{th} clock cycle. IP is the module which calculates the inner product modulo-2 of its inputs, thus in i^{th} clock cycle, it calculates the $<\mathbf{b}, C_{\mathbf{K_1},i}^{[m \times n]}>$, where $C_{\mathbf{K_1},i}^{[m \times n]}$ is the ith column of the circulant matrix $C_{\mathbf{K_1}}^{[m \times n]}$. The output of IP is stored in a shift register which does a left circular shift at every clock cycle. Initially, *sel* signal is 0, which inputs the secret key as it is. Afterwards, *sel* is 1, which inputs a right circular shifted value of the previous output. These simulate the behavior of the circulant matrix $C_{\mathbf{K_1}}^{[m \times n]}$. It requires n clock cycles to generate the n-bit vector. Similarly, $\mathbf{y} \| \mathbf{r}$, and $\mathbf{K_2}$ are inputs to $B2$ which calculates the value of $\mathbf{z}$.

4.4   Overall Hardware Module Operation

Initially, the RNG generates a m-bit random number that is loaded into *Reg_b*. This binary vector is then fed into block $B1$. Meanwhile, the module *generate_v* generates the random vector $\mathbf{v}$ following a Bernoulli distribution. After n clock cycles, the output of block $B1$, is XOR-ed with *Reg_v* to produce $\mathbf{y}$ which similarly calculates $\mathbf{z}$ after its concatenation with $\mathbf{r}$ and multiplication of concatenated result with $C_{\mathbf{K_2}}^{[(m-1) \times m]}$.

5   HTH Induced Safe Error Attack on the LCMQ Protocol

The objective of building a lightweight FPGA implementation of LCMQ protocol is to create a testbed on which we can later integrate our proposed HTH module. Therefore, the proposed hardware implementation and the subsequent HTH insertion act as a case study of LCMQ protocol vulnerability analysis on FPGAs. It must be noted that without loss of generality, such HTHs can also be developed for RFID tags, albeit with different methodologies.

An HTH design usually comprises of two phases: *Payload* and *Trigger*. Payload is the portion of the HTH circuitry that is responsible for inducing the functional failure or information leakage, while the trigger is used to activate the HTH. In an effective HTH, payload should have very low power and area overhead, ideally zero. Moreover, the HTH should be rarely triggered so that it can easily pass the verification test done after manufacturing of the chips or circuits. In this section, we mainly focus on the design of payload, but before that, we give a brief overview of the adversarial model and the trigger condition of HTH.

5.1   Adversary Model

As shown in [33], nexus between two or more stages of RFID manufacturing and deployment can be easily exploited in order to launch a tag impersonation attack. In our adversary model, we assume that the adversary is herself the malicious designer and maintains a malicious nexus with a personnel at a fabrication facility of the RFID tags. It is this personnel in the fabrication facility who injects a HTH designed by the adversary in order to reveal secret information to her. Hence, we can say that only these persons know the mechanism to activate the HTH. Such a model would be of great significance for deployments in defence mechanism [38].

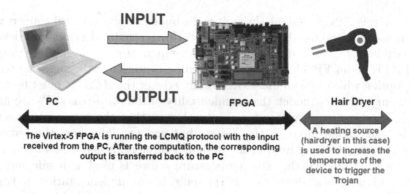

INPUT

OUTPUT

PC   FPGA   Hair Dryer

The Virtex-5 FPGA is running the LCMQ protocol with the input received from the PC, After the computation, the corresponding output is transferred back to the PC

A heating source (hairdryer in this case) is used to increase the temperature of the device to trigger the Trojan

Fig. 3. Proposed HTH triggering methodology

As the HTH in an Intellectual Property (IP) core renders comparison with a golden model extremely difficult, it is highly unlikely to detect the HTH using Side Channel Analysis (SCA) [39]. However, one must ensure that the gate count difference between actual design and the infected design should not be very high. In order to ensure this, we implemented the HTH using the LUTs on the FPGAs directly, which provides almost negligible overhead in terms of power as well as hardware resources.

The adversary uses the HTH to retrieve the key K_2 and then successfully impersonates according to the observation mentioned earlier. The triggering mechanism and mode of operation of the HTH is explained next.

5.2 Activation of HTH

Triggering of a HTH is usually done using two methods: (1) external triggering which is done based on output of the some sensors, (2) internal triggering where an internal logic is used to activate the HTH. Usually, triggering of HTH using internal logic incurs overhead in terms of gates and power consumption, hence an external triggering will be suitable for this case where the amount of gates required is already very low as the protocol is lightweight. Now, it must be noted that most of the modern systems where RFIDs are employed also requires incorporation of sensors to monitor the external environmental conditions. Now, an adversary can design a HTH which will get activated only when the external environmental condition (for example temperature) reaches certain value. The advantage of this type of triggering is that the overhead of such triggering is practically zero as such sensors are already available in the system. To prevent accidental activation of the HTH, an adversary can set the triggering condition at an abnormal environmental condition which is not achieved during normal operation.

Proposed Triggering Methodology: In our proposed HTH, we have used the external triggering methodology as described in [39]. Modern FPGA devices are now coupled with a temperature sensor which can be digitally monitored by the underlying FPGA designs through an in-built analog to digital converter. It is often used to monitor the system temperature so that a designer can develop safeguard in case of excessive increase in the temperature. As we validate the proposed HTH on an FPGA platform, this temperature sensor becomes an ready-to-use option which we can use to externally trigger the HTH. It must be noted that in our adversary model, the confidentiality of the third-party IPs are maintained. Therefore, an evaluator can only observe that the temperature sensor data is taken as an input to the design, but can not infer how the temperature sensor data is being used in the design. Therefore, it is not possible for the evaluator to decide whether the temperature sensor is used as a safeguard, or whether it is used as a trigger to a HTH circuit. In our implementation, to trigger the HTH we have rapidly increased the temperature of the FPGA using a hair dryer. It must be noted that the temperature reached by the device after being heated by the hair dryer can not be attained during normal operation, which prevents accidental triggering of the implemented HTH. A block diagram view of the proposed HTH triggering methodology is shown in Fig. 3. Once the HTH is activated, the circuitry then modifies some bits of the register by producing a safe error as discussed next.

5.3 Payload of HTH

We present an ultra-low hardware footprint HTH which occupies only 4 LUTs. Since, we are trying to obtain the secret key K_2, it is necessary for us to inject a fault in all of the m bits. However, if we add a multiplexer separately for all the bits, then that would lead to an linear increase in the overhead. In order to counter act this, we exploit the property of circulant matrices. Since, the input key is right shifted at each clock cycle, as explained in Sect. 4.3, a stuck at 1 fault induced in the 1st bit of right shift register in t-th clock cycle is equivalent in inducing a stuck at 1 fault in t-th bit of initial input key. We exploit this to induce stuck at 1 fault in all bits of input key by inducing it at the first position of right shift register at different clock cycles.

The malicious circuit is shown in the Fig. 2. The whole malicious circuit can be incorporated in the design using only 4 LUT's as shown in Fig. 4. The objective of the HTH is to inject a stuck at one fault at either $K_2[0]^{th}$ or at $K_2[80]^{th}$ bit at appropriate clock cycle determined by the value of least significant byte of $a[7:0]$. The working principle of the HTH payload is given below:

- The architecture of the LCMQ protocol requires a counter during the computation of inner product in $B2$ module to track the number of shifts. Now, when the HTH is triggered, two scenarios can occur:
  1. **a[6:0] equals counter value and a[7] = 0**: In this case, $K_2[0]$ gets injected by the stuck at 1 fault at $a[6:0]^{th}$ clock cycle. As previously mentioned, this is equivalent to injecting stuck at one fault at $a[6:0]^{th}$ bit of K_2.
  2. **a[6:0] equals counter value and a[7] = 1**: In this case, $K_2[80]$ gets injected by the stuck at 1 fault at $a[6:0]^{th}$ clock cycle. This is equivalent to injecting stuck at one fault at $(a[6:0]+80)^{th}$ bit of K_2.

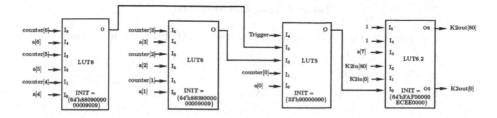

Fig. 4. LUT Diagram of Implanted HTH in architecture where $m = 163$.

Table 1. Power and execution time overhead

Overhead	Original design	Design with HTH	Increase in number
Power	0.539 W	0.539 W	0
Timing	3.789 ns	3.794 ns	0.13

- Figure 4 shows the HTH circuitry. The first LUT compare the value of $counter[2{:}0]$ and $a[2{:}0]$ and outputs 1 if they are same. Similarly, the second LUT outputs 1 if and only if $counter[5{:}3]$ and $a[5{:}3]$ are equal. The third LUT takes trigger, $a[0]$, $counter[0]$, and the output of the previous two LUTs as input. The output of the third LUT is 1 when trigger along with the output of the previous two LUTs are 1 and $a[0] = counter[0]$. If the output of the third LUT is one, the fourth LUT injects stuck at one fault at either $K_2[0]$ or $K_2[80]$ depending upon the value of $a[7]$. If the third LUT output is zero, the value of $K_2[0]$ and $K_2[80]$ remains unaltered.

It must be noted that the fault injection can also be carried out by only targeting $K_2[0]$. However the advantage of targeting either one of $K_2[0]$ and $K_2[80]$ is illustrated with an example. Let us assume that we want to inject fault at 114th bit position of K_2. If we only target $K_2[0]$, then we need to wait 114 cycles for the fault injection at the desired position and the corresponding least significant byte of a should be set to 114. However, in our methodology, if the value of a is $162 = 8'b10100100$, we can still inject fault at 114th bit of K_2 by setting $K_2[80]$ as 1 in 34th cycle. Thus our proposed methodology provides more flexibility in terms of location of fault injection. As LUT module of Virtex 5 FPGA supports 5 input and 2 output function, we can easily integrate our proposed methodology with it. After inducing the stuck at 1 fault, if the authentication succeeds then the adversary infers that the corresponding bit was 1, otherwise that corresponding bit 0.

6   Experimental Setup and Implementation Results

The hardware designs for both the hardware implementation of the LCMQ protocol and the proposed HTH were performed using *Verilog HDL* and executed

Table 2. Hardware overhead

Components	Original design	Design with HTH	Increase in number
LUT	714	717	0.4
SliceRegs	1507	1507	0
Slices	589	589	0.0

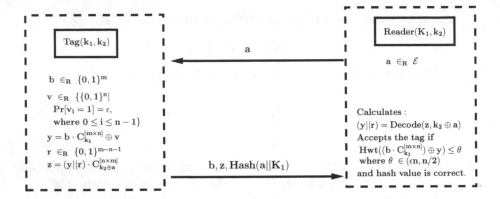

Fig. 5. A countermeasure to subvert the proposed attack at protocol level.

on Virtex-5 FPGA board. The results are shown for 80-bit security with parameter values $m = 163, n = 162, \theta = 18, \eta = 0.08$. The designs were synthesized and implemented using *Xilinx ISE 14.5*, and simulated using *Xilinx Isim*. The power estimation of the circuit was carried out using *Xilinx XPower Analyzer* and delay estimation using *Xilinx Timing Analyzer*.

Table 1 illustrates the percentage increase/decrease in the total power consumption and the critical path delays of the design before and after HTH insertion. Table 2 shows the comparison between the golden design and the overhead of the HTH circuit. We have assigned the *LUT combining* sub-property of the *Map property* to *Area* in the CAD software tool considering the reduced size of RFID tags. Theoretically 163 rounds of authentication should be sufficient to obtain all the 163 bits of the secret key $\mathbf{K_2}$. But in the experimental setup, the number of authentication rounds required to successfully retrieve $\mathbf{K_2}$ is approximately 2^{11}. This happens because the value of $\mathbf{a}[7:0]$ is equally likely to produce all the bits between 0 to 255. Hence, there will be some cases where the value of $\mathbf{a}[7:0]$ will be greater than 163 and hence, will not result in information leakage. But since, the adversary controls the triggering of the HTH, this does not decrease the potential of the attack.

6.1   Possible Countermeasure Against Proposed Attack

To subvert this attack, one potential countermeasure at the protocol level would be to force the adversary to reveal both $\mathbf{K_1}$ and $\mathbf{K_2}$ in order to successfully break the LCMQ protocol. As shown in Fig. 5, this can be achieved by calculating the hash value of $(a||K_1)$, and sending it along with b and z. As the reader has knowledge about both a and K_1, it can validate whether the hash value is correct or not along with checking the Hamming weights of $((\mathbf{b} \cdot C_{\mathbf{K_1}}) \oplus \mathbf{y})$ with respect to θ. If both the conditions satisfy, then only the reader accepts the tag as a legitimate one.

7   Conclusion

This paper addresses the issue of exploiting circulant matrix property to insert a stealthy HTH that could use safe error to obtain all secret keys, thus making impersonation of tag viable. First, we made an key observation that in an LCMQ protocol an attacker can impersonate without the knowledge of key $\mathbf{K_1}$, thus motivating a HTH designer to just target key $\mathbf{K_2}$. Subsequently, we gave an effective and efficient architecture of tag part of the LCMQ problem. We provided an ultra-lightweight HTH design which can induce safe errors surreptitiously to leak $\mathbf{K_2}$ potentially. We summed up by providing the hardware implementation of the LCMQ protocol and the design overheads, which confirm that the HTH in this type of setup is viable and efficient.

References

1. Bagadia, K., Chatterjee, U., Roy, D.B., Mukhopadhyay, D., Chakraborty, R.S.: Exploiting safe error based leakage of RFID authentication protocol using hardware Trojan horse. In: 2017 IEEE International Symposium on Hardware Oriented Security and Trust (HOST), pp. 167–167. May 2017
2. Hopper, N.J., Blum, M.: Secure human identification protocols. In: Advances in Cryptology - ASIACRYPT 2001, 7th International Conference on the Theory and Application of Cryptology and Information Security, Gold Coast, Australia, December 9–13, 2001, Proceedings, 2001, pp. 52–66 (2001). https://doi.org/10.1007/3-540-45682-1_4
3. Juels, A., Weis, S.A.: Authenticating pervasive devices with human protocols. In: Advances in Cryptology - CRYPTO 2005: 25th Annual International Cryptology Conference, Santa Barbara, California, USA, August 14–18, 2005, Proceedings, 2005, pp. 293–308 (2005). https://doi.org/10.1007/11535218_18
4. Bringer, J., Chabanne, H., Dottax, E.: HB^{++}: a lightweight authentication protocol secure against some attacks. In: Second International Workshop on Security, Privacy and Trust in Pervasive and Ubiquitous Computing (SecPerU 2006), 29 June 2006, Lyon, France, 2006, pp. 28–33 (2006). https://doi.org/10.1109/SECPERU.2006.10
5. Gilbert, H., Robshaw, M.J.B., Seurin, Y.: HB$^{#}$: increasing the security and efficiency of HB^{+}. In: Advances in Cryptology - EUROCRYPT 2008, 27th Annual International Conference on the Theory and Applications of Cryptographic Techniques, Istanbul, Turkey, April 13-17, 2008. Proceedings, pp. 361–378 (2008). https://doi.org/10.1007/978-3-540-78967-3_21

6. Duc, D.N., Kim, K.: Securing HB+ against GRS man-in-the-middle attack. Information and Communication Engineers, Symposium on Cryptography and Information Security (2007). http://caislab.kaist.ac.kr/publication/paper_files/2007/SCIS2007_Duc.pdf
7. Munilla, J., Peinado, A.: HB-MP: a further step in the HB-family of lightweight authentication protocols. Computer Networks, vol. 51, no. 9, pp. 2262–2267 (2007). https://doi.org/10.1016/j.comnet.2007.01.011
8. Leng, K.M.X., Markantonakis, K.: HB-MP+: a protocol: an improvement on the HB-MP protocol. In: Proceedings IEEE International Conference RFID, pp. 118–124 (2008). https://repository.royalholloway.ac.uk/file/1a749a12-a370-bc54-c2dd-5749004241ef/8/HB_MP_Protocol_An_Improvement_on_the_HB_MP_Protocol.pdf
9. Rizomiliotis, P.: HB - MAC: improving the random - HB$^\#$ authentication protocol. In: Trust, Privacy and Security in Digital Business, 6th International Conference, TrustBus 2009, Linz, Austria, September 3–4, 2009. Proceedings, pp. 159–168 (2009). https://doi.org/10.1007/978-3-642-03748-1_16
10. Hammouri, G., Sunar, B.: PUF-HB: a tamper-resilient HB based authentication protocol. In: Applied Cryptography and Network Security, 6th International Conference, ACNS 2008, New York, NY, USA, June 3–6, 2008. Proceedings, pp. 346–365 (2008). https://doi.org/10.1007/978-3-540-68914-0_21
11. Hammouri, G., Öztürk, E., Birand, B., Sunar, B.: Unclonable lightweight authentication scheme. In: Information and Communications Security, 10th International Conference, ICICS 2008, Birmingham, UK, October 20–22, 2008, Proceedings, pp. 33–48 (2008). https://doi.org/10.1007/978-3-540-88625-9_3
12. Deng, G., Li, H., Zhang, Y., Wang, J.: Tree-LSHB+: an LPN-Based lightweight mutual authentication RFID protocol. In: Wireless Personal Communications, vol. 72, no. 1, pp. 159–174 (2013). https://doi.org/10.1007/s11277-013-1006-2
13. Bringer, J., Chabanne, H.: Trusted-HB: a low-cost version of HB $^+$ secure against man-in-the-middle attacks. In: IEEE Transition Information Theory, vol. 54, no. 9, pp. 4339–4342 (2008). https://doi.org/10.1109/TIT.2008.928290
14. Rizomiliotis, P., Gritzalis, S.: GHB #: a provably secure HB-Like lightweight authentication protocol. In: Applied Cryptography and Network Security - 10th International Conference, ACNS 2012, Singapore, June 26–29, 2012. Proceedings, pp. 489–506 (2012). https://doi.org/10.1007/978-3-642-31284-7_29
15. Heyse, S., Kiltz, E., Lyubashevsky, V., Paar, C., Pietrzak, K.: Lapin: an efficient authentication protocol based on ring-LPN. In: Fast Software Encryption - 19th International Workshop, FSE 2012, Washington, DC, USA, March 19–21, 2012. Revised Selected Papers, pp. 346–365 (2012). https://doi.org/10.1007/978-3-642-34047-5_20
16. Gilbert, H., Robshaw, M.J.B., Sibert, H.: An Active Attack Against HB+ - A Provably Secure Lightweight Authentication Protocol. IACR Cryptology ePrint Archive, vol. 2005, p. 237 (2005). http://eprint.iacr.org/2005/237
17. Gilbert, H., Robshaw, M.J.B., Seurin, Y.: Good variants of HB$^+$ are hard to find. In: Financial Cryptography and Data Security, 12th International Conference, FC 2008, Cozumel, Mexico, January 28–31, 2008, Revised Selected Papers, pp. 156–170 (2008). https://doi.org/10.1007/978-3-540-85230-8_12
18. Avoine, G., Carpent, X., Hernandez-Castro, J.: Pitfalls in ultralightweight authentication protocol designs, In: IEEE Transition Mobility Computation, vol. 15, no. 9, pp. 2317–2332 (2016). https://doi.org/10.1109/TMC.2015.2492553
19. Li, Z., Gong, G., Qin, Z.: Secure and efficient LCMQ entity authentication protocol. In: IEEE Transition Information Theory, vol. 59, no. 6, pp. 4042–4054 (2013). https://doi.org/10.1109/TIT.2013.2253892

20. Boneh, D., Lipton, R.J.: Effect of operators on straight line complexity. In: Fifth Israel Symposium on Theory of Computing and Systems, ISTCS 1997, Ramat-Gan, Israel, June 17–19, 1997, Proceedings, pp. 1–5 (1997). https://doi.org/10.1109/ISTCS.1997.595151

21. Loubet-Moundi, P., Vigilant, D., Olivier, F.: Static Fault Attacks on Hardware DES Registers, IACR Cryptology ePrint Archive, vol. 2011, p. 531 (2011). http://eprint.iacr.org/2011/531

22. Piret, G., Quisquater, J.-J.: A differential fault attack technique against SPN structures, with application to the AES and KHAZAD. In: Walter, C.D., Koç, Ç.K., Paar, C. (eds.) CHES 2003. LNCS, vol. 2779, pp. 77–88. Springer, Heidelberg (2003). https://doi.org/10.1007/978-3-540-45238-6_7

23. Tunstall, M., Mukhopadhyay, D., Ali, S.: Differential fault analysis of the advanced encryption standard using a single fault. In: Ardagna, C.A., Zhou, J. (eds.) WISTP 2011. LNCS, vol. 6633, pp. 224–233. Springer, Heidelberg (2011). https://doi.org/10.1007/978-3-642-21040-2_15

24. Kim, C.H., Shin, J.H., Quisquater, J., Lee, P.J.: Safe-error attack on SPA-FA resistant exponentiations using a HW modular multiplier. In: Information Security and Cryptology - ICISC 2007, 10th International Conference, Seoul, Korea, November 29–30, 2007, Proceedings, pp. 273–281 (2007). https://doi.org/10.1007/978-3-540-76788-6_22

25. Gaspar, L., Leurent, G., Standaert, F.: Hardware implementation and side-channel analysis of lapin. In: Topics in Cryptology - CT-RSA 2014 - The Cryptographer's Track at the RSA Conference 2014, San Francisco, CA, USA, February 25–28, 2014. Proceedings, pp. 206–226 (2014). https://doi.org/10.1007/978-3-319-04852-9_11

26. Carrijo, J., Tonicelli, R., Nascimento, A.C.A.: A fault analytic method against HB+. In: IEICE Transactions, vol. 94-A, no. 2, pp. 855–859 (2011). http://search.ieice.org/bin/summary.php?id=e94-a_2_855

27. Berti, F., Standaert, F.-X.: An analysis of the learning parity with noise assumption against fault attacks. In: Lemke-Rust, K., Tunstall, M. (eds.) Smart Card Research and Advanced Applications, pp. 245–264. Springer International Publishing, Cham (2017). https://doi.org/10.1007/978-3-319-54669-8_15

28. Wang, X., Tehranipoor, M., Plusquellic, J.: Detecting malicious inclusions in secure hardware: challenges and solutions. In: 2008 IEEE International Workshop on Hardware-Oriented Security and Trust, June 2008, pp. 15–19 (2008)

29. King, S.T., Tucek, J., Cozzie, A., Grier, C., Jiang, W., Zhou, Y.: Designing and implementing malicious hardware. In: Proceedings of the 1st Usenix Workshop on Large-Scale Exploits and Emergent Threats, ser. LEET 2008. Berkeley, CA, USA: USENIX Association, 2008, pp. 5:1–5:8 (2008). http://dl.acm.org/citation.cfm?id=1387709.1387714

30. Jin, Y., Kupp, N., Makris, Y.: Experiences in hardware trojan design and implementation. In: 2009 IEEE International Workshop on Hardware-Oriented Security and Trust, July 2009, pp. 50–57 (2009)

31. Lin, L., Kasper, M., Güneysu, T., Paar, C., Burleson, W.: Trojan side-channels: lightweight hardware trojans through side-channel engineering. In: Clavier, C., Gaj, K. (eds.) Cryptographic Hardware and Embedded Systems - CHES 2009, Springer, Berlin, pp. 382–395 (2009)

32. Lin, L., Burleson, W., Paar, C.: MOLES: malicious off-chip leakage enabled by side-channels. In: 2009 International Conference on Computer-Aided Design, ICCAD 2009, San Jose, CA, USA, November 2–5, 2009, pp. 117–122 (2009). https://doi.org/10.1145/1687399.1687425

33. Ali, S., Chakraborty, R.S., Mukhopadhyay, D., Bhunia, S.: Multi-level attacks: an emerging security concern for cryptographic hardware. In: Design, Automation and Test in Europe, DATE 2011, Grenoble, France, March 14–18, 2011, 2011, pp. 1176–1179 (2011). https://doi.org/10.1109/DATE.2011.5763307
34. Johnson, A.P., Saha, S., Chakraborty, R.S., Mukhopadhyay, D., Gören, S.: Fault attack on AES via hardware Trojan insertion by dynamic partial reconfiguration of FPGA over ethernet. In: Proceedings of the 9th Workshop on Embedded Systems Security, WESS 2014, New Delhi, India, October 17, 2014, 2014, pp. 1:1–1:8 (2014). https://doi.org/10.1145/2668322.2668323
35. The big hack: How china used a tiny chip to infiltrate u.s. companies - bloomberg. https://www.bloomberg.com/news/features/2018-10-04/the-big-hack-how-china-used-a-tiny-chip-to-infiltrate-america-s-top-companies. Accessed on 07 Oct 2019
36. Berlekamp, E.R., McEliece, R.J., van Tilborg, H.C.A.: On the inherent intractability of certain coding problems (Corresp.). In: IEEE Transition Information Theory, vol. 24, no. 3, pp. 384–386 (1978). https://doi.org/10.1109/TIT.1978.1055873
37. Garey, M.R., Johnson, D.S.: Computers and Intractability; A Guide to the Theory of NP-Completeness. W. H. Freeman & Co., New York (1990)
38. Trust-Hub.org. https://www.trust-hub.org/home. Accessed on 07 Oct 2019
39. Roy, D.B., Bhasin, S., Guilley, S., Danger, J., Mukhopadhyay, D., Ngo, X.T., Najm, Z.: Reconfigurable LUT: a double edged sword for security-critical applications. In: Security, Privacy, and Applied Cryptography Engineering - 5th International Conference, SPACE 2015, Jaipur, India, October 3–7, 2015, Proceedings, 2015, pp. 248–268 (2015). https://doi.org/10.1007/978-3-319-24126-5_15

Invited Abstracts

Length Preserving Symmetric Encryption: Is It Important?

Debrup Chakraborty[✉]

Cryptology and Security Research Unit, Indian Statistical Institute,
Kolkata 700108, India
debrup@isical.ac.in

Abstract. A length preserving encryption scheme, as the name suggests, is a scheme where the lengths of the plaintext and ciphertext are equal. These schemes are inherently deterministic and thus provides "less" security than what is offered by encryption schemes which allows ciphertext expansion. It has been argued that length preserving encryption is essential for in-place encryption of sector/block oriented storage media like hard disks flash memories etc.

Tweakable enciphering schemes (TES) are a class of length preserving encryption encryption schemes which has been widely studied. TES has been formalized as the appropriate primitive for the application of storage encryption and it has been argued that they provide the maximum security possible for a length preserving scheme. In the last two decades there has been several activities in designing, implementation and proving security of TES. There have been some standardization activities also in this direction.

In the first part of this talk we will give an overview of TESs, discuss some notable constructions including their security and implementations. We will also discuss the current status of standardization of such schemes.

A length preserving scheme has several limitations compared to a scheme which allows length expansion. In the final part of the talk we will revisit the requirement of length preservation for disk encryption and show that a proper formating of the hard disks may allow the use of length expanding encryption schemes. We will present a specially crafted length expanding scheme called BCTR for this purpose and show its superiority compared to existing TESs.

© Springer Nature Switzerland AG 2019
S. Bhasin et al. (Eds.): SPACE 2019, LNCS 11947, p. 233, 2019.
https://doi.org/10.1007/978-3-030-35869-3

Towards Automatic Application of Side Channel Countermeasures

Francesco Regazzoni[✉]

ALaRI - USI, Lugano, Switzerland
`regazzoni@alari.ch`

Abstract. Security is one of the most important extra functional requirements that a system should provide. The importance of security will certainly grow in the near future, when IoT devices will pervade every aspect of our lives, including sensitive ones, and when cyber-physical systems will be massively deployed in our critical infrastructure.

Securing all these devices is however a complex tasks that goes beyond the simple inclusion of cryptographic primitives. These devices often have a limited amount of resources available for implementing security. Additionally, they are often deployed in an environment accessible to the attacker, making thus necessary the use of protections against physical attacks. Furthermore, CPSs and IoT devices often needs to fulfill other design requirements, such as reliability, real-time, low power, and low energy, that could be in contrast with security requirements.

So far, the problems involved in designing secure CPSs and IoT devices have been analyzed and addressed independently, by expert designers that were also in charge of the integration of the whole system. This approach however is not optimal, since it does not scale with the complexity of the systems and it does not allow, at least in a simple way, to capture potential security weaknesses introduced by the integration of countermeasures against different attacks.

Security can be achieved only with an holistic design methodology, addressing the problem at each level of the design flow with the necessary inclusion of a verification step. In turn, such a design approach can be effectively put in practice only if supported by adequate toolchains, capable of automatically apply countermeasures against known attacks and capable of automatically verify their correct application.

This tutorial concentrates on this problem from a side channel attacks perspective. Starting from the first works implementing hardware design flow for security [3], the initial steps towards automatically driving design tools using security variables [1] and the proposal of evaluation methodologies based on state of the art design tools [2], we will revise and summarize the research efforts toward the goal of automatic design of IoTs and CPSs secure against physical attacks and we will highlight future research direction in this important field of research.

Acknowledgment. This tutorial was partially supported by European Union's Horizon 2020 research and innovation program under grant agreement No 732105 (CERBERO).

S. Bhasin et al. (Eds.): SPACE 2019, LNCS 11947, pp. 234–235, 2019.
https://doi.org/10.1007/978-3-030-35869-3

References

1. Regazzoni, F., et al.: A design flow and evaluation framework for DPA-resistant instruction set extensions. In: Clavier, C., Gaj, K. (eds.) CHES 2009. LNCS, vol. 5747, pp. 205–219. Springer, Heidelberg (2009). https://doi.org/10.1007/978-3-642-04138-9_15
2. Sijacic, D., Balasch, J., Yang, B., Ghosh, S., Verbauwhede, I.: Towards Efficient and Automated Side Channel Evaluations at Design Time, pp. 16–31. Kalpa Publications in Computing (2018)
3. Tiri, K., Verbauwhede, I.: A logic level design methodology for a secure DPA resistant ASIC or FPGA implementation. pp. 246–51, Paris, February 2004

Author Index

Agrawal, Dishank 106

Bagadia, Krishna 214
Banik, Subhadeep 13
Batina, Lejla 86
Bhagwani, Harsh 123

Caforio, Andrea 13
Cassiers, Gaëtan 67
Chakraborty, Debrup 233
Chakraborty, Rajat Subhra 159, 214
Chatterjee, Ayantika 176
Chatterjee, Durba 142
Chatterjee, Urbi 214
Chowdhury, Dipanwita Roy 106

Daruwala, R. D. 34
Das, Abhijit 106
Das, Amitabh 159
Dutta, Aneet Kumar 123

ElSheikh, Muhammad 50

Govindan, Vidya 159
Guo, Chun 67
Gupta, Kishan Chand 195

Handa, Anand 123
Hazra, Aritra 142

Koteshwara, Sandhya 159
Kumar, Nitesh 123
Kvatinsky, Shahar 5

Mukhopadhyay, Debdeep 142, 214

Nagata, Makoto 1
Negi, Rohit 123

Pal, Debranjan 106
Pandey, Sumit Kumar 195
Parhi, Keshab K. 159
Pereira, Olivier 67
Peters, Thomas 67
Picek, Stjepan 9, 86

Reddy, B. Praeep Kumar 176
Regazzoni, Francesco 234
Roy, Debapriya Basu 214

Samanta, Susanta 195
Shahapure, Shravani 34
Shukla, Sandeep Kumar 123
Standaert, François-Xavier 67
Sule, Virendra 34

Weissbart, Léo 86

Youssef, Amr M. 50

Printed in the United States
By Bookmasters